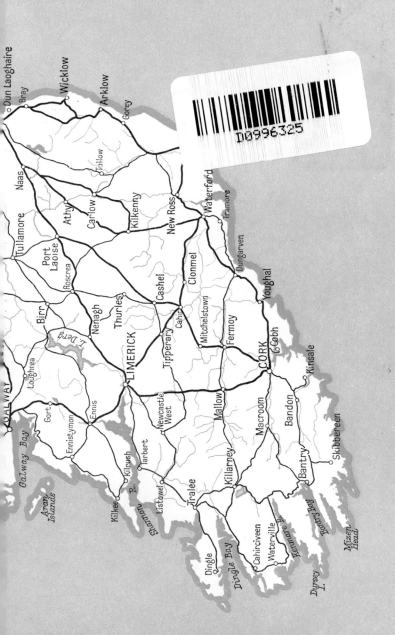

✤✤✤✤✤✤✤✤✤✤✤✤✤✤✤

Ireland

RED GUIDE

Fourth edition
© 1971 Ward Lock Limited—ISBN 0 7063 5070 7.

Printed in Great Britain by
Cox & Wyman Limited, London, Fakenham and Reading

Aer Lingus: Irish International Airlines

The Complete
IRELAND

****

*A survey of the
principal resorts and places
of interest*

Edited by Reginald J. W. Hammond

WARD LOCK LIMITED
London and Sydney

Maps and Plans

❦❦❦❦❦❦❦❦❦❦❦❦❦❦❦❦❦❦❦❦❦❦

4

Contents

✿✿✿✿✿✿✿✿✿✿✿

5

CONTENTS

6

CONTENTS

CONTENTS

9

Illustrations

✤✤✤✤✤✤✤✤✤✤✤✤✤✤✤✤

Photographs reproduced by courtesy of Bord Failte Éireann (Irish Tourist Board) and the Northern Ireland Tourist Board.

BY AIR TO IRELAND

There are four touch down points in Ireland, these are Dublin, Cork and Shannon in the South and Belfast in the North. Frequent services daily are operated by *Aer Lingus–Irish International Airlines* from ten points in Britain to the three in Ireland, and *British European Airways*, also, operate services to Dublin from London, Birmingham, Manchester, and from London to Shannon. Belfast air services are operated within British European Airways Domestic network.

Aer Lingus–Irish International Airlines services to Ireland offer the most comprehensive network. Such cities as London, Manchester, Birmingham, Bristol, Cardiff, Glasgow, Edinburgh, Liverpool and Leeds/Bradford have direct flights to Ireland. Additional services are operated by *British Midland, British United Airways, BKS* and *Cambrian Airways*.

Fuller information may be obtained on inquiry from Aer Lingus–Irish International Airlines at 223 Regent Street, London W.1; 67 Deansgate, Manchester 3; 19 Bennett's Hill, Birmingham 2; 19, Dixon Street, St. Enoch Square, Glasgow C.2, and from any of the British European Airway's offices, or your travel agent.

For passengers wishing to travel by air from the Continent, Dublin is linked either direct, or, via Manchester with 13 Continental centres; these include the major cities in Western Europe.

The North American network of Aer Lingus–Irish International Airlines links Dublin and Shannon with Boston, New York, Chicago and Montreal. There are frequent daily services during the summer months across the Atlantic, and during the winter at least a daily service to America. Extra flights are arranged to meet the heavy tourist traffic.

Indeed air services to Ireland are the most comprehensive for visitors to this friendly country.

SEA ROUTES TO IRELAND

The following are the regular sea routes to Ireland with all the year round services and with additional services during the summer months. In all cases there is accommodation for cars. Full particulars are available from the operating companies, from British Rail and agents.

Dublin (Dun Laoghaire) and **Holyhead**
   56 miles. 3 hours 15 minutes. Nightly. Also car-ferry service daily early May to early October. (British Rail L.M.R.)
Dublin (North Wall) and **Liverpool** (Prince's Dock)
   130 miles. 7 hours. Daily. British and Irish Steam Packet Co. Ltd.
Dublin (North Wall) and **Glasgow** (Anderston Quay)
   310 miles. 10 hours. Summer only. Burns & Laird Lines Limited.
Belfast (Donegall Quay) and **Ardrossan** (Winton Pier)
   85 miles. 4¼ hours. Weekdays. Burns & Laird Lines Ltd.
Belfast (Donegall Quay) and **Heysham**
   125 miles. 7 hours. Week-nights. British Rail (L.M.R.)
Belfast (Donegall Quay) and **Liverpool** (Prince's Dock)
   156 miles. 10 hours. Week-nights. Belfast Steamship Co. Ltd.
Belfast (Donegall Quay) and **Glasgow** (Lancefield Quay)
   194 miles. 9½ hours. Tuesdays, Thursdays and Saturdays. Burns & Laird Lines Ltd.
Belfast and **Preston**
   Sailing times according to tide. 12½ hours. Weekly. The Transport Ferry Service.
Cork (Penrose Quay) and **Swansea**
   7 hours. Daily. Car-ferry service. B & I Line.
Derry (Prince's Quay) and **Glasgow** (Broomislaw Quay)
   142 miles. 12½ hours. Wednesdays and Saturdays. Burns & Laird Lines Ltd.
Larne and **Stranraer**
   35 miles. 2¼ hours. Week-days. Caledonian Steam Packet Co. (Irish Services) Ltd.
Larne and **Preston**
   Sailing times according to tide. Daily except Sundays. The Transport Ferry Service.
Rosslare and **Fishguard**
   55 miles. 3¼ hours. Tuesdays, Thursdays and Saturdays. British Rail (W.R.).

Sailing Tickets and Operating Companies

At certain times during the summer season sailing tickets are necessary in addition to the travel ticket (The Transport Ferry Service excepted.) Application, well in advance, for both outward and inward journeys can be made to the operating companies or British Rail.

British Rail (London Midland Region), Holyhead or Heysham, according to route.
British Rail (Western Region), Paddington, W.2.
Belfast Steamship Co. Ltd., 9 Donegall Place, Belfast 1.
227 Regent Street, London, W.1.
Burns & Laird Lines Ltd., 52 Robertson Street, Glasgow.
9 Donegall Place, Belfast.
Caledonian Steam Packet Co. (Irish Services) Ltd., Stranraer Harbour.
B & I Line, 155 Regent Street, London, W.1.
Transport Ferry Service, 25 Whitehall, S.W.1.

Hotels and Accommodation

Hotels in Ireland range from the very simple to the luxurious, but in all there will be found a degree of comfort and service, a welcome and good fare, that together will ensure a happy stay. All hotels in Ireland are registered, and official lists of the principal establishments are issued annually by Bord Failte Éireann, Irish Tourist Board, 14 Upper O'Connell Street, Dublin, and the Northern Ireland Tourist Board, 6 Royal Avenue, Belfast. Also available are lists of the smaller guest houses, farms and private houses where less expensive though no less comfortable accommodation is available. Throughout this Guide we have indicated a selection of some of the hotels at the various centres, together with an indication of the number of rooms available. During the main summer months it is important to make early reservation particularly in the more popular districts.

Youth Hostels

There are over fifty Hostels in Ireland open to members of Youth Hostel Associations. They vary from castles to cottages, from shooting lodges to coastguard stations, from schools to barracks. Those in the Republic of Ireland are the property of An Óige (39 Mountjoy Square South, Dublin) and those in Northern Ireland of The Youth Hostel Association of Northern Ireland (Bryson House, Bedford Street, Belfast 2), from each of whom handbooks listing their hostels may be obtained.

13

USEFUL FACTS

Ireland, with a total area of 32,000 square miles, lies to the west of Great Britain, in the Atlantic Ocean. It is separated from Britain by the North Channel, the Irish Sea and the St. George's Channel. Its greatest breadth, from Annagh Head to Dundrum Bay is 180 miles and the greatest length, from Mizen Head to Fair Head, is 302 miles.

The country consists for the greater part of its area of a central limestone plain encompassed by a 2,000-mile coast line, and periodic hill and mountain groups. The highest of the mountain ranges are Magillicuddy's Reeks (Carrantuohill, 3,414 feet, is the highest point in Ireland), Wicklow Mountains (Lugnaquilla, 3,039 feet) the Galtee Mountains (Galtybeg, 3,018 feet), Mourne Mountains (Slieve Donard, 2,796 feet), Connemara Mountains (Twelve Pins (Bens), 2,695 feet), Knockmealdown Mountains (Knockmealdown, 2,609 feet), Comeragh Mountains (Knockanaffrin, 2,470 feet), Derryveagh Mountains (Errigal, 2,466 feet), and Sperrin Mountains (Sawel, 2,240 feet).

The Shannon River is the longest in the British Isles and flows for 240 miles from its source in Co. Cavan to Limerick and its long estuary to meet the Atlantic at Loop Head, Co. Clare. Again, Lough Neagh with an area of 150 square miles, is the largest inland water both in Ireland and the British Isles.

Ireland's climate is rather more equable than that of Great Britain, with cooler summers and milder winters. February is generally the coldest month and July and August the warmest.

Ireland is divided into four Provinces, each subdivided into counties, thirty-two in all, as follows: *Connacht* (Counties Galway, Leitrim, Mayo, Roscommon, Sligo), *Leinster* (Counties Carlow, Dublin, Kildare, Kilkenny, Laois (Leix), Longford, Louth, Meath, Offaly, Westmeath, Wexford, Wicklow), *Munster* (Counties Clare, Cork, Kerry, Limerick, Tipperary, Waterford) and *Ulster* (Counties Antrim, Armagh, Cavan, Donegal, Down, Fermanagh, Londonderry, Monaghan, Tyrone). The Constitution of Ireland, 1937, declares Ireland a sovereign independent democratic state, and twenty-six counties come within the authority of the Government of the Republic of Ireland. Six counties of the province of Ulster (Antrim, Armagh, Londonderry, Down, Fermanagh and

14

Tyrone) however, form the collective term "Northern Ireland" and are administered by a separate local Parliament from whom certain fiscal powers are reserved to the British Parliament.

A recent estimate of population amounted to 4,368,802, of whom 568,772 resided in Dublin and 416,000 in Belfast, the respective seats of government.

Railways

The national transport undertaking for the Republic of Ireland is Coras Iompair Éireann, which maintains a fast service of trains over a network connecting many major centres. In Northern Ireland, the Northern Ireland Railways Co. Ltd. maintains speedy and comfortable services to many points in the Six Counties. The main line railway between Dublin and Belfast is under the joint control of both undertakings.

Buses and Coaches

Both Coras Iompair Eireann and Ulsterbus Ltd. provide comprehensive services of buses and coaches with connections to all parts of their respective territories. Coach tours are also provided in addition to which are those operated by numerous local concerns. Some British coach companies also operate inclusive tours in Ireland. Combined coach and rail or coach-air tours are also available.

Shooting

Shooting is immensely popular throughout Ireland, and especially in the west. In many districts it is quite free, whilst in others permission is available at moderate charges. Many hotels have shooting rights which are freely available to their visitors. Full particulars of suitable grounds and letting arrangements can be obtained from the Irish Land Commissioners, Merrion Street, Dublin.

Horse Racing

There are over thirty race-courses holding meetings regularly in summer. The principal classic events are the Irish Derby, among the world's richest horse races, the St. Leger and the Guineas, which are run at The Curragh, County Kildare. Point-to-Point meetings are held in the spring and Steeplechase

15

meetings throughout the year. There is considerable bloodstock breeding in Ireland, Irish-bred race horses to a value of well over three million pounds being exported annually.

Hunting

Hunting is equally popular with horse racing, for all Irish people love their horses and ride or watch other people ride at every opportunity. There are two famous packs of Staghounds —The County Down and the Ward Union, the latter hunting the open country of Co. Meath. There are many packs of foxhounds, harriers and beagles with frequent meets. Hiring charges for hunters are very reasonable.

The Dublin Horse Show is held in August, and is the climax of Ireland's sporting season, and certainly one of the world's greatest horse shows.

National Games

Rugby, soccer, tennis and cricket are played extensively and facilities exist at most centres. The national ball games of Ireland, however, are hurling, Gaelic football and handball. Hurling is fast and spectacular. Played with teams of fifteen, it is similar to hockey or shinty, though considerably more strenuous. The women's version of the game is known as Camogie. Gaelic football, with teams of fifteen, is a combination of rugby and soccer, with the players catching the ball and running three paces before taking a kick. Handball is similar to fives and is popular in the more rural districts.

Greyhound Racing and Coursing

There are numerous tracks in Ireland with frequent meetings. The headquarters of the Irish Coursing Club is at Clonmel, Co. Tipperary, where many dogs are registered in the Irish Stud Book each year.

Angling

The many lakes and rivers of Ireland provide an abundance of fish—salmon, sea-trout, brown trout, and coarse fish (pike, perch, rudd and bream especially). There is a considerable amount of free-fishing throughout the country, brown trout and coarse fishing being almost everywhere free. The best salmon fisheries are strictly preserved, but there are still very

16

many places where the salmon fisher may fish entirely free. Many hotels have fishing rights which they freely pass to their visitors. For salmon and sea-trout, licences are necessary, these being obtainable on a yearly, monthly or weekly basis. Unique in Ireland is the free, or almost entirely free, fishing for brown trout. Some clubs and associations control their local waters and generally permission must be obtained from the respective secretaries.

Full information concerning licences, places to fish, etc., are obtainable from the Irish Tourist Office, 14 Upper O'Connell Street, Dublin, or the Tourist Information Centre, 6 Royal Avenue, Belfast 1.

Golf

There are well over two hundred golf courses in Ireland, many of them of championship standard and all in superlative playing condition. Green fees and other charges are generally lower than for comparable services in Great Britain. Principal courses have been indicated in the descriptions of the various centres, throughout this Guide. Most clubs have extensive fixture lists that will appeal to visiting players, while for the spectator there are numerous championship and professional tournaments to watch.

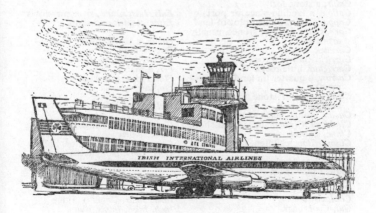

IRISH INTERNATIONAL AIRLINES

GLOSSARY

The following list gives a selection of words commonly used in the formation of place names together with their topographical equivalents.

Agha, a field
Aherlow, a valley
Aill, a cliff
Annagh, a marsh
Ard, a height
As, ess, a waterfall
Ath, a ford

Bal, Bel, entrance, mouth
Bal, Bally, Baile, a place or town
Bal, Bally, a path or way
Bane, Baun, white
Bawn, fortified enclosure
Beg, Beag, little
Ben, Pin, peak, mountain
Bog, soft
Boher, a road
Boherun, a lane
Bon, Bun, foot, end
Boy, yellow
Bray, a hill

Cahir, a stone fort
Callow, a landing-place or port
Cappa, Cappo, a tilled plot of land
Carn, Cairn, heap of stones, usually artificial
Carnock, square
Carrick, Carrig, a rock
Carrigans, little rocks
Carrow, a quarter (in land measurement)
Cashel, ancient stone fort, church boundary wall
Cavan, hollow place, cave
Claddagh, Clydagh, beach, sea-shore
Clane, sloping
Clann, Clan, children, descendants, race
Clar, Clare, level space
Claw, Cly, a fence
Clon, Cloon, meadow
Clough, shore
Cool, corner
Cul, Cool, back
Coon, harbour

Cor, round hill
Cree, Creagh, boundary, end
Crag, Creg, rock, crag
Creeve, tree
Crusha, cross, cross-roads
Curragh, Curra, marsh or low plain

Da, two
Dangan, Dingle, stronghold; (adj.) strong
Dare, Derry, oak, oak-grove
Derg, red
Desert, Dysert, wilderness, hermitage
Don, Dun, Down, fort
Donagh, Donough, Donny, church (usually one thought to have been founded by St. Patrick)
Doo, Dub, Duff, etc., black
Droghed, Drohid, Drehid, Drought, bridge
Drom, Drum, ridge

Enis, Inis, island, river meadows
Espic, Aspick, a bishop

Fahan, a green, lawn
Farran, land
Feakle, tooth, tooth-like crag
Fer, a man
Fith, Fid, Fee, a wood
Fin, fair, whitish

Gal, Goole, river
Gar, short
Garve, Garriff, rough
Glas, rivulet
Glen, Glan, Glyn, valley, hollow
Gort, Gurt, ploughland
Gorten, little field

Howth, head

Imer, Imor, Ummery, ridge
Inch, Inish, Ennis, island
Inver, estuary

18

Ken, *Kin*, head
Kil, *Kel*, church
Knock, hill
Knockan, hillock
Kyle, a strait

Lack, *Leck*, flagstone
Leath, *Leith*, *Lay*, *Le*, half
Lei, *Lee*, grey
Lem, leap or pass
Letter, wet hillside
Lis, an enclosure
Lough, *Loch*, *Low*, lake
Lougher, *Loughry*, rushes
Lurgan, a shin, strip of land
Lusk, a cave
Lyre, fork (of road or river)

Ma, *May*, *Moy*, *Maw*, *Mhagh*, an open plain
Mac, a son
Magher, a plain
Mam, *Maam*, *Maum*, a pass
Meen, level, gentle
Mel, sweet
Men, small
Mena, middle
Moate, mound
Mog, a plain
Mon, *Mount*, *Moon*, peat bog
Mor, *More*, big, great
Moy, a plain, expanse of land
Muck, a pig
Mullen, *Mullin* (*Vullen*, *Willin*, *Multy*), mill
Mullagh, summit
Mweel, *Muil*, bare

Naas, meeting-place
Navan, a grave
Noo, *New*, new, fresh

Og, youth
Oran, a spring
Oughter, upper

Owe, *Oul*, apple tree, orchard
Owen, (*Avon*), river
Ower, pale grey, dun, light brown

Pas, a pass
Pool, *Poul*, a hole

Rath, *Ray*, circular fort
Rea, *Reagh*, *Revagh*, grey
Rin, *Reen*, *Ring*, point
Risk, moor, marsh
Roe, red
Ross, *Rose*, *Rush*, promontory point; wood
Roosky, *Rusky*, marshy place

Sally, *Silla*, willow
Sean, *Shan*, *Shane*, old
Skeagh, whitethorn
Skellig, high crag or rock
Slieve, a mountain
Slighe, way or pass
Sligo, shelly river
Strad, *Straid*, a street
Stradbally, a village
Straffan, a small stream

Tamney, *Tawney*, *Turney*, fresh, green pasture
Tass, the south
Taugh, *Teach*, *Ti*, *Tagh*, (*Sta*, *Sti*), horse
Teampull, church
Ter, *Tyr*, territory
Termon, a sanctuary
Tipper, *Tubber*, *Tober*, a well
Thou, *Tan*, further side, lower part
Thurles, strong fort
Tom, *Toom*, *Tuam*, tomb, tumulus
Toor, *Tour*, tower/bleach green
Trim, *Trum*, alder-tree
Tull, *Tulla*, *Tully*, a hillock

Vally, path
Villy, path, tree

THE RED GUIDES

Aberystwyth
Anglesey and North Wales

Barmouth, Harlech, etc.
Bournemouth and District
Broads and Norfolk Coast

Channel Islands
Cornwall: North
Cornwall: South
Cornwall: West
Cotswolds

Devon: South
Dorset Coast

Exmoor and Doone Country

Infracombe and N.W.
   Devon
Isle of Man
Isle of Wight

Lake District
Llandudno, Colwyn Bay
London
Lyme Regis and District
Lynton and Lynmouth

New Forest

Peak District
Penzance and W. Cornwall

St. Ives and W. Cornwall

Tenby and South Wales
Torbay and South Devon

Wales, N. (Northern
   Section)
Wales, N. (Southern
   Section)
Wales, South
Wye Valley

Yorkshire Dales

SCOTLAND

Aberdeen, Deeside, etc.
Edinburgh and District
Highlands
Inverness, Strathpeffer, etc.

Northern Scotland
Oban, Fort William, etc.
Western Scotland

RED TOURIST GUIDES

Lake District (Baddeley)
Complete Scotland
Complete Ireland

Complete Wales
Britain

Portugal (Sarah Bradford)

Japan (William Duncan)

WARD LOCK LIMITED

DUBLIN
✣✣✣✣✣✣✣✣

Air Terminal.—Store Street Bus Station for Dublin (Collinstown) Airport.
Air services operated by Aer Lingus to Europe and North America, as
well as internal services between Dublin, Cork and Shannon. Booking
Office at 40, Upper O'Connell Street.

Banks.—*Bank of Ireland, National Bank, Munster and Leinster, Provincial,
Hibernian, National City*, and the *Royal*, all of them with principal offices
in or near College Green, and sub-offices throughout the city. The
Northern Banking Co., the *Ulster Bank* and others have branches in
Dublin. Banking hours are 10–12.30 and 1.30–3 (Fridays 5), closed
Saturdays.

Buses and Coaches.—Excellent services of local buses operate from numerous
starting points throughout the city. Long distance buses start from Central
Bus Station, Store Street, and connect with all towns of importance
throughout the country. Córas Iompair Éireann (C.I.E.) office at 59,
Upper O'Connell Street.

Churches, etc.—Principal places of worship. For particulars of service times
see local announcements.
Church of Ireland: St. Patrick's Cathedral, (*see* p. 28); Christ Church Cathedral;
University Chapel; St. Andrew's, St. Andrew's Street; St. Ann's, Dawson Street;
St. Bartholomew's, Clyde Road; St. Catherine's, Thomas Street; St. George's,
Hardwick Place; St. Mary's, Mary Street; St. Thomas', Marlborough Street;
and others.
Roman Catholic: Pro-Cathedral (*see* p. 36), Marlborough Street; St. Andrew's,
Westland Row; Carmelite Church, Clarendon Street; St. Audoen's, High Street;
St. Augustine's, Thomas Street; Franciscan Church, Merchants' Quay; St. James's,
St. James Street; St. Joseph's, Berkeley Road; St. Kevin's, Harrington Street.
There are a considerable number of others.
Baptist: Grosvenor Road, Rathmines; Phibsborough and North Circular Road.
Congregational: Inchicore Road, Kilmainham.
Friends: Eustace Street; Monkstown; Churchtown Road and Rathfarnham.
Methodist: Lower Abbey Street; St. Stephen's Green; South Great George Street;
and at Rathmines, Rathgar, Clontarf and Sandymount.
Presbyterian: Abbey Church, Parnell Square; Adelaide Road, Lower Abbey Street;
Donore Church, South Circular Road; Clontarf, Howth Road; Christ Church,
Rathgar; Sandymount.
Synagogues: Adelaide Road; Dolphin's Barn; Rathfarnham Road.
And establishments of various other denominations.

Distances.—Belfast 103, Bray 12, Cork 161, Drogheda 30, Dun Laoghaire
8, Howth 10, Killarney 191, Limerick 123, Londonderry 151, Lucan 9,
Port Laoise 53, Portrush 147, Rosslare 94, Slane 29, Wicklow 32.

Early Closing.—Wednesday and/or Saturday.

Entertainment.—
Cinemas. Near city centre are the *Savoy, Metropole* and *Carlton*, O'Connell
Street; *Capitol*, Princes Street; *Adelphi*, Middle Abbey Street; *Ambassador*, Parnell Square; *Grafton*, Grafton Street. There are numerous
cinemas throughout the suburbs.
Dancing. At *Clery's*, O'Connell Street; *Crystal*, South Anne Street;
Television Club, Harcourt Street; and at the leading hotels.
Theatres. Abbey Theatre, Abbey Street; *Gate Theatre*, Parnell Square;
Gaiety Theatre, South King Street; *Olympia*, Dame Street.

DUBLIN

Hotels.—Number of rooms indicated in brackets. Among the principal are—*Intercontinental* (314), Pembroke Road; *Gresham* (240), O'Connell Street; *Shelbourne* (200), St. Stephen's Green; *Royal Hibernian* (112), Dawson Street; *Russell* (34), St. Stephen's Green; *Anchor* (23), Parnell Square; *Central* (70), Exchequer Street; *Clarence* (70), Wellington Quay; *Four Courts* (75), Inns Quay; *Jury's* (154), College Green; *Moira* (36), Trinity Street; *Power's Royal* (30), Kildare Street; *Ivanhoe* (40), Harcourt Street; *Buswell's* (53), Molesworth Street; *Castle* (29), Gardiner Row; *Grosvenor* (19), Westland Row; *Mount Clare* (30), Clare Street; *North Star* (35), Amiens Street; *Ormond* (73), Upper Ormond Quay; *Moran's* (50), Talbot Street, and many others. A full list of hotels and guest houses may be obtained from Irish Tourist Office, 14, Upper O'Connell Street and 51 Dawson Street.

Information.—Irish Tourist Office, 14, Upper O'Connell Street. There is a Telephone Information Bureau for train and bus passengers (Dublin 47911).

Population.—568,271.

Post Office.—General Post Office, O'Connell Street. Branch offices in principal streets.

Sport.—

Baths.—Indoor baths at Tara Street, at Bride Street, Clontarf.

Golf.—There are several fine courses within a radius of 5 miles of the city, including the Castle Club, Rathfarnham, Clontarf, Elm Park and the Royal Dublin at Dollymount.

Greyhound Racing.—Stadiums at Harold's Cross Park and Shelbourne Park. Meetings on alternate days.

Horse Racing.—Three race courses close to Dublin: Phoenix Park (3 miles), Leopardstown (6 miles) and Baldoyle (8 miles).

Sailing and Rowing.—Dublin Bay is a chief centre for yachting. Annual regatta. Headquarters of Dublin rowing club mostly at Islandbridge. The Liffey provides good rowing stretches.

Tennis.—Many clubs at which visitors may play and public courts available in parks, etc.

Other Sports.—Hurling and Gaelic Football in Croke Park; facilities throughout Dublin for rugby, soccer, motor and cycle racing, gliding, fencing, etc. Salmon fishing in the *Liffey*, *Dargle* and *Vartry* rivers.

Stations.—Main line stations are:

Connolly Station for Howth, Malahide, Belfast, Derry, etc., and for Dun Laoghaire and south-east coast *via Westland Row.*

Pearse Station for Galway, Sligo and the west of Ireland, and for Dun Laoghaire boat trains, Bray, Wicklow and Rosslare.

Heuston Station for Cork, Killarney, Limerick and for the south and south west.

Youth Hostel.—Morehampton House, 78, Morehampton Road; also, open in July, August and over Easter week-end, 39, Mountjoy Square, South.

THE CITY OF DUBLIN

Most of the buses start from the City centre, a convenient starting-point from which to visit the sights of Dublin. Those

mentioned in the first route are all comprised within a distance
of about 3 miles. Buses serve the principal thoroughfares.

I.—O'Connell Street—Bank of Ireland—Trinity College—The Castle—Christ Church—St. Patrick's Cathedral

The most outstanding feature of **O'Connell Street** is its
unusual width. Down the centre are some notable statues, and
lofty buildings line its sides. Looking towards the north end,
we see part of the **Rotunda** and the **Parnell Monument,** the
latter a triangular shaft of Galway granite, 60 feet in height.
On the pedestal is a bronze statue by *Gaudens.* In the middle
of the street stands a white marble **Statue of Father Mathew,**
the "Apostle of Temperance", who had a great influence in
Ireland in the second quarter of the nineteenth century.

On the right, down O'Connell Street, the General Post
Office building displays a striking Ionic portico. The next
turning on the right is Middle Abbey Street, where are the fine
offices of the *Irish Independent,* leading to the site of the old
St. Mary's Abbey.

The *Statue of O'Connell,* at the south end of the street, is an imposing work of art. On a granite base rests a huge cylindrical pedestal
around which are typical Irish figures in bronze, the chief of which,
facing the bridge, is Erin, trampling her cast-off fetters under foot,
holding the Act of Emancipation in her left hand, and with her right
arm uplifted pointing to the Liberator above. Beneath is the single
word, "O'Connell." High above rises the colossal figure of the
patriot, draped in his cloak, with his left hand on his heart, his
favourite attitude. The base and pedestals are 28 feet high, and the
figure, begun by Foley, finished by Brock, and unveiled in 1882, is
12 feet high.

The *Liffey,* at the foot of O'Connell Street, is crossed by the
three-arched **O'Connell Bridge,** remarkable for its great width,
which exceeds its length.

Off the south side is the wide, but short, **Westmoreland Street,**
with some handsome shops. It leads to busy **College Green,**
the north side of which is occupied by the Bank, the east by
Trinity College, and the south by other banks and commercial
buildings. In the centre stands Foley's excellent statue of
Grattan.

The Bank of Ireland

(An attendant conducts visitors through the premises. Open free during Bank hours.

This fine building is one of the most notable architectural features of Dublin. It was originally the Irish House of Parliament, constructed between 1728 and 1739. Six lofty Corinthian columns support the east pediment (added in 1785), on the apex and angles of which are emblematic figures of Minerva, Justice and Liberty, the whole forming an excellent specimen of Corinthian architecture.

The *West Front* looks on Foster Place, and is of plainer design including only four Ionic pillars without statues on the pediment.

The chief or **South Front** consists of three sides of a quadrangle, colonnaded throughout. The tympanum of the central portico contains the Royal Arms; on the apex stands a figure of Hibernia, with Fidelity on her right hand and Commerce on her left.

In 1803, the Irish Parliament having been dissolved by the Act of Union, the building was sold to the Bank of Ireland.

Forming the east side of College Green is the long façade of—

Trinity College (Dublin University)

Trinity College was founded by Queen Elizabeth under a charter dated 1591. This site, on which the College now stands, was then nearly half a mile eastward of the city gates, and the official designation of the College is therefore "the College of the Holy and Undivided Trinity of Queen Elizabeth, near Dublin".

The first stone was laid in 1593, and students were admitted in 1594. For a century Trinity College remained small and poor, but towards the end of the seventeenth century it began to expand. It was rebuilt at this period in red brick; of these buildings one range (*see below*) remains, but the original Elizabethan buildings have quite disappeared. During the eighteenth century it was again rebuilt on a larger scale, and these buildings constitute the principal part of the College today. The nineteenth century saw further expansion and development, and from about 1840 to 1914 the College enjoyed in the learned world a reputation for scholarship (especially in the fields of classics and mathematics) quite out of proportion to its size and resources.

The College contains today over 4,300 students, of whom nearly a third are women.

Beyond the archway in the West Front is a large open space, of which the nearer (western) part is called **Parliament Square** (the cost of its building having been defrayed by grants from the Irish Parliament), while the further (eastern) part, beyond the campanile, is distinguished as **Library Square**. Parliament Square was built between 1752 and 1798. It is flanked on either side by the twin Corinthian porticoes (designed by Sir William Chambers, the architect of Somerset House in London) of the **Chapel** on the left (north) side, and the **Examination Hall** on the right. The ceiling of both buildings is decorated by handsome plaster-work. In the Examination Hall, which is used also for conferring of degrees and other public ceremonies, there are portraits of eminent persons connected with the College, and a large marble monument, executed in Rome by Christopher Hewitson, to Provost Baldwin (*d.* 1758).

Beyond the Chapel is the **Dining Hall,** with an Ionic pediment, approached by a broad flight of steps. In it hang portraits of past members of the University.

The **Campanile**, the gift of Lord John George Beresford, Archbishop of Armagh, was built in 1853. It houses the great bell, which was cast in 1744, and also a small bell that may have belonged to the Priory of All Hallows.

Beyond the Campanile is a red brick range known as the **Rubrics**, which dates from about 1700 and is the oldest part of the College now standing. On the left, beyond the Dining Hall, is the **Graduates' Memorial Building**, erected in 1900. Behind it is a plain square, built in 1790–1816, known as **Botany Bay** because the site was previously occupied by a kitchen garden.

The whole of the south side of Library Square is formed by the **Library**, (*open free, 10–5 Mondays to Fridays, 4 in winter, Saturdays 10–1 p.m.*).

The original nucleus of the Library were books bought in London in the years 1601–8, since when many important collections have been added. Under the Copyright Act the library is entitled to a copy of any book published in the British Isles. It now possesses over a million volumes.

Visitors are admitted only to the **Long Room** (on the first floor), a magnificent room 210 feet long, 41 feet broad and 48 feet high. Originally it had a flat, ornamented ceiling; the present barrel-vaulting dates from 1860. A series of marble busts flanks the book-stacks on either side.

Most of the books on the shelves of the Long Room date from before 1800. Nineteenth-century books are mostly in the gallery, and modern books on the ground floor. There is a rare books reading room on the second floor.

A series of glass cases contain many objects of interest. Of these the most celebrated is the Book of Kells, one of the most elaborately illuminated manuscripts in the world, and the greatest single monument of the unique Celtic art which was developed in Ireland during the Dark Ages. It consists of the four Gospels in Latin, and was executed in the monastery of Kells, County Meath in the eighth century. The Book of Durrow is less ornate; it dates from the seventh century. The leather satchel of the Book of Armagh, embossed with elaborate Celtic ornament, and the jewelled silver shrine of the Book of Dimma indicate the way in which these precious manuscripts were kept in ancient times. An ancient Irish harp of the type used by the wandering bards over 600 years ago is also exhibited.

In the main entrance to the Long Room is a shop where reproductions, slides and postcards may be purchased. The *New Library* completed in 1967, contains a large reading room and an Exhibition Hall.

Beyond the Library square is the **New Square**. At the north-west corner is the **University Press**, with an elegant Doric portico, built in 1734.

The south side of the New Square is formed by the **Museum Building**, which houses the schools of Engineering, Geology, Geography, etc. It is of interest as the first non-ecclesiastical building to be erected under the influence of the Gothic revival.

Beyond the Museum Building extends the **College Park**, which is occupied mainly by playing-fields. At the far end of it are the various **Scientific and Medical Laboratories.**

The **Provost's House**, facing into Grafton Street and set somewhat apart from the other College buildings, was built in 1760. It has one of the finest Georgian interiors in Ireland.

From College Green, the wide business thoroughfare of **Dame Street** runs away for a considerable distance.

The City Hall, or Royal Exchange, as it was once called, is a handsome but heavy-looking building in the Corinthian order, erected in 1769–79 on the site of the old Dame's Gate, the east gate of the city, and founded on a rock formerly known by the name of Stand Fast Dick.

With three fronts of Portland stone, the building is crowned by a central dome. The interior is imposing, the dome resting on a cylindrical lantern with circular windows. The statues include Grattan, by Chantrey (a splendid piece of work); Dr. Lucas, Daniel O'Connell and Secretary Drummond, by Hogan, an Irish sculptor; George II, by Van Nost; and others. The building has been used as a City Hall since 1852. The Charters of the City, dating from 1171, and the Assembly Rolls of the Corporation are preserved here.

Dublin Castle

The Castle yard is always open. State Apartments (*charge*), Monday to Friday, 10–12 and 3–4.30. Heraldic Museum (*free*), Mondays to Fridays 9.45–1 and 2.15–4.45. Church of the Most Holy Trinity (*free*), 8.15–12.45 and 2.15–6. Daily Mass at 8.45, Sundays 10.

The first fortress was built here in A.D. 840, by the Danes or Norwegians. Meiler Fitz-Henry, natural son of Henry II, started the building of a new castle in 1204. This was finished in 1215 by Archbishop de Loundres. Largely rebuilt about 1775, the castle has had a threefold use; as a citadel for the defence of the city and of the English interest, as the seat of government and the residence of the Viceroy, to which use it was put from the reign of Elizabeth down to 1922, and as the place where the courts of judicature and sometimes the high courts of Parliament were anciently held. State prisoners were once confined in the Castle; here, too, the stands of arms were kept. The State Papers, etc., have been kept in the Castle since the destruction of the Four Courts in 1922. A moat fed by the river Poddle, now underground, ran where the road in the Lower Courtyard now is.

The **Upper Castleyard,** once known as the "Devil's Half Acre", is a quadrangle 280 feet long by 130 broad. On the right is the **Bedford Tower,** surmounting an early Georgian building in which is embedded the Eastern gate-tower.

The **Genealogical Office and Heraldic Museum** contains a unique collection of heraldic devices, dress, china and glass, and many interesting documents.

The **State Apartments,** which during the British occupation accommodated the Viceroy and other Crown officials, is approached by a fine staircase. The **Presence Chamber** contains the throne, dating from William III. The **Ball Room,** or St. Patrick's Hall, so called since the institution of the Order of St. Patrick in 1783, is a splendid apartment 82 feet long, with notable paintings on the panelled ceiling. Other State rooms include the **Long Gallery,** the **State Drawing-rooms,** and the **Dining-room,** most of which have beautiful ceilings.

The **Lower Castleyard,** reached through an archway, is a large irregular area, 250 feet by 220 feet, but the buildings, with the exception of the Church, and the Record Tower, with walls 19 feet thick at the base, are poor.

The **Church of the Most Holy Trinity.** Formerly the Chapel Royal, this beautiful building, in the Decorated style, stands on the site of a garrison chapel of the sixteenth century, and was completed in 1814. The church

came into Roman Catholic ownership in 1943. The exterior is adorned with many carved heads and the interior is rich in Irish oak carving and stained glass.

Leaving the Castle, we continue up Dame Street and its continuation, Lord Edward Street, and cross the head of Fishamble Street, where stood a famous music-hall in which Handel's *Messiah* received its first performance in 1742, under Handel's own conductorship. At No. 3 Lord Edward Street, the poet Mangan was born. The house faces the east end of the ancient Priory Church of the Holy Trinity, commonly called—

Christ Church Cathedral

(Open to visitors daily, May to September 9.30 a.m. to 5.30 p.m. October to April 9.30 a.m. to 4 p.m. Choral services daily on weekdays. Matins 10.45 a.m., Evensong at 6 p.m. Sundays at 11 and 3.30).

This is the diocesan cathedral of the sees of Dublin and Glendalough. Its foundation is 150 years older than St. Patrick's. The Church of the Holy Trinity was first erected by Sitric, the Danish King of Dublin, and Donatus, the Bishop, in 1038. The Norman invaders, led by Strongbow, Earl of Pembroke, and Archbishop Laurence O'Toole, rebuilt the church on a larger and more magnificent scale, and succeeding prelates further added to it. In 1539, Henry VIII reconstituted it "the deanery and chapter of Christ Church." In 1871 a complete restoration was put in hand. The result is a magnificent pile of buildings bearing a close resemblance to the ancient cathedral. The plan is cruciform, with nave, transepts, choir and chancel, and a square battlemented tower rising from the intersection.

The interior is very fine. Six pointed arches on clustered columns separate the nave from the aisles, which are lit by lancet windows. The triforium and clerestory are also pointed with chevron mouldings. The roof is groined. The west window is pierced by five lancets. The screen and pulpit are handsome, and the general effect of the choir and chancel, with their stained glass windows, is very rich. Among the tombs the one that attracts most interest is that commonly called Strongbow's; it replaces the one destroyed by the fall of the roof in the sixteenth century.

The *Crypt*, which is the oldest part, dates from 1173. Many fragments of the old stonework may be distinguished, by their darker colour, in the pillars and other parts of the Cathedral.

The Tower contains a carillon of thirteen bells but not now played.

The modern Chapter House is on the north-east side. The ruins of the old Chapter House have been uncovered and may be seen in the gardens to the south of the Cathedral.

The Synod Hall is connected with the west end of the Cathedral by a covered way; it contains the Hall of Convocation of the Irish Church, and accommodation for the bishops, clergy and laity.

Westward from Christ Church, along **High Street,** is St. Audoen's Roman Catholic Church, while to the north are the ruins of **St. Audoen's Parish Church,** one of the oldest in Dublin. The remains of **St. Audoen's Arch,** part of a gate which the Burghers erected in 1315 at the invasion of Edward Bruce, may yet be seen.

Farther west, along **Thomas Street,** is the **Church of the Augustinian Friars,** one of the finest in the city (Robert Emmet was executed nearly opposite this in 1803). Beyond that is **Guinness's Brewery,** with entrance in James Street. *A limited number of visitors are admitted and conducted through the Brewery hourly, Mondays to Fridays, from 10 to 3.*

To the south of Christ Church, Nicholas Street leads through a largely rebuilt area to **St. Patrick's Park,** bestowed by Lord Iveagh, and just beyond is—

St. Patrick's Cathedral

(Open free to visitors every week-day from 9 a.m. to 6 p.m. Week-day Choral Services, 10 a.m. and 5.30 p.m., Saturdays at 10 a.m.; Sunday Services, 8.30 a.m., 11.15 a.m. and 3.15 p.m.)

This splendid cruciform building, which measures 300 feet long by 67 feet wide with a transept width of 157 feet, was erected on the site of the old parish church of St. Patrick in the twelfth century. It suffered much damage by fire and water, having been several times partially flooded by the now subterranean river Poddle. In 1370, after a disastrous fire, it was thoroughly renovated and restored by Archbishop Minot. Dean Swift will always be associated with St. Patrick's

Cathedral, as during his deanship he issued some of his most famous writings.

In 1860–4, St. Patrick's Cathedral, then in a dilapidated condition, was restored by Sir Benjamin Lee Guinness, the work being completed in 1902 by his son. The style is chiefly Early English, with a fourteenth-century tower and steeple 251 feet high. The flying buttresses are unusual in Ireland. The bells are noted for their beauty.

The entrance is usually by the south-west porch, near which is a seated statue of Sir Benjamin Guinness. The great length of the interior, the lofty groined roof, the pointed arches of the nave aisles, the triforia and clerestory openings, the banners of the Knights of St. Patrick over their canopied stalls in the choir, and the stained glass windows in the Lady Chapel beyond, and elsewhere, combine to produce a very fine and stately effect. There are a number of memorial tablets and monuments, a fine stone pulpit in memory of Dean Pakenham, and an old pulpit which was in use during Swift's time. In the south transept is a memorial of Wolfe, the writer of *The Burial of Sir John Moore*. The tower contains a clock and 14 bells. There are some fine pre-Reformation brasses in the south choir aisle. The Baptistery is the oldest part of the Cathedral. Looking east from the Nave, only thirteenth-century architecture, skilfully restored and repaired, is seen.

Some ancient stones and a Celtic cross of the ninth or tenth century were found at the **Well of St. Patrick** (now closed), with which water the saint is said to have baptized his Dublin converts.

The choral services of the Cathedral are deservedly famous.

Adjoining the Cathedral is a valuable Reference Library, known, from the Archbishop of Dublin who founded and endowed it, as **Marsh's Library** *(open free, except Tuesdays, from 10.30–12.30. Additionally from 2–4 on Wednesdays, Thursdays and Fridays.* It is especially rich in ecclesiastical literature of the fifteenth century and earlier, some of its treasures being unmatched even in the British Museum. It was the first (1703) public library in Ireland.

II. Grafton Street—St. Stephen's Green—University College, Dublin—National Museum—National Library—Mansion House—National Gallery—Custom House—Pro-cathedral

Grafton Street is the busiest in the city. Here will be found the leading shops. Off Grafton Street, at the Stephen's Green end, is Balfe Street, where a tablet indicates where Michael Balfe, the famous composer, was born in 1808. **Johnson's Court,** a narrow public passage, runs off Grafton Street and leads to the Carmelite **Church of St. Teresa,** where Hogan's masterpiece, "The Dead Christ," is treasured. This Court is noted as the place where Samuel Whyte established his first school, and where such celebrities as Richard Brinsley Sheridan, Samuel Lover, George Petrie the antiquarian, Thomas Moore the poet, Robert Emmet, and the Duke of Wellington were pupils.

West of Grafton Street, in South William Street, is the **Dublin Civic Museum** (*open Tues to Sats, 10–6; Sundays 11–2; closed Mondays*) occupying the former City Assembly House. The collection includes numerous prints, maps and coins, and other items of antiquarian and historical interest concerning the city.

St. Stephen's Green, at the south end of Grafton Street is the largest park within the city. This charming pleasure-ground of 22 acres was given to the public in 1880 by Lord Ardilaun. There are some good flower beds and a waterfall and stream on the northern side, and various memorials.

In South King Street, near the north-west corner of the Green, is the **Gaiety Theatre.** Around the Green are many fine buildings and residences, notably that of the **Royal College of Surgeons,** with a Doric front. Almost facing the College is a seated statue of Lord Ardilaun, by *Farrell.*

Buses run down this side of the Green and along its continuation, **Harcourt Street,** where, on the left at No. 87, is the **National Children's Hospital.**

Returning, and proceeding along the south side of St. Stephen's Green, we pass **St. Patrick's Nurses' Home,** the **Wesley College,** where George Bernard Shaw received his early education, and the Methodist Church. Farther on is the **University Church,** an ornate structure founded by Cardinal Newman in 1856 at the time he established the first Catholic University in the next building. A little farther on the **Department of External Affairs** occupies the former ornate **Iveagh House.** At the corner the first turn to the right leads to Earlsfort Terrace, where are situated the principal buildings of—

University College, Dublin

a constituent College of the National University of Ireland. The College had its origin in the Catholic University of Ireland, founded under the Rectorship of John Henry Newman in 1852. Until 1919 the main work of the College was carried out in what is now Newman House (Nos. 85 and 86 St. Stephen's Green), still used for the recreation of students. The foundation of the Royal University in 1879 led to the establishment of University College, Dublin, in what had originally been St. Patrick's House in the Catholic University (86, St. Stephen's Green). From 1883–1908 the College was in charge of the Jesuit Fathers. In 1908, under the Irish Universities Act, University College was incorporated by Royal Charter. The buildings in Earlsfort Terrace house the administrative and much of the academic work

of University College. The Engineering Faculty is in Merrion Street.
It was in the College Council Chamber that Dáil Éireann held, in
1921, the stormy session at which the Anglo-Irish Treaty was
ratified.

In recent years the College has acquired an estate of close on
300 acres at Belfield, Donnybrook, and a large new complex houses
the Science and Commerce faculties to be joined shortly by the Arts,
Administration and library departments. The Agriculture Faculty
farm is at Lyons Estate, near Celbridge.

On the east side of St. Stephen's Green is **St. Vincent's
Hospital,** which is under the care of the Sisters of Charity, and
some fine residential houses, in pre-Union days the homes of
Irish nobility. Leading north from the Green by the side of the
Shelbourne Hotel is **Kildare Street,** half-way along which, on
the right, are the National Museum and National Library, a
fine groups of buildings in the Italian Renaissance style on
either side of the Courtyard of old Leinster House.

THE NATIONAL MUSEUM

The museum is open free Tuesdays to Saturdays, 10–5, Sundays, 2–5. Closed Mondays, Christmas Day and Good Friday.

The National Museum originated from the amalgamation of the
collection of Irish antiquities assembled by the Royal Irish Academy
and the zoological and mineralogical collections of the Royal Dublin
Society. The present Museum buildings were completed about 1890
and the institution now contains the national collections of antiquities, fine arts (exclusive of painting), zoology and geology. The
main building is entered from Kildare Street, but the entrance to
the zoological section is from Merrion Street.

The exhibition of Irish antiquities occupies most of the ground floor of the
Kildare Street building and embraces displays relating to all phases of the
prehistoric, Early Christian and medieval periods. Immediately inside the
entrance is a circular vestibule containing a number of casts of the richly
decorated high crosses, dating from the eighth to the tenth century, which stand
at the sites of early monasteries in many parts of the country. The main
exhibition of antiquities in the central court is designed to show a representative selection of the surviving relics of human activity in Ireland,
beginning with the time when man first arrived here in the mesolithic period,
about 6,000 B.C. The flint tools and weapons of this period are succeeded
by the polished stone axeheads, pottery and other remains of the neolithic
period, which commenced about 3,000 B.C. The exhibition is particularly
rich in relics of the succeeding bronze age, when Irish smiths produced a
great variety of weapons, tools, personal ornaments and other items. From
the later stages of the bronze age, specially noteworthy exhibits are the series
of magnificent cauldrons, trumpets and shields, while the collection of gold
objects of the period is the richest in northern Europe. These comprise

crescents of sheet gold, called lunulae; twisted torques, ranging in size from bracelets to girdles; and a large number of miscellaneous objects, including hair-ornaments, necklaces, dress-fasteners and pins. The iron age material, though small in quantity, contains a number of superbly made trumpets, highly ornamented horse-bits, brooches and a spectacular gold collar and model boat found at Broighter, Co. Derry. The exhibition is particularly rich in items of the elaborate metalwork of the Early Christian period. Among these are: the Tara Brooch (eighth century), Ardagh Chalice (eighth century), Moylough Belt Shrine (eighth century), Lismore Crozier (twelfth century), Shrine of St. Patrick's Bell (twelfth century) and Cross of Cong (twelfth century). The day to day life of the people of the time is illustrated by examples of their personal belongings (combs, brooches, etc.), domestic equipment (wooden vessels, spindle-whorls, etc.), agricultural gear (ox-yokes, ploughshares, etc) and much else. The medieval material includes items of dress and footwear found in bogs, wooden religious statues, seals and finger-rings.

The study-collection of Irish antiquities contains hundreds of thousands of specimens of artifacts from every phase of the country's past and provides invaluable raw material for research into the life of its people. There is also an important and growing folk life section.

On the ground floor there is also an exhibition of historical material connected with events and figures of the past two centuries and including uniforms and regalia.

The collections of fine and applied art are in the first-floor rooms and on the gallery of the central court. They include representative collections of Irish silver, glass, costume and textiles. The numismatic collection contains specimens of all Irish coins and medals and is particularly rich in examples of the earliest Hiberno-Norse coinage. Clocks and watches by Irish makers are also exhibited, and the room devoted to musical instruments contains many examples of Irish origin. Of less specialized Irish interest are the exhibitions of furniture and ceramics, the latter of which contains material illustrating the products of the main Irish, British and continental centres of manufacture, together with a selection of wares from China, Japan and elsewhere. In addition, there are smaller exhibitions of jewellery, ivories, metalwork and stamps. The ancient civilizations of Egypt, Crete, Greece and Rome are illustrated by a selection of their most characteristic remains, including mummies, pottery, metalwork, religious objects and personal ornaments.

The **Zoological Collection** occupies a separate building, entered from Merrion Street. The ground floor is devoted to an exhibition of the Irish fauna, with specimens of all the native mammals, birds, reptiles, amphibia and fishes, together with a representative cross-section of Irish insects, crustaceans, molluscs, etc. Of unusual interest are a number of well-preserved skeletons of the Giant Irish Deer, which has been extinct since post-glacial times. On the upper floor and the surrounding galleries is an exhibition of mammals, birds, reptiles, fishes, insects, etc., from various parts of the world. The study collections are extremely extensive and, in addition to much comparative foreign material, embrace complete series of the entire fauna of the country and a very large assemblage of geological specimens.

From the vestibule of the National Museum, we follow the pathway leading to—

LEINSTER HOUSE

The public are admitted to the visitors' gallery when sessions are in progress on presenting a pass, which may be obtained from members of the Dáil.[1] The normal hours of meeting are on Tuesdays and Wednesdays from 3 p.m. to 10.30 p.m. and on Thursdays from 10.30 a.m. to 5 p.m. When sessions are not in progress visitors can be conducted through the Houses on application to Usher at Kildare Street Gate, 10–1 and 2–5, Mondays to Fridays. Overseas visitors by arrangement at gate.

Now the seat of the Irish Parliament, the building was erected about 1745 as a town residence for the first Duke of Leinster.

In 1815, this magnificent residence was bought by the Royal Dublin Society, who continued to use it as their headquarters until 1922, when the then new Irish Free State Government acquired the building, which has been the Oireachtas or Parliament House ever since.

From Leinster House it is but a few paces to—

THE NATIONAL LIBRARY

The Reading Room is open from 10 a.m. to 10 p.m. on week-days. Saturdays till 1 p.m. Closed for 3 week period late July—early August.

The Library contains over 500,000 books and miscellaneous collections of literature, besides files of Irish newspapers, old and new, and a very large collection of manuscripts relating to Ireland.

Adjoining the Library building is the **National College of Art,** where the Royal Hibernian Academy annually holds its exhibition.

Leaving the National Library, we pass about a hundred yards farther on the **College of Physicians** and the **Kildare Street Club,** and turning to the right along Leinster Street and Clare Street we reach the west side of **Merrion Square.** Three sides of the Square are occupied by residences, the west side being bounded by Leinster Lawn. At the northern end is—

THE NATIONAL GALLERY OF IRELAND

Free on weekdays from 10 a.m. to 6 p.m. (Thursdays until 9 p.m.) and on Sundays from 2 p.m. to 5 p.m.

Opened in 1864, the National Gallery now contains in the oils section alone nearly 2,000 paintings, among which are many universally acknowledged masterpieces. The Dutch and Flemish collections include superb works by Rembrandt, Franz Hals, Jan Steen, Ruysdael, Rubens, Van Dyck and Teniers.

Among early Italian works worthy of special notice are: *The Attempted Martyrdom of Saints Cosmas and Damian* by Fra Angelico.

[1] *Dáil Éireann* (pron. Dawl Airun), lit. "The Assembly or Parliament of Ireland."

Ireland (c)   33

A *Madonna and Child*—by Paolo Uccello; and a *Madonna and Child with Saint John*, attributed to Michelangelo. In addition, there are the superb *Portrait of Baldasarre Castigione* by Titian, the moving *Pieta* by Perugino, and works by Signorelli, Tura, Palma Vecchio, Moroni, Paolo Veronese, and later Italian masters.

In the French collection are major works by Nicolas Poussin, a beautiful painting by Claude Lorraine, a water colour by Cézanne, *Montagne Sainte Victoire*, and many other examples of French art from the fifteenth to the twentieth century.

In the Spanish room there is a famous *Saint Francis in Ecstasy* by El Greco, four masterly works by Goya, characteristic examples of the art of Morales, Zurbaran and Ribera, and portraits by Sanchez Coello and Pantoja de la Cruz.

No gallery has a more moving example of the Early Flemish School than the *Christ Saying Farewell to His Mother* by Geerhardt David, and there are many other fine examples from the studios of Flanders (as of the Rhenish and Danubian Schools) of the fifteenth and early sixteenth centuries.

The English school is very fully represented by nine landscapes and portraits by Gainsborough, seven works by Reynolds, four by Hogarth, three by Richard Wilson, and several pictures by other leading English painters of the eighteenth and nineteenth centuries. Scotland is most notably represented by Raeburn and Allan Ramsay.

The galleries have been enriched by important recent acquisitions, among them being: *Venice, Queen of the Adriatic*, by Tintoretto; *Holy Family* and a *St. Mary Magdalen* by Murillo; works by Louis le Nain, Nattier, Quentin de la Tour and Courbet. Twentieth century art includes a number of brilliant works by the late Jack B. Yeats and several examples of the Paris School—Picasso, Juan Gris, Segonzac, etc. There are also works by Orpen, Osborne and Paul Henry, contemporaries of Yeats, and in the Irish rooms many other notable pictures.

The collection of drawings ranges from the early Italians to Durer and Watteau and down to Whistler and Sargent.

The **National Portrait Gallery** an integral part of the National Gallery contains a splendid collection of paintings of distinguished Irishmen and English people who have influenced Irish history, together with drawings and engravings of historical interest.

We next enter Upper Merrion Street, where on the right are **Government Buildings,** the headquarters of the Republic of Ireland Government and of its principal offices, including the Prime Minister's Department, the Department of Agriculture, the Department of Justice and the Department of Finance.

In the quadrangle behind the Government buildings is the **College of Science,** now a part of the National University; opened in 1911, it is a handsome structure with well-equipped laboratories, separate lecture rooms, and a large lecture theatre.

Opposite Government Buildings, at 24, Upper Merrion Street, is **Mornington House,** the reputed birthplace of Arthur Wellesley, Duke of Wellington. A minute's walk brings us back again to

Merrion Square, with many fine Georgian houses, which have now mostly been converted for office use. Famous people who have lived in Merrion Square include Oscar Wilde at No. 1, Daniel O'Connell at No. 58, Joseph Sheridan le Fanu at No. 70, W. B. Yeats at No. 52 and later at No. 82, and at Plunkett House, No. 84, Sir Horace Plunkett.

Merrion Street leads to Westland Row and the Railway Station, near which is **St. Andrew's Catholic Church,** containing a fine group representing the Transfiguration—the work of Hogan, perhaps the greatest sculptor to whom Ireland can lay claim.

Returning along Westland Row and taking the first turning on the right we pass through **Lincoln Place,** and so to **Leinster Street.**

At the west end of Leinster Street **Dawson Street** runs off to the left. Here is **St. Ann's Church,** where the poetess Felicia Hemans is buried; she lived and died at No. 20, quite close to the Church. Close by also, at No. 19, is—

The Royal Irish Academy

Open free on week-days from 9.30 a.m. to 5.30 p.m.; Saturdays, until 12.45 p.m.

a Georgian house of unusual design. Plaster-work over the main staircase is very fine and the Meeting Room at the back contains the benches and chandeliers from the old Parliament House on College Green. Its Library preserves many rare manuscripts, including the *Stowe Missal,* which contains the form of the Mass and other prayers in use in Ireland from the fifth to eighth century. Its other valuable manuscripts include the *Cathach*, a copy of the psalms reputedly made by St. Choluim Chille himself, the *Book of the Dun Cow*, the *Annals of the Four Masters*, the *Leabhar Breac*, or the "Speckled Book," and the *Book of Ballymote*. A splendid collection of rare books dealing with science, literature and archaeology is a feature of the library.

Adjacent to the Royal Irish Academy is—

The Mansion House,

a fine building in the Queen Anne style containing some spacious apartments, notably the panelled *Oak Room* and the *Round Room*, 90 feet in diameter, the latter having been specially built by the Dublin Corporation in 1821 for the purpose of entertaining George IV. The Mansion House has been the official residence of the Lord Mayors of Dublin for many years, and the scene of important public meetings.

Beyond the Mansion House, on the opposite side of the street, is the **Royal Irish Automobile Club** (No. 32), and thence it is only a short distance to the upper end of Dawson Street, which opens on the north side of St. Stephen's Green.

We can from here return *via* Grafton Street (p. 29), the next on the right leading from the Green; or may take a bus back through Kildare Street, Nassau Street, Westland Row, Pearse Street, and College Green, to O'Connell Bridge.

Alighting at College Street (before reaching the Bridge), we walk the short distance to Pearse Street, where is the newly rebuilt Abbey Theatre and St. Mark's Parish Church. Hawkins Street, opposite Pearse Street, leads to **Burgh Quay,** where are the **Corn Exchange** and O'Connell's Conciliation Hall, the headquarters of the famous Irish leader during his agitation for the Repeal of the Union. The historic Hall is now the home of the daily newspaper *The Irish Press*. Burgh Quay is used as a terminus by the buses running to Bray and other centres on the east coast.

To reach the other side of the Liffey we cross either **O'Connell Bridge** or **Butt Bridge,** named after Isaac Butt, the pioneer of the Home Rule (for Ireland) Movement, and come to face—

The Custom House

completed in 1791 from designs by Gandon, and at one time considered the finest building of its kind in Europe. This fine building suffered the unfortunate fate of many others in Dublin during the stormy days preceding the signing of the Anglo-Irish Treaty, and was burned down in May 1921. It has, however, been restored and has reverted to its former purpose of accommodating local government offices. The building has a fine Doric portico, and the wings are flanked by two pavilions terminated with the arms of Ireland, beautifully executed. The keystones of the arches are decorated with colossal heads representing the principal rivers and provinces of Ireland. A magnificent dome rises from the centre, and standing at its apex is a statue of Commerce 16 feet high.

From the Custom House, eastwards are the offices of railway and shipping companies and landing stages for cross-channel boats. Northwards, Amiens Street leads to Connolly Station.

From Amiens Street we proceed along Talbot Street and turn right into Marlborough Street, where on the left is—

St. Mary's Pro-Cathedral

The Cathedral has a celebrated choir. Masses on Sundays and Holy Days are held from 7 to 12 noon; High Mass at 12.40. Evening masses, 5.45, 7 and 8.30.

the chief Roman Catholic church in Dublin. Built between 1816 and 1825, it is a splendid example of the Grecian-Doric style of architecture, and the portico is a copy of the Temple of Theseus in Athens. In the apse is a magnificent white marble altar by Turnerelli, and behind the High Altar, a fine stained glass window. Near St. Joseph's altar is a memorial to Dr. Troy, who founded the cathedral in 1815, and there are statues of Cardinal Cullen and Archbishop Murray. Two exquisite smaller altars are dedicated to the Sacred Heart and to the Blessed Virgin.

Opposite to the Cathedral is **Tyrone House,** an interesting Georgian House built in 1741 and now serving as the Headquarters of the Education Department. The large marble Pieta by Juffi was given by the Italian Government in gratitude for help during the Second World War.

III.—St. Mary's Abbey—Four Courts—Burke's Birthplace—King's Inns—Municipal Art Gallery—The Rotunda—The Gate Theatre

Starting again from O'Connell Street we turn up Henry Street, where a turning on the left leads to the site of the old **Abbey of St. Mary,** which stood for some seven hundred years.

Founded for Benedictine monks about 896, presumably by the Danes, it was transferred to the Cistercians in 1139 and under them became one of the richest in Ireland. It was suppressed by Henry VIII and its endowments confiscated, the buildings being long used as a quarry by the people living near. Of the once magnificent buildings only a few crumbling fragments, mixed with the surrounding houses, remain.

In Mary Street is **St. Mary's Church** dating from about 1697. Here was baptised Sheridan in 1751 and Sean O'Casey, playwright, in 1880. There is a fine old Harris organ. The old graveyard has been developed into a public park.

Crossing Arran Street into Chancery Street, where is the **Fish and Vegetable Market,** we turn to the left down Charles Street, opposite Richmond Bridge, and then to the right, along King's Inn Quay, where are the splendid buildings of the Courts of Justice called—

The Four Courts

Bus from O'Connell Bridge will also bring one here.

The Courts were erected in 1786 from designs by James Gamdon. The hall of the Four Courts is a perfect circle 64 feet in diameter, with entrances to the Courts formerly known as the Exchequer, King's Bench, Chancery, and Common Pleas leading from it. A grand dome supported outside by a colonnade of Corinthian pillars rises above this circular hall. The statues over the portico represent Moses,

37

supported by Justice and Mercy, with Wisdom and Authority at the angles.

Like the Customs House and other public buildings, this architectural masterpiece suffered destruction during the late hostilities in Ireland, and many priceless documents were destroyed.

Excellent restoration work has been carried out and the building has again become the home of the Irish Law Courts.

By still continuing westward along Arran Quay the visitor will find, at No. 12, the **Birthplace of Edmund Burke** (1729). No. 11 was the birthplace of another celebrated Irishman, John Halliday, author of *The Scandinavian Kingdom of Dublin.* On this quay also is the fine **St. Paul's Roman Catholic Church,** which contains a handsome altar and a painting in the semi-dome of the apse. Beyond **Queen's Bridge,** is **Usher's Island,** on the Liffey.

Barrack or **Victoria Bridge** next spans the Liffey. **King's Bridge,** still farther west, is a handsome structure built in memory of George IV's visit to Ireland. On its south side are the **Kingsbridge Terminus** of the C.I.E. Railways. Close by are **Steeven's** and **St. Patrick's (Dean Swift's) Hospitals;** and on the north the **Blue Coat School,** founded by Charles II for the children of poor citizens; and **Collins Barracks** and **Soldiers' Home.** One of the entrances to **Phoenix Park** is quite close to this bridge.

Turning to the right up Church Street, just past the Four Courts, we have on the left **St. Michan's Church,** a seventeenth-century structure with a fine tower, on the site of an old Danish church. The vaults, which may be inspected (*fee*), contain numbers of bodies in a partly mummified state, preserved by some curious desiccating properties peculiar to the atmosphere of the vaults. Emmet is believed to be buried here, though the family burial-place is at St. Peter's. St. Michan's has some interesting old plate and a curious cutty stool, or stool of repentance, for the punishment of transgressors. There is said to have been subterranean communication between St. Michan's and the Castle in olden days.

Farther along Church Street is the **Franciscan Capuchin Monastery.**

At the top of Church Street we turn to the right, along North King Street and Bolton Street. At the end of Henrietta Street, on the left-hand side of Bolton Street, are the **King's Inns,** the Dublin Inns of Court. The striking building contains a fine dining hall and a library. To the west of the Inns there is a whole nest of public buildings, and at the junction of Dominick Street with Bolton Street is **St. Saviour's Church,** containing a fine Pietà by Hogan.

Bolton Street leads into Dorset Street (Sheridan was born at No. 12), where is **St. George's Church** (*Sundays at 8, 11 and 7*), considered by many the most beautiful and elegant of the Dublin churches. The principal feature is the lofty and graceful spire, 200 feet high.

From the church Temple Street leads to Gardiner Place. Nearby, in Gardiner Street, is the Jesuit **Church of St. Francis Xavier.** Turning to the right from Gardiner Place we reach Great Denmark Street. In this street is **Belvedere House**—now a Jesuit College—one of the finest old residential houses in Dublin. Continuing, we emerge in Parnell Square, opposite the **Presbyterian Church,** a handsome building in the Decorated Gothic style, with a lofty spire. On the north side of the square is **Charlemont House,** one of the finest examples of Georgian architecture in Dublin and now the home of—

The Municipal Gallery of Modern Art

Open free from 10 to 6 p.m. Tuesday to Saturday inclusive; 11 to 2 p.m. Sunday; closed all day Monday.

The Gallery was the first established in the British Isles exclusively for the exhibition of Modern Art (including foreign Art). It was opened in 1908 and temporarily housed in No. 17 Harcourt Street. In 1927 the Government presented to the City Charlemont House in Parnell Square, and an Art Gallery was formally opened in 1933. Charlemont House was the only town house in Ireland built by Sir William Chambers and was completed in 1763. This fine

Georgian mansion was designed in the best tradition of the period. It has a semi-elliptical façade in cut stone, the wings curving out to pillars on which are placed wrought-iron lanterns. The interior has been altered on the ground floor to lead into the ten fine rooms of the modern gallery.

The collection of modern paintings owes its existence largely to the generosity and public spirit of the late Sir Hugh Lane. Since the Gallery was opened, a room had been kept empty and prepared for the return to Ireland of the famous Lane pictures, held in London following the disputed will case. An agreement now concluded between the Government of Ireland and the Trustees of the National Gallery, London, provides that for a period of twenty years at least half of this outstanding collection may be seen in the Gallery. The pictures are divided into two groups, and each group is loaned to Dublin alternately for five-year periods.

In the permanent collection the Barbizon, French, Impressionist and Modern Continental Schools are represented. There are eleven Corots, together with works by Monet, Fantin-Latour, Daubigny, Sidaner, Harpignies, Monticelli, Boudin, Mancini, Daumier, Boldini, Millet, Mauve, Troyon, Rouault, Pierre Luc-Rousseau, Jean Lurcat, Bonnard, Utrillo, Vlaminck, Segonzac, Picasso, Clave, etc.

The British School is represented by pictures by Constable, Millais, Watts, Leighton, Wilson Steer, George Clausen, Bertram Nicholls, Frank Brangwyn, Rothenstein, Augustus John, Whistler, James Holland, Walter Sickert, John Nash, C. R. W. Nevinson, William Scott, D. Y. Cameron, W. Nicholson, Glyn Philpot, John Piper, Matthew Smith, etc.

Among the Irish artists are to be found pictures by Nathaniel Hone, Sir William Orpen (including a self portrait), John Butler Yeats, Sir John Lavery, Walter Osborne, Sarah Purser, Jack B. Yeats, Gerald Festus Kelly, Harry Clarke, S. C. Harrison, John Keating, P.R.H.A., Patrick Tuohy, Roderick O'Connor, W. J. Leech, Paul Henry, Patrick Hennessy, Frances Kelly, Mainie Jellett, Nano Reid, Daniel O'Neill, Father Jack Hanlon, George Campbell, Louis Le Brocquy, Norah McGuinness, Camille Souter, Noel Sheridan, Barrie Cooke, Leslie McWeeney, Michael Farrell, Cecil King, Sean MacSweeney, T. P. Flanagan, and two stained glass panels by Evie Hone.

The Gallery also contains an interesting collection of contemporary Irish portraits, and a small but valued collection of sculpture.

Passing down the east side of the Square we reach the circular building known as the **Rotunda,** part of which houses a cinema. Adjoining is the **Rotunda Hospital,** of great repute for maternity work. A few steps northwards bring us to the Gate Theatre buildings. The **Gate Theatre** is a Repertory house that has become one of the premier theatres of its kind in the British Isles.

DUBLIN EXCURSIONS
❀❀❀❀❀❀❀❀❀❀❀❀❀❀❀❀❀❀❀❀❀

Route IV—Phœnix Park—The Zoological Gardens—The Old Viceregal Lodge—Irish National War Memorial—Lucan —Leixlip—Celbridge—Maynooth

There are several bus routes to Phœnix Park from the city centre. The Botanic Gardens at Glasnevin may conveniently be visited on the way to or from the Park.

Phœnix Park

Some 1,752 acres in extent and about seven miles in circumference, it is the largest public park in Europe, one of the finest and most beautiful in the world, the pride and glory of Dublin, and the great playground of its citizens.

The great extent of the Park may be realized when it is known that, besides the large tracts open to the public—the People's Gardens, the cricket and polo grounds, extensive review grounds, etc.—it also contains **Árus an Uachtaráin,** the official residence of the President of Ireland (formerly the Viceregal Lodge), the Zoological Gardens, a Chest Hospital, offices of the Ordnance Survey, and, near the North Circular Road entrance, an immense depot and barracks of the "Gárda Síothchána" (pron. *Gaurda Sheecawna*)—the Irish Civic Guard Forces.

From the Parkgate Street entrance a broad, tree-lined avenue leads right through the Park, a distance of 2½ miles, having its exit at the Castleknock gate, and connecting with the main road to Navan. Many other roads traverse the Park in every direction, affording delightful drives or walks.

The **People's Gardens** lie between the Parkgate Street and the North Circular Road entrances to the Park. It is a beautifully laid out and planted enclosure, with an ornamental sheet of water. On the left of the Gardens is the massive **Wellington Monument,** 200 feet high.

Just beyond the People's Gardens is the entrance to—

The Zoological Gardens

Admission.—*Charge.* The Gardens are open week-days 9.30–6, and Sundays, 12–6. Closes sunset in winter. Restaurant.

These charming Gardens are laid out with ornamental shrubs and flowers on gracefully undulating grounds. In the centre is a large lake containing many different species of ducks and geese. The collection of animals is extensive and valuable, most of them being housed either in modern up-to-date buildings or in barless outdoor

enclosures. The Dublin Zoo is famous for breeding lions, over 600 cubs having been born and reared here and sent to other Zoological Gardens throughout the world.

For the children there is a Pets Corner, Pony Rides and Pony Express.

The Gardens are run by the Council of the Royal Zoological Society of Ireland, which has a membership of over 5,000 and they were first opened in 1831. There are many social events, Dinner Dances, Breakfasts, and Barbecues. The Annual Garden Party and Marquee Ball is one of the highlights of the season.

To the north of Phœnix Park is **Dunsink Observatory**, built in 1785. *Open to the public 8 p.m.–10 p.m., on first Saturday of the month from September to April, inclusive.* It runs jointly with the observatory at Armagh, Northern Ireland, a telescope at Bloemfontein, South Africa.

Between the Chapelizod Gate and Parkgate, the beautiful lower road near the Liffey runs. Beyond, near the Knockmaroon Gate, is one of the most beautiful and least-known parts of the Park, the **Hawthorn** or **Fairy** (Furry) **Glen**.

A return can be made via the south side of the Liffey by the bridge to the **National War Memorial Park** (1914–18).

We can also leave the Park by the south-west gate at **Knockmaroon** to enter the steep slope known as the **Strawberry Beds**. These extend for some distance along the steep north bank of the Liffey, past the little village of **Palmerston** and its quaint, tiny, ruined church on the south side of the river, to **Woodlands**.

The bus can be taken to Lucan a few miles farther on, or back to Dublin.

The picturesque old-world village of **Chapelizod** is said to date from the time of the British King Arthur, and to derive its name from *La Belle Iseult*, or Izod. In this quiet little village the first Lord Northcliffe was born on July 15, 1865. Close to Chapelizod are the **Hermitage Golf Links,** one of the finest courses around Dublin.

At Parkgate (or at the Chapelizod or Knockmaroon gates, as may be most convenient), bus should be taken for the seven-mile run through the little villages of Chapelizod and Palmerston to—

Lucan

Spa Hotel (40 rooms), 9-hole golf course; trout and salmon fishing). The town is prettily situated in a wooded vale on the south side of the Liffey. It contains a church with tower and spire, and a one-arched stone bridge, designed by Brunel, over the river.

Lucan was at one time noted for its sulphur spas, but it is now chiefly known as the centre of a good hunting district.

Two miles farther stands **Leixlip,** on the north bank of the Liffey, where a great deal of hydro-electric development is taking place.

Not far away is the St. Wolstans estate, where there is a fourteenth-century bridge and a few fragments of the old *Monastery of St. Wolstons* (1208). West of Leixlip is **Castletown,** demense of the Conolly family (*Weds, Sats, Suns, Bk. Hols in summer 2–6 p.m.*). From the front of the mansion a fine avenue of limes leads by the main gate south-westwards to little **Celbridge**—it was at the abbey here that Swift's "Vanessa" (Esther Vanhomrigh) lived. *Conolly's Folly*, an obelisk, is visible from many directions.

From Leixlip it is a run of some four miles to Maynooth, with good views of the *Rye* river and the extensive demesne of **Carton** (*house, garden, Shell House, Sats, Suns in summer 2–6 p.m.*), former seat of the Duke of Leinster.

Maynooth

Maynooth is a modern form of a very ancient Irish word incorporating the name of a king of the first century. Here may be seen the **Roman Catholic College** (St. Patrick's), a fine old fifteenth-century church with a very strong tower, and the extensive remains of **Maynooth Castle,** a stronghold of the powerful Kildare Geraldines. The ruins are close to the main entrance of the College. On the opposite side of the road is the Protestant Church, the square tower of which is all that remains of the ancient Roman Catholic edifice. The walls of the Castle are eight or nine feet thick. The older part was built about 1230; it was enlarged and the towers added in 1426. Gerald the Great, the eighth earl, left lands to endow a college, and his son built one. This College was suppressed by Henry VIII, in 1538, but in 1795 were laid the foundations of St. Patrick's College, which is now a recognized college of the University and a training centre for the Irish priesthood.

The **College Church** at Maynooth, built in Gothic style, was consecrated in 1891. It has a fine rose window in the west front and some good carved oak stalls.

A return to Dublin (15 miles) can be made by bus.

Route V.—Glasnevin and the Botanic Garden. For those wanting to explore the north-west suburbs of the city a bus can be taken from Eden Quay to the gates of **Glasnevin Cemetery** (also known as Prospect Cemetery) in which are buried Daniel O'Connell, John Philpot Curran, Charles Stuart Parnell, and many other notable Irishmen. The grave of Parnell, which on the anniversary of his death is visited by some of his admirers, lies opposite the door of the mortuary chapel. Leafy avenues intersect in all directions and striking monuments are everywhere to be seen, the most conspicuous being that to O'Connell. The route to the cemetery passes the large *Mater Misericordiae Hospital* and *Mountjoy Prison*; then it follows Botanic Road to—

The Botanic Gardens, Glasnevin

Admission free. Week-days—9 till 6 in summer, Sundays—11 till 6; weekdays in winter, 10 till 4.30, Sundays 11 till 4.30.

The Gardens, instituted by the Royal Dublin Society in 1795, are now under the Department of Agriculture, and cover about 50 acres of undulating ground. They occupy the site of a mansion and grounds once the home of the poet Tickell (1725–40). This house, near the entrance to the gardens, is now the residence of the Director. Swift, Stella (Esther Johnson), Addison, Sheridan, Mrs. Delaney and other celebrities lived near; the fine yew-tree walk in the gardens is known as Addison's Walk.

The gardens, watered by the little river Tolka, are charmingly laid out with flower beds, shrubberies, rockeries, water gardens, with beautiful lilies, spiraeas, rushes, etc., and are divided into departments in which the visitor will meet with plants native to China, Japan, South Africa, Australia, New Zealand, Mexico, India, and other countries. There are fine palmhouses and conservatories; orchids and tree-ferns are successfully cultivated, and the collection of cacti and succulent plants is one of the finest in Europe.

Route VI.—Clontarf and Dollymount. From the city centre the route is by Amiens Street and North Strand, then across the Royal Canal and the Tolka river where it empties itself into the Bay. On the right is **Fairview Park,** converted from scrubland. The road then skirts the edge of Dublin Bay and gives a view of the harbour and *Pigeon House Fort*, now the city electric power station. The populous suburb of **Marino** is on the left, and a short distance farther on is the pleasant coastal suburb of **Clontarf** (from *Cluain Tarbh*, "bull's meadow"). Clontarf Castle, a handsome castellated mansion, was rebuilt in 1835 on the site of an ancient castle. A desperate battle was fought between the Danes and the Irish at Clontarf in 1014.

Dollymount, a short distance beyond Clontarf, has extensive and smooth sands, the scene of many a shooting match. Near the **North Bull Wall** (9,000 feet long), which stretches out into the Bay towards the **Poolbeg Lighthouse,** are the golf links of the Royal Dublin and of the St. Anne's Golf Clubs. **Howth** lies beyond.

Route VII.—Kilmainham and Clondalkin. Kilmainham is in the immediate neighbourhood of Kingsbridge, on the western side of the city, and is reached by bus from College Green. Brian Boru encamped here before the battle of Clontarf, and the former Abbey of Kilmaingnend (as the name was anciently spelt) was one of the most important of its kind in Ireland.

Clondalkin is of interest on account of its ancient **Round Tower,** the nearest to Dublin. The structure, probably ninth century and 84 feet high, is one of the best preserved in Ireland. The door is 15 feet from the ground, 12 feet of this height being solid masonry. At the base the tower is 45 feet in circumference, and the walls are 3 feet thick. About two-thirds up, the interior diameter suddenly narrows. The top is finished with the usual conical cap. This is one of the few round towers that can be ascended.

Clondalkin was the scene of the famous duel between Daniel O'Connell and D'Esterre, in which the latter was shot dead, while the moral shock to O'Connell coloured the whole of his after life, and gave him a horror of bloodshed.

In the neighbourhood is the ancient *St. Brigid's Well*, to which pilgrimages are made.

Howth

Distances.—Dublin 10, Drogheda 49½.
Early Closing.—Thursday.
Golf.—Howth Club, 18 holes. Sutton Club, 9 holes.

Hotels.—*Claremont* (24 rooms), *St. Lawrence* (24), *Royal* (19), *Cliff* (16), *Marine*, Sutton, (28).
Population.—5,750.

Howth (pronounced *Hoathe*) is a small seaside resort noted for its invigorating air, boating, fishing and golf. It has a large harbour, steep streets, a castle and fine cliff walks. On the summit of Howth Hill is a cairn reputed to mark the burial place of King Crimhthan Niadhnair (A.D. 90). From here there are magnificent views of Dublin city, the mountain ranges of Dublin and Wicklow, and, in clear weather, the mountains of Mourne and the Welsh mountains. There are good walks along the northern side of the hill, and from Sutton along the south-western edge, passing **St. Fintan's Church,** a ninth-century foundation, to the **Baily Lighthouse.** Many pleasant tracks cross and encircle the hill. For non-walkers, buses run from Sutton and Howth stations, and the route affords magnificent views as it nears the summit of the hill. Baily Lighthouse was built in 1814 on the site of an old stone fort which was once a beacon light point, and it too is a very fine view point. A mile north of Howth Head lies the rocky island of **Ireland's Eye** (Ey is a Gaelic affix meaning island) which is the haunt of many sea birds. It has a good sandy beach and is a popular picnic place. Beyond it is **Lambay Island** (see p. 48).

Overlooking the harbour is the **Abbey Church,** built probably about A.D. 1240 on a Danish foundation of 1042. It contains some interesting monuments. On the south side are the remains of a sixteenth-century building known as Howth's College.

Howth Castle (*not open*) is approached by a long avenue of Irish yew trees. The Keep and Gateway Tower, sole remnants of the original castle, were built about 1230. Since then each century has seen the addition of a new wing or a major alteration until 1911 when Sir Edwin Lutyens undertook restoration and built the West Tower. The castle is owned by the St. Lawrence family who first settled in Howth in 1177. In the grounds is a famous Beech Hedge over half a mile in length and 30 feet high. *A Rhododendron Walk is open to the public: daily April 2.30–6; May–June 11–9; July–September 11–6, charge.*

Picturesquely situated on the Howth promontory is the rising little resort of **Sutton,** with an hotel, golf, tennis and bracing air.

DUBLIN AIRPORT

Dublin Airport is situated at Collinstown in flat, open country six miles north of the city. Formerly the site of a military aerodrome, it was opened for air traffic in 1940. Its buildings include a modern Central Terminal providing the usual facilities for passengers and visitors, including several restaurants, lounges, bars and shops. Passengers and visitors number well over a million a year. There are three concrete runways, 7,000, 6,800 and 4,500 feet long respectively. The airport is the home base of the Irish national airline, Aer Lingus—Irish International Airlines.

DROGHEDA AND THE BOYNE VALLEY

❄❄❄❄❄❄❄❄❄❄❄❄❄❄❄❄❄❄❄❄❄❄❄❄❄❄❄❄❄❄❄

Access.—From Dublin, Drogheda may be reached by road (29 miles) *via* Swords and Balbriggan or by rail (32 miles), leaving from Amiens Street Station and passing through **Malahide, Rush** and **Lusk, Skerries** and **Balbriggan.** From Drogheda the main line continues to **Dundalk,** but bus services run along the Boyne Valley to **Navan, Kells** and Oldcastle.

Motor coach excursions from Dublin to the Boyne Valley run several times a week.

Malahide

is a popular resort near Dublin with a sandy beach and safe bathing (*Grand* (61 rooms), *Royal* (10 rooms)). There are excellent golf links on the mainland at **Portmarnock,** and those known as the Island links, reached by ferry. Malahide and Portmarnock are among the few seaside places near Dublin with a sandy shore. On the lovely expanse of sand, known as the *Silver* or *Velvet Strand*, beautiful shells are to be found. **Malahide Castle** (Lord Talbot de Malahide—*no admission*) is a fine battlemented building with circular towers. It has a medieval Great Hall, and its Oak Room contains panels carved with scriptural subjects.

Adjoining the Castle is the ruined **Manorial Church,** often miscalled the "abbey", a single-aisled building of nave and chancel, divided by a handsome arch. For centuries this church has been the burial-place of the Talbots. Inside is the altar-tomb and effigy of one of the Talbot ladies, Maud Plunkett (the heroine of Gerald Griffin's ballad, "The Bridal of Malahide"), whose newly-wed husband was slain in battle a few hours after the marriage ceremony, thus making her "maid, wife and widow in one day."

Three miles west of Malahide, on the direct Drogheda road, is **Swords,** where St. Columba founded a monastery in the sixth century. In the grounds of the Protestant church is a fine **Round Tower,** some 75 feet high, with a restored cap.

The purpose of these curious **Round Towers,** of which there are still 118 in Ireland, chiefly along the north-west coast and in the central parts, has long been disputed, but it is now generally agreed that they were built from the ninth to the thirteenth centuries as watch-towers (all have windows very high up, just under the conical roof, looking north, south, east and west) and as treasure houses and places of refuge against the Danes. They are all much alike, solidly built of blocks of stone, with a single small doorway high up—6 to 18 feet above the ground—reached by a ladder, which could be easily withdrawn in case of assault. They were nearly always built near churches and monasteries, and are called bell towers in the early Irish records. They were divided into storeys, communicating by ladders. In some the stones are rounded and carefully laid; others are more roughly built of undressed stones. They are generally about a hundred feet high, and taper from the base to the summit. The doorway faces the

47

church to which the tower belonged. The towers at Lusk, Swords and Clondalkin are now the only ones in Co. Dublin.

The **tower** or belfry, forming a separate part of the modern church, dates from the fourteenth century and is the only remaining part of the old monastery. A short distance away are the ruins of the **Archbishop's Castle,** surrounded by embattled walls with towers at their angles. Swords is the oldest town in the county, and until 1327 the Archbishops of Dublin lived here—after that date they lived at Tallaght.

For those returning to Dublin from Swords or Malahide, there is an opportunity to visit the **Holy Well of St. Wereburghe,** a seventh-century saint, daughter of the King of Mercia. About four miles south of Malahide is the quaint little **Church of St. Doulough,** a medieval building on an ancient foundation. This church was built by the Danes and does not stand due east and west. It has a double stone roof (an Irish architectural feature), a crypt with the saint's tomb, a hermit's cell in the roof, and a penitential bed in the thickness of the wall. Near the church is the **Holy Well of the Blessed Virgin,** under a stone cone; and in the roadway are the stone basement and socket of an ancient **Cross.**

A railway viaduct from Malahide crosses the north of the creek to **Portrane.** Seaward there is a good view of **Lambay Island** and its lofty cliffs. The island is about 4 miles in circumference and has an area of 617 acres. Owned by Lord Revelstoke, it is used as a bird sanctuary.

Near the next station, **Rush and Lusk,** we see on the left the remains of a Round Tower and an old church. This circular belfry is built into the steeple of the church. It is 80 feet high and of great antiquity.

Shortly the ruined **Baldungan Castle** appears on a hill to the left. In 1641 Thomas Fitzwilliam, a lessee of the Lords of Howth, fortified but failed to hold this castle against Colonel Jones, the Parliamentarian leader.

North again, by road or rail, is—

Skerries

Distances.—Dublin 19, Balbriggan 4, Belfast 87, Drogheda 15, Dundalk 37. **Early Closing.**—Thursday.

Hotels.—*Holmpatrick House* (39 rooms), *Lambay Lodge* (34). **Population.**—3,000.

Skerries has in recent years grown from a modest fishing village to a prosperous seaside resort. Its splendid beach offers ideal bathing; there is a good 18-hole golf course, and an annual regatta attracts many visitors. The town is sheltered from the north by the **Red Island** headland, on which is a martello tower and a large holiday camp. For the historian and antiquary Skerries offers much that is of interest. On one of the three islands off the coast—**St. Patrick's Island** (locally called "Church Island")—St. Patrick is said to have landed in the course of his journey to Tara. Adjacent to Skerries also

O'Connell Street, Dublin

Dun Laoghaire

Bray, Co. Wicklow

Glendalough, Co. Wicklow

are the site of the ancient oratory of St. Mobhi (or Movo), who died in 630, and a holy well dedicated to the saint.

Five miles off the coast is the **Rockabill Lighthouse**, built on the summit of a large rock standing sheer up out of the water.

Passing **Balbriggan** (9-hole golf course), noted for the fine hosiery made here and as the place where the victorious King William encamped his army after the Battle of the Boyne (*see* p. 51), we reach **Gormanstown**, with its castle and surrounding trees, and the bright little watering-places of **Laytown** (nearby is the Mosney Holiday Village) and **Bettystown** (*see* p. 51). The line crosses the pretty valley of the river Nanny and turning inland reaches the ancient and historic town of—

Drogheda

Access.—From Dublin by rail (Conolly Station) or by bus.
Churches, etc.—*Roman Catholic, Church of Ireland, Presbyterian.*
Distances.—Dublin 30, Ardee 15, Balbriggan 11, Belfast 73, Navan 17, Cork 184, Dundalk 22, Skerries 15.

Early Closing.—Wednesday.
Golf.—18-hole course at Baltray, 3½ m.
Hotels.—*White Horse* (19 rooms), *Boyne Valley* (18). *Rossnaree.*
Population.—17,908.
Youth Hostels.—At Mellifont, 6 miles and at Port Oriel, 8 miles.

The word Drogheda (pronounced Drawhedda) is a corrupted form of the Irish *Droichead Atha,* meaning "the Ford Bridge." The place is a seaport corporate town lying on both banks of the Boyne—the most famous river in Irish history. Though a busy, modern town, Drogheda has considerable historical and antiquarian interest. It is best known to tourists as a centre for exploring the famous Valley of the Boyne.

That Drogheda is a place of considerable antiquity seems evident from the historical belief that in A.D. 911 the town was fortified by Turgesius the Dane. For centuries afterwards its advantageous position continued to be recognized by the reigning monarchs, for history records that in 1220, when making a renewed grant of Meath to Walter de Lacy, Henry II retained in his own possession the town and castle of Drogheda. Here many of the English Viceroys kept their Courts and held their parliaments, which enacted some of the most remarkable statutes in Irish history, among others the notorious "Poynings Law," passed in 1495, which made the Irish Legislature subservient to that of England and which continued in effect till 1782. It was here that Richard II, in 1394, received within the walls of the Dominican Friary the submission of O'Neill, Prince of Ulster and his subordinate chiefs. In Drogheda, too, Cromwell began his career in Ireland, in 1649, with a bloody massacre. Within 3 miles of the town the famous Battle of the Boyne was fought in 1690.

The **Walls** of Drogheda, originally a mile and a half in circumference, have almost entirely disappeared, and the parts that remain bear unmistakable evidence of Cromwell's shot. Of the gates which gave entrance to the town, only **St. Lawrence's Gate** is standing today: it is a curious but perfect structure, and still forms a handsome approach to the town.

Other portions of the old walls may be seen near St. Mary's churchyard, of which they form the southern boundary.

In addition to these remnants of antiquity are: the ruins of an old **Augustinian Priory,** founded in the reign of Edward I; the majestic **Magdalen Tower**—the only existing fabric of the Dominican Friary, or abbey of the Preaching Friars, built in 1224 by Luke Netterville, Archbishop of Armagh; and **St. Mary's Abbey,** formerly devoted to the Carmelites. Other objects of interest near the town are an old grass-grown rath, the legendary fortress of Gobhan Saor, the Vulcan of Irish mythology; and Clough Patrick or **St. Patrick's Stone,** on which the saint prayed or preached, before baptizing his converts at a well in St. Patrick's Well Lane. Two miles from Drogheda, on the banks of the Boyne, is **Rossnaree**, the "wood of the Kings," the reputed burial-place of King Cormac Mac Art, claimed to be the most enlightened monarch who ever reigned at Tara (*see* p. 54).

Some of the modern buildings of Drogheda will also interest the visitor with an eye for architectural beauty. The **Oliver Plunket Memorial Church of St. Peter** in West Street is a handsome edifice.

The foundation stone was laid on July 10, 1881, on the occasion of the bi-centenary celebration of the death of Dr. Oliver Plunket, Catholic Archbishop of Armagh and Primate of Ireland, who during the reign of Charles II, and after a doubtful trial for treason, was hanged at Tyburn.

Another building which will attract attention is the **Tholsel,** once a courthouse and now occupied by the Hibernian Bank. **St. Mary's Church,** James's Street, and **St. Peter's Church** (Protestant), are also noteworthy. A conspicuous feature of the town is the handsome railway viaduct 1,700 feet long and spanning the Boyne at a considerable height above the water.

As an industrial centre Drogheda is far ahead of most towns of its size in Ireland. This is due largely to its situation in a district rich in agricultural potentialities and to its fine harbour, which enables it to carry on an extensive export trade with Liverpool and other cross-channel centres. Its principal industries are brewing, linen and cotton making, and the manufacture of cement, chemical manures and fertilizers. In addition, there are grain mills, sawmills, malt-houses, an oil and cattle-cake mill, three boot and shoe factories, a men's clothing factory, three factories manufacturing women's clothing, and a factory for the manufacture of sparking-plugs.

The Boyne is a noted salmon river, its main centres being at Navan, Trim and Slane. The best stretches are strictly preserved, but permission to fish for trout, etc., is freely given.

The pleasant little seaside resorts of **Laytown and Bettystown** are little more than four miles to the south of the town, and ten minutes' run by train on the Dublin line. The two places adjoin to form a joint resort whose fine bathing strands and other amenities attract many visitors. Around Laytown pleasant walks can be enjoyed, and especially popular is the trip to **Ballygarth Castle.** Here excellent fishing for trout is to be had, free, in the little *Nanny* stream. Near Laytown is Butlin's Holiday Village (Mosney) with its own station. Close by is **Mornington** beside the mouth of the Bague. There is an excellent 18-hole golf course ¾ mile from Bettystown.

The **Battle of the Boyne** was fought between William III's Protestant and James II's Jacobite armies about 3 miles to the west of Drogheda, on the banks of the river. To reach the site pass through West Street and continue straight ahead after leaving the town.

After the failure of the siege of Derry, James resolved to stake his kingdom on a pitched battle at Drogheda. His army was posted on Donmore Hill, on the south bank, in front of which the river forms a triangle. William, with a well-trained force, reached the north side of the Boyne on June 30, 1690, and encamped on Tullyesker Hill opposite the army of James. Early in the morning he rode down the beautiful King William's Glen to reconnoitre and breakfast and was struck by a ball fired by James's scouts, and the news spread that he was killed. The wound, however, was slight. On the next morning the attack was made; 10,000 of William's men were sent to cross the river at Slane, some distance up the stream; another force, under General Schomberg, crossed at Old Bridge; a third, between the two islands below the bridge; and the fourth, under William, to the east of Tullyesker Hill. Both sides fought well, but the Jacobite artillery was greatly outnumbered and the undisciplined infantry were seized with panic, though the cavalry displayed great gallantry. After several attempts

51

William's party, the Orangemen, forced a passage, but Schomberg was killed. Towards evening the Irish wings were driven back upon their centre, Donore Hill. At length, losing hope, they beat a retreat, which was skilfully and coolly effected, there being little or no pursuit. James had taken to flight as soon as he found things going against him. So ended the famous Battle of the Boyne, which virtually established William on the throne, while giving a fatal blow to the Jacobite fortunes. In all, about 1,500 men were killed.

About a mile and a half to the west of Boyne Bridge (*Youth Hostel*), on the farther side of the river Mattock, stands the tumulus of **Dowth**, a conical mound about an acre in extent which, since it was opened in 1847, has been the object of much antiquarian curiosity. A caretaker lives nearby. A passage, 28 feet long, leads to a circular chamber or vault 16 feet in diameter and about 12 feet in height. The sides of this internal chamber are formed of large standing stones, the roof being constructed of overlapping slabs after the style of the beehive dwellings of early monastic establishments. Many of the stones have beautiful carvings consisting of spirals, concentric circles, zigzags and lozenge patterns, as well as straight lines resembling Ogham characters. Off the main chamber are three smaller crypts, one of which gives access to another series of vaults and recesses.

Near the mound are **St. Bernard's Holy Well** and a ruined **Church** that has a curious figure built into its south wall. The remains of a castle, a rath and a stone circle are also nearby.

Two miles and a half farther west is—

Newgrange, another mound, rising from its surroundings to a height of about 70 feet and covering an area of about two acres. Originally the mound was encompassed by a circle of thirty-five pillar-stones of enormous size, which stood apart, like those at Stonehenge; of these, only twelve now remain in position, near the entrance to the tumulus.

Lying on the north of the passage-way is an immense slab inscribed with elaborate spiral carvings. The passage, 62 feet in length and 4 feet in height, leads to a hexagonal chamber about 20 feet in height and measuring 21 feet across at its greatest width, with a dome-shaped roof formed of horizontal slabs. Three smaller recesses lead from the larger vault, as at Dowth, and in each chamber or cell an oval-shaped stone basin rests on the floor. The most extraordinary features of the interior are the elaborate stone carvings in every direction, the spiral pattern being the most prominent.

A mile farther west is the **Knowth Mound,** another important tumulus.

Five miles to the north-west of Drogheda are the ruins of—

Mellifont Abbey (*Youth Hostel* close by),

picturesquely situated on the left bank of the Mattock stream.

The site of this historic abbey was chosen by St. Malachy, Archbishop of Armagh, in compliance with the wishes of St. Bernard, Abbot of the Cistercian Monastery at Clairvaux. The site selected by the Archbishop was readily granted by Donagh O'Carrol, Prince of Oriel, who also handsomely endowed the monastery, the building of which began in 1142. In 1157 a great synod was held within the walls of Mellifont and the church was solemnly consecrated; and thus was inaugurated the first colony of Irish

Cistercian monks, whose monasteries in Ireland subsequently increased to forty-two.

Three Plantagenet Kings—Henry II, John and Henry III—granted charters to the Abbey of Mellifont, whose abbots sat in the early Irish Parliaments with the rank of an Earl. The conquest of Ireland by the Anglo-Normans, however, brought troubles to the Abbots of Mellifont, until finally in 1539 the royal edict of suppression closed the doors of the famous Abbey for ever.

In 1566 the Abbey and its extensive possessions were leased by Queen Elizabeth to Sir Edward Moore, whose son, Sir Garret—the first Lord Moore—converted it into a fortified castle.

The existing ruins consist chiefly of the *Lavabo* and the *Chapter House*, the former an octagonal building in Norman style and the latter a beautiful conception of the later decorated period of Gothic architecture. Little remains of the Abbey Church.

Another circular mound and the ruins of a thirteenth-century church may be seen in the field above the Abbey.

New Mellifont. After 400 years the Cistercians returned to Mellifont. In 1939 they acquired the property known as Oriel Temple at Collon, some 4 miles north of the old Abbey, and established there a new house of the Order under the name of New Mellifont, now more usually known as Mellifont Abbey (Collon).

Five miles to the north of Drogheda is—

Monasterboice

where there are the ruins of a monastery founded by St. Bute or Boetus, who died in 521 on the day that St. Columba was born. In 1097 it was destroyed by fire (and its precious library burnt) and only partially rebuilt; it apparently fell into utter ruin about 1117. There now remain the walls and gables of two very old Churches and a Round Tower, 110 feet in height, which dates from the ninth century. The door is about 6 feet from the ground and modern stairs enable the visitor to reach the top. But the pride and glory of Monasterboice are the marvellous Celtic Crosses. The *West Cross* is 21½ feet high and is covered with fine sculpturings of scriptural subjects and Celtic ornamentations cut into the stone. *Muiredach's Cross*, though not so high, is monolithic, and the sculpturings are better preserved. Abbot Muiredach, who had the Cross made, died about 923. The *North Cross*, 16 feet high, has a new shaft fitted, but the old one can be seen nearby.

Nine miles from Drogheda, by the road leading due west, is—

Slane

a village situated on the Boyne and overlooked by the **Hill of Slane,** on which are the ruins of a church and a monastery. The hill commands a fine view of the Boyne Valley, and to the south we can see the rounded **Hill of Tara** (*see* below). It was on the Hill of Slane that St. Patrick, on Easter Eve A.D. 433, in defiance of the pagan king's proclamation, lighted the Paschal fire, which led to the Saint's duel with the Druids at Tara and the triumph of Christianity over paganism in Ireland.

Near the village are the ruins of the hermitage of St. Erck, the first bishop of Slane, said to have been consecrated by St. Patrick.

Slane Castle is a modern mansion beautifully situated on the north bank of the Boyne, about a mile west of Slane. A little farther on is the demesne of **Beauparc.** Above a weir are the ruins of **Castle Dexter;** further on is a steep limestone rock, the **Maiden Rock,** which commands a fine view of Slane Castle, Beauparc and the river.

From the Hill of Slane the towers of Trim may be seen, and some ten miles distant the—

Hill of Tara,

the historic site of the capital of ancient Ireland. Here was the royal residence of the pagan kings of Ireland, the site, so the chroniclers tell us, being first chosen by Slainge, a monarch of the Firbolgs, nearly two thousand years before the dawn of the Christian era. The spot continued to be the seat of each succeeding Ard-Ri or High King of Ireland until Tara was abandoned in A.D. 565.

Besides being a royal residence, Tara was the seat of government, and it was here that all meetings and events of prime national importance took place. The "Feis of Tara," which was in effect the National Parliament of the Celtic tribes, was a triennial event. At this assembly of the chieftains, bards and learned men of the nation, laws were enacted or revised, historical records were examined and tribal disputes settled.

At the height of its greatness many spacious buildings adorned this historic hill, most of them being erected or restored by Cormac Mac Art. Nothing, however, now remains but a few grass-grown mounds. The largest of these is known as the "Teach Miodhchuarta," which served as a **Banqueting Hall** and is by far the most interesting of the monuments at Tara. Its site can still be distinctly traced, and antiquarians have computed its dimensions at no less than 800 feet in length and from 60 to 80 feet in breadth, with six or seven wide entrances at either side.

On the summit of the hill is **Rath na Riogh,** "the Rath of the Kings," a circular fort within which are two smaller raths—"Cormac's House" and the "Foradh" or Dais. The "Mound of Hostages" is beyond the "Foradh," to the north, and a pillar stone, the Lia Fáil or Stone of Destiny, has been moved from its original position here to the summit of Cormac's House.

The **Lia Fáil** is the legendary test-stone of the ancient Irish Kings. On it they placed their feet as a symbol of sovereignty, and if they were of truly royal descent the stone signified its approval by bellowing loudly; otherwise it remained dumb. Tradition further says that this mystic stone was removed at the beginning of the sixth century to Scone in Scotland and is now under the Coronation Chair in Westminster Abbey. But it is probable that the stone standing in Tara is the original Lia Fáil.

Still northward is the **Rath of the Synods,** where religious ceremonies appear to have been held. Excavations were carried on here not many years ago by a few optimists in the hope of discovering the Ark of the Covenant! Another rampart, **Rath Laoghaire,** is supposed to have been the private residence of Laoghaire, who was High King when St. Patrick came to Ireland and who gave his name to Dun Laoghaire, the old and new name of Kingstown (*see* p. 58).

A modern church (wholly out of place) has been built on the hill, and here also stands a monument to St. Patrick.

Eight miles from Slane by road is **Navan,** from whence a road strikes north-westwards to **Kells** and **Lough Ramor** passing through a region rich in historical associations. A little beyond Navan is **Donaghpatrick,** with its great rath, for here, too, was an ancient royal residence. The church occupies one of the most ancient ecclesiastical sites in Ireland. St. Patrick preached here.

At Kells, where St. Columba founded a monastery in the sixth century, may be seen the famous sculptured *Crosses of Kells.* Near the church is *St. Columba's House* and a *Round Tower.* (For Book of Kells, *see* p. 25).

Two miles from Bective, between Dublin and Navan, is **Bective Abbey,** a Cistercian monastery founded about 1150. The cloisters are well preserved.

Trim, about 9 miles from Navan, is a good centre for salmon and trout fishing in the *Boyne,* and has great anti-quarian interest. The conspicuous yellow *Steeple,* a ruined tower, stands on the site of an abbey founded by St. Patrick. Some parts of the old wall and two of the town gates remain. The *Castle* was built in 1173 and rebuilt half a century later, and is well worth visiting. Trim was one of the strongholds of the "Pale."

From Drogheda the railway runs north through Dunleer and Castlebellingham to **Dundalk** (18-hole golf course), the last station on the Republic side of the border.

DUBLIN TO BLESSINGTON AND POULAPHOUCA

Blessington lies some 18 miles south-west of Dublin, and is reached by the **Terenure** road. At Terenure we bear right, and in a further 4 miles reach—

Tallaght

whose modern appearance is deceptive. The old square tower on the right of the road is the sole remaining fragment of **Bancroft Castle,** now part of a farm-house. By the Church, also, are the remains of an **Abbey** built in 1324, later the palace of the Dublin primates until 1821.

The Tallaght Hills seem to have been the burial-places of the earlier races of Ireland, and cairns, megalithic tombs and burial mounds carry reminders of ancient days.

From Tallaght the road rises through richly-wooded country past **Corbally Bridge** to **Brittas,** where it passes into County Wicklow. To the left are fine views of the mountains, and in 6 miles we reach—

Blessington

(*Downshire House.* Population, 546) a picturesque village of one long street. East of the village lies the northern part of **Poulaphouca Lake,** which provides the city of Dublin with 20 million gallons of water each day.

About 4 miles south of Blessington, at the upper limit of the lake, are the **Poulaphouca Falls,** where the Liffey forms a succession of waterfalls. The surroundings are beautiful, and the falls are still impressive, though the volume of water has been much reduced by the construction of a **Dam** for the Liffey hydro-electric scheme, whose main power-station stands below the falls.

DUBLIN TO DUN LAOGHAIRE AND
BRAY BY THE COAST

⚜⚜⚜⚜⚜⚜⚜⚜⚜⚜⚜⚜⚜⚜⚜⚜⚜⚜⚜⚜⚜⚜⚜⚜⚜⚜⚜⚜⚜⚜⚜

Dun Laoghaire and Bray are easily reached by rail and road. From Merrion the line follows closely the curve of Dublin Bay as far as Dun Laoghaire, affording a succession of beautiful views, with the bold promontory of Howth well in sight on the left and occasional glimpses of the Dublin and Wicklow hills on the right. The main road passes beside the Show Grounds at **Ballsbridge** and enables visitors to get a close-up view of the extensive Show premises of the **Royal Dublin Society,** where the world-famous Dublin Horse Show is held annually in August.

The **Royal Dublin Society** was founded in 1731 for the purpose of pro-moting agriculture, industry, science and art in Ireland. It is a large and influential Society, and is known chiefly for its famous Horse Show and for its almost equally popular Spring Show and Industries Fair, held each year in May. It is now rapidly establishing itself as a venue for International Conferences.

Facing the Show Grounds are the spacious premises of the Irish Hospitals Trust, wherein are held the famous Sweepstake Draws.

About a mile further on the road converges on the railway, running parallel with it past **Merrion.** On the right of the Merrion Road is Shrewsbury Road, where, at No. 20 the **Chester Beatty Library** is housed. (*Admission free, Monday to Friday, 10–1 and 2.30–5; Saturday 3–6.*) The buildings were erected between 1953–1957 for the very fine collection made by Sir A. Chester Beatty of Oriental and European illuminated manuscripts, ancient documents and books, works of art, furniture, and other objects of interest and beauty.

After **Booterstown** (*Bay*, 5 rooms), the spacious grounds and buildings of *Blackrock College*, founded in the sixties' by French and Alsatian priests, are passed, before **Blackrock** is reached. On the left, just before reaching the town, is Blackrock Park; and opposite, on the right, is *Frascati*, where the romantic Lord Edward Fitzgerald lived with his wife Pamela, daughter of the Duke of Orleans. Leaving the town, the road continues through Newtown Avenue, where many historic houses are situated.

Passing **Seapoint,** a bathing place popular with Dublin people, we reach **Salthill,** or **Monkstown,** a favourite residential suburb. The Moorish turret of the church is a prominent object. Inland are the remains of *Monkstown Castle*, founded by the monks of St. Mary's Abbey, Dublin, in the twelfth century.

A short distance further on by the coastal road we pass the base of the West Pier of Dun Laoghaire Harbour, and are now in **Old Dunleary,** a little fishing village out of which has grown the fine modern town of Dun Laoghaire—the gaelic form of the ancestral village name.

Dun Laoghaire

Distances.—Dublin 8, Bray 7, Cork 168, Wicklow 27, Belfast 110.
Early Closing.—Wednesday.
Hotels.—*Royal Marine* (102 rooms), *Ross's* (48), *Pierre* (26), *Salthill* (35), *Avenue* (35), *Ardeen* (20), *Lismara* (21), *Loch Lomond* (21), and many others.
Population.—51,772.
Churches, etc.—
 Church of Ireland: Mariner's Church; Christ Church.
 Roman Catholic: St. Joseph's; St. Patrick's (Glasthule); St. Michael's.
 Presbyterian: York Road; *Methodist; Congregational.*

Sport and Entertainment.—Golf course (18 holes) at Eglington Park; bowling greens in Moran Park; well-equipped sea-baths; numerous bathing stations; yachting and boating (principal yachting centre in Ireland), races from May to September, annual regatta; good sea fishing; racing; cinemas; dancing; band concerts; museum.

Tourist Office.—Information and Room Reservation at Marine Road.

The general aspect of the town is impressive. The spacious harbour, beautiful church spires, stately terraces of handsome houses and cheerful streets make a fine picture. This is completed with the wide expanse of Dublin Bay as foreground and a background of charming woodland and mountain scenery.

The **Harbour** with two massive pincer-shaped piers which stretch out away into the bay was constructed between 1817 and 1859. At the sea end of the East Pier is a lighthouse which every 15 seconds flings a brilliant beam of light across the bay. Nearly opposite, on the extreme promontory of Howth Head, is the Baily lighthouse, and away out at sea is the Kish lighthouse.

The piers are favourite promenades, for they command fine panoramic views. Near the entrance to the East Pier are the **Beach Gardens,** the **Marine Gardens** and the **People's Park,** tastefully laid out with flower-beds and ornamental shrubs and trees. Overlooking the harbour is the **Marine Parade,** a raised esplanade stretching from the railway station to Sandycove, where there are good bathing facilities, a James Joyce museum, and evening illuminations. Adjoining the Marine Parade are the **Pavilion Gardens,** with the **Pavilion Cinema,** and close by is the **Lifeboat Station.** Along the coast in both directions from Dun Laoghaire are several martello towers.

In and near Marine Road are several buildings worthy of notice: the **Mariner's Church,** the **Town Hall,** the **Post Office** and the **Municipal Technical Schools.**

From Dun Laoghaire the road route to Dalkey (2 miles) gives a good view of the ruins of **Bullock Castle,** which probably dates from the twelfth century. Half a mile from it is—

Dalkey

Hotels.—*Cliff Castle* (23 rooms),   Population.—9,000.
   Colamore (20),
   Shangri-la (20),

A pleasant little place, consisting of the old town and the Coliemore or harbour and a number of charming villas scattered on the hillside, Dalkey was once a place of considerable mercantile importance, and the chief landing-place of passengers from England. The only reminders of this era are the remains of a castle and fragments of an ancient church. A road leads uphill from the centre of the town to Sorrento Park, from which there are lovely views. *Dalkey Avenue,* near the old castle, leads to Dalkey Hill—another good view point. **Torca Cottage** (plaque) on Dalkey Hill was the home of G. B. Shaw from 1866–74.

Below is Dalkey Island, a quarter mile off the coast. On it are fragments of a tiny oratory dedicated to Saint Benedict, in the oldest style of Celtic Church architecture, and a martello tower on the site of an old Milesian fort. It commands a very charming view of the coast scenery, with the hills behind.

Farther out is the little **Muglins Island,** with a lighthouse. Close, too, are Lamb Island, Clare Rock and Maiden's Rock.

About a mile from Dalkey Station is **Killiney Hill** (512 feet) from the top of which there is a magnificent view.

From Dalkey, it is not far to—

Killiney

(*Killiney Castle* (80 rooms); 9-hole golf course; population, 500), charmingly situated, with a fine beach 2 miles long above which stands a martello tower. Killiney Hill (*see above*) can also be climbed from here. In a field on the right of the road to Bray, half a mile from Ballybrack, is a cromlech, and higher up the hill is a so-called Druidical Chair. Above the station

and surrounded by a high wall are the remains of an ancient church and cross, probably dating from the fifth century.

From Killiney the road runs parallel with the coast, through Shankill, to Bray.

DUBLIN TO BRAY BY THE INLAND ROUTE

In addition to the coastal road there are two other main routes from Dublin to Bray. The most direct—an excellent road—is that via Donnybrook Bridge to **Stillorgan** (5 miles) (*South County Hotel*), the birthplace of William Orpen (1878–1931), and from there to **Foxrock**. Nearby is the very fine **Leopardstown Racecourse** (the name is a corruption of Leper's Town—a hospital for lepers once existed here). A mile further on is **Cabinteely,** at the foot of Killiney Hill. A mile south-west of Cabinteely is **Carrickmines,** where are the ruins of a castle, a church said to be of Danish foundation, a very fine cromlech (in the private grounds of Glendruid) and also a 9-hole golf course. But the main road leads from Cabinteely through **Shankill** to the descent of the **Bray valley.**

The inland route offers the scenery of the Dublin mountains instead of sea views. Leave Dublin by Harcourt Street, and pass through the residential suburbs of **Milltown** (18-hole golf course) and **Dundrum** to **Stepaside** (6 miles) at the foot of Three Rock Mountain; thence via **Kilgobbin,** where there are the ruins of an ancient church, to **Kilternan,** where there is a large dolmen and a curious church. We next enter the rocky defile known as **The Scalp** and descend to cross the river to **Enniskerry,** where the road forks left for Bray. Buses run from Dublin via the Scalp to Enniskerry; or from Dundrum the walker who is equal to a ten-mile tramp can enjoy a delightful walk to Bray via Three Rock and Two Rock Mountains, then through The Scalp where, near Enniskerry, a road turns left for Bray.

Farther inland the walks and drives along the valleys of the two ranges of Dublin's Hills are even more beautiful. These hills are usually rounded and boggy. The highest is **Kippure** (2,473 feet and topped by the Irish Television Transmitter), on the extreme southern boundary of the county. On Mount Venus is an enormous cromlech.

Bray

Access.—Rail and bus service from Dublin; *via* Dun Laoghaire and Killiney, 16 miles; *via* Dundrum, the Scalp and Enniskerry, 17 miles. Bus *via* Stillorglin, 12 miles.

Churches, etc.—
Roman Catholic: Church of Most Holy Redeemer, Main Street; St. Peter's, Dublin Road; Our Lady Queen of Peace, Putland Road.
Church of Ireland: Christ Church, Church Road; St. Paul's, Main Street. *Presbyterian:* Quinsboro' Road; *Methodist,* Florence Road; *Plymouth Brethren,* Florence Road.

Distances.—Dublin 12, Belfast 115, Cork 176, Dun Laoghaire 7, Enniskerry 4, Greystones 5, Wexford 71, Wicklow 19.

Early Closing.—Wednesday.

Hotels.—*Bray Head* (52 rooms), *Royal Starlight* (104), *International* (70), *Esplanade* (37), *Kinvara* (32), *Lacy's* (10), *Strand* (14), *Mayfair* (10), and many others.

Population.—12,659.

Post Office.—Chief Office in Quinsboro' Road.

Sport and Entertainment.—9-hole and 18-hole golf courses. Good bathing and boating. Freshwater angling and sea fishing. Salmon fishing in the River *Dargle.* Tennis, putting, bowls, horse racing, dancing, cinemas .

Bray, the "Gateway to the Garden of Ireland," is one of the most popular seaside resorts in Ireland. The town is delightfully situated in a richly coloured vale, bounded on one side by the sea and closed in on the other by the peaks of the Wicklow Hills. Its bay is guarded on the south by the precipitous promontory of Bray Head and on the north by the charming hill of Killiney. The bare and breezy summit of **Bray Head** (almost 800 feet and topped by the *Flagstaff Cairn*), approached by a firm pathway, commands a series of charming views.

The esplanade runs from the mouth of the Dargle to the foot of Bray Head. In front is the mile-long walk known as the Promenade. From the long beach of firm sand there is safe bathing. There is also good bathing at **Naylor's Cove** beneath Bray Head. Diving and swimming competitions attract many entries.

The principal buildings in the town are Christ Church, a fine Gothic building with an elegant spire, the Church of the Most Holy Redeemer, and the Town Hall in Main Street.

There is a fine walk round Bray Head, the slope of which forms an extensive natural park where one may wander among rocks, trees and heather, or climb the many paths to the summit, or ascend it the easy way by cable car.

On the northern slope of the Head are the ruins of a thirteenth-century church called Raheen-a-Cluig (the little church of the Bell), now partially restored. Another ancient church, St. Crispin's, is on the southern side, towards Greystones.

Greystones

Early Closing.—Wednesday.
Population.—with Delganey, 3,952.
Sport and Entertainment.—Two 18-hole golf courses, fishing, boating, pony-trekking, tennis, dancing, cinema.
Hotels.—*La Touche* (50 rooms), *Woodlands* (23), *Burnaby* (15).

Five miles south of Bray Head is Greystones, an attractive residential town and seaside resort lying in a pleasantly wooded part of the Wicklow coast. Part of the town retains its old atmosphere and appearance of a quiet fishing village. There is an excellent sandy beach which, sloping gradually to the water, provides safe bathing. There are good recreational facilities, and there are several attractive walks in the neighbourhood.

TO WICKLOW AND WEXFORD
❀❀❀❀❀❀❀❀❀❀❀❀❀❀❀❀❀❀❀❀❀❀❀❀❀❀❀

From **Bray,** both road and rail run south to Wicklow. The railway follows the coast, via Greystones (p. 62). The road follows the coastal plain via **Delgany** (*Horse and Hound*, 16 rooms; 18-hole golf course) and **Newcastle.**

Inland, County Wicklow offers a rich variety of interesting tours and scenic beauty—rugged mountains, wooded glens, rivers and lakes. A few miles west of Bray is the pretty village of **Enniskerry** (*Leicester Arms* (5 rooms), *Powerscourt Arms* (6 rooms)), from which one may explore the narrow—

Glen of the Dargle

a rocky and well-wooded ravine about 2 miles in length. A favourite viewing point is the massive rock known as *Lovers' Leap*. The Dublin water supply (from Roundwood Reservoir) is carried in conduits supported by a suspension bridge over the river. There is a Youth Hostel at the head of Glencree, 6 miles from Enniskerry, and one in the southern slope of Knockree.

Nearby is the **Powerscourt Estate** (*Estate and gardens open Easter to October, charge*) extending over an area of 14,000 acres. The main entrance is just above Enniskerry village. A beech avenue leads past the stately mansion (*private*) to the gardens and pleasure grounds. The beautiful gardens have sweeping terraces and embankments, statues and a lake. Of special interest here are the Japanese and Italian ornamental gardens. There are fine views of the Sugar Loaf Mountain and the Wicklow Hills.

Beyond the house (*not open*) the drive continues beside the river through shrubberies and plantations to the *Deer Park*, and to the celebrated *Waterfall* (*charge*), where a line of white foam falls almost vertically from a rocky cleft 398 feet above.

About 4 miles south of Enniskerry is the village of **Kilma-canoge,** and from here one may make the ascent of the—

Great Sugar Loaf (1,659 feet)

This is an easy climb, except perhaps for the steep and stony conical top; from here the view is extensive, from the mountains of Mourne in the north to Wicklow Head in the South. Great Sugar Loaf may also be reached from Greystones by way of Delgany and the **Glen of the Downs,** a densely wooded defile about one mile in length.

A rather longer tour starting from the region of Bray would be as follows:

From Enniskerry, take the road to the west, leaving **Knockree** (1,127 feet) on the left and **Prince William's Seat** (1,875 feet) on the right. The road continues along the north side of the **Glencree Valley,** with Kippure (2,473 feet) on the left, to the old barracks.

Here turn left. The road passes **Lower Lough Bray,** a mountain tarn 1,225 feet above sea level and the source of the Glencree river. A mile to the south, and still higher up, is **Upper Lough Bray.** Both loughs are ice-formed, and immense blocks of granite may be seen nearby.

Continuing southwards, past the source of the river *Liffey*, one reaches in 3½ miles the **Sally Gap,** 1,630 feet above sea level; the name is derived from "sallow" meaning willow. Here bear left and go down the pass, crossing the *Annamoe* river, with the round head of **Djouce** (2,384 feet) and the long **War Hill** (2,230 feet) on the left. Below, on the right, lies **Lough Tay,** but the main road continues south-eastwards to **Anna Carter Bridge,** where one turns right for—

Roundwood (*Wicklow Hills Hotel* (12 rooms)) a pleasant village in a wooded valley lying to the west of the great **Vartry Reservoir** of the Dublin Corporation. The reservoir covers 400 acres and presents the appearance of a mountain lake.

From Roundwood the main road runs north to **Bray,** and south to **Laragh** and **Glendalough.** Or, by taking the road eastwards *via* **Vartry Reservoir, Ballyduff Crossroads, Killiskey** and **Ashford,** one reaches—

Wicklow

Distances.—Arklow 16, Belfast 134, Bray 19, Cork 160, Dublin 32, Roundwood 10, Wexford 54.
Early Closing.—Thursday.

Hotels.—*Grand* (18 rooms), *Strabreag* (12).
Population.—3,340.

Wicklow derives its name from the Danes, by whom it was called *Wykinlo*, or the Viking's Loch. The town has a chequered history, and for several hundred years was a bone of contention between the Anglo-Norman invaders on the one hand and the O'Tooles and O'Brynes on the other. It is an old and small

Patrick Street, Cork

Cobh, Co. Cork

Gougane Barra, Co. Cork

Blue Pool, Glengarrif, Co. Cork

town, with good shops and hotels, and a fair harbour, enlarged and improved. It is much frequented in summer for its excellent bathing and has a 9-hole golf course on the cliffs south of the town. The stirring events of the 1798 Rebellion are recalled by the memorial to "Billy" Byrne in the market-place. The piers form a pleasant promenade and a shelter for yachts. The long spit of green turf by the side of the lagoon, known as the **Murrough,** makes a capital natural promenade. Fishing on the Three Mile Waters and Potter's River is free.

The road from the station to the town passes on the left the ruins of **Wicklow Abbey,** a Franciscan Friary founded in the time of Henry III. The old part of the town is at the entrance to the harbour, at the far end of the street. On the headland above are the remains of Wicklow Castle, or **Black Castle,** as it is generally called, a picturesque ruin dating from the twelfth century.

There are fine walks and drives about here. The **Silver Strand,** 2 miles away, and the cliffs and caves there and at **Wicklow Head,** where seals may be seen, are favourite resorts.

The Devil's Glen

The road from Wicklow, passing through **Rathnew** (*Hunter's* (16 rooms)) leads to **Ashford,** 4 miles from Wicklow. This is a pretty village. Close by is **Mount Usher,** a beautiful garden, where flourish semi-tropical shrubs and many rare and lovely trees, ferns and flowering plants, especially water plants, since the river *Vartry* runs through the garden. (*Admission charge.*)

From Ashford it is about a mile to the entrance gates at the foot of the **Devil's Glen.** (*Pedestrians only.*) The coach or car should go round by the road to the head of the Glen, while the visitor walks up.

For about 1½ miles the path runs by the side of the stream, then it mounts the side of a rocky defile with precipitous banks some 400 feet above the stream. At the upper end of the Glen the path affords a fine view of the picturesque **Waterfall.**

Ten miles south-west of Wicklow, and reached by rail or road, lies **Rathdrum** (*Barry's* (6 rooms), *Whaley Abbey* (9 rooms)), a little town situated above the beautiful valley of the *Avonmore.* To the north of the town the river flows through the wooded ravine called the **Vale of Clara** (pronounced "Clah-ra"). At the end of the Vale lies **Laragh,** and from here a road runs west to—

Glendalough,
the "valley of the two lakes" and the seven churches (*Roya*
(34 rooms); *Youth Hostel*).

Fishing (mainly for small brown trout) on the Upper and Lower Lakes is
free to visitors at the Royal Hotel.
As there are other Glendaloughs in Ireland, the full address of Glendalough, Co. Wicklow, should always be used.

In this deep, solitary glen, situated in the heart of a wild,
mountainous region, are found two lakes, the ruins of seven
churches which have stood for upwards of twelve hundred
years, and a round tower nearly a thousand years old.

The **Lower Lake** is a small, shallow sheet in the centre of
the valley and easily accessible; but the **Upper Lake,** the
centre of attraction, is a long, narrow, deep tarn from the left
side of which the mountain rises so abruptly that it is foolhardy
to try to scale it. On the right-hand side runs a road through
a fine plantation overlooking the dark, solemn lake. The
mountains that hem in the Glen are **Brockagh** (1,833 feet),
Glendassan, and **Camaderry** (2,296 feet) on the north, and
Derrybawn (1,567 feet), **Mullacor** (2,176 feet), and **Lugduff**
(2,148 feet) on the south.

The history of the valley is the history of St. Kevin, who took the cowl
about the year 520 and withdrew to this lonely glen to lead a hermit's life.
He is said to have lived to the age of 120. As his fame grew, a monastic
city sprang up and became a famous centre of learning. For several hundred
years the city flourished, but in the tenth century it was repeatedly plundered
by the Danes, and in the twelfth century it was looted by a party of Anglo-
Normans. At length, in 1214, it was annexed to the See of Dublin, and from
that time gradually decayed, becoming at length a hiding-place for outlaws
and robbers.

The ruins of Glendalough are certainly among the oldest Christian
buildings in Europe.

Passing through an old archway by the side of the hotel, we see
most of the ruined buildings and churches close together. The first
building is called the **Cathedral,** and is believed to be 1,200 years old.

On the south side of the Cathedral is the large monolith of granite
known as **St. Kevin's Cross.**

The **Round Tower** is 110 feet high and 52 feet in circumference.
The doorway is 10 feet above the ground-level; there is a narrow
window at each of the five storeys, and four windows in the topmost.
The conical cap is the only part that has given way, and this was
reconstructed in 1876 from the stones found within.

South-west of this is **Our Lady's Church,** or St. Mary's Church,
believed to have been the oratory built for St. Kevin, and his resting-
place. The chevron moulding of the east window remains.

St. Kevin's Kitchen, the small stone structure with high pitched roof
and bell turret south of the Cathedral, is perhaps the most interesting

building, as it has not only stood intact for hundreds of years but contains interesting collections of sculptured stones, crosses, and domestic implements found during restorations. This, of course, is not a kitchen, but one of the churches.

Following the path over the stream, we see a stone with a circular depression. This is the **Deer Stone**, which, according to local tradition, was filled with milk for the saint by the mountain deer during a famine.

Turning to the right, we skirt the small **Lower Lake**, some way past which a cleft in the rocks may be noticed. This is called the **Giant's Cut**, from a tradition that some fabulous hero tried the strength of his arm and the temper of his axe on this cliff. The path to the left leads to the little **Pollanass Waterfall**, on the *Lugduff Brook*.

Descending again, we cross the stile into a field, turn to the left, and, following the path to the left up the hillside, reach what remains of the stoutly-built **Rhefert Church**, or "Sepulchre of Kings." This was the principal burial church of the city and of the O'Toole chieftains of this district.

Again descending, we can take a boat from the mouth of the stream along the **Upper Lake** to **St. Kevin's Bed**, but the view from the boat is finer if one starts from the opposite corner. A decidedly awkward path (no place for the nervous) leads to the "Bed," a tiny cell in the cliff which can be seen satisfactorily from the boat if it stands off a little from the cliff. According to tradition, St. Kevin retired to this cliff-bed to avoid the attentions of a certain lady.

A little distance beyond are the remains of a building called **Temple-na-Skellig**, or "The Church of the Rocks," where, tradition relates, St. Kevin used to spend the season of Lent in solitude.

Returning by the path along the north side of the Glen, we can visit the remains of **Trinity Church**, or the "Ivy Church" as it is also called, and the site of another Round Tower beyond the hotel. Then, passing again through the cemetery and turning to the left along the little Glendassan stream, we soon reach **St. Kevin's Well** and the ruins of **St. Saviour's Priory** or Monastery. In the latter may be seen many beautifully carved stones and fantastic sculpturing.

Vale of Avoca

If the main road above Rathdrum station is followed southwards we soon pass **Avondale**, the birthplace of Parnell and now a Forestry School. Farther on, we see **Castle Howard** across the river. Midway between Rathdrum and Avoca (3 miles from each) is the **Meeting of the Waters**, immortalised by Moore—

"There is not in the wide world a valley so sweet
As that vale in whose bosom the bright waters meet."

Here the *Avonmore* and the *Avonbeg* unite to form the *Avoca* river.

67

Two miles beyond **Avoca** village (*Moore's Vale View* (11 rooms), *Redmonds* (5 rooms); *Youth Hostel*) is **Woodenbridge,** situated at the junction of the *Avoca* and *Aughrim* rivers. This second "Meeting of the Waters" is even more beautiful than the first, as here four valleys unite. Woodenbridge has a hotel (*Valley* (11 rooms)) and a 9-hole golf course, and fishing in the *Augrim* is free.

From Woodenbridge the road follows the river south-eastwards for 5 miles to—

Arklow

Distances.—Belfast 148, Cork 144, Dublin 45, Gorey 12, Rosslare 51, Wexford 38, Wicklow 16.
Early Closing.—Wednesday.
Golf.—9-hole course.
Hotels.—*Hoyne's* (33 rooms), *Royal* (34), *Marine* (13), *Bridge* (9), *Bay* (29).
Population.—6,100.

Arklow is a place of considerable antiquity and historical interest, and was once the most populous town in Co. Wicklow. Fishing and shipping were its principal industries, and to these has been added a thriving pottery industry.

But thanks to its beautiful position at the mouth of the *Avoca*, to its mild climate, sandy beaches and beautiful surroundings, Arklow is rapidly becoming a major tourist resort, with an *Entertainment Centre* that includes sea-water swimming pool, boating lake, tennis courts, ballroom, etc.

A popular walk is along the South Strand to **Arklow Rock,** from which there is a fine view of the mountains and the sea.

ARKLOW TO WEXFORD

The main road follows the railway, but a coastal route (38 miles) may be followed by branching off to **Castletown.**

By main road or railway one passes through **Gorey, Ferns** and **Enniscorthy.** Gorey is the station for **Courtown,** a popular seaside resort, with a 9-hole golf course, 3 miles to the east. **Ferns,** though now a village, was once the capital of Leinster. It has the ruins of an ancient **Augustinian Abbey,** founded by Dermot MacMurrough in the twelfth century, and **Ferns Castle,** one of the first towered keeps in Ireland. The rectangular keep is defended at the angles with round towers.

Enniscorthy

Distances.—Dublin 73, Ferns 7, Gorey 19, Kilkenny 36, New Ross 21, Wexford 15, Wicklow 46.
Early Closing.—Thursday.
Museum.—In Castle.
Golf.—9-hole course 2½ miles from the town.
Hotels.—*Portsmouth Arms* (25 rooms), *Slaney* (18), *Murphy-Floods* (12).
Population.—5,750.

Enniscorthy is a pleasant market town on the river *Slaney,*

which is spanned by an imposing bridge of six arches. The **Castle,** whose keep is well preserved, was built in the thirteenth century, rebuilt in the sixteenth, and captured by Cromwell in 1649. **St. Aidan's Cathedral** is a fine modern building. Overlooking the town is the historic **Vinegar Hill,** where the Wexford insurgents were finally defeated in 1798 by the British.

Wexford

Distances.—Arklow 38, Belfast 186, Cork 117, Dublin 83, Enniscorthy 15, New Ross 24, Rosslare 11, Waterford 39.

Early Closing.—Thursday.
Hotels.—*Talbot* (160 rooms), *White'* (46), *County* (20).
Population.—11,542.

Wexford is situated where the river *Slaney* widens into a spacious harbour. It is an ancient town of winding streets and was originally a settlement of the Danes in the ninth century. Of the fortifications of Wexford, which once included four castles and five fortified gateways, scarcely anything remains except the **West Gate Tower.** The fragments of the walls near the West Gate emcompass the churchyard of **Selskar Abbey,** founded at the end of the twelfth century on the supposed site of a former Viking temple.

It was in this abbey that the first Anglo-Irish treaty was signed, in 1169, when Wexford was surrendered to Robert

69

Fitzstephen. King Henry II spent the Lent of 1172 within its walls as a penance for the murder of Thomas à Becket.

One of the most notable spots in the town is the small square known as the **Bull Ring**, which, as its name implies, was the scene of the bloodthirsty sport of bull-baiting indulged in by the Norman nobles of the town. Wexford has a fishing harbour and is a centre for the manufacture of agricultural machinery. At **Curracloe,** on Wexford Bay, there is a splendid six-mile stretch of sandy beach.

Rosslare

Distances.—Cork 128, Dublin 94, Rosslare Harbour 5, Wexford 11, Belfast 193.
Hotels.—*Strand* (71 rooms), *Golf* (24), *The Cedars Guest House* (17).
Golf.—18-hole course on Rosslare Strand.
Population.—480.

Almost at the extreme south-easterly point of Ireland, with its 8-mile long *Strand*, Rosslare is the rendezvous of visitors from all parts during the summer. Its magnificent stretch of glinting silver sand is unmatched scarcely anywhere along the Irish coast, and this, amongst its many other amenities, has established the town as a popular holiday resort.

Its 18-hole golf course is splendidly laid out.

Rosslare Strand must not be confused with **Rosslare Harbour,** which is some 3 miles farther south and is the terminus of the boat service (car ferry) from Fishguard (*Harbour View,* 20).

At **Splaugh Rock,** a mile or so south-east of Rosslare Harbour, is the best bass fishing in Europe.

From Rosslare tours can be made to **Carnsore Point,** the south-eastern "corner-stone" of Ireland, where there are the ruins of St. Vogue's Church, a Caiseal (stone fort), a holy well, and stone with incised cross. Adjacent is **Lady's Island Bay**— a narrow sea loch—containing two small islets, Inish and Lady's Islands. In the latter are the remains of an Anglo-Norman Castle and an Augustinian Priory dedicated to the Blessed Virgin, whence the island got its name.

WEXFORD TO WATERFORD (38 miles)

From Wexford the main road runs westward 23 miles to **New Ross** (*see* p. 81), a very ancient small town and an inland port on the river *Barrow*. From New Ross the road runs south to Waterford.

An alternative route from Wexford is the Waterford Ferry road, *via* **Tullycanna, Tintern Abbey,** and **Ballyhack** (25 miles), whence a ferry (passengers and cycles only) crosses Waterford Harbour.

DUBLIN TO CARLOW AND KILKENNY
❀❀❀❀❀❀❀❀❀❀❀❀❀❀❀❀❀❀❀❀❀❀❀❀❀❀❀❀❀❀❀❀

The route *via* Athy is that running through Naas (21 miles), Kilcullan (28 miles), Athy (43 miles), Carlow (55 miles) and Leighlinbridge (63 miles) to Kilkenny.

Dublin is left through Kilmainham with Clondalkin to the right and views of the Dublin Hills on the left. Beneath Saggart Hill is **Rathcoole** (14 miles) and in a further 7 miles—

Naas

Distances.—Belfast 124, Carlow 31, Cork 140, Athy 22, Dublin 21, Kildare 13.

Early Closing.—Thursday.

Golf.—9-hole course 3 miles to the north of the town.

Hotels.—*Osberstown House* (10 rooms), *Nas Na Riogh* (13), *Royal* (14).

Population.—4,529.

Post Office.—Main Street South.

Racecourses.—Punchestown, 3 miles south-east. Naas, 1 mile.

Naas, the administrative town of County Kildare, is an ancient place. Just outside the town is the *North Moat*, a mound which was once the site of the palace of the Leinster kings. There are some remains of an old Norman **castle**, now incorporated in the rectory. **Punchestown Racecourse**, 3 miles south-east, is well known for steeplechase meetings and attracts its annual visitors for the National Hunt races.

Three miles north of Naas is **Sallins** through which the Grand Canal passes. A mile to the east of the village is the Leinster Aqueduct, by which the canal crosses over the *Liffey*.

Seven miles on from Naas is **Kilcullen**, where the bridge over the *Liffey* dates from 1318. Here the road forks, the left-hand road going direct to Carlow and the right-hand one to Athy. The Carlow road passes through **Ballitore, Timolin** and **Castledermot**. The rather longer right-hand road leads through Seven Stars and Fontstown to **Athy** (*Leinster Arms* (20 rooms); 9-hole golf course), a market town on the river *Barrow* where the river links up with the *Grand Canal*. At the bridge over the river is **White's Castle,** built about 1507 by the 8th Earl of Kildare. To the north, on the opposite side of the river, is **Woodstock Castle,** built 200 years earlier and noted for the thickness of its walls.

Just before the river we turn left and follow the east bank to—

Carlow

Distances.—Athlone 70, Athy 12, Cork 116, Dublin 52, Naas 31, Kilkenny 24, Waterford 47.
Early Closing.—All day Thursday.
Golf.—18-hole course 2 miles from the town.

Hotels.—*Roya* (44 rooms), *Crofton* (30), *Kilfane Guest House* (7).
Hunting, Shooting and Fishing and Boating are available.
Population.—11,000.

Carlow was an important stronghold of the Anglo-Normans, and one can still see the remains of the **Castle** built to protect the borders of the Pale. The development of the town, the chief centre of County Carlow, has been helped by the fact that the Barrow is navigable for 76 miles. Carlow takes pride in its beet sugar factory, which was the first to be established in Ireland. Of the castle only the west wall with two 60-foot towers remains. The most noteworthy building is the **Roman Catholic Cathedral of the Assumption,** with its lantern tower. In the cathedral is Hogan's monument to Bishop Doyle. Adjoining the cathedral grounds is the parkland surrounding **St. Patrick's College,** for the education of priests. The parish **Church of St. Mary's** (Church of Ireland) is an imposing nineteenth-century building with a fine spire. Two miles north-east of Carlow, at **Browne's Hill,** is a fine dolmen. Its sloping capstone weighs about 100 tons and is the largest of its kind in Ireland.

South of Carlow is **Leighlinbridge,** pleasantly situated in the Barrow Valley. By the stone bridge are the remains of **Black Castle,** built in 1181, one of the earliest of Norman defences in Ireland. A quarter mile south is a fine rath, *Dinn Righ*, marking an ancient seat of the Leinster kings.

Kilkenny

Angling.—Kilkenny Angling Association controls some salmon and trout fishing and issues tickets to visitors for stretches near the city.
Distances.—Belfast 176, Carlow 24, Cashel 35, Cork 92, Dublin 75, New Ross 27, Thomastown 11, Waterford 30.
Early Closing.—All day Thursday.
Golf.—18-hole course of Kilkenny Club

1 mile from city.
Hotels.—*Clubhouse* (40 rooms), *Carmel* (14), *Castle* (21), *Central* (9), *Metropole* (21), *Railway* (9), *Rose Hill House* (14), *Newpark* (46).
Population.—11,500.
Post Office.—High Street.
Youth Hostel.—At Foulksrath Castle, Jenkinstown, about 8 miles from Kilkenny.

Kilkenny, *Cill Chainnigh* = church of St. Canice, headquarters town of Co. Kilkenny, is the most famous city of Ireland. Apart from its two cathedrals and castle, there are many buildings of historic interest in the city. Kilkenny was made famous by the finest quality marble obtained from quarries in the near vicinity.

72

The town formed part of the territory which Strongbow acquired by his marriage (*see below*). His daughter and heiress married William, Earl of Pembroke, who built the original castle. William's daughter married Gilbert de Clare, Earl of Gloucester, from whose family the property passed by marriage to Hugh le Spencer, who sold it to the Butlers in 1391. Of the several parliaments held at Kilkenny, that of 1367 is noteworthy for the Statute of Kilkenny, which among other provisions made it a capital offence for an Englishman to marry an Irishwoman. In 1642 assembled a "rebel" or Catholic Parliament, from which the name "City of the Confederation" arose. The Lord Lieutenant, Ormonde, was about to conclude a treaty on the King's behalf when the Papal Legate arrived with money and arms, and the result was the siege and capture of the city by Cromwell's army in 1650.

The Dublin road enters Kilkenny on the east, passing the station and the partly ruined St. John's Church to St. John's Bridge over the *Nore* river. From here there is a fine view of the castle prominently set on the west bank.

Kilkenny Castle

(*Enquire at Office.*) This structure was erected in 1192 by Strongbow's son-in-law, William le Mareschal, on the same site as the former fortress of Strongbow himself. Though considerable portions were rebuilt in 1835, some of the original stonework may be seen in the towers. Set on three sides of a quadrangle, it retains three of its four original corner towers. From the fourteenth century it was the chief seat of the Butler family. It is now state property and the grounds developed as a National Park.

From the castle, the Parade leads directly down to the High Street, wherein is the **Town Hall** (Tholsel) which at one time served as an exchange. It has a curious clock tower and its front arcade extends over the pavement. **Rothe House** (restored) is a fine example of a Tudor merchant's house (1594).

Turning left out of High Street, beyond the Post Office, is James Street, at the far end of which is **St. Mary's Roman Catholic Cathedral** consecrated in 1857. It is a rich building, though the shortness of the nave is to be regretted. The total length is 175 feet, and breadth, including aisles, 90 feet. The central tower is 200 feet high. To the left of the Lady Chapel is a huge statue of the Virgin by Benzoni.

From the Cathedral Blackmill Street leads to the **Dominican Church,** which incorporates the slender tower and some fine fourteenth-century windows of the old *Black Abbey,* built here by William le Mareschal in 1225.

In Abbey Street is **Black Freren Gate,** the last remaining of the gates of the old city walls.

North of the little Bregagh stream (covered) is—

St. Canice's Cathedral (Church of Ireland)

The Cathedral stands on high ground and is undoubtedly the finest building in the city. Founded at the close of the twelfth century, it is believed to stand on the same site as a church founded by St. Canice in the sixth century. Externally, the most striking features are the stepped battlements and the *Round Tower* (100 feet), standing close to the south transept. Within the Cathedral there are some notable floor slabs. The groined roof of the Central Tower springs from four piers, and is exceedingly beautiful. The cathedral font is of fine Kilkenny marble.

North-west of the Cathedral is **St. Canice's Library,** with over 3,000 sixteenth- and seventeenth-century volumes bequeathed by Bishop Otway and Bishop Maurice.

Excursions from Kilkenny. Excellent tours may be made from Kilkenny, both in the immediate vicinity and further afield. Seven miles north-east is the **Cave of Dunmore,** an interesting series of limestone caverns the second of which has a high stalactite pillar. Ten miles south-west of Kilkenny is **Callan,** a busy market town on the *Kings River.* On the Kilkenny side are the remains of an Augustinian Abbey founded in 1468. At **Kells,** 5 miles east of Callan, are the large and interesting ruins of a fortified twelfth-century priory. For Thomastown, *see* p. 82.

Twelve miles north of Kilkenny is **Castlecomer,** a town begun by the Wandesforde family in the seventeenth century. It is situated in a wooded valley in the centre of the former Leinster coalfields, from which a good quality anthracite was mined. There is a 9-hole golf course.

DUBLIN TO LIMERICK, CORK OR KILLARNEY

To Limerick: *Via* Naas, Kildare, Port Laoise, Roscrea and Nenagh.
To Cork: *Via* Port Laoise, Cashel, Mallow or Fermoy.
To Killarney: *Via* Limerick (as above), or *via* Roscrea, Thurles, Cashel and Mallow.

The first part of the main route for all three destinations is *via* **Naas** (*see* p. 71) to **Port Laoise.** The right-hand road previously mentioned leads in a short while to **Droicead Nua, or Newbridge** (*Grand* (6 rooms)), on the *Liffey*, with its one long main street. A former garrison town, it is now one of the chief industrial centres for County Kildare. It has factories engaged in rope and cutlery manufacture, and also houses the Experimental Station of the Irish Turf Board. The board's chief function is the production of machine turf, or peat, for use in power stations, factories and homes.

South of the road from Droicead Nua to Kildare lies the **Curragh,** a great stretch of turf extending over 5,000 acres. It is an important military training centre, the Aldershot of Ireland, but is probably best known for its famous *Racecourse*, on which in June the classic Irish Sweeps Derby is run. Other classic races run here are the Irish 2,000 Guineas and 1,000 Guineas in May, the Irish Oaks in July, and the Irish St. Leger in September. In all, some fifteen meetings are held between April and November. At the eastern end of the plain is the well-known **Curragh Golf Club's** 18-hole course, one of the leading provincial courses.

Kildare

Distances.—Athy 14, Belfast 133, Cork 127, Dublin 34, Kilkenny 44, Monasterevin 7, Naas 12, Port Laoise 20, Tullamore 30.
Early Closing.—Wednesday.

Golf.—Cill Dara 9-hole course 1 mile from the town.
Hotels.—*Railway* (12 rooms), *Derby House* (20 rooms).
Population.—2,730.

Kildare, on the west side of the Curragh, is a market town and busy centre of the horse breeding and training world. Its **Cathedral** (St. Brigid—Church of Ireland) on the north side, is a cruciform building with a central tower (1229). Reconstructed between 1871 and 1896, it follows the design of the thirteenth-century Anglo-Norman building, of which some evidence may be seen embodied in the present building. Close to the Cathedral is the fine **Round Tower,** 103 feet high. It is perfect, except that its cap has been replaced by a battlement.

Two miles south of Kildare on the Fontstown road is **Tully House,** with very fine Japanese Gardens (*charge*). Adjoining is the **Irish National Stud,** a Government horse-breeding establishment.

North of Kildare are the low sandstone **Red Hills,** highest points of which are Dunmurry Hill (768 feet), **Gra**nge Hill (743 feet), Hill of Allen (676 feet) and Boston Hill (538 feet). **Rathangan** is a small town on the edge of the **Bog of Allen,** a wide expanse of bogland stretching north-westward, and a centre of the peat industry.

From **Monasterevin** the Port Laoise road strikes south-westward, but a road north of it leads to **Portarlington** (*East End* (12 rooms)), a town (population 2,804) on the *Barrow*. Four miles south of it is *Emo Court*, former seat of Lord Arlington, from whom the town is named. The house is now a Jesuit establishment. A prominent feature at Portarlington is the high cooling tower of a turf-fired generating station—the first of its kind in Ireland. A 9-hole golf course is situated 1 mile from the town. West of Portarlington is **Mountmellick** (*Leix Arms*), a town founded by the Society of Friends on the Port Laoise–Tullamore road. For **Tullamore,** *see* p. 168.

Port Laoise (*County* (10 rooms) and *Kelly's* (19 rooms)), chief town of County Laoise (Leix), is at an important junction of roads. Here the routes from Dublin to Limerick and Cork divide. It is typically Irish and has worsted manufacture and flour-milling interests. Four miles from the town is a 9-hole golf course, at Heath.

The Rock of Dunamase, 4 miles east of Port Laoise off the Carlow road, is an old fortress. The 200-foot steep rock is topped by the extensive ruins of the castle of Diarmuid MacMurrough. **Stradbally** has a single mile-long street from which the Carlow road rises to *Windy Gap* (632 feet), from where there are extensive views of the Barrow valley and Slieve Bloom mountains.

The direct Cashel road goes southward through **Abbeyleix** (9 miles), an attractive little town with a quaint Market House in its square. The town takes its name from a former abbey founded here in 1183 by Conohor O'More. In the **de Vesci** demesne, south of the town (*grounds open to the public*), is the tomb of Melaghlin O'More, a chieftain of Laoise in the thirteenth century. There is a 9-hole golf course nearby. For **Cashel,** *see* p. 78.

For **Limerick** the main road winds westward to **Roscrea** (*see* p. 168) whence the route is described in the reverse direction on p. 167.

For **Cork** or **Killarney** we branch southward from Roscrea for **Thurles**. In 12 miles is **Templemore** (*Mullally's* (15 rooms)), a small town (population 1,775) taking its name from the Knights Templar. In the old Priory Park are the ruins of the Templars' Castle and a fragment of the abbey church. Overhanging the town is the **Devil's Bit Mountain** (1,577 feet), showing clearly the notch supposedly made by the devil's teeth when he bit out what he afterwards dropped on the plain to form the Rock of Cashel (p. 78).

Thurles

Distances.—Belfast 180, Cashel 13, Cork 74, Dublin 92, Kilkenny 30, Limerick 40, Roscrea 21, Templemore 9, Tipperary 26.
Early Closing.—Wednesday.

Golf.—18-hole course at Turtulla, 1½ miles.
Hotels.—*Hayes* (48 rooms), *Munster* (10), *Castle* (7), *Anner* (15).
Population.—6,743.

Thurles is a market town on the *Suir* and the seat of the Roman Catholic Archbishop of Cashel. Adjoining the bridge are the remains of an old castle keep. There is another keep, *Black Castle*, near the square. The only building of note is the **Roman Catholic Cathedral** on the left, beyond the bridge. It is a fine Italian–Romanesque-style building, built between 1857 and 1875, and stands on the site of an ancient foundation of 1300. Its square 125-foot-high campanile is a landmark seen from many miles around.

The town is well known as a sporting centre. Hurling and Gaelic football are played at the large stadium. There is good fishing for salmon and trout in the *Suir*, pheasant and duck shooting, and several packs of foxhounds hunt the district. There is an 18-hole golf course at Turtulla to the south, and 1½ miles west is *Thurles Racecourse*, which has popular meetings throughout most of the year. Dog Racing: Tuesdays and Saturdays.

Thurles to Holy Cross Abbey (4 miles)

Holy Cross and Cashel (p. 78) form a good excursion from Thurles. Cashel is on the same road as Holy Cross, 9 miles beyond its Abbey. The Cashel road crosses the railway by the station, and again 2 miles farther on. Then it follows the *Suir* to the little village of Holy Cross.

Holy Cross Abbey, founded in the late twelfth century for Cistercians by Donnell O'Brien, King of Munster, is a beautiful and interesting fourteenth-century ruin of which a great part, including window tracery and groining, is well preserved. It is on the bank of the *Suir*, which flows past the east end. The plan of the Abbey church is cruciform with a central tower. The western limb has north and south aisles, and on the east side of each arm of the transept are chapels.

Externally, the most striking features are the west window of the nave, consisting of six lights and filled above with tracery formed of elongated hexagons, and the east window of the choir, which has six lights and honeycomb tracery reminiscent of the Lady Chapel at Wells.

Internally, the church consists of a nave of four bays, with a round arcade on one side and a pointed one on the other. The choir includes a third of the nave and extends some distance west of the tower, which rests on four pointed arches and has a ribbed vault. A stair leads up the tower to a small chamber. An elaborate monument in the choir is thought to be the tomb of the rebuilder of the abbey. The north transept displays a flamboyant character in the windows, and there is curious tracery in the window of the northernmost of the two side chapels. The south transept also has two eastern chapels with flamboyant windows, but the most interesting feature is the narrow compartment between the chapels; this has three pointed arches, supported by twisted columns on each side, and an elaborately groined roof. The purpose of this room is uncertain, but it may have been a mortuary or the shrine of the relic of the true Cross, sent by the Pope to Donnell.

Cashel

Distances.—Belfast 191, Cahir 11, Clonmel 15, Cork 61, Dublin 100, Limerick 37, Mallow 50, Roscrea 34, Thurles 13, Tipperary 13.
Early Closing.—Wednesday.

Fishing.—Trout and salmon in the *Suir*.
Hotels.—*Grant's Castle* (19 rooms), *Cashel Palace* (13), *Cashel Inn* (40).
Population.—2,679.
Post Office.—Main Street.

Cashel is a small town on the east and south of the famed **Rock of Cashel,** a mass of carboniferous limestone rising about 100 feet above the plain, with a small cliff on the town side. Though a titular city—it is the seat of the Protestant Bishop— it has little in itself to attract the visitor other than the great ecclesiastical ruins on the Rock. These include the Cathedral, Cormac's Chapel, Hall of the Vicars Choral, a tenth-century Round Tower, and St. Patrick's Cross (*Flood-lit at night*).

The Cathedral, thirteenth-century, consists of a short nave, side transept with pointed windows, a tower resting on pointed arches, and four chapels. In the south wall of the choir is the wall-tomb of Archbishop Miler Mac-Grath, Archbishop of Cashel in 1626. The Cathedral was burnt in 1495 by the Earl of Kildare, who hoped his enemy, Archbishop Creagh, was inside. From the transept a staircase gives access to the fortified parts of the structure.

Adjoining the Cathedral on the south side is—
Cormac's Chapel (Cormac McCarthy, King of Munster) begun in 1127 and consecrated in 1134. It is Hiberno-Romanesque work, and a unique

structure in Ireland. The plan comprises nave, square transeptal towers, chancel, and a small eastward extension from the altar. Externally, the roofs are steep stone ones, diminishing in height eastward. Internally they are groined with ribs springing from short columns, and along the walls runs an enriched round-headed arcade.

The **Round Tower** at the north-east corner of the transept is a perfect specimen. Built of sandstone, it dates from the eleventh century and rises just over 80 feet high. It has the usual conical cap and the doorway is 12 feet above the ground.

To the south-west of the Cathedral is **St. Patrick's Cross,** probably twelfth-century, with a figure representing St. Patrick on the one side, and on the other the Crucifixion.

Near the entrance to the enclosure is the **Hall of the Vicars Choral,** an extensive fifteenth-century building in two parts of two storeys each; used to accommodate minor officials of the Cathedral.

At the foot of the rock are the ruins of **Hore Abbey,** founded in 1272 by the Archbishop of Cashel for Cistercians. The church, which is cruciform with a central tower, is singularly plain.

In the town, opposite the Town Hall, is *Grant's Castle Hotel,* now converted but retaining in the upper storey battlements and gargoyles of the fifteenth-century Quirk's Castle. The **Protestant Cathedral** was built in 1784, its spire being added in 1812. In the vestry is a small *museum* of local interest, while in the grounds is a seventeenth-century library. The *Dominican Priory* was founded in 1243. It has a beautiful east window.

Eleven miles south of Cashel is **Cahir** (*see* p. 86) at the junction of the Waterford–Limerick and Cashel–Mallow roads. For routes onward to Cork or Killarney, *see* p. 86.

WATERFORD

🍀🍀🍀🍀🍀🍀🍀🍀🍀🍀🍀🍀

Distances.—Dublin 99, Cappoquin 38, Carrick-on-Suir 17, Cork 78, Dungarvan 29, Fermoy 59, Kilkenny 30, Tramore 8, Wexford 39.

Early Closing.—Thursday.

Festival.—International Festival of Light Opera in September.

Golf.—Waterford Golf Club, 18-hole course at Newrath, half-mile north of the city.

Hotels.—*Bridge* (32 rooms); *Granville* (52), *Metropole* (25), *Dooleys'* (22), *Tower* (83).

Post Office.—Head Office at the Quay. Several sub-offices.

Population.—29,842.

Youth Hostel.—At Arthurstown: Cottages Nos. 3 and 4, Coastguard Station. Ferry from Ballyhack across Waterford Harbour.

Waterford Glass.—Visits may be made to the factory of Waterford Glass Ltd. to see the leaded glass blown and cut by hand. Appointment necessary.

Waterford is an ancient city of Danish origin, well placed on the south side of the River Suir.

Waterford was founded by Sitric, the Dane, about the year 853, though no trace of his early fortifications remains. When Dermot MacMurrogh, King of Leinster, was driven from his kingdom in 1167, he went to Henry II, under whom he promised to redeem and hold his dominions. Under letters from Henry, MacMurrogh came to terms with Richard de Clare, better known as Strongbow, a point of their agreement being that the latter take Eva, MacMurrogh's daughter, as his wife, and thus become heir to Leinster. Strongbow landed at Waterford in 1170, and a few months later succeeded to his principality, which by then had been enlarged. Henry II, jealous of his successful subject, landed at Waterford in 1171 and Strongbow made peace with him. After receiving the submission of the Irish chiefs the King left in 1172. After this the walls of the city were extended and a mint established. Perkin Warbeck, Pretender in the reign of Henry VII, tried in vain, in 1492, to take the city, and again, in 1649, Cromwell was unsuccessful in his attempt to capture it. Ireton, however, stormed the city in 1650, and forty years later it was occupied by William III.

At the junction of the Mall with the Quay is *Reginald's Tower* (museum) a remnant of the Danish defences. Built and named after a Danish governor, Reginald MacIvor, in 1003, it was restored in 1819. It was in the great hall here that Strongbow was married to Eva in 1171. Christ Church Cathedral (Church of Ireland) occupies the site of the Danish church built in the second half of the eleventh century. It was rebuilt in 1773, and partially restored in 1891. The Roman Catholic Cathedral in Barronstrand Street, near the Clock Tower on the Quay, is spacious and has a high, vaulted roof. At the west end of the Quay the *Suir* is crossed by a concrete bridge.

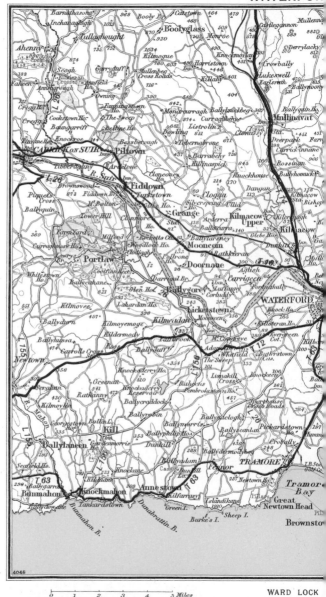

0 1 2 3 4 5 Miles

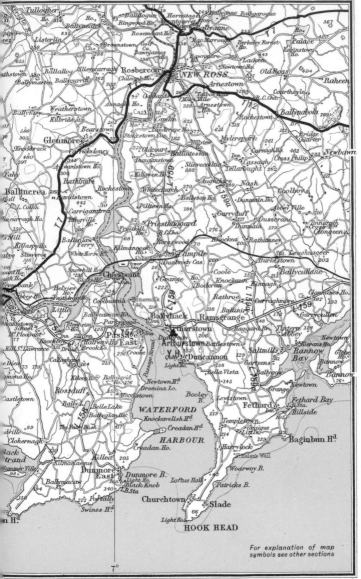

AND DISTRICT

For explanation of map symbols see other sections

WATERFORD EXCURSIONS

To Tramore

The road south (T63) from Waterford leads in 8 miles to
Tramore, a popular holiday resort of 3,270 inhabitants.
(Hotels: *Grand* (50 rooms); *Majestic* (41 rooms); *Atlantic*
(23 rooms); *Hibernian* (18 rooms), etc.). There is an excellent
golf course. The town occupies high ground at the north-west
corner of Tramore Bay, in which there is a 3-mile stretch of
firm sand. To the west of the bay are the Doneraile cliffs with
the attractive Doneraile Walk leading to the popular Foyle
bathing place. Farther south is Great Newtown Head, at the
top of which is the *Metal Man*, a 14-foot iron figure set on a
pillar as a warning to shipping. The point eastward across the
bay is *Brownstown Head*, while westward may be seen Helvick
Head, and beyond it, in the distance, Mine Head and Ardmore
Head. Eastward of the town are the Burrows, dividing the bay
from Back Strand, a sea-water lagoon. Sports facilities include
bathing, golf, horse racing, tennis, hunting and shooting. Race
meetings at Whitsun (two days) and in mid-August (four days).

To Dunmore

Eleven miles south-east of Waterford by L158. About 3
miles out of Waterford a left branch road leads to Passage
East, but L158 forks right for **Dunmore East** (*Haven, Ocean,
Strand*), a pleasant resort offering some good sea fishing. On
the west side of the entrance to Waterford Harbour, there was
during last century a mail-packet terminus for the Milford
Haven service. It still has its long pier and lighthouse. South
of the pier is the Black Knob promontory, with Merlin's Cave
easily accessible.

WATERFORD TO NEW ROSS, by road, 15 miles.

The road is dull at first, but about 7 miles from Waterford
the scenery improves as the valley of Glenmore is reached.
The road then descends to run beside the *Barrow* for about a
mile. Road and river part company for a time to rejoin at
Rosbercon, which has a long bridge to New Ross.

New Ross (*Royal, Phoenix*) is a busy town of some 4,600
people, on the *Barrow*. It was founded by Isabella, Strongbow's
daughter, its name distinguishing it from Old Ross, a village

5 miles to the east. The town is built on a steep hill-side, and many of its quaint streets are stepped and winding. There is some port activity and a 9-hole golf course, but for visitors it is more important as a convenient base for exploring the beautiful scenery of the *Nore* and *Barrow,* which join about 3 miles above the town.

NEW ROSS TO INISTIOGE AND THOMASTOWN
(Jerpoint Abbey)

This is a delightful route up the valley of the *Nore.* The road ascends above the left bank of the *Barrow* and passes the old keep of Mountgarrett Castle, with a good view of the meeting of the Nore and Barrow. At 4 miles from New Ross a road diverges right to Graiguenamanagh, but we keep straight on and then cross the river by a ten-arched bridge to **Inistioge,** a small village in a delightful setting. Here was founded, in 1210, an Augustinian monastery, of which two towers, one now incorporated with the parish church, remain. In the second are reminders of the Tighe family, among them an effigy by Flaxman of Mrs. Mary Tighe (*d.* 1810), authoress of "Psyche."

There is a fine walk of about 5 miles from Inistioge to **Brandon Hill** (1,694 feet), which is approached by following the Graiguenamanagh road and turning off right in 3 miles. From the summit a grand view takes in the river valleys and the Leinster and Blackstairs Mountains.

It is a pleasant $5\frac{1}{2}$ miles from Inistioge, by road, beside the Nore to **Thomastown,** a small town of some 1,200 inhabitants. Once, it was a walled town of importance, but today only the ruins of the walls and castles built by Thomas FitzAnthony remain. Behind the Protestant Church in the main street are the remains of the old parish church, founded at the same time as the castle. In the grounds of the Roman Catholic Church is the high altar from Jerpoint. Thomastown is well known as a hunting and salmon-fishing centre. To the west, over the Nore, is the Mount Juliet stud farm, with the grave of the famous racehorse, *The Tetrarch.*

Jerpoint Abbey, $1\frac{1}{2}$ miles south-west from Thomastown, is among the most interesting ruins in Ireland. It was founded in 1158 for Cistercians by Donough, Prince of Ossery (*d.* 1185), and a great part of what remains is of that date. The superstructure of the fine tower, with curious battlements and corner turrets, is assigned to the fifteenth century. There are six wide, pointed arches between the nave and the north aisle. Several tombs with effigies are of interest, including that of Bishop O'Dullany (the first abbot) holding his crozier on which is a serpent. Of considerable influence and wealth at the Dissolution in 1540, the Abbey and grounds passed to the Ormonde family.

Beyond Thomastown road and rail keep close company, *via* Bennettsbridge, for 11 miles northward to Kilkenny (*see* p. 72).

WATERFORD TO DUNBRODY ABBEY

Dunbrody is easily reached from Waterford by road to **Passage East,** a small township on the Waterford side of the river, at the head of the harbour. Here a small ferry plies to **Ballyhack,** a fishing village on the Wexford bank. The abbey lies to the left of the New Ross road about 2½ miles north of Ballyhack.

Dunbrody Abbey, 8 miles south of New Ross, was founded in 1182 by Hervey de Monte Marisco, Marshal to Henry II, who gave it to the monks of Buildwas, in Salop, who in turn ceded their rights to St. Mary's Abbey, Dublin. The abbey had the right of sanctuary, and became known as the Monastery of St. Mary of Refuge. Its situation is a little desolate, but the remains are among the finest of their kind in Ireland. The church is cruciform, with a central tower, and the East window is a lancet triplet of grand proportions. There is an aisled nave and three chapels opening off each transept. The chevron mouldings of the pointed nave arcades should be noted.

South from Ballyhack, beyond **Arthurstown** (*Youth Hostel*), is **Duncannon,** a pleasant resort with a sandy beach.

WATERFORD TO LIMERICK

❀❀❀❀❀❀❀❀❀❀❀❀❀❀❀❀❀❀❀❀❀❀❀❀❀

Distances.—Carrick-on-Suir 17, Clonmel 30, Cahir 40, Tipperary 54, Limerick 79.
Services.—By rail *via* Limerick Junction in about 3 hours. By road 79 miles (bus service).

As far as Limerick Junction this is a very picturesque route, the Suir Valley being well wooded and set off by its background of mountains. The towns on the route each offer something of interest, with accommodation available at all of them. For the first thirty miles, to Clonmel, there are alternative roads either side of the Suir, the one north of the river being the faster, though not as fine as the other on the score of scenery. South of the river, 15 miles out of Waterford, is the village of **Portlaw,** and adjoining it, **Curraghmore,** the fine seat of the Marquess of Waterford (*grounds open on certain days*) and early home of Admiral Lord Beresford (1846–1919). Beyond **Fiddown,** with its ¼-mile-long bridge, is picturesque **Piltown,** and close at hand, Bessborough Park, the former residence of Lord Bessborough.

Carrick-on-Suir, with a population of 4,870 is a quiet town situated at a pretty stretch of the river. Most of it stands on the north, Tipperary, bank, but its suburb, Carrickbeg, lies on the opposite, County Waterford, side. Two bridges connect them. *Carrick Castle* is a fifteenth-century ruin with an Elizabethan mansion built on to it by the Butlers, Earls, and later Dukes, of Ormonde. There is a good 9-hole golf course south of the town, while good trout and salmon fishing is available on the Suir and the Clodiagh tributary.

Carrick-on-Suir is a good centre for walks and climbs in the Comeragh Mountains. A popular excursion is to **Lough Coumshingaun,** a finely set tarn which may be included with the ascent to *Knockanaffrin* (2,597 feet), highest point of the range.

Six miles north of Carrick-on-Suir, in a gap in the hills, is the village of **Ahenny,** with two eighth-century High-Crosses carrying curiously involved spiral and fret designs.

Beyond Carrick the valley of the Suir contracts, but the road on either bank may be followed. On the more beautiful south

84

side are wooded creeks backed by the Comeragh Mountains; on the right, the mass of Slievenamon (2,364 feet). We pass **Kilsheelan,** which takes its name from an ancient church and opposite which is the fine demesne of Gurteen le Poer, once the home of the statesman Richard Lalor Shiel (1791–1851).

Clonmel

Access.—C.I.E. main line services and bus routes.

Churches.—St. Mary's (*Roman Catholic*); St. Mary's (*Church of Ireland*); Presbyterian.

Early Closing Day.—Thursday.

Golf.—9-hole course on south side of river.

Hotels.—*Hearn's* (29 rooms), *Ormonde* (30), *Larkin's* (10), *Slieve-na-mon* (15), *Minella* (43), *Suir Vale* (10).

Population.—11,026.

Post Office.—Gladstone Street.

Principal town of County Tipperary, Clonmel is a clean and pleasant place and an important centre for local trade. The chief part is on the north bank of the Suir, but the town also includes Moore and Suir Islands in the river and a suburb on the south bank.

Its features of interest can be seen within a few hours, but it is a good place to stay in, for there are many pleasant walks and excursions to be made from it and there is good salmon and trout fishing in the *Suir*.

Cluain Meala (clue-in malla), Honey Meadow, was of some importance as early as the ninth or tenth century, and its walls defied Cromwell for a time when he stormed it in 1650. The West Gate and parts of the walls are still standing. Lawrence Sterne, author of *Tristram Shandy*, was born at Clonmel in 1713, and in 1817 the first of Bianconi's Cars, which revolutionized Irish traffic (or rather created it), was put on the road from Clonmel to Cahir. George Borrow, the great writer, spent much of his grammar school days here while his father was stationed in the town.

The station is to the north of the town, some distance from O'Connell Street and Parnell Street, the main thoroughfares. Towards the west end of O'Connell Street is the ancient West Gate (rebuilt 1831) arching over the roadway. This is the only one remaining of the original four gates of the town. Of interest are the Main Guard, built to house the town garrison and designed by Wren, the modern Town Hall, and the Parish Church (Church of Ireland). The last is Pre-Reformation, with a fine east window. The Franciscan (Catholic) Church in Abbey Street has its original tower and some early tombs. There is an interesting *Museum* in Parnell Street. Added attraction for visitors is a greyhound track in the town, horse-racing at Powerstown Park, good fishing in the Suir and local streams, and a certain amount of hunting. The Tipperary

85

FETHARD

Foxhounds and Clonmel Harriers have frequent meets in the neighbourhood. Good climbing and hill walking can be enjoyed. The Comeragh Mountains are immediately to the south, the Knockmealdowns south-west, and Slievenamon a few miles to the north-east.

Nine miles north of Clonmel is **Fethard,** a curious old town with a considerable part of its original walls still standing. The Protestant Church, fourteenth century, is the nave of the original building. In the town are some well-preserved remnants of an Augustinian Priory, with various sixteenth- and seventeenth-century tombs.

Clonmel to Ardfinnan (8 miles), Clogheen (15 miles), Ballyporeen (19 miles) and Mitchelstown (27 miles). A fine excursion south-west of Clonmel. In 8 miles is **Ardfinnan** (Finan's Height), where a long bridge crosses the Suir, dominated by the ruins of Ardfinnan Castle, finely situated on a bold rock. An important strategic centre, it was built about 1184 by Prince, afterwards King, John. It was reduced to ruins by Cromwell, 1649–50. The road now winds up from the Suir. The Knockmealdown (left) and the Galtee Mountains (right) bound the wide fertile valley lying between them. Beyond the Shanbally stream, which runs into the *Tar* river, we reach **Clogheen,** a large village at the head of the breath-taking road zig-zagging its way through the Knockmealdown Gap to Lismore. We bear right, however, for **Ballyporeen,** 3 miles north of which are the famed **Mitchelstown Caves** (*see* p. 95).

Continuing the main route to Limerick, we come in 10 miles from Clonmel to **Cahir** (*Kilcoran Lodge* (16 rooms); *Cahir House* (25 rooms); *Galtee* (28 rooms)), a trim little town on the Suir in a charming neighbourhood. The main route here is crossed by the Dublin–Cork trunk road. Of principal interest are the Castle and Park.

The Castle (*permission to enter from Estate Office*), dating from 1142, stands on an island in the Suir. The massive square keep and high walls present a striking effect.

Cahir Park, with its lovely grounds, stretches for some distance along both banks of the Suir.

On the river, a little above the railway bridge, are remains of an old priory founded during the reign of King John.

Both the Suir and the Aherlow provide occasional salmon, and trout fishing, a good bit of it free, is good. Cahir is convenient for exploring the Galtee Mountains (*see* p. 95), which extend westward, and there are frequent hunt meets.

Beyond Cahir the road to Tipperary skirts the eastern end

of the Galtee Mountains and runs past the Glen of Aherlow, from where the view of the Galtees is very fine—hill behind hill in gentle cones. The country is a rich pastoral vale onwards to Tipperary.

TIPPERARY

Distances.—Glen of Aherlow 4½, Athassel Priory 9½, Cashel 13, Cahir 14, Limerick Junction 2½, Limerick 25, Waterford 55.
Early Closing.—Wednesday.
Golf.—9-hole course to south of town.

Hotels.—*Royal* (25 rooms), Bridge Street; *Dobbyns'* (19).
Population.—4,507.
Racecourse.—At Limerick Junction, 2 miles.

The town of Tipperary is well situated in the fertile Golden Vale, or Vein, with the Slievenamuck hills to the south. Dairy farming, woollens and linoleum manufacturing are the principal occupations, but the town is also known for horse-breeding and as a centre for some good hunting. There is also salmon and trout fishing in the Suir a few miles west of the town. There are few buildings of note. A thirteenth-century Augustinian abbey shows few remains, and in the same grounds is the burnt-out Abbey School. In the town is a monument of a bronze, seated figure of C. J. Kickham (1826–82), patriot poet.

Tipperary came to notice in the Land League agitations of last century, when tenants of Mr. Smith Barry set up a temporary settlement which they called "New Tipperary" just outside the town. This "Plan of Campaign," as it was then known, against rent payment was, however, unsuccessful.

Four miles north of Tipperary, at Soloheadbeg, is a fine memorial commemorating the outbreak, in 1919, of the War of Independence. A short distance farther north, at the Donohill cross-roads, is a good example of a Norman motte.

Glen of Aherlow.—From Tipperary there is a fine circular trip of about 20 miles to **Galbally,** by road over Slievenamuck up the glen and returning by the road north of the range. There is a *Youth Hostel* at Ballydavid Wood, near Bansha, and trout-fishing in the *Aherlow.* Either of these roads can also be taken as part of a longer but picturesque route to **Buttevant** and **Mallow.**

Tipperary to Cashel.—In the eastward direction the main street of Tipperary becomes the Cashel road in just under 6 miles. Along it, on the right, is the ruin of *Thomastown Castle,* where Father Theobald Mathew, the great "apostle of temperance," was born in 1790. There is a statue of him at the nearby cross-roads. Beyond Thomastown is the village of **Golden,** 1½ miles south of which is **Athassel Priory.**

Athassel Priory was founded for Canons Regular at the end of the twelfth century by William de Burgo, and, as the ruins show, was an important establishment. The chief remains are those of the church, whose choir still retains some of its lancet windows. The nave, with aisles 117 feet by 58 feet, and the square tower, originally higher, are not especially noteworthy, but a doorway with pointed arch above is a worthy exception. A tomb with effigy is said to be that of the founder. West of the church and south of the nave are remains of further buildings.

At Golden the Suir is crossed, and for the last few miles into *Cashel* (*see* p. 78) its Rock is a conspicuous landmark.

Onward from Tipperary to Limerick road and railway are not far apart. In 2 miles is **Limerick Junction,** with its popular racecourse. A mile farther on is **Oola,** and then beyond **Pallas Green** the Slievefelim Mountains become prominent on the right. Roads to the right at Pallas Green or Dromkeen, 2 miles farther, lead to **Cappamore,** 4 miles north of which is *Glenstal Abbey*, close to the village of Muroe. The Benedictine Abbey is known for its daily services and for its boys' school. Next on the main route are **Boher** and **Killonan.** Near the latter, 4 miles short of Limerick, the Nenagh–Roscrea loop of the line to Dublin branches off.

For **Limerick,** *see* p. 160.

WATERFORD TO CORK BY THE COAST
❧❧❧❧❧❧❧❧❧❧❧❧❧❧❧❧❧❧❧❧❧❧❧❧❧❧❧❧❧❧❧❧❧❧❧❧❧❧

The first part of this route along T 63 is described for the first 8 miles to Tramore on page 81. Then the road cuts inland behind Great Newtown Head to reach the coast again at **Annestown,** a pretty village with a good sandy beach. North of this village stands ruined *Dunhill Castle*, once the chief fortress of the Power family. It capitulated to Cromwell's army in 1649. Our road keeps close to the shore to **Bunmahan,** with a long smooth stretch of sand. At each end of the bay are high, jagged cliffs. **Stradbally,** 3 miles farther, is the site of an ancient friary. Then comes Clonea Bay with smooth, sandy beach and its castle on a low cliff.

Dungarvan

Distances.—Cappoquin 11, Cork 49, Dublin 128, Rosslare Harbour 80, Shannon Airport 93, Tramore 26, Waterford 29, Youghal 19.
Early Closing.—Thursday.
Hotels.—*Devonshire Arms* (23 rooms), Bridge Street; *Lawlors'* (17); *Ormonde* 14).

Population.—5,380.
Sport.—Sea-water swimming pool, sea fishing (bass, skate, ray, etc.), angling for brown trout, shooting, hunting, tennis and golf.
Transport.—C.I.E. bus route. Local road services.

Dungarvan, the administrative headquarters for Waterford County, is a busy market town on Dungarvan Harbour, at the mouth of the *Colligan*. A suburb, Abbeyside, on the east side of the river is connected with the town proper by a causeway and bridge. Of Abbeyside, or McGrath's Castle, only a small part remains. An Augustinian Priory of the thirteenth century shows some well-preserved remnants. Its square tower is incorporated with the Abbeyside Catholic Church. Beside the Colligan is the massive circular keep of Dungarvan Castle, originally built by King John in 1185. Adjoining are the former British military barracks, destroyed in 1921. Dungarvan has a fine harbour and a fair amount of port activity, but for visitors it is best known as a convenient centre from which to explore the Monavulliagh–Comeragh ranges.

The main road, T 12, strikes south-westward from Dungarvan towards the Drum Hills and passes close to the summit (662 feet). At the foot of the hills a left-hand road (L 177) passes through Ringville to *Helvick Head*, the 232-foot-high promontory sheltering Dungarvan Harbour on the south. The main road, however, continues across the hills *via* **Gorteen**, Kiely's Cross Roads, and Cleary's Cross Roads to the New Youghal Bridge.

From Kiely's Cross Roads the left-hand turning leads in 6 miles to **Ardmore** (*Cliff House* (20 rooms), *Melrose* (10 rooms)), a pleasant little resort at the southern end of sandy Ardmore Bay. Ardmore is noted for its ecclesiastic antiquities. A monastic settlement was founded here in the seventh century by St. Declan,* Bishop of Ardmore, and a tiny *Oratory* marks his traditional burial-place. The building, about 13 feet by 9 feet, is of rude masonry, with high-pitched gables. **The Cathedral** is chiefly notable externally for the curious carvings, in two groups of niches, on the west wall of the entrance, whilst inside one feature is the fine pointed chancel-arch. The nave is in Romanesque style, but the chancel shows traces of work contemporary with the Oratory. Inside the building are two Ogham stones. Ardmore ceased to be a bishop's see in 1150.

The **Round Tower,** 97 feet high, has four storeys, each marked by projecting bands. Its door is some distance above ground level.

Half a mile eastward, towards Ardmore Head and a little beyond Cliff House, are the remains of *Temple Disert*, once a large church (*c.* thirteenth century), and close by is *St. Declan's Well*, bearing three rough crucifixes. On the beach below the village is a glacial boulder known as *St. Declan's Stone*.

For **Youghal** see p. 114. The route onward then to Cork is described in the reverse direction on the same page.

Waterford to Dungarvan (Alternative). For those working towards Killarney there is a quicker and shorter inland road (T.12) from Waterford, by-passing Dungarvan, *via* Kilmacthomas on the Mahon. This roads winds round the southern point of the Monavullagh Mountains and gives good views of Dungarvan and the harbour.

---

* It is claimed by some that St. Declan was a pre-Patrician saint—which fact pushes the foundation of the monastic settlement back to the fifth century.

DUNGARVAN TO CAPPOQUIN, LISMORE, FERMOY AND MALLOW

From Dungarvan the Killarney road (T 30) keeps close with the railway for 11 miles to—

Cappoquin

The name means "Conn's tillage plot" (*P. W. Joyce*). The little town (*Conway's* (10 rooms)) has a population of about 800 and is delightfully situated, the surrounding country being very picturesque, with many pleasant houses. Cappoquin is a good centre for anglers. Salmon-fishing is in private hands but trout-fishing may be freely enjoyed within a minute's walk. Bacon-curing is the chief industry.

The most interesting excursion from Cappoquin is to **Mount Melleray Abbey** about 3 miles northward.

The Abbey stands about 750 feet above sea-level, on the southern slope of the Knockmealdown Mountains. It was founded by Cistercian monks expelled from France in 1831. At that time the land was largely unreclaimed mountain. The visitor can see for himself to what a state of cultivation it has since been brought by the labours of the monks. They farm 700 or more acres of what was once wild, bare land. The community numbers

110 monks, over forty of whom are priests. Visitors who desire to make a Retreat may stay in the Men's or Ladies' Guesthouse. It is essential to make bookings beforehand with the Guestmaster.

A new monastery church was consecrated for public worship in 1952. It is built of stone from Mitchelstown Castle, erected by the Earl of Kingston early in the nineteenth century. The castle was burned in 1922 though the stones resisted the fire. The monks of Melleray bought the ruins and had the stone brought over the mountains to their abbey.

Cappoquin to Lismore

The distance by road is 4 miles.

The roads between Cappoquin and Lismore are among the most beautiful in Ireland. There is one on each side of the river.

That on the north runs close to the water for nearly a mile, and is then separated from it by meadows. It is more like an avenue than a road. Nearing Lismore, it again approaches the river and crosses it by **Lismore Bridge,** on which it is well worth while to stop for the view.

The road on the south side of the river affords delightful views of the opposite and more wooded part of the valley. Cross Cappoquin Bridge and then turn to the right. In a mile we come to the brink of the river, just opposite *Salterbridge House*, and for the next mile and a half travel by the side of the stream. Abreast of a wooded islet the road turns to the left, while on the right is the rath, **Round Hill,** an ancient stronghold formerly known by the name now borne by the neighbouring town—Lismore (the great fort).

Lismore

Distances.—Dublin 135, Cork 36, Fermoy 16, Shannon Airport 78, Waterford 42.
Early Closing.—Thursday.

Hotels.—*Lismore* (20 rooms), *Ballyrafter* (8),
Population.—894.

a clean, well-built market-town is pleasantly situated in the valley and noted for the surrounding scenery, its fishing, and its castle. This is a good centre for the Blackwater fishing and for rough shooting, and there is hunting with the West Waterford Foxhounds. There are many fine houses about.

Lismore Castle is one of the seats of the Devonshire family. It occupies a magnificent situation on a wooded cliff rising almost perpendicularly from the water's edge. In the entrance gateway, called the *Riding House*, two horsemen mounted guard in former days, and the spaces for them by the side can still be seen. There is an avenue of tall yew trees in the grounds.

The Castle was founded in 1185 by Prince (afterwards King) John, and four years later was almost destroyed by the local inhabitants. It is not known who repaired it, but the restored building was long held by the Bishops of Lismore (a place of great religious fame from time immemorial), and served them as a residence. In 1587 it passed into the possession of Sir Walter Raleigh, and fifteen years later was sold by him to Richard Boyle, afterwards first Earl of Cork, by whom it was rebuilt. In 1627 the earl's youngest and famous son, Robert Boyle, was born within its walls. He was the only pacifist of that family. During the Civil War the castle was captured and burnt, but ten years after its destruction it was rebuilt, and in 1689 gave shelter for a night, it is claimed, to James II when he fled from the Boyne to Kinsale. Another version, however, has it that James left Waterford *via* Duncannon on a ship for Kinsale, where he embarked for France. On the death of the Earl of Cork, in the middle of the eighteenth century, Lismore Castle became the property of the fourth Duke of Devonshire through his marriage with the then earl's daughter. It was practically rebuilt by the sixth Duke.

At the eastern angle of the river-front is *King James's Tower*, so called because it gave brief shelter to that sovereign. Behind this is *King John's Tower*, said to have been the scene of the first parliament held in Ireland under the presidency of that Prince. At the western angle of the river face rises the *Carlisle Tower*, named after the Earl of Carlisle, Lord-Lieutenant of Ireland in the middle of the nineteenth century, by whom the foundation-stone was laid. The view of the woods, the Blackwater, and the mountains from the great bay window of the drawing-room and from the upper windows, is very beautiful. The Banqueting Hall, with its striking ecclesiastical window, oak roof and seats, is a very fine apartment.

Lismore Cathedral (Church of Ireland) is mostly of seventeenth-century work, the "great" Earl of Cork having spent a large sum on it; but the spire is more modern, while, on the other hand, some of the pillars in the nave belong to the thirteenth century. It stands on a height to the east of the town and is chiefly remarkable for its inscribed (Gaelic) slabs of the ninth and tenth centuries. The Mac-Grath tomb, in excellent preservation, dates from the first half of the sixteenth century. In the wall on the south-western side of the cathedral is an archway thought to be of tenth-century work.

Lismore was once the site of a noted monastery and a university with some 4,000 students, and it is said that Alfred the Great studied here. The town was plundered by the Danes. St. Carthagh's holy well is in a garden near the Cathedral. **St. Carthagh's Catholic Church** sometimes described as a Cathedral (though the bishop's see is at Waterford). It is a modern building of striking design. St. Carthagh was the founder of this See in the seventh century, and the church is believed to occupy the site of his cell. It is built of sandstone.

Lismore to Fermoy

This journey of 16 miles by road takes one through much beautiful scenery. The way out of Lismore is by the bridge over the Blackwater. At 5½ miles from Lismore is **Ballyduff Bridge,** near which, on the southern side of the river, is **Glencairn Abbey,** in charming grounds open to visitors. Part of the building rises perpendicularly from the brink of the river. From the bridge two roads run to Fermoy, north and south of the river. The south road is undulating and has some pretty spots. About a mile from the bridge the ruined **Ballyduff Castle** may be seen on the southern bank of the river, and about 2 miles farther on the ruins of **Mocollop Castle.** This road south of the Blackwater is very rough.

The north road passes Kilmurry House and then skirts the grounds of **Moore Park,** formerly the seat of the Earls of Mountcashel. Fleetwood, Cromwell's general, was given extensive property here but it passed from his descendants. Moore Park is now the National Dairy Research Centre run by the Agricultural Institute. The road now turns south-westward to pass the ruin of **Carrigabrick Castle.**

Fermoy

pleasantly situated on the Blackwater, was formerly a large military centre but nowadays has a more peaceful pursuit in distributing market produce from the surrounding agricultural district. The town (*Royal* (20 rooms); *Grand* (10 rooms)) is an excellent centre for anglers, and some fishing is free. Boating and golf can also be enjoyed. At **Glanworth** is the keep of an old Castle and a Dominican Priory of the thirteenth century.

North of Fermoy (10 miles) over the Kilworth Mountain is **Mitchelstown** (bus service), with an important creamery. There is a 9-hole golf course 1 mile away.

Mitchelstown Castle, built by the Earl of Kingston (nineteenth century), was occupied until 1922, when it was burned. The owners decided not to restore it. The splendid grounds were divided into smallholdings. The castle, probably the last of its size built in Ireland, was pulled down and the dressed stone sold to Mount Melleray Monastery.

The celebrated Mitchelstown **Caves,** in the mountain limestone, are 5 miles from the town, off the main Mitchelstown–Cahir road.

The "new" caves, among the largest in the British Isles, are especially rich in stalactites. It is well to take a torch, though candles are provided. A low, narrow passage gives place to a tunnel leading to a large, circular chamber called the House of Commons. Near this another passage leads past a number of fluted musical columns appropriately named the "Organ" to the House of Lords, a capacious cavern containing many beautiful and fantastic formations. From the House of Commons access is obtained to Sadler's Cave, containing an immense stalactite that has been humorously named "Lot's wife," and thence to Kingston Gallery, a very remarkable tent-like cave with a beautiful arched roof. A short distance from the "new" caves is the older "Desmond's" Cave, which was a refuge for the Irish in Elizabethan times. It was in this cave that an Earl of Desmond was captured.

The Galtee Mountains. This grand mass of old red sandstone mountains rises on the north of the Cahir road. The highest point is *Galtymore* (or *Dawson's Table*), 3,015 feet. It is both the best place to aim for and as easy as any of the principal summits to reach. The popular route is by Mountain Lodge Youth Hostel to the southern spur of Galtymore, and from there, somewhat to the left, to the ridge a little west of the highest point. Galtymore itself is a conical summit, but Galtybeg, just east of it, is still more of a cone. To the west of Galtymore is *Lough Curra*; between it and Galtybeg is the smaller *Lough Diheen*, and beyond Galtybeg *Lough Borheen*. Of these tarns, Lough Curra has cliffs of some 1,000 feet rising almost to the summit of the range. *Lough Muskry*, also on the north side of the ridge and about 3 miles east of Galtymore, has even higher cliffs. The view in clear weather is magnificent in all directions.

Fermoy to Mallow. This road, although pretty and with the Nagles Mountains (1,406 feet) close on the left hand, does not compare with the road west from Cappoquin. It passes Castle Hyde and Cregg Castle on the left, on the approach to the Blackwater. At the road junction (5 miles from Fermoy) the left hand one goes past the ruin of *Ballyhooly Castle*. Over the Blackwater, turn right at the cross-roads beyond. On the north side of the river are **Castletownroche** and the Glen of Awbeg, but on our road we have *Carrigacunna Castle* and **Killavullen.** From the bridge at Killavullen there is a fine view.

MALLOW

Mallow

Distances.—Dublin 149, Cork 22, Killarney 42, Waterford 78, Shannon Airport 57.
Early Closing.—Wednesdays.
Churches.—*St. Mary's* and *Church of the Resurrection* (Roman Catholic). *St. James's* (Church of Ireland).
Golf.—18-hole course.

Hotels.—*Central* (40 rooms), *Hibernian* (25).
Hunting.—Weekly meetings.
Population.—5,520.
Post Office.—Bank Place.
Racing.—Meetings at Easter, mid-June and late Summer Bank Holidays.

Mallow is a considerable road and rail junction on the Cork, Killarney and Limerick routes from the east. It is situated on the north bank of the Blackwater, a good salmon river which here, as a broad stream, flows through a wide wooded valley. At one time a considerable spa, it is now known as an angling and hunting centre. The racecourse to the west of the town is the venue of regular meetings. Worthy of note in the town itself are the half-timbered Clock House, the Spa House, and a remnant of the Castle in the grounds of the modern mansion of the Jephson family. About a mile downstream is the *Rock* rising abruptly from the Blackwater, its summit commanding exquisite views of the river. The spot where the rock drops sheer to the water is known as "Lovers' Leap."

Mallow to Killarney. Beyond Mallow the road follows closely the River Blackwater westward leaving **Banteer** on the left and with grand views on the left of the Boggeragh Mountains to **Rathmore** in County Kerry.

For **Killarney**, *see* pp. 133–135.

96

CORK
♣♣♣♣♣

Access.—Cork Harbour from Liverpool, 239 miles, or Fishguard, 138 miles. Ferry service Swansea-Cork.

Airport.—Four miles south of city at Ballygarvan on the Kinsale Road. Daily services to principal English and Continental cities.

Angling.—Good salmon and trout fishing available in River Lee and tributaries. Excellent sea-fishing at Ballycotton and neighbouring resorts. Coarse angling at "The Lough" in city.

Banks.—*Bank of Ireland, Munster and Leinster, Provincial, National,* and *Hibernian;* all in South Mall with sub-branches. *Ulster Bank* in Patrick Street.

Bathing.—At sea-side resorts within and near harbour. At *Lee Baths* (open air) and *Eglinton Street* (indoor), near City Hall.

Bowling.—Three clubs within the city with flat greens.

Buses.—City services from St. Patrick Street. Depot for County and long distances services, Parnell Place. Daily services to Dublin, Waterford, Killarney and intermediate towns.

Cinemas.—*Palace,* MacCurtain Street; *Savoy* and *Pavilion,* Patrick Street; *Capitol,* Grand Parade; *Ritz,* Washington Street; *Lee,* Winthrop Street; *Cameo Panorama,* Military Road.

Distances.—Belfast 252, Blarney 6, Cobh 15, Fermoy 23, Glengariff 62, Killarney 54, Limerick, 63, Mallow 22, Tipperary 53, Waterford 78, Youghal 31.

Dancing.—*Arcadia,* Lower Road; *Gresham Rooms,* Maylor Street; *Clarence Hall, Imperial Hotel,* South Mall; *Metropole Ballroom,* MacCurtain Street; *City Hall Ballroom,* Albert Quay; *Cameo Club,* Military Road; *Palm Court Ballroom,* Caroline Street.

Golf.—*Little Island* (18), 6 miles east of city on the Middleton Road. *Douglas* (18), 3 miles S.E. of city; *Muskerry* (18), 8 miles W.; *Monkstown* (9), 9 miles S.E. Many others (9 holes) throughout the County of Cork.

Hotels.—*Imperial* (82 rooms), *Metropole* (124), *Intercontinental* (96) *Victoria* (70), *Country Club* (25), *Windsor* (28), *Arbutus Lodge* (20) *Moore's* (25), *Park View* (10), *Silver Springs* (72); many boarding houses

Information Centre.—
Irish Tourist Office, 109, Patrick Street (Phone 20676).

Population.—122, 146.

Post Office.—Head office in Oliver Plunket Street. Open week-days, 8 a.m.– 6.30 p.m. Sundays, 9–10.30 a.m. and 5–7 p.m. Several sub offices.

Railway Station.—For Dublin, Killarney, etc., Lower Glanmere Road.

Ireland (g)   97

Shooting.—Excellent wild fowl shooting along coasts and river mouths. Rough shooting throughout the County. Apply Messrs T. W. Murray, Gunpowder Stores, 87, Patrick Street, Cork.

Tennis.—Many clubs available in the city and throughout the County.

Youth Hostel.—1 Redclyffe, Western Road, Cork. Next nearest hostels are at Summer Cove, Kinsale, 18 miles.

Cork derives its name from *Corcaig*—a marshy place. It is built around the head of the tidal waters of the River Lee. Spenser, who occasionally stayed in Cork when Clerk of the Council of Munster, spoke of it as the "beautiful citie of Cork," but in his day it was a small town huddled inside walls, remnants of which still exist. There was one main street running from the South Gate to the North Gate and numerous lanes running east and west. Many of these small byways have been cleared and several river channels filled in and built over, but Broad Street where Spenser lodged still exists in name, although the old houses have all disappeared. The city grew rapidly in the seventeenth and eighteenth centuries. Today, the two main river channels are crossed by many bridges and the best part of Cork lies outside the old city walls—mainly between Grand Parade in the West and Custom House in the East. Cork Harbour is an important port able to accommodate transatlantic liners. It has a large export trade, mainly of agricultural products. The chief industries of the city are brewing, distilling, bacon-curing, ship-building, textiles and motor engineering.

Historical Note.—At the end of the sixth century St. Finnbarr, a native of Connaught, founded a monastery and church on the south bank of the River Lee. This flourished for 200 years until progress was halted by the invasion of Norsemen in A.D. 820. The invaders established a trading settlement nearby which became a thriving Danish stronghold.

In 1172, an Anglo-Norman invasion ousted the Danes, but after some turbulent years both Danish and Anglo-Norman settlers became absorbed by the native population. Cork became a prosperous city, with a strong spirit of independence and a defiance of English authority that earned for it the title of "The Rebel City". At the outbreak of the civil war between Charles I and Parliament Cork sided with the King, but was forced to surrender to Cromwell in 1649. When Marlborough besieged the city in 1690 it was forced to submit after five days of severe losses.

By the eighteenth century it had recovered its prosperity and was famous for its glass manufacture. In the nineteenth century Cork was affected by the great famine of 1847, and the Fenian movement of 1865–67. The city took a prominent part in the War of Independence; in 1920 two Lord Mayors sacrificed their lives and much of the city was burned. Today, the government of Cork is controlled by a City Council and a City Manager. The civic head or Lord Mayor is elected each year by the Council.

A TOUR OF THE CITY

The features of Cork best worth seeing are:

PUBLIC BUILDINGS

City Hall.
County Hall.
Court House.
Crawford Municipal School of Art and Art Gallery.
University College and Honan Chapel.
Municipal Library.
Public Museum (Fitzgeralds Park).

STREETS

St. Patrick's.
Grand Parade.
MacCurtain Street.
The Quays.
South Mall.

PROMENADES AND OPEN SPACES

The Marina, south side of Lee.
The Mardyke, western end of city.
The Fitzgerald Park on Mardyke.

CHURCHES

St. Finbarr's Protestant Cathedral, Bishop Street.
SS. Peter and Paul R.C., just off St. Patrick's Street.
St. Ann's, Shandon, near Shandon Street.
St. Mary's R.C. Cathedral, near Shandon Street.
St. Mary's R.C., Pope's Quay.
Franciscan Friars, Liberty Street.
Holy Trinity, Father Mathew Quay.
St. Patrick's, Lower Road.

The north and south channels of the River Lee form an island that is connected with the mainland by eighteen bridges, the principal being **St. Patrick's Bridge** and Parnell Bridge. The city is at the western end of the island, with St. Patrick's street as its main thoroughfare.

Starting from the south side of St. Patrick's Bridge, we first notice the **Statue of Father Mathew,** a fine work in bronze, by Foley, erected in 1864 and said to be an exceptionally good likeness of the man.

The great Irish Apostle of Temperance was born at Thomastown Castle, Co. Tipperary, in 1790, his father being agent to, and a relative of, Lord Llandaff He was ordained in his twenty-third year, attaching himself to the Capuchins. After a short charge at Kilkenny he came to Cork, and for twenty-four years led a busy and uneventful life among the poorest classes of the city, his sterling character and unbounded generosity making him respected and loved. At the age of forty-seven a Quaker in the City begged him to lend his support to a temperence movement they had inaugurated. His success as a temperance advocate was immediate and astounding. In less than three months he had enrolled 25,000 teetotalers. During the ensuing nine months 126,000 people were enrolled, and before long it was calculated that half the population of Ireland, then much greater than now, had taken the pledge. Not only in Ireland, but in Scotland, England, and the United States, the Father won hosts of adherents. He died at Cobh (Queenstown) on December 8, 1856. A simple cross marks his grave in St. Joseph's Cemetery, about a mile from the City, a burial-ground which he himself established.

St. Patrick's Street,

lined with good shops, is the main street of the city. This

street suffered considerably in the Irish troubles, and one side
has largely been rebuilt on modern lines. The curved shape is
accounted for by the fact that the street is built along what was
once a deep and important branch of the river, in which ships
were loaded and unloaded. The goods were delivered into
warehouses on the Quay levels while the merchants lived in the
upper storeys of the buildings. With one exception the "steps"
or stone stairs that gave access from the outside to the residential
parts of premises have disappeared from the main thoroughfare.
A few others remain around corners in side streets. The river
at that time was open up to an old Castle, which still retains
this name, though now a drapery stores.

Winthrop Street leads from St. Patrick's Street to Oliver
Plunket Street, where stands the **General Post Office**, a handsome stone-fronted building. Farther on, facing the South Mall,
are the Commercial Buildings, now part of a hotel.

Back in St. Patrick's Street, however, a short passage on
the right leads to the Roman Catholic Church of **St. Peter and
St. Paul,** a handsome Gothic building designed by Welby
Pugin. The interior is richly decorated.

A few yards farther we turn left into the **Grand Parade,** the
widest street in Cork. It stands on what was once a large dock,
arched over in 1780. Up to that time the western side was
known as Tuckey's Quay and the eastern as the Mall—then
a pleasant promenade shaded with trees. In the middle of the
roadway is an immense circular fountain; a little farther south
is the library, and at the end will be seen the **National Monument,** in memory of various Irish patriots. The principal meat,
fish and vegetable **Markets** adjoin the Parade.

Westward of Grand Parade the wide Washington Street
leads to the **Court House.** At Victoria Cross is the tall **County
Hall.**

Opposite the National Monument on the Grand Parade
is the **South Mall,** another broad thoroughfare, in which there
are banks, insurance offices and other business premises. A
War Memorial stands at the western end. Close by, on Father
Mathew Quay, stands the—

Father Mathew Memorial Church

also called the Church of the Holy Trinity. It is a beautiful
limestone building, and when seen from across the water
immediately arrests the eye by its curious open front and

pinnacled tower. The spire is 200 feet high. The church contains a fine stained-glass window in memory of O'Connell, the "Liberator." Nearby is the Municipal School of Commerce.

Crossing the South Channel by **Parliament Bridge,** with its single arch, and turning to the right, or westward, by Sullivan's Quay to Bishop Street, we see high up on the left the dingy wall of *Elizabeth Fort*, one of the fortifications of the old city. Just beyond is by far the most noteworthy and imposing building in Cork—

St. Finbarr's Cathedral

the Church of Ireland Cathedral of the diocese. It occupies the site of a church said to have been erected by the saint to whom Cork is said to owe its foundation (*see* p. 98). The entrance is at the western side of the enclosure. *Voluntary guides available from 3 p.m.*

The design has been truly described as "utterly un-English in character." The west front in particular suggests Bayeux or Rheims. William Burges, A.R.A., was the architect, and, considering the past connection of France with the South of Ireland, it was a happy inspiration on his part to adopt so successfully the French Early Pointed style. The Cathedral was consecrated by Bishop Gregg in 1870.

The central tower surmounted by a plain octagonal spire 240 feet high; the two western towers and spires, lower, but of similar design; the magnificent west front, with its statuary and beautiful portals; the semicircular apse at the east end; the large rose windows

at the end of each transept; the great number of other windows, filled with stained glass; and the massive buttresses—these and every detail, charmingly blended, form a harmonious whole. The richly-carved West Front, with its three recessed portals, massive rose window and stately twin spires, is specially noteworthy. The figures on either side of the middle portal represent the Wise and Foolish Virgins, with lamps in their hands, the Bridegroom standing in the centre.

Internally, the church is very lofty and imposing. The bishop's throne is of carved oak on a plinth of red Cork marble, and the mosaic pavement of the semicircular apse is particularly good. The stained-glass windows of the aisles and transepts represent scenes from the Old Testament. An unusual feature is the position of the organ, which is 14 feet below ground level in the north transept. A brass tablet on the floor near the pulpit marks the tomb of the Hon. Elizabeth Aldworth (1695–1775); she is said to be the only woman ever initiated into Freemasonry.

In 1690 the old Church was garrisoned by the English, and the guns of the Irish fort close by did it considerable damage. In the ambulatory of the present building can be seen on a bracket a cannon-ball which was found embedded in the former steeple.

Facing the west end of the cathedral is the entrance to the **Bishop's Palace,** a plain Georgian house built in 1782 and standing in extensive grounds.

Nearby is the **Municipal Technical Institute,** and opposite it are the Convent and Schools of the Mercy Order of Nuns. These buildings occupy the site of the Dominican Priory of St. Mary of the Isle. Somewhere in the grounds lie the remains of Edmund Mortimer, Earl of March, who died here on St. Stephen's Day, 1381.

In the suburb of Greenmount to the south-west of these buildings is a lake some 14 acres in area known as "The Lough." It is a sanctuary for water fowl and the scene of model yacht racing.

About half a mile west of St. Finbarr's Cathedral, by way of Gill Abbey Street and College Road, is—

University College

The main entrance is on the Western Road, and buses from the Father Mathew statue pass the gate. *The grounds are open to the public on week-days, 10–5, and Saturdays, 10–1.*

The buildings form three sides of a quadrangle. There are various departments, including a Dairy Science Building, situated in the extensive grounds.

The college houses a large library, including some early books printed in Cork, laboratories and lecture halls. There are various collections of natural history, geological, mineralogical and other exhibits which visitors may view by request. The **Honan Chapel,** or Collegiate Chapel of St. Finnbarr, is a small but beautiful building erected out of bequests from the Honan family. A miniature round tower is incorporated on the eastern end. The rich interior decoration includes stained-glass windows the design and colour of which are considered the finest of their kind in Ireland.

Leaving the College grounds by the Western Road entrance, we reach—

The Mardyke

a mile-long promenade running between the two channels of the river.

The entrance to **Fitzgerald Park** is midway on the north side of the Mardyke. The grounds are extensive, well ornamented with shrubs, flower beds, a miniature pond and fountain, stately trees and a children's recreation ground. There are many attractive views of the river and the picturesque district of Sunday's Well, which can be approached by **Daly's Bridge** at this point.

The **Cork Public Museum,** in Fitzgerald Park, was opened in 1945 and houses objects of local interest. Various phases of the history and growth of the city of Cork are depicted, and there is an interesting archaeological section. *The museum is open on Week-days, 11–1 and 2.15–5, Saturdays and Sundays 11.30–1.*

Sunday's Well is a popular residential suburb lying on the southern side of the long hill upwards from the river. The name is derived from a spring once believed to possess miraculous virtues. The well is closed, but the site is indicated by a tablet. In this quarter are the Cork Waterworks and a number of imposing public buildings. The prominent structure of red sandstone with limestone dressings is **St. Vincent's Roman Catholic Church.** Near it are the **Good Shepherd Convent,** and a picturesque Protestant Church (St. Mary's, Shandon) whose spire is well seen from the river.

East of Sunday's Well Road, Blarney Street leads to Shandon Street and—

St. Ann's, Shandon

Admission to the tower to see the bells and have them rung (*fee*).

No one can miss seeing Shandon Church, for the tower is prominent from almost every part of the city. The church, built in 1722, is a plain building occupying the site of an earlier church destroyed during the Revolution of 1690. The tower is unique, for two sides are built of the local red-brown sandstone, and the other two of local limestone.

The bells of St. Ann's gave rise to Father Prout's song and also provided William Black with a title for his novel, *Shandon Bells.* There are quaint inscriptions on the bells, one of which states that "Abel Rudhall, of Glo'ster, made us all." The tower clock has four dials and can be seen from nearly all parts of the city.

Just beyond and above Shandon Church is **St. Mary's Roman Catholic Cathedral.** It has a massive and lofty tower—built of local sandstone relieved by local limestone linings. The style is early Neo-Gothic Revival and the combination of materials is to an extent characteristic of Cork building in the nineteenth century. It is the finest pre-Emancipation church in Cork; the interior is reminiscent of Italian decorative influences. A monument by John Hogan near the choir screen commemorates Dr. Moylan, founder of the Cathedral (founded 1808 on the site of a previous church), and in the open space in front of the main entrance is a bronze statue of Bishop Delany, D.D.

Returning to Pope's Quay by Roman Street, we come to the **Dominican Church of St. Mary,** the Ionic portico of which stands out so clearly from St. Patrick's Bridge.

Across the river is the new Opera House replacing that destroyed by fire in 1955. Nearby in Emmet Place is the **Crawford Municipal School of Art.** Visitors are admitted on week-days from 10 a.m. to 5.30 p.m. to view the Sculpture and Picture Galleries containing a collection of modern paintings and works by Cork artists.

Adjoining Emmet Place is the **Coal Quay,** now a misnomer; but at one time the river was navigable here, thus enabling coal vessels to dock. The famous Coal Quay "Market" is actually situated in nearby Cornmarket Street and bears a close resemblance to a Spanish bazaar, both in the mode of selling and the variety of articles displayed. Everything can be had, from a needle to an anchor—household equipment, fruit, vegetables, clothing, books, and an incredible assortment of junk. Morning is the best time for a visit, when from their booths the sellers, mostly women, describe with considerable wit and volubility the merits of their wares.

So far nothing has been said about the eastern end of the town and its chief attraction, the Marina. We will, therefore, suppose a start to be made again from Father Mathew's statue. We turn this time eastward along the **Merchant's Quay,** which borders the south side of the Lee, and passing through Parnell's Place (terminus for country bus services) cross the **Parnell Bridge** to **Albert Quay.** Here we see—

The City Hall

In December, 1920, the City Hall and the Carnegie Free Library which stood near it at the corner of Anglesea Street and Albert Quay were burned, as was about £1,500,000 worth of other property. The Library was replaced within a few years by a building in the Grand Parade near the National Monument. The new City Hall was not begun until 1931, and took four years to complete. It is a dignified building, if perhaps a little on the austere side externally.

A little farther on in Anglesea Street are what were once the entrances to the Corn Market and Hay Market. The Corn Market was controlled by a Committee representing merchants and growers. Now it has ceased to function, as nowadays the growers sell direct to merchants and accept their weighing. The Hay Market operates nominally, but the trade has declined.

Eastward of the quay is *The Marina*, a tree-lined promenade commanding delightful peeps of the Lee and the attractive houses and gardens on the opposite bank. There are several boat-houses here.

Across the water are the wooded, hilly suburbs of **Montenotte** and **Tivoli.** Raleigh lived at Tivoli for a time, and it is said that trees planted by him still survive. Miss Curran, the betrothed of poor Robert Emmet, lived at a house (demolished) known as Woodhill. Her story inspired Moore's song, "She is far from the land where her young hero sleeps," and Washington Irving's essay, *The Broken Heart.*

EXCURSIONS FROM CORK
✤✤✤✤✤✤✤✤✤✤✤✤✤✤✤✤✤✤✤✤✤✤✤✤✤

Cork and Kerry are two of the largest counties in Ireland. Both have a broken and lovely sea-coast; both are mountainous, and both have a very beautiful river with the same name, the Blackwater. The Lee in Cork is a fine river, expanding near its mouth to form Cobh Harbour.

I.—Cork Harbour, Cobh, Monkstown, Crosshaven, etc.

Cobh is reached by rail *via* Little Island, Cobh Junction and Fota Island. A fine steel bridge of several spans connects **Fota** and the **Great Island,** on which Cobh is built. Excellent views of the river, now widening into the Lower Harbour, are on the right.

The road route to Cobh (15 miles) follows the railway as far as Cobh Junction; then there is a detour of a few miles, road and railway meeting again at Belvelly. Here is the ruin of **Belvelly Castle.** Built in the fourteenth century, it was owned for a time by Sir Walter Raleigh; then it passed to the Barrys. Nearby is a Martello tower, built to resist invasion by the French. There is a ferry service from Monkstown to Rushbrooke, and from Passage West to Carrigloe. There is a steamer service from Cork to Cobh on Sundays in summer.

Cobh

Distances.—Cork 15, Dublin 169, Shannon 94, Belfast 261.
Early Closing.—Wednesday.
Hotels.—*Commodore* (42 rooms), *Westbourne* (20), *European* (12), *Atlantic* (10).

Population.—5,608.
Post Office.—Casement Square.
Sport and Entertainment.—Fishing, shooting, hunting, golf. Cinemas, dancing, etc. Yachting races; annual regatta.

Cobh is the principal harbour on the south coast of Ireland. The town is built on Great Island and is the most important Irish port of call for trans-Atlantic liners. From this harbour the first steamer to cross the Atlantic, the *Sirius*, left Passage West in April, 1838, taking 18½ days for the voyage. In the nineteenth century it was a rather obscure fishing village. It was called "the Cove of Cork," which inland dwellers, who never saw the sea and did not know what a cove might be, translated into "the Comb of Cork." It was renamed Queenstown in 1849 to commemorate Queen Victoria's visit, but in 1922 the Irish designation, with supposedly Gaelic spelling, was re-adopted.

Cobh was badly hit by the withdrawal of the British Navy after the Anglo-Irish Treaty of 1921, which allowed Britain limited port facilities. One or two destroyers remained to represent her navy and small maintenance garrisons remained in the forts at the entrance to the harbour and on Spike Island. In 1937–38, under another agreement, Britain relinquished her port rights, and all her "token" forces were withdrawn.

During the 1914–18 War Queenstown (the name was as yet unchanged) was a base for the British, and, after April, 1917, for the American fleet. It was from the harbour that destroyers were sent out on May 7, 1915, to rescue the survivors of the ill-fated *Lusitania*, sunk off the Old Head of Kinsale by a German submarine. Hundreds of the passengers, alive and dead, were brought in here. Many of the victims were buried in the old Clonmell graveyard, a mile from the town. A modest tablet marks the place. A more elaborate monument has since been erected in the town.

The graveyard mentioned contains the tomb of the Rev. Charles Wolfe, author of the well-known poem "The Burial of Sir John Moore." Not far from his grave lies John Tobin, dramatist, who died in 1804.

Seen from the water, Cobh, dominated by its stately Cathedral, is very attractive. The town is built on terraces in the hillside, rising tier behind tier, the houses commanding a fine view across the spacious Harbour. Far away to the south, beyond Spike Island, the bottle-neck entrance to the Harbour may be seen, with Carlisle and Camden Forts on either side and the white lighthouse on Roche's Point at the extreme end. Very large modern vessels can enter the Harbour with perfect safety.

Apart from its importance as a port of call for Atlantic liners, Cobh offers many attractions as a holiday resort. It lies in a sheltered position amongst lovely surroundings and is an ideal touring centre, with good entertainment facilities. The Promenade is a pleasant enclosure with bandstand and seats. Much sailing is done within the harbour and at sea by members of the yacht and sailing clubs at Crosshaven across the water. A "popular" regatta in August brings crowds into the town.

The business section of the town, including the larger hotels and shops, faces the quay. Immediately opposite the beach is Haulbowline Island, the headquarters of the Irish Navy, and farther south is Spike Island, an army defence coastal station.

Apart from the interesting Protestant Church, the only notable building is the conspicuous and richly decorated

107

Roman Catholic Cathedral, finely situated at the summit of a steep hill, 150 feet above the Harbour.

The Cathedral is dedicated to St. Colman. The style is a florid Gothic (the architect was Pugin) the light and spacious interior, with its many statues, being as pleasing to the eye as the exterior. The first stone was laid in 1868 and after fifty years' labour the building was completed and consecrated on August 24, 1919. The tall spire, 300 feet high, is surmounted by a gilt copper cross 12½ feet high.

The length of the Cathedral is 210 feet, the height 100 feet. The outer walls are of blue Dalkey granite and the columns of Irish marble. The design of the exterior is early Decorated French Gothic. The west front contains a deeply recessed and elaborately carved arch with rose window. The statues of Apostles and Saints were added by the late Bishop of Cloyne; the very beautiful high altar was erected to commemorate the 50th year of his priesthood. The carillon of forty-two bells is very fine. The mouldings, carved capitals, stained-glass windows and ornamentations give the interior a very rich effect. The apse with its window and marble reredos is very striking. An open triforium extends the whole length of the building. A notable feature is the continuation of the nave walls as a screen across the transepts.

Great Island, on which the town stands, is 5 miles from east to west and 2 from south to north. The circuit of the island, with varied and pleasing views, may be made in a drive of about two hours or less. **Carlisle Fort** frowns above on the east, on Dogsnose Point, while to the west is a much indented coast-line, backed by hills and woods, and Weaver and Ram Point, the latter crowned by **Camden Fort,** between which and Currabinny is a wide creek running inland as far as some woods a mile or so away. This is the **Carrigaline River,** or the Owenboy, and it runs inland for about 20 miles.

Opposite Carrigaloe on Great Island, and linked with it by ferry, is **Passage West,** which was once a prosperous and important town with busy docks and shipyards. Now it has only 2,500 inhabitants. However, after some years of acute depression the town shows signs of recovery. Its neighbour, **Glenbrook** (*The Club* (11 rooms)), a mile farther south, is a favourite residential area. Both these towns are connected with Cork by buses running *via* Douglas, where there are woollen mills for tweeds and worsteds.

Monkstown

half a mile farther south, is believed to derive its name from a colony of Benedictine monks. The place contains the ruins of **Monkstown Castle,** an Elizabethan fortified residence. Tradition declares that Anastasia Goold, whose lord, one John Archdeacon, was fighting under Philip of Spain, conceived the idea of erecting this castle to while away the time and to surprise him on his return. She shrewdly stipulated that the workmen should buy all their food from her. They either lived very extravagantly or were greatly overcharged, for the lady's profits were so considerable that it was found when the work was done that the house had only cost her a groat. The castle is in good repair and occupied by the *Monkstown Golf Club*. Monkstown is connected with Great Island (Rushbrooke) by a ferry service, and with Cork by the bus service *via* Douglas. Monkstown Church, in Early-English style, on a picturesque elevation, is said to have been the first Protestant place of worship built in the neighbourhood after the Reformation.

Crosshaven

Distance.—13 miles from Cork.
Hotels.—*Grand* (31 rooms), *Bunnyconnellan* (31), at Myrtleville; *Church Bay* (11), *Maryland Guest House* (6).
Population.—950.

Sport.—Excellent facilities for fresh and sea-water fishing, bathing and boating. International sailing fixtures frequently held in harbour. Royal Cork Yacht Club.

Crosshaven is a favourite summer resort with Cork residents. It is reached by a bus starting from Parnell Place and crossing Douglas and Carrigaline.

Carrigaline is on the Owenboy river where, in 1587, Sir Francis Drake and five sloops sought to escape from a powerful Spanish fleet. The enemy followed him into Cork Harbour, which they scoured in vain, exploring, as they thought, every creek, winding and channel, but Drake was not to be seen. For days the search continued, until at length the Spaniards, attributing his disappearance to magic, thought well to disappear also. Upon which out came Drake with his merry men from behind those very woods which seem to mark the water's limit! The secluded spot, about 2 miles from Crosshaven, has since been known as **Drake's Pool**. It is convenient as anchorage for yachts and sailing boats of moderate draught.

Crosshaven lies in a sheltered position at the mouth of the Owenboy river. From it a net-work of roads and lanes leads to the following small and delightful resorts with their bathing nooks and beautiful scenery—**Church Bay, Weaver's Point, Myrtleville, Fennell's Bay** and **Fountainstown. Robertscove,** a well-known beauty spot, lies 9 miles south of Crosshaven.

The coast may be followed northward round to Camden Fort (renamed Dun Ui Mheachair). There is a pretty cliff walk southward to Myrtleville Bay. Overlooking Church Bay is the powerful Dun Teampall Bride (Templebreedy Fort) commanding the waterway used by transatlantic liners.

Templebreedy church, built in 1778, stands on the hill between Church Bay and Fennell's Bay providing a distinctive landmark.

II. To Aghada, Roches's Point, Cloyne and Ballycotton

Aghada

Aghada, "long ford" (pronounced *A-had'-a*, with accent on second syllable), is a pretty seaside village picturesquely situated on the eastern side of the estuary.

A drive from Aghada to Roche's Point the bold headland at the eastern entrance to Cork Harbour, affords good views of the Harbour. **Roche's Point Lighthouse,** familiar to Atlantic passengers, is the signalling station for homeward-bound vessels. A meteorological station has been established near the lighthouse. A good road leads to **Whitegate,** where there is a large oil refinery serving the oil tankers from the modern pier and jetty.

The drive to Cloyne and Ballycotton is pretty and the roads are good. At **Castlemary,** a mile or so from Cloyne, an interesting Druidical cromlech may be seen, with a capstone 15 feet by 8. A number of gold ornaments were found about here.

Cloyne (5½ miles) is remarkable for its 100-foot-high **Round Tower,** adjacent to the Cathedral. Free, safe access.

The origin and use of these towers, of which there are more than a hundred in Ireland and scarcely any elsewhere, was a question that long puzzled antiquaries, but probably they were erected as watch-towers and as places of refuge and treasure houses for the monks. They are always found in proximity to ecclesiastical buildings. See also pp. 47–8.

Cloyne Cathedral belongs to the Church of Ireland, and the diocese, a very ancient one, is united to that of Cork. The building dates from the thirteenth century but has been extensively restored. A former bishop was Berkeley, the famous eighteenth-century metaphysician. He was buried at Oxford, but there is an ornate modern monument to him in the Cathedral. The bishop is represented by a recumbent figure. The remains of an oratory in the graveyard are said to be the burial-place of St. Colman and to date from the sixth century.

There are two roads from Cloyne to Ballycotton (7 miles; 12½ from Aghada), the more circuitous known as the Shanagarry road. The Lighthouse is seen long before the destination is reached. The motorist will find lovely wooded countryside hereabouts. The roads are well signposted.

Ballycotton

Distance.—24 miles from Cork (bus from Parnell Place).
Hotels.—*Bay View* (25 rooms), *Congress* (12), *Holiday Inne* (7).

Population.—425.
Angling.—Famous for deep-sea fishing. Sea-angling competitions held from June to September.

Ballycotton is situated in the south-east corner of County Cork on a prominence overlooking the Atlantic. The cliffs to the west are wild and bold and the sea has scooped out little bays here and there as if for the special convenience of bathers. At low tide long stretches of seaweed-covered rocks are exposed. There is an excellent harbour, with massive pier and breakwater, though it seems all too large and expensive for the comparatively few fishing vessels and yachts that shelter here. The **Lighthouse** stands on a pretty island, separated from the town by a narrow channel. Its friendly light flashes every 10 seconds, and is visible 20 miles away. To the east can be seen the cliffs that mark the entrance to Youghal Harbour.

Ballycotton is famous for sea fishing and many members of the British Sea Anglers' Association come here every year. Particulars can be obtained from hotel managements at Ballycotton. Fish caught here include halibut, skate, conger, ling, cod, haddock, blue shark, etc.

Several walks may be taken from Ballycotton. At **Shanagarry,** 2 miles north, are the remains of the Penn family's home (founders of Pennsylvania). **Knockadoon** is a good camping ground, and has some fine cliff scenery. Farther west the pleasant village of **Ballymacoda** overlooks Youghal Bay.

III. To Blarney Castle

Distance.—About 5 miles north-west of Cork (bus service).
Hotels.—*Castle* (10 rooms),

Muskerry Arms (5), *Waterloo Inn* (5), *Hotel Blarney* and guest houses.
Castle.—Admission charge. Open daily.

Blarney is a place of pilgrimage for all seekers after eloquence, whether they believe or not in the widely-reputed virtues of the Blarney Stone.

The most picturesque route is along the line of the old light railway. Turn west into Washington Street and drive or ride ahead to Carrigrohane (4 miles). On the right flows the Lee, and beyond it is a ridge of hill on the side of which are several institutions and private houses. Two miles out from Victoria Cross will be seen across the river an old graveyard where Jerome Collins, the Arctic explorer, is buried. He died on an expedition.

At Leemount there is a choice of roads. One can take that

to the left, which for 3 miles overlooks the Lee Valley, and turn right at the direction post. The other continues straight on and passes by the Muskerry Golf Club (18-hole course).

Blarney Castle

Little of the Castle is left except the **Keep**, a square, well-preserved structure 120 feet high. It is capped by machicolated battlements built out as a sort of staging from which could be dropped stones and other trifles on to the heads of assailants. The keep stands on a limestone rock, with the *Coomaun*, or crooked river, winding round it. A staircase on the right hand with small vaulted rooms let in the walls, often 9 feet thick, leads to the top. One is known as the Earl's Chamber.

In the neighbourhood there are extensive remains of other buildings, and some caves and secret passages will be shown by the attendant.

The Castle, the third on the site, dates from about 1446 and was built by the then powerful Cormac MacCarthy, surnamed *Làider*, "the strong." It was besieged by Cromwell's forces under Ireton and was then almost completely dismantled.

The addition of the very useful and expressive word "blarney" to the English language has been accounted for as follows:

"The word 'blarney,' meaning pleasant 'deliderin' talk,' is said to have originated at the court of Queen Elizabeth. MacCarthy, the then chieftain over the clan of that name who resided at Blarney, was repeatedly asked to come in from 'off his keeping,' as the phrase in the State Papers goes, to adjure the system of Tanistry by which the clan elected the chief, and take

tenure of his lands direct from the Crown. He was always promising with
fair words and soft speech to do what was desired, but never could be got
to come to the sticking point. The Queen, it is told, when one of his
speeches was brought to her, said: 'This is all Blarney; what he says he never
means.'"

The **Blarney Stone** is set in the parapet on the southern side of the
tower.

The rite of kissing the Blarney Stone has been robbed of much
of its thrill since the days when the visitor was lowered head down-
wards over the parapet, or was lowered through the opening between
the parapet and the main wall. All one has to do is to lie on one's
back, take hold of two bars attached to the wall, lower the head and
shoulders and kiss the underside of the stone.

The history of the Blarney Stone is obscure. Local tradition is confused,
but the probability is that the MacCarthys, once the most powerful clan in
Munster, possessed an inaugural stone upon which they set high value.
(Compare the stone under the Coronation Chair in Westminster Abbey.)
The Muskerry branch was the strongest in the fifteenth century when the
castle was built. It is such as any feudal baron with great estates might have
built anywhere in the British Isles. If Cormac *Làider* (the strong) attached
importance to a stone that was venerated by his ancestors it is natural that
he should have it fixed in a place of safety, and where it is would have been
the safest spot in the building.

That, however, did not prevent the MacCarthys from losing their estates
and castle on account of their adherence to the Stuarts. The last Lord
Muskerry of the MacCarthy line died at Altona, below Hamburg, on the
Elbe, about 1723. The estate was bought from the Crown by one Jeffreys
and later passed, through marriage, into the Colthurst family.

There is an excellent view over the surrounding country from the
tower. The view extends over a rich, undulating country, intersected
by the rivers *Martin, Coomaun* and *Shournagh.* To the north-west
rise the Boggeragh Mountains.

The **Rock Close,** near the foot of the Castle, is prettily wooded.
There are ancient ilex and yew trees amongst weird stone
formations. It is open to visitors (*fee*).

Blarney Village is set around a pleasant green and has a
prosperous tweed factory, which visitors may usually inspect
on application. Blarney Lake, within the grounds, is well
stocked with coarse fish—pike, perch, rudd and roach. It is
said that the MacCarthys dropped their treasures in the lake
rather than let them be captured.

There are some pleasant walks in the neighbourhood. To the
north along the valley of the River Martin is Waterloo Bridge
with a Round Tower (executed by Father Mat Hoogan 1776–
1849). Four miles north-west of Blarney are the Lisnaratha
earthworks and a pair of standing stones.

YOUGHAL AND THE BLACKWATER
✱✱✱✱✱✱✱✱✱✱✱✱✱✱✱✱✱✱✱✱✱✱✱✱✱✱✱✱✱✱✱✱✱

Youghal (pronounced *Yawl*), with its memories of Sir Walter Raleigh, and the lovely Blackwater are easily reached from Cork, by road (bus service).

Beyond the riverside suburbs of Tivoli and Dunkettle the road skirts the northern shore of **Lough Mahon,** and there are many pretty peeps down the harbour. Due east from Cobh Junction and Carrigtwohill is **Midleton** (*Eastferry House*), a hunting centre with an extensive distillery, flour and woollen mills. Midleton lies at the outlet of the *Dungourney* and *Owennacurra* rivers, and the latter, particularly, shows some pretty wooded gorges. In a further 6 miles the Youghal road passes through **Castlemartyr,** with its Carmelite College and nearby Imokilly Castle. Next comes Killeagh, above which is *Glenbower Wood*, a good picnic spot in the *Dissour* valley.

Youghal

Access.—*Rail:* from Dublin via Limerick Junction to Cork, then bus. Bus and coach connections with major towns.

Distances.—Belfast 249, Cappoquin 19, Cobh 29, Cork 31, Dungarvan, 19, Dublin 146, Lismore 19, Midleton 17, Waterford 48.

Early Closing.—Wednesday.

Entertainments, sports, etc.—Bathing, boating, fishing, shooting, golf (9 holes), tennis, carnivals, dog-racing, cinemas, dancing, etc.

Ferry.—To Monatrea, on east side of Youghal Harbour.

Hotels.—*Devonshire Arms* (13 rooms), *Atlantic* (15), *Adelphi* (40), *Marine* (13), *Harbour View* (13), *Avondhu Guest House* (8) *Gougane Barra Guest House* (12),

Population.—5,108.

Post Office.—North Main Street. Sub-office in Strand.

Youghal is an interesting town situated on the west bank at the mouth of the River Blackwater. It is a popular summer resort with a 5-mile beach of fine sand, beautiful coast line, and many entertainment and sporting facilities. Youghal consists of two distinct parts. The Strand, popular with visitors, overlooks Youghal Bay, which is bounded on the east by hilly ground at the river mouth, and on the south by a low shore of sand extending to **Knockadoon Head** (135 feet), 4 miles off, and its small islet, Capel Island. The older part, Youghal proper, consists of one long Main Street and a parallel river frontage.

The town received its first charter from King John in 1209, and is said to derive its name from *Eochaill*, the Irish word for yew-wood, the hills having been formerly covered with those trees. It was a wealthy and important city, strongly fortified, and a large part of the walls, originally built by the Normans, still stand on the western and northern sides. The town was

114

occupied in 1579 by the Earl of Desmond, but later Ormond drove him out, rebuilt the walls and placed a strong garrison here. It was taken and retaken again and again. When Charles I was executed the Puritans in the town sided with Cromwell, who entered in 1649 by the Water Gate and for a time made the town his headquarters. Jones, one of his generals, died here. Youghal today has an important salmon fishery and thriving factories producing silk and cotton goods, stained glass, pottery and carpets.

On the site of the ancient South Gate now stands the **Clock Gate**, erected by the Corporation in 1777. In Main Street, on the right-hand side as one comes from the Clock Tower, is **Tynte's Castle**, an ancient tower built by English settlers in the fifteenth century. A few yards from this a narrow street on the left leads to **St. Mary's Collegiate Church.**

This occupies the site of a church that stood here before the Norman invasion, and it was rebuilt by the eighth Earl of Desmond, who founded a college in connection with it in 1464. It was restored in 1619 by the "great" Earl of Cork. The massive tower adjoining the Church, but not part of it and probably built for defence, has a height of 50 feet and is known as Cromwell's Tower. The interior of the Church is very beautiful, especially the choir, which contains an east window unsurpassed in Ireland for size and beauty of form. It has a curious pulpit. The nave and aisles are now used as the parish church. The roof is of dark Irish oak. In the south transept (vestry) are the tombs of Richard Bennett and his wife, and some very ancient monuments. On the opposite side of the same transept—or chantry of our Blessed Saviour—is the florid monument to the first Earl of Cork—the "great" earl, as he is usually called—who is represented in a recumbent position between his two wives, while underneath are the diminutive figures of his nine children (for four of whom he managed to get peerages), and over the arch his mother. The Countess of Desmond, whose tomb is near the west door, is said to have been 140 years of age when she died in 1604. The churchyard is very ancient and is reputed to be haunted. There are numerous ancient tombstones.

Adjoining the churchyard is Myrtle Grove (private), built in 1586, at one time the residence of Sir Walter Raleigh, who was mayor of the town in 1588. It was while living here that he is reputed to have planted the first potatoes in Ireland, having brought some from Virginia; and beneath the yews in front of the house, it is said, he startled his domestics by smoking tobacco, which he also introduced from America.

The *College* just mentioned in connection with the Church still stands, close to the Church.

Just beyond the town walls, at the north end of Main Street, are the west gable of the church and a few fragments of **North Abbey,** a Dominican monastery founded in 1268. South Abbey thoroughfare commemorates the Franciscan foundation of 1224, of which no trace now remains. About a quarter mile farther north, only fragmentary traces exist of St. John's Abbey, a fourteenth-century Benedictine abbey.

At the far end of the town a very broad causeway and bridge lead across the river, at low tide a marshy swamp.

From Youghal one can cross the river by the ferry and go on to **Ardmore** (6 miles), with its interesting ecclesiastical remains, described on p. **90**. **Ferry Point** is a pretty holiday spot with fine sea views.

The Blackwater River

The *Blackwater* has a length of over 80 miles, though only sixteen are navigable. It rises above Kingwilliamstown (also known as Ballydesmond) not 20 miles from Killarney, and crosses the entire breadth of county Cork from west to east, taking a sudden turn southwards at Cappoquin.

Parts of the Blackwater give some of the finest fishing in Ireland, though some of the best reaches are preserved. Salmon and trout abound. Fishing can be had at reasonable rates. Make local inquiries.

Youghal to Cappoquin. From Youghal to Cappoquin there is the high-road which follows the western or left bank of the river. As an alternative, at Camphire the ferry can be taken across to Villierstown; thence by road to Cappoquin.

It is a beautiful motor run from Youghal to Mount Melleray (p. 91) along the Blackwater as far as Cappoquin, returning by Lismore and Tallow. Motorists should explore here, and not merely rush through. For Cappoquin, *see* p. 91.

Several interesting ruins may be found at short distances off the main road from Youghal to Cappoquin—**Rhincrew Castle**, once a preceptory of the Knights Templar, founded by Raymond le Gros, a companion-in-arms of Strongbow; the picturesque ruins of **Temple Michael Church** and **Castle**; the extensive ruins of **Molana Abbey**, where Raymond le Gros lies buried, and the fine mansion of **Ballinatray**. Farther on **Strancally Castle** (7 miles from Youghal) rises over the deepest part of the river, and its ivied ruins among the mossy rocks have a peculiarly venerable and pleasing appearance. The modern Castle of Strancally is surrounded by extensive woods, above which rise its towers and battlements; here is the **Murdering Hole**, a natural fissure in the rocks. After passing the bridge over the River *Bride*, we reach **Camphire** nearly opposite the neat village of **Villierstown**. Farther on, overlooking the river on the left, is **Dromana Castle**, with wooded surroundings. In the grounds, which are open, are the remains of the old castle. Here was born the Countess of Desmond, said to have lived 140 years.

Tourin Castle lies on the right, and we can distinguish in the distance the spire of the Abbey of Mount Melleray. From Camphire to Cappoquin is considered by many the finest part of the Blackwater, the many islets adding greatly to its picturesqueness. In the grounds attached to Affane House, a short distance up the *Finisk* (right), Raleigh is said to have planted the first cherry tree (brought from the Canary Isles) seen in Ireland.

116

CORK TO GLENGARRIFF
(AND KILLARNEY)
❀❀❀❀❀❀❀❀❀❀❀❀❀❀❀❀❀❀❀❀❀❀❀❀

Route by the coast to Kinsale, Clonakilty, Skibbereen and Bantry.

There is a magnificent stretch of coast to the south-west of Cork with many attractive resorts. Leave Cork by Evergreen Street, and turn right at Turner's Cross; the route descends to Fivemilebridge, crosses the Owenboy river, and runs along the Stick river to **Belgooly,** which stands at the head of the Oyster-haven estuary. After crossing the estuary, the route reaches—

Kinsale

Angling.—Freshwater fishing in Bandon River and tributaries; excellent sea-fishing grounds between the harbour and Daunt's Rock.
Distances.—18 miles from Cork (daily bus services), Dublin 178, The Old Head 10.
Early Closing.—Thursday.

Golf.—9-hole course on the Cork road (2 miles from Kinsale).
Hotels.—*Actons* (63 rooms), *Murphy's* (12), *Dempsey's Guest House* (10), *Trident* (40).
Population.—1,600.
Youth Hostel.—At Summer Cove (2 miles).
Regatta.—Popular regatta on August Bank Holiday.

The town is built on the slope of Compass Hill at the mouth of the river Bandon. It has a quaint appearance, its houses, many of Spanish inspiration, rising tier above tier on sites ex-cavated out of the solid rock, some being perched on projecting crags. The streets follow the windings of the river. The ruins of the old fort, which was thought impregnable until it fell into the hands of Marlborough in 1690, are a picturesque feature. There is a charming public walk, shaded by trees, around **Compass Hill,** which commands a series of good views of the harbour, including a ruined fortress on the opposite bank and the villages of **Scilly** and **Summercove** (the favourite quarters of summer visitors).

The chief object of antiquarian interest in the town is the **Parish Church** of St. Multose, built by the Normans about 1170. The church is cruciform, with a curious ancient tower at the west end, the upper stage, of smaller dimensions than the lower, ending in a broach spire. In the porch of this tower are the old town stocks. In 1894 a stone with a sculptured figure supposed to represent St. Multose was found. The font is very old. The church is mentioned in a Papal decretal in 1199, but of course has since been largely rebuilt. It contains some interesting memorials.

Other points of interest in the town are **Desmond's Castle** (or French Prison), which is a good example of a sixteenth to eighteenth-century town house, and the ruins of a **Carmelite Friary** dating from 1314. The **Museum** is housed in the Old Courthouse (*open daily from 11 till 1 and 2 till 5*); it contains many objects of local and historical interest.

Kinsale was formerly governed under a charter of Edward III (dated 1333) by a "sovereign" (mayor) and other officials. It has an interesting history. It took part in all the struggles between the English and the "native Irish," from the time when Strongbow first subjected it to the English crown to its capture by Marlborough. In 1601 a Spanish force under Don Juan d'Aquilla captured Kinsale. They were besieged by mixed English and Irish Forces and those latter were surrounded by an Irish Army under the northern Chiefs O'Neill and O'Donnell. Through lack of co-ordination on the part of the Irish, the Queen's army won the battle. James II landed at Kinsale on March 12, 1689, to begin the campaign that ended so disastrously for him at the Boyne. For centuries Kinsale was the most important port on the coast, and though it has long since given way to Cobh its harbour is spacious and well sheltered.

Opposite Kinsale is the ruin of **Ringrone Castle,** built by Milo de Courcey, the ancestor of Lord Kingsale, the premier baron of Ireland (the title goes back to 1181).

The **Old Head of Kinsale** protects the harbour on the west. It is a bald promontory whose name—derived from *ceann saille*, "a headland in the sea"—is happily descriptive. It is only 256 feet high, but commands a magnificent view. The best but not the shortest way is by the village of Ballinspittle. An old Signal Tower is on a narrow strip of land leading on to the Old Head and the extreme point is crowned by a lighthouse.

On Friday, May 7, 1915, some 8 miles off the Old Head, the great liner *Lusitania* was torpedoed by a German submarine. Some 1,195 passengers died and only 764 lives were saved. A small number of survivors were picked up by Kinsale fishing boats.

Westward from Kinsale the road at first skirts the Bandon River, then crosses it to **Ballinspittle,** where there is the prehistoric Ballycateen fort with triple ramparts.

Just beyond, a road turns off for **Garrettstown Strand** (*Coakley's Atlantic* (23 rooms), *O'Neill's* (18)), a favourite seaside resort with grand bathing and a 9-hole golf course. Eight miles farther along the coast road is **Timoleague,** where salmon and trout fishing can be had in the River *Argideen*, and where are the remains of a very fine abbey, erected in 1372 by the MacCarthys and dedicated to St. Molaga (hence the name, derived from *ty-Molaga*, "the house of Molaga"). It was the largest of many religious houses in County Cork. The remains comprise nave, choir and south transept, with a beautiful square tower 68 feet high added by Edward Courcy, Bishop of Ross, in 1518. There is a squint in the transept, 5 feet long, for the use of lepers, whose hospital was a mile away. The situation is very beautiful, the sea washing up to the walls.

A coast road extends east from Timoleague on the south side of the creek, and leads in 2¾ miles to **Courtmacsherry,** a pretty village set against a background of wooded slopes and magnificent cliffs. Bathing, boating, and shooting amenities are good, and across the harbour (ferry service) is an 18-hole golf course.

The main road westward from Timoleague leads in 6 miles to—

Clonakilty

Distance.—33 miles from Cork. Bus services.
Early Closing.—Wednesday.

Hotels.—*O'Donovan's* (10 rooms), *Emmet House* (11), *Dunmore House* (10).
Population.—2,422.

Clonakilty is one of the chief towns of west Cork and is rapidly becoming a popular resort, with excellent bathing facilities.

The town lies at the head of a small inlet, the mouth of which is defended by **Inchydoney Island** (connected with the mainland by causeways), on which are the remains of an old church. On **Galley Head,** the western horn of the bay, is a lighthouse 69 feet high. A mile to the north of Clonakilty a Druidical temple may be seen, and there are several ruined castles.

A good road to the west leads in 8 miles to—

Rosscarbery

Angling.—Most important shore angling centre in the south of Ireland.

Hotel.—*Carbery Arms* (10 rooms).
Bathing.—Safe sandy beaches.

Rosscarbery was once the site of a "famous university, whereto resorted all the south-west part of Ireland for learning's sake." The place acquired great celebrity from St. Fachtna, abbot of Moelanfaidh, in County Waterford, who founded an abbey here in the sixth century. The Protestant bishopric of Ross is now united to that of Cork and Cloyne; the Cathedral, of Perpendicular architecture with a square tower and octagonal spire, is used as the parish church, but has retained its cathedral status in the diocese of Ross.

There are many ruins in the neighbourhood and several

119

items of archaeological interest, such as stone circles, dolmens, etc. Rosscarbery is pleasantly situated and has a thriving farm industry. There is a pleasant walk by Rosscarbery Bay to **Castle Freke,** the one-time home of Lord Carbery and now a holiday camp. The cliff scenery all round here is magnificent, and a good coastal road runs 12 miles west to Skibbereen, passing the beautiful inlet known as Glandore Harbour. **Unionhall** and **Glandore** villages are picturesquely situated on either side of the harbour, at the head of which is **Leap,** of old considered the boundary between civilization and lawlessness; hence a local proverb, "Beyond the Leap, beyond the law." Numerous ancient ruins can be seen in the neighbourhood, including **Kilfinnan Castle** (restored), with walls 13 feet thick.

Skibbereen

Distance.—53 miles from Cork. Bus services.
Early Closing.—Thursday.
Fishing.—For salmon and sea trout in the river *Ilen* (*free*).

Golf.—9-hole golf course, 1½ miles south-west of the town.
Hotels.—*Eldon* (16 rooms), *West Cork* (19).
Population.—2,028.

Skibbereen, standing at the spot where the Ilen widens out to form the creek, is a market town. The ruins of **Abbeystrowry Abbey** on the bank of the river are worth visiting. A walk or drive that should not be missed is that to **Lough Ine,** about 4 miles south-west, a kind of marine *cul de sac* with a very narrow inlet from the sea. The country is wild and desolate in the extreme, but the immediate surroundings of the lough are picturesque. In the centre is an islet on which are the ruins of an old castle of the O'Driscolls. A Marine Biology Station has premises both on the island and on the shore.

From Skibbereen, excursions can conveniently be made to **Toe Head,** east of the lough, which commands a beautiful view. Here there is a graveyard for children only. Beyond is the sea with many small islets and the **Stags,** three rocks of great height. The Head is at the end of the western promontory which shuts in **Castle Haven,** at the head of which is **Castletownsend,** a pretty village deriving its name from the Townsend family, who succeeded the O'Driscolls as lords of the property. In 1602 the harbour was the scene of a naval engagement between the Spaniards and the English fleet. It saw some fighting in 1690, when King James II tried to recover his realm of Ireland. On the western side are the ruins of **Glenbarrahane Castle** and of the **Chapel of St. Barrahane,** with a holy well. It was at Castlehaven that some of the Irish Chiefs embarked for Spain after the disaster of the battle of Kinsale, 1601–2. Castletownsend was the home of the late Miss Edith Somerville, the Irish writer.

From Skibbereen another road goes south-west to—

Baltimore

which owes its charm to the romantic cliff walks in the neighbourhood. It is an excellent yachting and fishing station and
most picturesque. The ramifications of the great harbour are
difficult to understand on account of the many islands in it,
some of considerable size. The whole of this coast is very
indented and irregular, with magnificent cliffs. The best viewpoint is at the curious round **Beacon** at the extreme south-west
point of the cliff, opposite **Innisherkin** or **Sherkin**, largest of the
numerous islands which is about 3 miles long by 2 broad, and at
one time contained a Franciscan abbey and a castle, both now
in ruins. Care in ascending is necessary, as the cliff is steep
and there are some nasty chasms in places. Sherkin has become
popular with Cork residents in recent years. The sea bathing is
excellent. The island to the south-west, beyond Sherkin, is
Cape Clear Island. The Fastnet Rock Lighthouse lies beyond.

Baltimore was sacked in 1631 by Algerian pirates and a
number of the inhabitants were taken off as captives.

A rock commanding the harbour is crowned by the ruins
of Dunashad Castle, an old fortress of the clan O'Driscoll.
The Harbour extends northward almost to Skibbereen.

Schull

Fifteen miles west of Skibbereen is Schull, reached by bus.
There is a population of about 400. *Barnett, East End, The
Haven* (guest). Boating and sailing can be enjoyed and the
sea-fishing is good. Behind the village is the prominent *Mount
Gabriel* (1,339 feet).

Cape Clear Island

which may be visited from Baltimore (by Ferry, daily on Mondays,
Wednesdays, Fridays and Saturdays at 2.15 p.m. (other excursions in
summer), returning to Baltimore at 6 p.m.) or from Schull, is 3 miles
long by 1½ broad at its widest part, with an extremely rugged and
precipitous coast. At its southern extremity it presents an inaccessible
cliff to the sea, and—as every schoolboy knows—is the first land
sighted by vessels on their approach from America. St. Keiran was
born here. On the summit of **Fastnet Rock,** about 3¼ miles to the
south-west, is a grey granite lighthouse whose light is 160 feet above
high-water mark and is visible for 25 miles. Its white light flashes
every 5 seconds. The O'Driscolls were the former rulers here, and
one of their castles, **Dunamore,** is on a rock off the island of Cape
Clear. The 200 inhabitants of this island still retain unchanged some

121

of the old customs and many can only speak Irish. They are all fearless sailors. (*Youth Hostel* at South Harbour.)

Far to the west of Schull is **Mizen Head,** the extreme south-western point of Ireland. The first view of this headland, 765 feet high, is peculiarly exciting. At the top is an old signal tower. To the east, separated from it by Barley Cove, is **Brow Head,** with a telegraph station. **Three Castle Head,** the extreme point of Dunmanus Bay, is so named from three old fortresses of the Mahony sept. The village of **Goleen,** about 12 miles from Schull, is the nearest headquarters for the exploration of these crooked sea-indented and almost unknown promontories. One of the inlets beyond Goleen, **Crookhaven Bay,** is the safest harbour in the south of Ireland. It has a lighthouse at the entrance.

Between Skibbereen and Schull is **Ballydehob,** once a copper-mining centre. It stands at the head of a long creek, from which a road runs northward to—

Bantry

Distance.—57 miles from Cork; bus service daily.
Early Closing.—Wednesday.

Hotels.—*Vickery's* (20 rooms), *Anchor* (16), *Bantry Bay* (10), *West Lodge* (40).
Population.—2,300.

Bantry lies in a sheltered position at the head of Bantry Bay. It offers good facilities for bathing, yachting, boating and fishing. There is a beautiful view down and across the spacious bay, with its background of sharply defined peaks—Hungry Hill, the Sugarloaf, and the long range of the Caha Mountains, said to hide 365 lakes.

Bantry House, finely situated over the bay, is the principal attraction of the town. The entrance gates are on the Town Square, near the Castletown pier. The grounds offer impressive views over the bay, while in the house itself is the Earl of Bantry's celebrated collection of tapestries, furniture and other *objets d'art.* House and grounds are open (*fee*) during summer.

Drive round Dunmanus and Bantry Bays, about 35 miles. This is a six hours' drive over a winding, hilly road. Lunch can be taken in the car, but there is a little hotel at **Ahakista,** on the northern shore of Dunmanus Bay, 12 miles from Bantry. The chief charm of the drive is the fact that the sea is close at hand all the way, except for the first 7 miles or so to **Durrus.** We drive past a succession of pretty coves, with fine views of Dunmanus Bay, **Mount Gabriel** (1,339 feet) and the rugged coast-line, to Three Castle Head and Mizen Head. About two-thirds of the way along the promontory we reach the village of **Kilcrohane,** and turning to the right begin the steep ascent of **Seeyn** (1,136 feet). The zigzag upward road winds so much that the scrambler by path has only about half the distance to go.

The backward view is magnificent, but is surpassed by that which meets the gaze in front when the summit is reached. The whole stretch of Bantry Bay, certainly one of the finest in the world, lies below. Across the water is the strongly fortified Bere Island, sheltering the harbour and town of Castletown Berehaven (*see* p. 129). Behind the island tower the Slieve Miskish and Caha Mountains. To westward is the boundless ocean, and eastward we have, as we turn and slowly descend, a sight of the Bay as far as Whiddy Island. The road during the first part of the homeward journey is about 1,000 feet above the sea, which it directly overhangs.

Bantry Bay is 21 miles long and from 6 to 8 wide. The depth of water at the entrance is about 40 fathoms. It affords very safe anchorage, having no rocks or sandbanks and being sheltered by Bere Island. Up to 1936–37, British military forces occupied Bere Island.

The bay is historically interesting as having been the scene of two attempted invasions by the French. In 1689–90 their fleet entered, bringing to Ireland the ex-king of Great Britain, James II. In a short time the English fleet, under Admiral Herbert, bore down in pursuit; but, being inferior in force, were compelled to sail out again after a brisk engagement. But it was at Kinsale that James II and his Franco-Irish army disembarked. In 1796 the French with about fifteen thousand men intended for the invasion of Ireland again put to sea, appointing Bantry Bay as their rendezvous. They were scattered by a storm, and only a remnant of the armament reached the Irish coast; and General Hoche, the commander-in-chief, not having joined them, the vessels which had cast anchor did not disembark their forces. Having lost an opportunity of landing without opposition, they sailed again for France on the 27th of January after a stay of five days in the bay.

Whiddy Island lies at the head of the bay, opposite the town. It has an area of about 1,000 acres. There are some relics of an old church, with a cemetery attached, and on the eastern point are the ruins of a castle built in the reign of Henry VI by O'Sullivan Bere. A large part of the western side of the island has been developed as an oil tank storage base by Gulf Oil. There is accommodation for mammoth 300,000 ton tankers.

Cork to Bantry (Inland route)

An alternative inland route from Cork to Bantry can be followed *via* Bandon and Dunmanway. Leave Cork City by Washington Street and Western Road, then turn left at Victoria Cross, pass through Wilton, and ascend the hill. Descend to Ballinhassig and continue to **Inishannon,** on the Bandon river. From here the road runs alongside the river, passing the ruins of **Kilbeg Castle** and **Dundaniel Castle** (built 1476), to—

Bandon

Distances.—20 miles from Cork. Bus service. Bantry 37, Dublin 180, Killarney 48, Kinsale 12.
Early Closing.—Thursday.

Fishing.—Centre for trout and salmon angling in the *Bandon*.
Golf.—9-hole course.
Hotel.—*Munster Arms* (12 rooms).
Population.—2,294.

Beautifully situated on the river Bandon, and an important agricultural centre, Bandon was for a long time almost exclusively Protestant, and on that account was called the "Southern Derry". The church of Kilbrogan, built in 1610, was the first built in Ireland for the reformed worship. The first Earl of Cork recommended Bandon to royal favour and protection, on the ground that "no popish recusant, or unconforming novelist, is admitted to live in all the town"; and Smith, writing in 1750, left on record that "in the town there is not a popish inhabitant, nor will the townsmen suffer one to dwell in it, nor a piper to play in the place, that being the music formerly used by the Irish in their wars." Oliver Cromwell visited Bandon during his Irish campaign. He was enthusiastically welcomed by the Bandonians. The room in which he slept was preserved intact down to living memory.

From Bandon the road skirts the estate of Castle Bernard and passing through the villages of **Enniskean** and **Ballineen.** There are several ruins to be seen in the neighbourhood, including the **Round Tower of Kinneigh,** about 3 miles north. The tower is about 70 feet high and is round at the top, but the bottom 18 feet are hexagonal. The next town on the route is—

Dunmanway

Distance.—37 miles from Cork, Glengarriff 26, Macroom 19, Skibbereen 17.
Early Closing.—Thursday.

Hotels.—*Bostonian* (9 rooms), *Castle* (7).
Population.—1,406.

Formerly the centre of a prosperous linen trade, Dunmanway is now a market town. Situated at the entrance to wild, hilly country, it attracts the tourist who is keen on pheasant, duck and snipe shooting. There are also fine fishing facilities, both in the Bandon river for salmon and trout, and in the many lakes for trout and coarse fish. From Dunmanway the road continues to **Drimoleague,** 12 miles from Bantry, and the junction for Skibbereen and Baltimore. **Bantry** is described on pp. 122–123.

CORK TO GLENGARRIFF AND KILLARNEY
BY THE TOURISTS' ROUTE VIA MACROOM

Cork to Macroom (24 miles)—Macroom to Glengarriff (40 miles)—Glengarriff to Kenmare (17 miles)—Kenmare to Killarney (21 miles)

For fares, timetables, etc., apply at Bus Office, Parnell Place, Cork, or at Killarney. It is advisable to check up on bus route times, for alterations are often made at short notice.

We describe the journey in the westward direction, as the scenery ahead is distinctly better this way. The long chain of lakes at Inchigeela, the holy lake of Gougane Barra, and the Pass of Keimaneigh, make this route very interesting, and it also passes through extremely fine scenery.

There are two routes to Macroom. One is by Washington Street and Western Road to Victoria Cross, where some of the buses bear left to Dennehy's Cross, thence right and out by the Model Farm Road to Ballincollig, Ovens, Crookstown and Macroom.

The other and more picturesque route is by Carrigrohane, Leemount, Inniscarra, Dripsey, Coachford, Carrigadrohid and so to Macroom.

Beyond **Ballincollig** on the southern road is **Ovens,** where some caves are worth exploring. Five miles farther is Farnanes, a mile from which along a narrow road at the eastern end of village are the ruins of **Kilcrea Abbey,** founded in the fourteenth century by MacCarthy of Blarney. From Farnanes the road continues to Macroom, or alternatively the north road may be reached at Carrigadrohid by turning right at Ballincollig.

The northern road from Cork keeps closer company with the River Lee and is in consequence more picturesque. Between Inniscarra and Carrigadrohid is the new River Lee Hydro Electric scheme which has completely altered the historic Lee Valley. **Carrigadrohid's** claim to notice is an old castle which stood out against the Cromwellians under Lord Broghill. The besiegers captured Dr. MacEgan, titular bishop of Ross, and Broghill promised him liberty if he advised the garrison to surrender. He was taken before the castle, but far from advising surrender he urged the soldiers to hold out to the last for the Catholic faith. Needless to say, that after this the Bishop got short shrift. Carrigadrohid is a grand centre for salmon fishing. Trout fishing is free, but there is competition for salmon. Inquire locally or in Cork.

From Carrigadrohid the road cuts across a small peninsula to—

Macroom

Distances.—Cork 24, Glengarriff 39, Kenmare 35, Killarney 30, Inchigeela 9.

Early Closing.—Wednesday.

Golf.—9-hole course.

Hotels.—*Castle* (18 rooms), *Victoria* (14), *Coolcower* (6), *St. Gobnaits* (5).

Population.—2,200.

The name "Macroom" is variously translated as "the plain of the croom (oak)," and "the crooked oak," from the large forest of oaks which at one time grew here. The town is pleasantly situated near the junction of the rivers Lee and Sullane.

Macroom Castle, said to have been built in the reign of King John by the MacCarthys, is interesting as the birthplace of Admiral Sir William Penn, the father of the founder of Pennsylvania. It was acquired by the late Lady Ardilaun (who claimed descent from the McCarthys), and renovated. It was occupied as an occasional residence until 1920. It was burned by Republicans in 1922, and has not been restored. Rinuccini, the famous Papal Nuncio, stayed here for a short time on his way to Kilkenny in 1645. A picturesque golf course has been laid out in the Castle grounds by the riverside.

Macroom to Glengarriff

Leaving Macroom, we have a view to the right of the **Boggeragh** and **Derrynasaggart Mountains.** The island-dotted river below, to the left, is the *Lee*. At Toon Bridge we notice the ruined tower of **Dundarieke Castle,** a fortress of the Mac-Carthys. Presently, on the left is **Castle Masters,** and farther on, the highest pillar stone in Ireland—20 feet.

Inchigeela, 10 miles from Macroom and 35 from Cork, is mostly resorted to by anglers, trout being plentiful in the neighbouring lakes and rivers. Boats can be hired.

After leaving Inchigeela village we pass, close to the road, a chain of no fewer than six lakes or "broads," the largest of which is **Lough Allua.** The lakes are really an expansion of the Lee. With their fringe of rushes, white water-lilies and setting of firs, the waters are very picturesque. The curiously shaped height to the left, which has been for some time conspicuous, is the **Shehy Mountain** (1,797 feet). The mountains now close in on either side. Three miles westward of Ballingeary (well known for its summer school in connection with the Irish language movement) we stop at Gougane Barra cross-roads, 20 miles from Macroom.

Gougane Barra

The name means St. Finbar's rock-cleft. The road does not actually

126

pass the celebrated "holy lake," which lies embedded in the mountains a mile distant from the cross-roads, in the direction indicated by the signpost.

The **Lake**, a deep tarn a mile long, lies in a sequestered spot surrounded on all save the eastern side by steep mountains—relieved here and there by green patches—that rise abruptly to a height of nearly 1,800 feet. The dark shadows of these great overhanging cliffs are reflected in the glassy surface of the water.

The Lake is a favourite resort for anglers, the fishing in this and the neighbouring lakes being free. There are two hotels beside the lake, *Gougane Barra* (20 rooms) and *Cronin's* (9 rooms).

In the middle of the lake is a small wooded island joined to the mainland on the south side by a causeway. This island was, at the end of the sixth century, the chosen retreat of Saint Fin Barre, the patron saint of Cork. On it are the ruins of a religious foundation of *c.* 1770 consisting of a rectangular court or cloister.

St. Finnbarr or Fin Barre (the name means beautiful hair) grew up near Gougane, and became famed for his holiness. Told by an angel to go to the place where Cork now is, he followed the river Lee and established a monastery there that became famous for its learning and flourished for centuries. He was buried in Cork.

Returning to the main road, we at once enter on the best part of the drive.

The **Pass of Keimaneigh**, "the pass of the deer," is a stern defile more than a mile and a quarter in length and bounded by steep rocky hills. It is probably the finest of its kind in Ireland, though some give preference to the Pass of Ballaghbeama in Kerry. The mountain appears to have been split by some mighty convulsion, and there is only just room in the deep cleft for the narrow road and the torrent that foams beside it.

The summit of the pass is 700 feet above sea-level and is the highest part of the route. On emerging, we round the unmistakable Shehy Mountain and have the river *Owvane* for company all the way down the long descent to Bantry Bay. From here onwards the road winds along the shore and the view of Bantry Bay and the islands and hills around is, in clear, weather, superb. About midway we pass the **Castle of Carriganass** ("rock of the waterfall"), a former seat of the O'Sullivans. At the head of the bay, at **Ballylickey** Bridge, the road turns left to **Bantry** (3½ miles), and right to **Glengarriff**. (7 miles).

For the route onward to **Kenmare** and **Killarney**, *see* pp. 130 and 131.

Direct route from Macroom to Killarney (31 miles)

The road runs north-west *via* **Ballyvourney,** climbs the Derrynasaggart Mountains to 958 feet, where it enters County Kerry, and descends to the Flesk Valley. Here the road undulates through open country with the Rathmore road running in on the right 5 miles short of Killarney.

GLENGARRIFF
❧❧❧❧❧❧❧❧❧❧❧❧

Distances.—Cork 62, Killarney 38, Dublin 222, Macroom 39, Kenmare 17.
Early Closing.—Tuesday.
Golf.—9-hole course 1 mile from village.
Post Office.—Near Poulgorm.
Population.—431.
Hotels.—*Glengarriff Castle* (19 rooms), *Eccles* (65), *Casey's* (22), *Golf Links* (30), *Harvey's Poulgorm* (29), *Bay View* (45), and others.

Heights of Mountains near Glengarriff:
Sugar Loaf . . . 1,887 feet
Cobduff . . . 1,244 „
Hungry Hill . . . 2,251 „
Shrone Hill . . . 919 „

Glengarriff ("the rugged Glen") is said to be the most beautiful spot in Co. Cork. The bathing, boating and sea-fishing are excellent, and there is some good trout fishing to be had.

Glengarriff is a simple village set in a deep Alpine valley about 6 miles in length and a quarter in breadth. The enclosing hills are of the wildest, singularly broken and irregular in their outline. Glacier-borne rocks, some of enormous size, are flung together in strange confusion, but the roughness is relieved by luxuriant foliage, for the bases of the hills and every crevice and hollow are filled with trees and shrubs. The arbutus, the yew and the holly seem native to the place, as also do many semi-tropical plants. The glen is surrounded on the north, east, and west by mountains, and is thus effectively sheltered from the winds. It opens southward on to a lovely inlet of Bantry Bay, and the breezes that reach it from this quarter have all been tempered by the Gulf Stream. The air is consequently genial and soft, without being enervating or relaxing.

There are two churches in the village—the Church of Ireland with an unusual stained-glass window, and a Roman Catholic church at the western end of the village.

Cromwell's Bridge is picturesque when seen from the road, but far more so from the water. It can only be reached by water, however, when the tide is in—then the branches dipping low into this armlet of the sea and the reflections, with the ivy-grown arches, make a lovely picture. To reach it by land, go through the village; where the roads fork at the farther end turn down to the left, crossing **Poulgorm Bridge** (blue pool), with its view looking down on Cromwell's broken bridge. The name commemorates the legend that this bridge was built at short notice on Cromwell's orders.

If the main road to Castletown is followed for a quarter of a

Upper Lake, Killarney

Lough Caragh, Co. Kerry

Parknasilla, Co. Kerry

Slea Head, Dingle, Co. Kerry

mile or so, lovely views are seen across the harbour and its
many islets to Glengarriff Castle. Turning sharply to the right
through a gate, a walk or drive of about 2 miles brings one
towards the **Eagle's Nest** (2,005 feet), which can then be
ascended (about 3 miles). The climb is worth the trouble.

Farther along the Castletown road Derryconnery School
House is soon reached opposite Garinish Island, and after a
short ascent the view becomes wilder and grander. Gabhal
Mhór (Sugarloaf) Mountain and the Caha Range rise in front,
Shrone to the side, and the lovely Bay lies at the foot. A
favourite boat excursion from Glengarriff is across the Bay
to **Garinish Island** or Ilnacullin, with its old fort and martello
tower built during the Napoleonic Wars and its wonderful
Italian garden. *Open 10–5.30; landing charge.*

In the Glengarriff district there is the best of sport for rod and
gun. All the lakes and rivers have trout—particularly Lough-a-
Vaul on the Castletown road, and Barley Lake which drains into
the Glengarriff river about a mile above Glengarriff Lodge.

For those who prefer to wander, there is the drive or walk of about
3 miles to **Glengarriff Lodge** or **Lord Bantry's Cottage**, with its pretty
grounds. Follow the main Kenmare road, and in about half a mile
from the village turn sharply to the left at the entrance to the demesne,
through which cars are allowed to drive. A footpath under the trees
leads to **Lady Bantry's View**, a view-point looking towards the Caha
range, which divides Co. Cork and Co. Kerry. This is one of the
most charming views to be had within a short distance.

A longer trip is to the **caves** (9 miles by sea) and the lofty **Adrigole
Waterfall** (12 miles) and **Hungry Hill** (2,251 feet), the highest point
of the Caha Mountains, with the prettily-wooded Adrigole harbour
at its foot. There are many other good mountain climbs.

A lonely road leads down the Bay to **Castletown Berehaven** (22
miles), a small town (*Berehaven* (16 rooms); 9-hole golf course)
formerly known in connection with autumn naval manœuvres. The
road skirts the north coast of the Bay at the foot of the Caha Mountain for 12 miles, then turns more inland. Glacial action can be
plainly seen on the smooth-faced rocks by the road and many perched
blocks are passed. To the south-west of the Caha Mountains is the
Slieve Miskish range. **Berehaven,** one of the finest natural harbours
in the Kingdom, remained a British naval base until 1938, when it
was handed over to the Irish government. There are fortifications
on Bere Island, which is named after Beara, a mythical Spanish
princess.

At the western or seaward entry of the haven stand the ruins of
Dunboy Castle. It was destroyed after a long siege in 1602. A return
can be made by the road over the Slieve Miskish Mountains to the

south shore of Kenmare river, and thence eastward by way of Ardgroom and Kilmakilloge Harbours, Derreen (a wooded desmesne), and Clonee Lakes to Kenmare (33 miles). From Kenmare back to Glengarriff is 18 miles.

Ascent of the Sugarloaf.—The climber may care to make the ascent of Gabhal Mhór (Great Fork)—the **Sugarloaf** (1,887 feet). The distance is about 7 miles from Glengarriff village, but a whole day will be occupied and lunch should be taken. As there are several routes to the summit, a guide is desirable; but a fairly simple ascent may be made by following the Berehaven road until about a mile beyond the inlet known as **Coolieragh Harbour.** Here turn to the right and ascend the south-eastern slope of the mountain. A fine view is gained of the whole of Bantry Bay.

The Healy Pass. A longer but interesting variation of the direct route from Glengarriff to Kenmare, which follows, is *via* **Adrigole** and the Healy Pass; this pass, completed in 1931, was named after Mr. Tim Healy, the first Governor-General of the Irish Free State. At the summit of the Pass one enters Kerry. From here fine views open out as we descend to **Lauragh,** where the main road follows the coast to Kenmare. The total distance is 31 miles.

The **Beara Peninsula** stands for a further 12 miles or so westward of Castletown Berehaven the road continuing almost to the tip at Dursey Sound. Across the Sound is **Dursey Island.**

GLENGARRIFF TO KENMARE (17 miles)

The road at first follows the Glengarriff Valley, and then climbs steeply to the **Caha Mountains.** The **Sugarloaf** (1,887 feet) rises to the left. Six miles from Glengarriff we enter a 600-foot-long tunnel that takes us into County Kerry, and this is followed by three shorter tunnels as the road descends the Sheen Valley. The Kenmare Estuary is crossed by a suspension bridge to—

Kenmare

Distances.—Glengarriff 17, Killarney 21, Macroom 35, Dublin 211, Cork 58.
Early Closing.—Thursday.
Golf.—9-hole course.

Hotels.—*Great Southern* (60 rooms), *Lansdowne Arms* (14), *Central* (10), *Wander Inn* (10).
Population.—1,113.

Kenmare is a small market town at the head of the beautiful estuary of the same name. It is about half-way between Glengarriff and Killarney (buses running between these places daily during the season) and the terminus of the Kerry coast tour. Kenmare is an excellent tourist centre, and the district offers good angling, shooting, bathing and climbing.

Originally known as *Nedeen*, it owes its existence to Sir William Petty, the ancestor of the Marquis of Lansdowne. Petty, having obtained a grant of land, planted a colony of Englishmen here in 1670. They established a fishery and iron-works on an extensive scale, but were harassed by the Irish, and surrendering after some resistance were allowed to embark for Bristol scantily supplied with provisions. On the conquest of Ireland by William III, the colony was re-established and the fishery resumed; but the forests were soon exhausted, and the iron trade declined through want of fuel.

Kenmare consists of a main street leading from the market square, with a few others diverging from it. There is a good pier. The bay, or river, is crossed by a ferro-concrete bridge built on the cantilever principle. The Roman Catholic Church is a fine building, with a lofty spire. The adjoining **Convent of Poor Clares** is one of the best-known institutions in the town owing to the famous lace made there. Picturesquely situated on the shore of the Kenmare river is a good 9-hole golf course.

There are many beautiful drives about Kenmare—to **Derren** (16 miles) along the shore of Kenmare Bay, returning by the attractive upper road to **Headford**, with fine rock scenery; to **Windy Gap** on the Killarney road, and to **Goulane** on the old road to Killarney.

KENMARE TO KILLARNEY (21 miles)

From Kenmare the road ascends to **Moll's Gap**, where it turns eastward and in a few miles leaves **Loosecaumagh Lake** on its right. From here the scenery becomes more luxuriant, as Killarney comes into view (*see* p. 133). The road skirts **Upper Lake, Long Range** and **Middle Lake,** with **Torc Mountain** and **Torc Waterfall** on the right, Muckross House and gardens on the left, and finally crosses **Flesk Bridge** to **Killarney** (38 miles from Glengarriff).

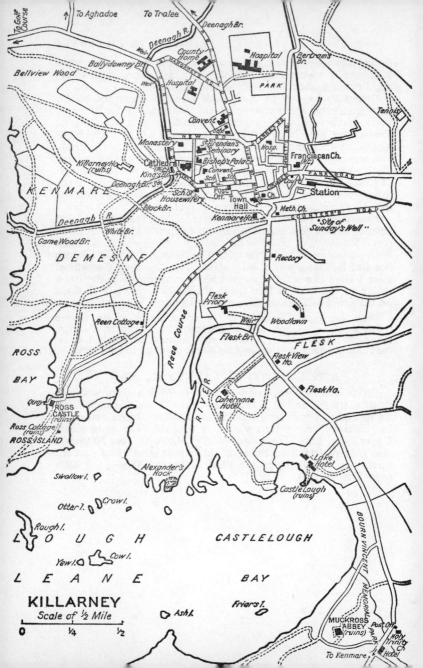

KILLARNEY
♣♣♣♣♣♣♣♣♣♣

Access.—Served by bus and rail from most areas. Through trains to and from Dublin (not Sundays), Cork and Tralee.

Angling.—Fishing is free on all three lakes. Salmon, trout and perch are to be had. Season, 17th January–12th October. A small charge is made for a 12-mile stretch of river fishing. Apply Secretary, *Lough Leane Anglers' Association.*

Banks.—*Munster and Leinster*, Church Place; *National*, New Street; *Provincial*, Main Street.

Bathing.—At Bunrower, Sandybottom, Fossa, Western Demesne and other places along the lake shore.

Churches, etc.—*Church of Ireland*: Parish Church of St. Mary; Holy Trinity, Muckross; Aghadoe Church. *Methodist. St. Mary's Roman Catholic Cathedral. Franciscan Church.*

Cinema.—*Casino.*

Dancing.—Town Hall, *Gleneagle's*, and at various hotels. Exhibitions of Irish dancing twice weekly.

Distances.—Dublin 191, Cork 54, Belfast 271, Bantry 49, Kenmare 21, Limerick 68, Parknasilla 31, Sneem 29, Waterville 51.

Early Closing.—Thursday.

Golf.—First-class 18-hole golf course on northern shore of Lough Leane.

Hotels.—*Europe* (92 rooms), *Great Southern* (200), *Cahernane* (40), *Castlerosse* (40), *International* (120), *Lake* (72), *Muckross* (42), *Arbutus* (30), *Glen Eagle* (63), *Belvedere* (14), *Grand* (30), *Scott's* (28), *Castlerosse Hotel* (40), *White Gates Guest House* (10) and many others.

Population.—6,800.

Post Office.—New Street.

Racing.—Killarney races held in May and July. Racecourse on Ross Road.

Shooting.—(On payment) for woodcock, pheasant, grouse, wild duck, wild geese and snipe.

Tennis.—Courts at several of the hotels.

Theatre.—Repertory at Town Hall.

Tours, etc.—Motor coach tours start from the Railway Station for the Dingle Peninsula and the Beara Peninsula. There are many organized tours by car and boat, and by jaunting cars taking one to four passengers and visiting lesser known parts of the district. Ponies and bicycles are available for hiring. Killarney offers the climber and hill walker the finest mountain climbing in Ireland; guides are available.

Youth Hostel.—Aghadoe House. Next nearest hostel at Black Valley, 9 miles.

Killarney is a fair-sized market town and a centre of some activity on this account, but it owes its fame principally to its situation in a district of some of the loveliest scenery and most beautiful excursions in Ireland, or indeed in the British Isles. It is set in the valley of the river Flesk about a mile from Lough Leane, the largest of the world-famous Lakes of Killarney. Though there are few buildings of importance in the town the small streets have nonetheless a distinct charm of their own. Killarney is greatly dependent on the tourist industry and there are good comfortable hotels and numerous guest houses.

The **Parish Church of St. Mary** (Church of Ireland) is in the Early English style, and stands on the ancient site of *Cill Airne* (the Church of Airne). There is also a Methodist Church.

133

The **Catholic Cathedral (St. Mary's),** designed by Pugin, is a limestone building in revised Gothic style containing a fine organ. It is cruciform in shape, with a massive square central tower and fine spire. The Earls of Kenmare are buried here, the sixth being better known as Viscount Castlerosse, journalist and director of the *Daily Express* newspaper. Adjoining the Cathedral is the **Bishop's Palace.**

The **Franciscan Friary** and **Church** stand in ornamental grounds near the railway station. Opposite stands a memorial to four Kerry poets—Pierce Ferriter (1653), Geoffrey O'Donoghue (1677), Aodhgan O'Rahilly (1728) and Eoghan Ruadh O'Sullivan (1784).

There are three **Convents** (Sisters of Mercy, Presentation, and Loreto) and a Presentation Monastery, each with schools attached. The **Diocesan Seminary of St. Brendan** is close to the Cathedral. The Sisters of the Presentation Convent excel in making Irish lace and art needlework, and visitors are always welcome to see the work in progress and to make purchases. The proceeds are devoted to the maintenance of the convent. There is a **Technical School** near the Post Office.

Of the private residences the chief is **Kenmare House,** replacing a former mansion destroyed by fire in 1913. The site is on the crest of a hill at the west end of the town. Surrounding it is a splendid park of vast extent skirting the Lower Lake.

Muckross House, an Elizabethan mansion in white Portland stone, overlooks the Middle Lake and is close to Muckross Abbey. The vast estate was given to the Irish nation by the last owners, and it is now known officially as the **Bourne-Vincent Park** or **National Park.** (*See* page 139).

Flesk Castle and **Southhill House** occupy high positions a little to the south of the town. The castle has been partly demolished by its owner, only the walls now remaining. **Lake View House** and **Aghadoe House** are on the northern shore of the Lower Lake. The latter was burned down during the Irish unrest, and is now re-built as a Youth Hostel.

Cahernane House, beyond the Flesk, has now been converted into a hotel. Originally it was the mansion of a branch of the Herbert family.

Many shops make a great display of articles manufactured from bog-oak and the wood of the arbutus, and these, together with the lace made here, are favourite souvenirs of a visit to Killarney. Several new local industries have established themselves in recent years.

THE KILLARNEY LAKES

The world-famed Lakes of Killarney are situated in the county of Kerry—the fourth in size and most romantic in character of Irish counties. It includes within its borders the most westerly point of Europe and the highest of the Irish mountains, Carrantuohill, 3,414 feet above sea-level ("The top of Ireland").

The great charm of Killarney is the infinite variety of its scenery. The extraordinary wealth of trees and rare flowering plants, in some places growing apparently out of the solid rock, the noble shapes and great height of the mountains, and the varied and gorgeous colouring, are the first things to impress one in Killarney.

The finest general view of the lake country is that from the high ridges at the southern end of the Upper Lake, on the road from Kenmare.

There are three lakes—the **Upper Lake, Middle** or **Muckross Lake,** and **Lower Lake** or **Lough Leane.** The Upper and Middle Lakes are connected by a tortuous stream, the **Long Range,** ending in the rapids under the Old Weir Bridge.

The lakes, fed by many mountain streams, lie in a valley bounded by the Tomies and Purple Mountains on one side and the Fordal-Torc-Mangerton group on the other. The Lower Lake or Lough Leane is 5 miles long by 2–3 miles broad, and has thirty islands, large and small. The Middle Lake has four, and the Upper, whose water is 5 feet higher than that of the other lakes, has eight. The Lower Lake discharges into the Atlantic by the river Laune at Castlemaine Harbour.

The lakes are described in connection with the Killarney excursions detailed on following pages.

KILLARNEY EXCURSIONS
✤✤✤✤✤✤✤✤✤✤✤✤✤✤✤✤✤✤✤✤✤✤✤✤✤✤✤✤✤

The name *Cill Airne*, "the Church of St. Airne," stands for the whole of the mountainous and romantic district around the lakes.

Scattered throughout the district are found numerous memorials of the greatness or piety of the past—the stone circles in which the Druids celebrated their mysterious rites; the venerable abbeys of Aghadoe, Innisfallen and Muckross; the ivy-clad ruins of Castles. These enhance and blend with the views of woods and lakes.

We give a description of some of the chief tours: of these, the Gap of Dunloe, with the row back down the three lakes, is almost the only one that requires a whole day.

I.—Gap of Dunloe—Black Valley—Logan Stone—Upper Lake —Long Range—Old Weir Bridge—Middle Lake

Leaving the town by New Street, we pass on the right the Cathedral and the Bishop's Palace, and half a mile farther reach **Ballydowney.** Soon the Lower Lake and the towering mountains come into view, and on the hill to the right can be seen the ruins of Aghadoe (*see* p. 144). On the northern shore of the Lower Lake we turn to the left, and crossing the river *Laune* by a bridge are shortly in full view of the celebrated Gap of Dunloe. The road turns sharply to the left. On the right is **Dunloe Castle,** on the summit of a small hill. Originally erected for the defence of the Gap, it withstood some severe struggles during the reigns of Henry VIII and Elizabeth I. In the grounds is a group of Ogham Stones, from a souterrain discovered in 1838.

Gap of Dunloe. We now reach the entrance to the renowned Gap of Dunloe, a wild gorge some 4 miles long running almost due south, strewn with boulders, and separating the Macgillicuddy Reeks from the Tomies and Purple Mountains. The gates of this romantic and gloomy valley are almost perpendicular rocks, which in places approach so closely that they scarcely allow room for the road. Vehicles usually stop at **Kate Kearney's Cottage.** From here, the journey is generally continued on foot or on ponies, though cars can continue as far as *Arbutus Cottage.*

Along the valley great rocks rise on either side in wild confusion apparently ready to topple over and crush the visitor. The narrow torrent is twice crossed by the road, the brawling waters intensifying the desolate but impressive character of the scene. Huge boulders appear above the path,

and shattered fragments of rock strew the mountain slopes. The **Purple Mountain,** with all its chromatic beauties; the **Tomies,** with glowing lights and intense shadows; the **Reeks,** with their aspiring summits; then the black unruffled lakelets, cold and silent, combine to make a picture which has no equal in Killarney. It is a scene of utter solitude and desolation. The small Loe stream crosses the valley, expanding in places into gloomy sheets of water known as the **Cummeen Thomeen Lakes,** remarkable for their inky blackness. The most southerly, **Black Lough** (a direct translation of Lough Dubh) or the **Serpent Lake,** exceeds the others in this respect and in coldness. The other lakelets abound in fish, but this has none. The echoes at Cushvally Lough must not be missed. Repetitions spring from the mountains, caverns and hollows; a perfect torrent of thunder rushes from the peaks and ravines and is hurled back by the precipices of the Purple Mountain. The colouring of the Purple Mountain is often ascribed to the heather, but the name was really given because of the purple colouring of the slates and stones. This hill, 2,739 feet high, is best climbed from the Gap.

From the cottage, leaving **Auger Lake,** the road rises some 400 feet. Close to the first bridge, where the Gap narrows so as scarcely to leave room for the road and the stream, are some very curious rocks called the **Turnpike.** Here again are marvellous echoes. Then the pass widens.

At the Summit (795 feet) of the pass, we descend. The wooded valley of Gearhameen and the Upper Lake gradually come in sight: the contrast between the gloomy Gap and the lovely lakes is very marked. Lower down is a glorious view of the **Black Valley** (*Youth Hostel* 1 mile from Gap of Dunloe) (a mis-translation of *Cumeenduff*). This is an almost Alpine glen amidst precipitous mountains. Close to the road the **Logan Stone,** or Balance Rock, can be seen. There is good angling for salmon and trout on the Upper Larne. At the foot

137

of the hill the Black Valley road turns to the right. A detour along this is well worth the time spent. There are many lakes; the longest is **Lough Nabricderg,** or the Pool of the Red Trout—for these lakes abound with trout. Following the road along the course of the river, we make for what is still known as **Lord Brandon's Cottage,** whence a short path leads to the Upper Lake and the landing-stage.

This is also a good spot for the ascent of Purple Mountain, a boggy climb. The *Gearhameen* river runs between the Upper Lake and the Gap of Dunloe and gives lovely views of wooded foreground and great hills behind.

Before entering the woods of Gearhameen, or Gurmaheen, a branch road to the *right* leads through the lovely **Owenreagh Valley,** or glen. Cyclists and hikers should take this road. The surface is fairly good and the scenery nearly equal to what we have passed through. The road winds along by the bed of the river, with luxuriant undergrowth and great heights rising above. Often the road seems completely cut off by rocks and trees. At about 4½ miles a turn to the left over a bridge leads to the **Windy Gap,** on the Kenmare Road, whence there is a fine run to Killarney (14 miles). The more courageous can continue over the pass to **Lough Brin,** and thence to the Sneem road, returning (to the left) *via* the Windy Gap to Killarney. As an alternative, follow the Sneem road (right) to Geragh cross-roads, and thence north through the Ballaghbeama Gap, Glencar, Lough Acoose and Beaufort to Killarney.

The Upper Lake. Embarking and rowing down-stream we soon find ourselves on the Upper Lake at one time known as MacCarthy Mor's Lake, studded with islands and encircled by mountain-peaks. It was this Upper Lake that Sir Walter Scott considered the "grandest sight he had ever seen." **MacCarthy Mor's Island** is first of the twelve islands. Then comes **Ronayne's Island;** others include **Eagle Island, Oak** and **Juniper Islands,** and **Arbutus Island.** The exit from the lake is by a narrow channel called **Colman's Eye,** where the giant Colman is said to have leaped across and left the marks of his footprints on the rocks.

The Long Range connects the Upper and Middle Lakes and combines the beauty of all three. It is 2 miles in length. In places, yellow and white water lilies abound, and on the banks grow royal ferns (*Osmunda*) and strawberry trees (*Arbutus*). Winding through lovely scenes, we float down a placid stream above whose wooded shores the mountains rise majestically. There are many islands here, too, with fanciful names. Soon we reach the **Eagles' Nest,** a conical hill rising some 1,100 feet on the left. The base is covered with evergreen, and the naked summit forms a tremendous precipice. Here there is another famous echo.

Again we glide on, but the current grows swifter and the noise of rushing waters reaches the ear. Soon the **Old Weir Bridge** is in sight, and we near the arch, the waves splashing and gurgling. Now the boatmen give a stronger, firmer pull; then another, and the oars are shipped. We shoot the rapids, and in another moment are again in calm water. The stream divides, one channel skirting Dinis Island and entering Lough Leane, the other passing under the bridge into Muckross Lake, the spot also known as the **Meeting of the Waters.**

We land on **Dinis Island,** where we can have tea, and stay to admire the view of the old bridge and the tropical vegetation.

The Middle Lake. Re-embarking, we cross the Middle Lake, also called **Muckross Lake** and **Torc Lake.** The curious and picturesque **Colleen Bawn Caves,** on the northern shore, will interest the visitor. The story, play, and opera about Colleen Bawn are based on a real tragedy, but it did not occur here. These rocks are limestone and fantastically water-worn. On the south, **Torc** (1,764 feet), with its woods, may be seen. Rowing under Brickeen Bridge, we enter **Glena Bay,** and crossing the Lower Lake pass **Innisfallen Island** to land at Ross Castle. From here we may return to Killarney by road.

II.—Muckross Abbey and Park—Dinis Island—Meeting of the Waters—Torc Waterfall

Leaving Killarney by the Kenmare road, we cross **Flesk Bridge** and reach in 2 miles the entrance to **Bourn Vincent Memorial Park** on the right. Cars and motor-cycles may enter as far as the entrance to Muckross House (car park). Muckross means "the promontory of the wild swine." About half a mile from the entrance, in the Park, are the ruins of Muckross Abbey.

Muckross Abbey (or Friary) is more correctly described as the Friary of Irrelagh, or Oir Bhealash (Erva-Lock), meaning "the Eastern Pass or way." The Abbey is said to occupy the site of a church destroyed by fire in 1172; no more beautiful site could have been chosen. It was founded by MacCarthy Mor (pronounced More, meaning "great"), the famous Irish chieftain, for the Franciscan Friars c. 1448. It was formally suppressed in 1542 by Henry VIII, and again by Elizabeth in 1585, but from an inscription on a tablet inserted into the north chancel wall it would appear that the Abbey was repaired in 1626.

The Friars continued in occupation until 1652, when the Abbey was destroyed by Ludlow, Cromwell's general, who also captured and destroyed Ross Castle (p. 142). The building comprises both Church and Monastery, the whole being known as the Abbey. Its venerable associations and picturesque situation make it one of the most interesting places in Killarney, if not in the whole of Ireland.

A beautiful doorway forms the entrance to the nave of the **Church,** which is 100 feet long and about 25 feet wide. In the centre is a strong, square tower rising from lofty arches. The beautiful east window of the chancel is seen through the Gothic arch of the tower or belfry. The window is divided into four lights by interlaced mullions. The High Altar was placed beneath the window, but no trace of it remains. The broken basin of the piscina, on a level with the present floor, can still be seen. The graves and tombs in the **Chancel** are the oldest in the Abbey. The large high tomb in the centre is that of the *O' Donoghues of the Glens.*

A narrow doorway on the left from the tower leads to the **Cloisters,** the best preserved and perhaps most interesting part. They form a square of 36 feet, surrounded by a vaulted corridor or ambulatory 7 feet wide. This is lighted by twelve semicircular arches on the east and south sides, and ten pointed ones on the west and north, springing from double columns. The arches and pillars are of grey limestone. In the centre of the square is a magnificent **Yew-tree**, which, tradition asserts, was planted by the friars at the foundation of the Abbey. It has now been weathered to half its former height, but its spreading branches fill the whole of the enclosure.

From the Cloisters three flights of stone steps lead from the angles of the ambulatory to the living apartments on the first floor of the Monastery. These will be easily recognized, and consist of Kitchen, Refectory or Dining Room, and Dormitory. Close to the Tower is a smaller room where a stone channel for carrying the water from the roof of the church can be seen, built into the wall at one end. The library is supposed to have been over the Reception Room, but the floor has fallen in. Actually, few ruins in Ireland are in a better state of preservation than Muckross.

Returning to the main driveway, we continue through the—

Bourn Vincent Memorial Park. The former Muckross demesne, which included the greater part of the mountains, lakes, woods and glades that have made Killarney famous, was presented to the Irish nation as a national park by Mr. and Mrs. William Bowers Bourne of California, and their son-in-law, Mr. Arthur Vincent. It is the finest and certainly the most beautifully situated park in Ireland. Every foot of the way is of exquisite and varied beauty—with the lakes, hills, trees, ferns growing on walls and tree trunks, richly clothed islands, and wonderful distant views. The gardens of Muckross House are beautifully laid out. The *Lady's Walk*, along the shore of the Lower Lake, is one of the most beautiful walks in Killarney.

The next left turn leads to **Muckross House and Gardens** (*all the year daily*). To the right is **The Denis Road** running through a peninsula, about 3 miles in length, separating the Lower from the Middle Lake. After passing the lakelet of **Doolagh,** and the **Colleen Bawn Rock** (in the Middle Lake, on the left), we see the workings of some old copper mines. The undulating road now brings us to **Brickeen Bridge** ("bridge of the little trout"). Here the Middle Lake discharges into the Lower Lake, the difference in the levels of the waters being only one foot.

Another mile brings us to **Dinis Island and Cottage** with its luxuriant vegetation and tropical plants. At the **Cottage** (which, with the Colleen Bawn Rock and the curious Caves, was rendered famous by Boucicault's play *The Colleen Bawn* and Benedict's opera the *Lily of Killarney*) refreshments can be obtained.

From near the cottage there is a charming view of the picturesque **Old Weir Bridge** over the famous rapids. Here the waters from the Upper Lake and the Long Range divide, running on the right to the Lower Lake, on the left of the Middle Lake. The spot has been called **The Meeting of the Waters.**

Following the footpath to the right, we reach the whirlpool known as **O'Sullivan's Punch Bowl,** where there is a very fine echo. Returning and following the stream to the Middle Lake, we come to the rustic structure known as the **Toothache Bridge,** so called from the legend that whoever touches his gums with the waters flowing beneath will never suffer from toothache. Outside the iron gate a path through the wood leads to the Old Weir Bridge.

Returning to the car, we now follow the road that skirts the Middle Lake for a mile and then joins the main road from Kenmare to Killarney (p. 131). Soon we arrive at a gate lodge, from which a path leads to the—

Torc Waterfall. A walk of less than ten minutes through a glade with some of the finest fir-trees in the district leads to the fall. Though the noise of the waters is heard from some distance, the fall is completely concealed until one is quite close; then, through a vista in the leafy screen, it bursts on the eye in all its beauty, plunging down a rock some 60 feet in height. A winding path, with many seats mounts high over the fall and affords a view of the upper reaches of the stream. Near the top a magnificent panorama is seen of the Middle and Lower Lakes, with their guardian mountains, winding shores, and fairy islands.

The return to Killarney is continued *via* **Muckross Village,** which is 2½ miles from Killarney. The hotels here make excellent centres, being close to Muckross Abbey and the Memorial Park and within walking distance of Torc Waterfall and Dinis Island. The little church of **Killeghie,** close by, enjoys the reputation of being one of the smallest in Ireland. The word signifies the "Church of Death" and the building was plainly intended as a mortuary chapel.

III.—Eagles' Nest—Tunnel—Lady's View

This excursion is another and very beautiful way of touring the three Lakes. The latter part of the tour resembles that of Route I, but no rough walk through the Gap of Dunloe is involved as we arrive at the Upper Lake from the opposite direction. *Arrangements must be made for a boat to be waiting at Derrycunnihy.*

Starting from Killarney, we take the Muckross road, with Torc mountain (1,764 feet) and the more distant Mangerton (2,756 feet) on our left. After skirting the southern shore of Middle Lake we bear left. There are splendid views of the mountains as we drive by the Long Range, the stream connecting the Upper with the Middle or Torc Lake. The Eagles' Nest Mountain (1,100 feet high) is on the opposite shore, richly clothed with verdure for the greater part, though the summit is bare. The road now ascends, reaching 2 miles farther on **The Tunnel,** an arch cut through an enormous rock under which the road passes. From the top of the tunnel one of the finest views of the Upper Lake and its islands and surrounding hills is gained, the background formed by the rugged summits of the Reeks, Carrantuohill rising like a dome above the other jagged peaks, with the Black Valley at its base. The **Upper Lake** is the smallest of the lakes—2½ miles long by ½ mile broad—but many consider it the most beautiful. On the opposite bank may be seen the pathway leading from the Gap of Dunloe to the landing-place, and the mountain streams flashing down the furrows of the Purple Mountain.

About a mile farther we reach **Derrycunnihy,** "the oak wood of the rabbits". Taking the steep, rough passage to the right, we are presently in what many consider the prettiest spot in Killarney. In the midst of dense foliage a cascade, less high but wider than the Torc Waterfall, plunges down a deep, rocky chasm.

Before we leave our car, however, we continue the journey along the main road. We pass the Chapel, and in about a mile come to the old Mulgrave Police Barrack, which was known as the most beautifully situated police station in the world. About 200 yards farther we reach a point, a little to the right of the road, called **The Lady's View** affording a good long panorama of the three lakes, the long Range Looscanagh Lake a little farther on, and the mountains. This is the farthest point of the tour, but the road continues to Kenmare, branching off at **Moll's Gap** for Sneem. We now return the short distance to Derrycunnihy—just described—where a boat may be taken for the trip through the Upper Lake, Long Range, Middle and Lower Lake to Ross Castle, as described in the tour through the Gap of Dunloe (p. 136).

IV.—Lower Lake—Ross Castle—Ross Island—Innisfallen Abbey and Island—Mahony's Point—O'Sullivan's Cascade— Glena Bay

The Lower Lake is studded by some thirty islands of varying form and character, some luxuriant with foliage, others barren rocks. The Lake is more than 5 miles long by about 3 broad; its proper name is **Lough Leane** ("the lake of learning"), probably derived from the fact that there were three religious establishments on its shores, viz. Muckross, Aghadoe, and Innisfallen.

Though its surroundings are not so grand as those of the Upper Lake, many prefer the Lower Lake to the other two.

Leaving Killarney by the Muckross road we take the first turning on the right, and reach in a mile and a half—

Ross Castle (*small charge*) a noble and picturesque ruin in a lovely situation and still in fairly good preservation. Tennyson is said to have written part of *The Princess* here. This stately keep was probably built by an Anglo-Norman baron in the fourteenth century, and it is commonly referred to as an O'Donoghue stronghold. The event for which Ross Castle is memorable in history is its siege by and surrender to General Ludlow in 1652. The strength of the place and the difficulty of approaching it would probably have tested the endurance of the Cromwellian troops had not the garrison been intimidated by an ancient prophecy that the castle would be impregnable until it was attacked by ships of war.

> "And Rosse may all assault disdain,
> Till on Lough Lein strange ship shall sail."

It is said that armed vessels were built at Kinsale and Bandon and transported overland to the lake.

The Keep is nearly perfect; it consists of a massive square tower with a spiral stone staircase. A fine view can be had from the top. Originally the keep was enclosed by an embattled curtain wall, having round flanking towers at each side.

Ross Island (*Toll*), actually a peninsula, runs out into the lake for

more than half a mile. A road (over 2 miles long) connects it with the town, and a drive runs through the Kenmare estate and leads to the point opposite Innisfallen Island known as the **Library,** so called from the fantastic appearance of the Rocks, the shape of which resembles books. The disused workings of the copper mines can be seen about half a mile from the Castle, on the south. There are pools of intensely green water. The area of the island is 164 acres, and it is about a mile in length.

Innisfallen Island. This is certainly the most charming of the isles on Lough Leane. Several of the groves are so luxuriant as to be almost impenetrable. The holly tree is extraordinarily luxuriant, evergreens abound, and the scarlet clusters of the mountain ash are as fresh and delicate as the arbutus berry. The island lies about half a mile from the shore, at Library Point, and covers 21 acres.

The ruins of **Innisfallen Abbey,** near the landing-stage, show that it was at one time very extensive. The Abbey was built in the sixth century by St. Faithlenn and afterwards inhabited by Canons-Regular of the order of St. Augustine, who compiled the celebrated *Annals of Innisfallen,* which with the *Annals of Tighernach* (who died A.D. 1088), form the real history of Ireland after the introduction of Christianity.

The *Annals of Innisfallen* were composed *circa* 1215 to 1320, but were begun two centuries earlier by Maelsuthain O'Cearbhaill (or Maelsochan O'Carroll), "the chief Doctor of the Western world," who died in A.D. 1009.

The little Church, or **Oratory,** with the sculptured doorway, which stands apart, on the right, on a low cliff overhanging the shore of the Lake, is said to be older than the **Abbey** ruins, and is regarded as a good example of the Hiberno-Romanesque style of architecture.

Leaving the Island, we row across the Lake to **Mahony's Point**

143

and **Cottage,** delightfully situated under the shadow of Aghadoe. Surrounded by exquisite shrubs, there is a most imposing avenue of magnificent trees forming a huge canopy extending to the water's edge. Here is a fine 18-hole golf course.

From here we proceed along the Fossa or north-western shore past Lake View House to the mouth of the *Laune,* which drains Killarney Lakes into the sea, and down this river to Dunloe Castle and Cave (*see* p. 136).

Heading our boat for the lake again we proceed along the Tomies shore in all its wonderful beauty to **O'Sullivan's Cascade.** The total height is about 70 feet divided into three leaps. The fall, with its beautiful surroundings, is perhaps the finest in the district. Beneath a projecting rock is a little grotto, overarched by trees, from which the view of the fall is very fine.

Returning to the boat we skirt the shore of **Tomies Mountain** (2,413 feet) and passing the rock on the mountain side known as the **Minister's Back,** and **Stag Island, Burnt Island** and **Darby's Garden,** enter the beautiful **Glena Bay.** The name signifies "the glen of good fortune." The scenery is almost equal to that of Innisfallen, and certainly is unsurpassed by any shore view on the Lower Lake.

From this point the **Shehy Mountain** (1,820 feet) can be ascended. **Glena Mountains,** really a part of the Purple Mountain, are the haunt of the red deer, which may frequently be seen near the water's edge at the Upper Lake and the Long Range.

From here we can proceed, if time permits, by the Back Channel to Dinis and the Middle Lake, and then return to Ross Castle.

If the return is made direct from Ross Castle the drive back to Killarney by the high road goes through banks of rhododendrons for over a mile.

V.—Aghadoe—Ross Castle—Ross Island

Leave the town *via* High Street and the Tralee Road, and at Cleeny (about three-quarters of a mile) turn left straight up the steep ascent of the **Madam's Height.** At the top turn left again, and proceed directly to the—

Ruins of Aghadoe (pronounced Ah-ā-doe), 2½ miles distant. The word means the "field of the Two Yews." The view of the lakes and mountains from here is very fine, and no more beautiful site for a church could have been found than that occupied by this shrine, of which so little is known.

The ruins of Aghadoe consist of a round tower, church and castle. Only part of the lower storey of the **Round Tower** remains. The stones, laid in regular courses, are large and well dressed; the masonry is much better than that of either the adjacent church or castle.

The **Castle,** or "military tower," also called **"The Pulpit,"** to the south of the church, is about 30 feet high; the walls are 6 feet thick and contain a flight of stairs within. The castle stands in an earthen enclosure and evidently belongs to a very early date.

The **Church** is 80 feet long by 23 broad. It consists of nave and choir,

Thomond Bridge over Shannon, Limerick

Kilkee, Co. Clare

Killary Harbour, Co. Galway

Ennistymon, Co. Clare

divided by a wall once pierced by a door. The nave is believed to date from the seventh century, the choir from the thirteenth. As a matter of fact, the church is really two buildings (though now joined) of different periods—the eastern church or choir is much later and is in the Pointed style; the other and earlier is in the Hiberno-Romanesque style, built long before the arrival of the Normans. In the south wall of the nave is an Ogham stone.

Continuing our journey, we pass the modern church of Aghadoe and Aghadoe House (a Youth Hostel). We can take the direct road into Killarney at the foot of the hill, or pass through the West Demesne and golf links, and skirting the lake for a considerable distance arrive at Ross Castle. We then drive round Ross Island (p. 143), and afterwards return to the town.

VI.—Druidical Remains at Lissivigeen—Glenflesk—Robber's Den—Lough Guitane

The district known as Glenflesk to the south-east of Killarney, is well worth visiting. This beautiful glen, richly timbered, is about 7 miles to the south-east of Killarney. One leaves Killarney by the main road to Cork, and after about two miles a turning to the left, near Woodford Bridge, leads to Lissivigeen Stone Circle, or the "Seven Sisters." The stones are about 3 feet high; the average breadth is the same. They enclose a circle 17 feet in diameter and are placed within a rath 78 feet in diameter.

Regaining the road and crossing the railway, we see the ruins of Killaha Castle on high ground to the right. This was formerly a stronghold of the O'Donoghues and commanded the entrance to Glenflesk. The remains of the old Church are close by.

Two miles beyond the Glenflesk Chapel is Filadown, a picturesque spot once the retreat of a celebrated outlaw, Owen MacCarthy.

A return to Killarney may be made by the road skirting the northern shore of Lough Guitane (the lake of the little cot or boat), a lovely and lonely lake some 5 miles round, lying under the shadow of Stoompa, a mountain 2,281 feet high. The lake has four islands. Both the lake and the river which flows from it afford the angler good sport. Surrounded by barren hills, gloomy glens and weird rocks, Guitane would anywhere be considered a remarkable lake. The ravine behind it, between Mangerton and Crohane hills, is called Coomnageehy "the Valley of the Winds."

VII.—Ascent of Mangerton (2,756 feet). No other excursion will give the tourist so good an idea of Killarney. Though the hill itself is rounded and less picturesque than many, the views from it are very grand. The path is fairly plain. The distance is about 7 miles; cars can go rather less than half-way, but ponies make the entire journey.

The route is through Muckross Village, where we turn to the left and after about 2 miles of varying ascent reach a stream where the road ends, giving place to a very rough pathway. Cars can go as far as this point.

About a mile on, we come in sight of Lough Guitane (p. 145). The mountain now becomes bleak and rugged, but more and more interesting, the views increasing in grandeur as we go higher. After some tough climbing we reach a plateau, and another half-mile brings us to the curious lake on the west of Mangerton known as the Devil's Punch Bowl.

The Devil's Punch Bowl is a deep-set tarn 2,200 feet above sea-level. It is about a quarter of a mile long, deep down in a dark gorge, and looking from the overhanging steeps intensely black. The water is icy cold and as unrippled as if it were frozen. No fish are found in it. The echo is fine, but rather peculiar; it seems to ring round and round as it bounds and rebounds from rock to rock. The Punch Bowl is supposed to be the crater of an extinct volcano, and is over 700 feet deep. It supplies Killarney with water. At one point the Devil's Stream emerges through a great chasm and falls to form, lower down, the Torc Cascade. From the Punch Bowl the ascent to the summit is easy, for we tread on peaty soil.

The return can be made by the descent south to Kilgarvon, or *via* the rocky ridge to the Horse's Glen on the east.

VIII.—Ascent of Carrantuohill (3,414 feet). Though the view from the summit of Carn Tual, more correctly, Carrantuohill ("the inverted reaping-hook"), is not finer than that from Mangerton, the climb is perhaps a greater favourite, for Carn Tual is 658 feet higher. The name comes from the curious serrated shape of the edge as it is seen from Killarney, with the great masses of projecting saw-like teeth set backwards. It is the highest mountain in Ireland. The lakes are not visible from its summit, but the view of the hills is very fine.

The mountain is about 15 miles south-westward from Killarney. The road leads by the northern shore of the Lower Lake, crosses the Laune at **Beaufort Bridge** and turns to the right at the village. Take the next turning to the left, following a beaten track by the side of a stream—the Gaddagh—and the road gradually winds up among the mountains, the peak being in view all the time. A guide can be engaged here, though experienced climbers should have no difficulty in following the well-defined tracks. The sudden descent of mist can, however, prove disconcerting. Continuing for about two miles we reach, on the right, the **Hag's Glen**, some 2 miles long, and farther on are two gloomy lakelets where the hag is said to bathe and to wash her clothes. The path becomes rougher and steeper, and we have to climb the course of a mountain stream known as the **Devil's Ladder.** Some caution is necessary, as the stones and boulders are easily displaced. Having scaled the "ladder," we reach the summit (3,414 feet) easily in half an hour. It is crowned by a little cairn, the first stone of which was placed by King Edward VII, then Prince of Wales.

Another ascent is by a bridle road turning off to the right from the entrance to the Gap of Dunloe, or some prefer the ascent from Caragh Lake.

The return journey is usually made by the same path, but the descent can also be made on the southern side of the Reeks into the **Black Valley** (p. 137), which opens into the Gap of Dunloe. This is not easy, however, as the cliffs are steep and craggy.

ROUND THE KERRY COAST
✻✻✻✻✻✻✻✻✻✻✻✻✻✻✻✻✻✻✻✻✻✻✻✻✻✻✻✻

The Iveragh Peninsula—Ring of Kerry—Valentia Island— Cahirciveen to Parknasilla and Kenmare

The Kerry Peninsula (also known as the Iveragh Peninsula) lies between the bays of Dingle and Kenmare, and affords a variety of magnificent scenery. Surrounded by the coastal road—the "Ring of Kerry"—are some of the finest mountains in Ireland.

The Ring of Kerry road-circuit of 110 miles may be taken in the following direction: Killarney—Killorglin—Glenbeigh— Cahirciveen—Waterville—Parknasilla—Kenmare—Killarney.

From Killarney the road to **Killorglin** (13 miles) follows the Laune Valley, with fine view of the Reeks to the left. **Killorglin** is a small town, prettily situated and with the ruins of an old Knights Templar castle. The town is at its most lively and crowded during the annual *Puck Fair* on August 10–12th, when a billy goat or "puck" is enthroned.

For 26 miles the coastal road runs along the southern shore of beautiful Dingle Bay. On the opposite side of the estuary are the lofty hills of the Dingle Peninsula, and in the far distance **Brandon Mountain** (3,127 feet) raises its imposing height almost straight from the sea.

About 5 miles from Killorglin is—

Caragh Lake

a beautiful sheet of water, some 5 miles long and in places a mile across, with wooded banks and hills rising high beyond. The pretty river Caragh, connecting the lough with the sea, is famous for salmon and trout. There are at least seven fishing lakes within reach.

Good rough shooting—grouse, woodcock, snipe, duck, etc. —can be had in plenty on the neighbouring moors and mountains, for the shooting over some 25,000 acres is reserved for visitors. There is a 9-hole golf course at **Dooks,** some 3 miles away. This curious name means "sand dunes." Dooks is close to the sea, with an excellent strand for bathing. From Caragh one has the best view of **Carrantuohill** (3,414 feet), the highest mountain in Ireland (*see* p. 146).

All about are delightful walks or drives. A very pleasant short excursion is to drive or row to the south end of the lake to **Blackstones Bridge,** under which the river dashes down through masses of black rock.

Two miles or so southward from Blackstones is **Glencar** where there is a good hotel (*Glencar* (40 rooms)), on high ground in delightful woodland surroundings. The district is a paradise for anglers and climbers, and there is also a *Youth Hostel*.

Beyond Glencar is **Acoose Lake,** with the high road to Killarney running alongside. The water from **Coomloughra Lake,** 1,500 feet above the sea, flows through Lough Acoose.

Carrantuohill (3,414 feet) is a good four hours' expedition. On the very rough road up one sharp turn, awkward for cars and looking impossible for motor-coaches, is called the **Devil's Elbow.** The views become increasingly wide and beautiful— Caragh Lake and its many wooded islets are seen, and then from near the summit Killarney Lakes and mountain beyond mountain, the Reeks and many other hills, with a wild foreground. (*See* p. 146.)

Gortmacloran (nearly 1,000 feet), on the east side of the lake, will satisfy the less ambitious. Caragh river is fed by several streams rising on **Coomeragh** (2,355 feet).

A drive along the road to Waterville should be taken as far as **Ballaghisheen Pass**—a fine but severe climb. Another magnificent mountain drive is by the road southward through the **Ballaghbeama Pass** (pronounced Blocka-beama) on to Blackwater Bridge and Parknasilla (22 miles). The mountains rise precipitously some 1,500 feet on either side of the pass, which is 852 feet above sea-level and one of the wildest and most impressive in Ireland. Lough Brin lies below, and the road follows the wooded Blackwater till it enters the sea.

Another drive, a circular one, is round the east side of Caragh Lake to Blackstones Bridge, then through the **Windy Gap** (884 feet) to Glenbeigh, and then back.

Returning to the coastal road, beyond Dooks one comes to—

Glenbeigh

which is a growing and charming little watering-place with two good hotels (*The Hotel* (20 rooms), *Towers* (21 rooms)) and a fine strand of over 4 miles for bathing. The place takes its name from its situation at the mouth of the river *Beigh*, which rises some 5 miles south-westward in the crag-surrounded loughs known as Coomasaharn, Coomaglaslaw, and Coomna-cronia. **Coomasaharn Lake** is certainly worth a visit, on account of the great overhanging precipices. Here, too, there is good fishing, some of it free, and a 9-hole golf course.

Leaving Glenbeigh the road ascends and, rounding the mountain, comes close to the coast, giving fine views of Dingle Bay and its background of lofty mountains. We continue to ascend to **Mountain Stage** (so named from its having been the stage-house in the days of carts and coaches). The road seems to cling to the mountain-side and in places almost to overhang the sea. After some miles we reach **Kells,** overlooking a very pretty inlet of the bay. Then comes a long descent to Cahirciveen with the Iveragh mountains rising beyond, and Valentia river and Dingle Bay below.

Cahirciveen is built at the foot of the **Bentee** (1,649 feet). It is a thriving agricultural centre, with 1,649 inhabitants. (Hotels: *O'Connell's* (16 rooms), *Harp* (16 rooms)). It is an excellent locality for walking, climbing, driving and bathing. There are splendid trout streams and numerous lakes and salmon rivers, for the most part free and within a compass of 10 miles of the town. The sea fishing is excellent. There is also free shooting—grouse, snipe, cock, duck and plover—over an extensive area.

The only building of note is the extremely fine **Catholic Church,** dedicated to the memory of Daniel O'Connell, the "Liberator." About a mile away to the north-east is **Carhan House,** now in ruins, where O'Connell spent his childhood.

Across the estuary the ruins of the fifteenth-century **Ballycarbery Castle** can be plainly seen. The white strand at Ballycarbery, a beautiful stretch of silver sand, is an ideal bathing resort. It is a lovely sheltered cove quite free from currents and absolutely safe for bathing.

Beyond it to the north-west rises **Doulus Head** (400 feet high), a promontory on the far side of the estuary. There are great caves in these rocks and the waves are said to reach a greater height than at any other place in Ireland. About here, Finn, the mighty warrior, fought many of his battles, and there are a number of prehistoric forts, notably **Leacanabuaile Fort** at Kimego West, north of Ballycarbery Castle. This was excavated in 1939–40.

Within easy distance and under Knocknodober Mountain are two pretty inlets of Dingle Bay—**Coonanna** and **Cooncroum,** with small fishing harbours. At the latter, the cables from America come ashore, crossing thence to Valentia. They are visible at low tide. Desolate **Cloonaghlin Lake** and lovely **Derriana**—a mountain tarn with a pretty wooded islet and many water-lilies—are worth visiting from here, or more easily from Waterville.

From **Reenard,** the former rail terminus, a ferry crosses to Knightstown on—

Valentia Island

Hotel.—*Royal* (32 rooms), Knightstown.   Ferry.—Reenard to Knightstown.

The island is separated from the mainland by a strait less

than half a mile wide. It is about 7 miles in length by 3 miles broad and formerly belonged to the Knight of Kerry, after whom Knightstown is named. Most of the inhabitants live by farming and fishing. Its old name is "Dairbhe" ("Oaks").

The harbour is deep and sheltered, but the entrance is narrow; it used to be a favourite haunt of smugglers and pirates. The best cliff scenery is on the north of the island—the **Fogher Cliffs** are the finest.

An enjoyable stay can be made at Valentia. Between the two World Wars it was regarded as too remote for the ordinary tourist. Since 1945 it has been re-discovered, and in the high season the demand for accommodation far exceeds the supply. Bathing, boating, golfing and first-rate sea-fishing can be had, and the cliff scenery is magnificent. As might be expected from its westerly situation, the winter climate of the island is exceptionally mild.

The shores are indented with bays and cliffs and guarded by isolated rocks against which the waves of the Atlantic surge with uncontrolled fury. **Bray Head,** with a rebuilt signal tower and steep black cliffs, the most westerly point, rises steeply 792 feet above the sea; from it there is a glorious view. Eight miles to the south the Skelligs loom like pyramids above the ocean, and all the islands in sight have an extraordinary and abrupt outline—stern, yet picturesque. Northward we see **Slea Head** and the Dingle Mountains, and the **Blasket Islands** rising over the waves, some looking like batteries and castles, others resembling Gothic houses.

There is a fine drive of about 2½ miles to the Slate Quarries (no longer worked). The road from Knightstown mounts steadily, and gives good views of Glanleam and its lovely grounds below, with the sea and islands beyond and farther on the wireless station. From the old quarries a footpath on the mountain side should be followed for about half a mile, when grand views of the Fogher cliffs may be seen.

The **Lighthouse** (light visible 10 miles) at the entrance to the harbour between Valentia and Beginish (the little island), and the **Monument** (an Irish cross) to the memory of a Knight of Kerry, are both built on wild high ground. The lighthouse stands on **Cromwell's Fort,** as the headland is named, a reminder of the fact that the Protector erected forts at each end of the island to safeguard the coast and to prevent the captains of hostile privateers from using the island and its harbour as a hiding-place. At **Glanleam,** a private estate, formerly the seat of the Knight of Kerry, are some gigantic fuchsias. The climate is so mild that the myrtle, arbutus, tree ferns, and other tropical plants flourish.

Basaltic rock formation crops up on Beginish Island, at the entrance of Valentia Harbour. Here and in one other spot in Kerry are the only places where it is found throughout the south and west of Ireland. There are many caves in the rocks.

On **Church Island,** in Valentia Harbour, are the remains of an early monastery, an oratory, and some beehive cells.

Valentia has the distinction of being the east terminal station of the first Atlantic Cable. After three attempts a cable was successfully laid from the island in 1858 to Trinity Bay, Newfoundland. There are now several cables from the Cable Station at Knightstown.

A Trip to the Skelligs

These rocky, slate islands—"the most western of Christ's fortresses in the ancient world"—lie to the south of Valentia. A visit to them forms one of the most interesting sea-excursions possible, but can only be made in fair weather. It is from the sea that the precipitous headlands can really be best seen. Leaving Cahirciveen, or Knightstown, as the case may be, we go through the tortuous channel between the island and the mainland, and our exit to the ocean is made under the lofty cliffs of **Portmagee,** which rise steeply from the sea some 850 feet. There is a fish-curing station here. Then we pass **Puffin Island,** the **Lemon Rock,** and many others remarkable for their wildness.

The two islands, the **Great Skellig,** or **Skellig Michael,** and the **Little Skellig,** are about 12 miles from Portmagee. The **Little Skellig** is a bare, fantastic rock with a great arch under which the sea foams. This island is almost inaccessible, and is a gannet sanctuary. **Skellig Michael**—dedicated to St. Michael, the guardian against the powers of darkness and the patron saint of high places—is an enormous mass of precipitous slaty rock, with two pyramidal summits: one 714 feet high, the other 100 feet lower.

The landing-place is a little cavern in a cove on the north-east side. It is safe, however, only in fair weather, for the Atlantic waves often rise here to a height of 20 feet. This landing-place and the good path—guarded by a parapet—leading to the lighthouse have been made by the Commissioners of Irish Lights. This road runs about half-way round the island; a turn to the right near the lighthouse leads by a steep ascent to the upper part of the island. The old ascent up the face of the cliff, by some 620 stone steps cut in the face of the rock, was much more dangerous.

There is just one patch of green to relieve the bareness of the island: this is called **Christ's Saddle,** and from here the Way of the Cross with its fourteen stations was ascended by pilgrims. From here are two paths, one leading to the highest peak, the other to the ruins, for to this remote spot St. Finian and others retired for worship and meditation. On a plateau high up, with retaining walls on the steep cliff side, may be seen the still venerated remains of **St. Finian's Abbey**, with its arched stone roof. The ruins include six beehive cells —clinging as it were to the rocks, and of unmortared, dovetailed stones—two wells, an oratory, some burial-places, several rude crosses, and the more modern **Church of St. Michael.** On a projecting crag at the summit is a cross; it used to be an act of great devotion and some danger to crawl along the pinnacle and kiss the cross.

This remote spot was devastated by the Danes in 812, and the monks were left to starve in their cells. The **Lighthouse** (46 feet high) on the Great Skellig is 175 feet over the sea, and the light (a triple white flash every 10 seconds) is visible 18 miles away.

CAHIRCIVEEN TO WATERVILLE

The drive along the western and southern coast of Co. Kerry is extremely interesting. At first there are fine views of Valentia Island and the Bay; the road then turns inland. Three miles from Cahirciveen we pass the branch road **to Portmagee,** and after a further 2 miles, the branch road to **Ballinskelligs.** Continuing on the main road, we reach the sea again, and the road crosses the *Inny*, a fine salmon and trout river that drains a large district and falls into Ballinskelligs Bay. Two miles farther, passing the Cable Station, we reach—

Waterville

Hotels.—*Southern Lake* (59 rooms), Population.—600.
  Butler Arms (71), *Bay View* (29). Early Closing.—Wednesday.

The village of Waterville stands on a neck of land between the sea and beautiful Lough Currane (accent on second syllable). It is a tempting holiday resort, commanding magnificent sea, mountain and lake views. There is excellent sea-bathing and a fine level strand. The 9-hole Golf Links are about a mile from the village.

Waterville is a favourite angler's resort, for the district is famous for salmon and trout in the many lakes and rivers, and for sea-fishing. Fishing is for the most part free. Hotel visitors have the exclusive right of fishing in preserved rivers, and free shooting—grouse, snipe, cock, duck and plover—over an extensive area.

Ballinskelligs, on the other side of the Bay and at the end of the peninsula, has a good hotel (*Sigerson Arms* (13 rooms)) and a Youth Hostel, a lovely strand with safe bathing, good sea fishing, and fine coast scenery.

A few minutes' walk from Waterville is—

Lough Currane, about 17¼ miles in circumference and, next to the Lower Lake at Killarney, the largest in Co. Kerry. There are several small islands. On the largest, **Church Island,** are the ruins of an oratory, and at the other side of the island is a beehive hut built by St. Finian in the sixth century. The oratory (probably of the twelfth century) is a fine example of Hiberno-Romanesque work with its elaborately carved pillars.

Lough Currane—said to be the best early angling water in Ireland —is fed by the river *Cummeragh,* the outlet of **Lough Derriana** and **Lough Cloonaghlin** and other mountain tarns, which can all be visited from Waterville. They abound in trout, and salmon may also be taken in Lough Currane and the River Inny.

There is a delightful drive of about 5 miles along the shore of Lough Currane to **Lough Coppal** ("the Horse lake").

From the upper end of Lough Coppal, a high pass—most of the way only possible on foot—leads across to Sneem and then to Staigue Fort. The drive to Lough Coppal (which also has trout) is by a well-made road, close to the lakes most of the way, with high rocks overhanging it in places and many perched blocks.

Excursions from Waterville

1. By car to **Derrynane,** where a pleasant walk of about a mile and a half along the shore of Derrynane Bay leads to Lord Dunraven's cottage.

2. Drive along the side of Lough Currane by the **Ivy Bridge,** cross the **Coomeragh** and go on to **Isknamaclery Lake;** which has a view also of Lough Namibrachdarrig on the right and of Loughs Namona and Cloonaghlin on the left. A walk on to **Derriana Lake** can be taken, or a drive back along the Coomeragh to Derriana Lodge and so to Waterville.

3. Drive to **St. Finian's Glen,** noting the fine view of the Iveragh Moun-

tains, the Macgillicuddy Reeks, and later the Skelligs. The return can be made by Bolus Head, visiting the ruins of **St. Michael's Abbey,** Ballinskelligs Castle and the Atlantic Cable Station.

4. **Staigue Fort.** This route is the same as that already described along Lough Currane for some 6 miles to Lough Coppal—from here a 4-mile *walk* leads to the fort. The return can be by road *via* West Cove and Derrynane.

5. There is a splendid drive between Waterville and Caragh Lake, through Ballaghisheen Pass (*see* p. 148).

WATERVILLE TO PARKNASILLA

Leaving Waterville, we begin the finest and most beautiful part of the drive. The road winds upwards for about 3 miles, till at **Coomakesta Pass** it is 700 feet above the sea. It would be difficult to imagine a finer view than that seen from the top of the pass.

Between Waterville and Derrynane four huge *Standing Stones* may be seen on the left-hand side, just off the main road.

The road descends for 5 miles to the shore at **Derrynane Bay,** a small inlet of the Atlantic separated from Ballinskelligs Bay by Hog's Head and from the Kenmare estuary by Lamb's Head. The romantically situated ruins of **Derrynane Abbey** are on the pretty Abbey Island—or peninsula, for it is only at high tide that it is surrounded by water. The monastery is said to have been founded in the sixth century by St. Finian, but the ruins are no older than the thirteenth century. Derrynane means "Finian's Oak Wood."

Before reaching Caherdaniel a detour to the right leads by a steep descent to **Derrynane House** the home of Daniel O'Connell. It is an irregular pile of buildings, partly castellated.

Caherdaniel is pleasantly situated—the old fort or cahir is pre-Christian. The road continues past **West Cove** and **Castlecove** (*West Cove Guest*), inlets of the Kenmare river. Just above West Cove is the ruined *Church of St. Crohane.*

Staigue Fort. A turning to the left near West Cove leads in 2¾ miles to Staigue Fort, a prehistoric stone fort and one of the most perfect antiquities of its kind in Ireland. It is supposed to be at least 2,000 years old, and has been attributed to the Phoenicians. Modern archaeologists, however, are inclined to hold that it was built by some more ancient resident people for defence against both human and animal foes. It stands on a commanding eminence about 500 feet above the sea. The walls are of unmortared schistose stones, 15 feet thick at the base, narrowing to 7 at the top, and 18 feet high. The fort is 84 feet in diameter on the inside and 114 outside. The visitor will be struck with the massive masonry and the perfectly symmetrical building. It has one doorway and two small rooms in the thickness of the walls; several double flights of steps lead to the top.

The Kenmare River

or **Bay,** is an arm of the Atlantic penetrating inland for some 30 miles and giving good anchorage right up to Parknasilla. At the widest part it is 5 to 6 miles across. It is one of the most beautiful of the many bays which indent these shores, though some give preference to Bantry Bay. The road on towards Parknasilla is very winding, and there are generally numbers of Kerry cattle straying along it. About half-way a charming valley leads up to **Coomcallee** (2,134 feet), a sharp and precipitous mountain with a pretty lake at its foot.

Sneem, 22 miles from Waterville, is a village prettily situated at the head of the estuary formed by the *Sneem* river and two or three mountain streams. It contains a Roman Catholic church with a curious campanile, a Protestant church, a comfortable hotel (*Fitzgerald*) and other accommodation.

A picturesque mountain road (29 miles) runs from Sneem *via* the Windy Gap (Moll's Gap) and the Lady's View (p. 142) and provides a useful route for those wishing to return to Killarney.

The coast road turns south-eastward, and in 2 miles reaches—

Parknasilla

Distances.—Waterville 24, Derrynane 16, Cork 74, Killarney 31, Dublin 222. Golf.—9-hole course in hotel grounds.

Hotel.—*Great Southern* (83 rooms). Tennis, Pony Trekking, water skiing, etc.

The name means the "meadow of willows." Sheltered by the Askive Mountains, the situation of Parknasilla is delightful. It stands in a nook between the bay and Knockanamadane Hill (895 feet), with wooded hills rising all round, the broken coast studded with tree-covered islets. Just below the hotel is a boat slip and a little farther away are facilities for very good bathing. Everywhere are lovely little inlets of the sea and wooded islands with rustic bridges and shady walks.

Excursions across the bay can be made to the beautifully wooded **Garinish Island,** to the island **of Rossdohan,** which has tropical shrubs and faces the burnt-out shell of Derryguin Castle on the mainland, and across the Kenmare river to Derreen. Boat trips can be made to the Caves, Derrynane, Ardgroom, etc., or to **Reenkilla** and **Garinish Island,** and then by car to **Glanmore Lake,** skirting Derreen on the return. Another trip is to **Ormonde's Island,** and from there along the shore to **Clonee Lake, Inchiquin Glen** and Cascade. The drives are many: to Staigue Fort, to Sneem and Tahilla, returning by the ancient fort of Dunquilla; from Sneem a walk or pony to the top of **Beoun Mountain,** with magnificent views, as there are also from the summit of **Finnaragh.** In the opposite direction there is a fine drive to **Blackwater Bridge** and Waterfall. The Blackwater Valley can be followed to **Lough Brin,** returning by Tahilla.

Parknasilla to Kenmare

We pass **Tahilla** with its chapel and post office and then the head of **Coongar Harbour,** sheltered by **Rossmore Island,** one of the largest in the estuary. The best part of the drive is reached at a distance of 6 miles as we descend the wooded slopes of the *Blackwater*, one of the many rivers of that name in Ireland, and distinguished from others as the "Kerry" Blackwater. It runs merrily along a deep wooded ravine, with thickly-wooded banks so high that the two-arched bridge by which we cross is quite 60 feet above the water. The river forms many pretty cascades in its course to Kenmare Bay— now so rapidly narrowing as to be little more than a mile across. But before mingling its fresh water with the sea, the Blackwater again expands into a little harbour, useful to small coasting vessels. The river is famous for salmon and is strictly pre-served. It rises in fine surroundings in an amphitheatre of steep mountains called **The Pocket.**

There is a road from Blackwater Bridge through the Gap of Ballagh-beama to **Glencar** (15½ miles). (*See* p. 148.)

Near the bridge over the Blackwater is **Dromore Castle,** a Gothic building with charming views and beautiful grounds in which are the ruins of Cappanacuss Castle. Just off the coast are the **Greenan** and the **Dunkerron Islands,** the former joined to the shore at low water. After passing Tem-plenoe, and 2 miles from Kenmare, we pass the ruins of **Dunkerron Castle,** like Cappanacuss once a seat of the O'Sullivans.

KILLARNEY TO TRALEE

From Killarney the road to Tralee runs northward for 20 miles through lowland country with no features of outstanding interest. It passes **Farranfore** (9 miles), whence buses go to Glenbeigh and Valentia.

Tralee

Distances.—Killarney, 20 miles (bus and rail service), Dingle 31, Cork 74, Limerick 64.

arly Closing.—Wednesday.

Hotels.—*Benner's* (50 rooms), *Manhattan* (23), *Grand* (31), *Meadowlands* (25), *Imperial* (17), *Harmons'* (8).

Population.—11,213.

Post Office.—Edward Street.

Tralee is the capital of Kerry, a progressive modern town and a good centre for touring. It has a long and chequered history, bound up as it was with the Earls of Desmond until Elizabethan times, but few old houses survive.

There is a fine **Town Park** of 75 acres and a 9-hole **Golf Course** nearby, at Mount Hawk.

Five miles to the north-west of Tralee is **Ardfert,** a see founded by St. Brendan in the sixth century. Here are the ruins of a thirteenth-century cathedral.

THE DINGLE PENINSULA
❀❀❀❀❀❀❀❀❀❀❀❀❀❀❀❀❀❀❀❀

The Dingle Peninsula, which stretches for 30 miles westward of Tralee, is the most northerly of the mountainous promontories which form the indented coast of south-west Ireland. It is particularly notable for its scenery of mountain and coast and is of interest on account of its antiquities. There are bus services along the north and south coasts from Tralee or *via* Farranfore.

Although mountainous, the peninsula is easily travelled. Roads skirt the south and a very large part of the northern coast, while two roads cross the centre. An attraction of a tour here is its variety: now one travels through deep gorges, then climbs precipitous cliffs, and often rides beside the waves of the mighty Atlantic Ocean.

The first part of a circular road tour from Killarney round the peninsula leads us up a very steep hill, with Aghadoe House on the left and the ancient Abbey of Aghadoe away to the right. Thence to Milltown and **Castlemaine** across the River Maine, with the Tralee Mountains on one side and the Macgillicuddy Reeks towering on the other, until we strike the Atlantic near the little village of **Inch** on the northern side of Dingle Bay. This is in a sheltered spot on the river side of the promontory and is noted for its 4-mile stretch of sand. (*Strand Hotel* (12 rooms).)

From Inch the road to Dingle is *via* **Annascaul**. Dingle Bay gleams beneath, and magnificent views may be had from the lake of Annascaul in the surrounding hills. Near **Lispole**, farther on, can be found **Coumanare**—a sheet of water hidden by the pretty Listorgan hill. At **Ballintaggart** we are in full view of—

Dingle

Distances.—Tralee 31, Cork 105, Annascaul 11, Castlemaine 24, Killarney 40.

Population.—1,500.

Hotels.—*Benner's* (27 rooms), *Milltown House* (5) *Riverside* (7) *Alpine Guest House* (10), *Aisling Guest House* (7).

Riding.—Ponies etc available.

A little town, Dingle was once a fortress, being in ages past surrounded by a wall, hence its name "Daingeen"—a fortress. Boating, fishing and bathing in nearby sandy coves are amongst its attractions. The majestic mountains rising from the shore here form a regular amphitheatre.

Nestling amongst the low-lying hills in the midst of unrivalled scenery westward from Dingle are several little villages: **Ballydavid, Ballyferriter, Ventry** "the fair strand."

157

West of Ventry is—

Slea Head

Here we have a scene of indescribable splendour. The ocean dashes against an impenetrable barrier of towering cliffs. Offshore are several islands from mere rocks to the **Great Blasket Island,** a former Earl of Desmond property but later passing to the Ferriter family.

The Blaskets are not now generally inhabited, the Irish-speaking community having moved to a new settlement on the mainland in 1953. They are active fishermen, though at heart, storytellers. Famous among them has been Maurice O'Sullivan, who wrote a really fine book in Irish which has been translated into English as *Twenty Years Agrowing.*

The antiquarian will revel in this western part of the Dingle area, so many are the places of interest. The district is dominated by **Mount Brandon,** the second highest mountain in Ireland (3,127 feet). It is named after St. Brendan, who lived from 484–576. From here he sailed to seek the "land of the blest," and legend says that he discovered America. A pass called "the way of the saints" was constructed from Kilmalkeder to the top of Brandon, which had become a far-famed scene of pilgrimage. From the top of the hill there are magnificent views.

At Gallerus there is the so-called "Gallerus Oratory," built in the Early-Christian period of unmortared stones. The walls were brought to a point and though the builders could not have been expected to understand principles of the arch, their structure has well survived the wear and tear of time. About two miles from Gallerus at **Kilmalkedar** are other ancient remains, ruins of a church and several standing stones with Ogham inscriptions. On the side of Connor Hill is **Coumanare** (the valley of slaughter), where spear-heads were found in the earth, relics of a battle fought on this spot in pre-Christian times. Close to Cahir Conroy is to be seen a dolmen, or burial chamber, generally called **"Fin Mac Cool's Table."** Another dolmen known as the **"Giant's Grave"** is farther down the hill, while at Ballintaggart there are nine Ogham stones each with deep-cut crosses on them. There are two standing stones called by the inhabitants "The Gates of Glory" to be found on the Dingle to Ventry road. There are several hundreds of these objects in this neighbourhood.

DINGLE TO TRALEE

From Dingle a road to the north-east ascends the **Connor**

Pass (1,500 feet), from which there are magnificent sea views. At the foot of the pass a road to the left leads to **Cloghane** and **Brandon**. The main road, however, continues east to **Stradbally,** shortly after which a diversion to the left leads to—

Castlegregory, *Galvin's* (6 rooms), *Kennedy's* (4), *O'Connor's* (5), a village named after Gregory Hoare, who had a castle here in the sixteenth century, but of which no trace remains. There are several other guest houses. Bass fishing here is first-class.

North of Castlegregory a peninsula juts into the sea to end in **Rough Point.** With Illauntannig, Illaunbarnagh, Illaunimult and the **Magharee Islands,** or Seven Hogs, to the north, it has in its guardianship the Bay of Tralee on its right. The bold Mount Brandon towers over Brandon Creek to the west. **Lough Gill** bisects the promontory where it joins the mainland, and to the south of this lake **Beenoskee** rises in its lofty magnificence to a height of 2,700 feet from a range of heather-tinted hills. Castlegregory is blest with a climate all its own. Here the sea-coast is truly delightful. A little farther are six miles of exquisite silvery sands, with unrivalled bathing.

The delightfully wooded districts of **Fermoyle** and **Hillville** are less than 5 miles west of Castlegregory, with the Bay of Brandon on the northern side.

Half-way up the mountain, below which the road is built across the face of a steep cliff many hundreds of feet high, is **Coumanare** with its black-hued expanse of water called Pedlar's Lake. In the valley are three pretty lakes, one shaped like a heart, and so called; these lakes and the river forming the outlet contain brown and white trout, and also salmon, and are a happy hunting-ground for the adventurous angler. The crags towering over this road on Connor Hill are a wonderful sight, rising to over 500 feet; the foot of the precipice—far beneath—is hidden from the level of the road. In this district, on the south side of the pass to Connor Hill, at Ballyhoneen, is the dolmen already referred to called the "Giant's Grave," and to the east of it is the very interesting glen of **Moghanabo.**

From Castlegregory the coast road runs east to Tralee (15 miles), passing through **Camp,** with a view of the **Slieve Mish Mountains** on the right, and finally through the pretty village of **Blennerville** to Tralee (p. 156).

159

LIMERICK
❧❧❧❧❧❧❧❧❧

Access, etc.—The Railway Station and Bus Terminus adjoin in Parnell Street. There are rail and road connections with all main centres.

Airport.—Shannon Airport at Rineanna, Co. Clare, 15 miles. Frequent bus services. *See* p. 170.

Banks.—*Bank of Ireland, National Bank, Provincial Bank, Munster and Leinster Bank* and *Ulster Bank*, all in O'Connell Street. *Limerick Savings Bank*, Glentworth Street.

Churches, etc.—
Roman Catholic: St. John's Cathedral, Cathedral Place; St. Michaels', Denmark Street; St. Munchin's, North Strand; St. Mary's, Athlunkard Street; St. Patrick's, Clare Street; Church of our Lady of the Rosary, Ennis Road; Church of our Lady, Queen of Peace, Janesboro; Redemptorist, Mount St. Alphonsus; Jesuit, The Crescent; Dominican, Baker Place; Fransciscan, Lower Henry Street; Augustinian, O'Connell Street.
Church of Ireland: St. Mary's Cathedral, Bridge Street; St. Michael's, Pery Square.
Presbyterian, Upper Henry Street; *Methodist,* O'Conrell Street; *Baptist,* O'Connell Avenue; *Gospel,* Upper Mallow Street.

Distances.—Adare 11, Cork 63, Croom 12, Dublin 123, Ennis 23, Galway 65, Killaloe 14, Killarney 68, Listowel 44, Nenagh 25, Shannon Airport 15, 160, Tipperary 25, Tralee 64.

Early Closing.—Thursday.

Golf.— *Limerick Golf Club* (18 holes) at Ballyclough, 2½ miles south. *Castletroy Golf Club* (18 holes) on Dublin Road, 3 miles.

Hotels.—*Ardhu House* (31 rooms), Ennis Road; *Cruises'* (82), O'Connell Street; *Hanratty's* (25), Glentworth Street; *Royal George* (60), O'Connell Street; *Shannon Arms* (20), Henry Street; *Intercontinental* (96), Ennis Road; *National* (35). Baker Place; *Cecil* (12); *Geary's* (18), Thomas Street. There are others, and numerous Guest Houses.

Population.—55,912.

Post Office.—Lower Cecil Street, and several sub-offices.

Racing.—Racecourse at Greenpark.

Tennis.—There are several clubs at which visitors may play, including *County Club*, Ennis Road and the *L.P.Y.M.A.*, Ennis Road.

Theatre, etc.—Amharclann na Feile, O'Connell St. Several cinemas. Dancing at Stella Ballroom, Shannon Street, Cruise's Hotel and Jetland Ballroom.

Youth Hostels.—Nearest hostels are at Glin, 31 miles, and Mountshannon, on Lough Derg, 29 miles.

Limerick, third in size of the cities of the Republic, is situated at the beginning of the Shannon estuary, at that river's junction with its tributary, the Abbey river. This junction divides the city into three distinct districts, joined by four bridges. The modern residential and commercial part is south of the Shannon and is known as Newtown Pery and Irish Town, the latter forming part of the old city with English Town, on King's Island, on the opposite bank of the Abbey river. The suburbs of Lansdowne and Thomondgate are on the Co. Clare side of the Shannon.

Limerick is an important port and industrial centre, largely thanks to its great waterway, the Shannon river, and its proximity to the busy Shannon Airport, 15 miles away at Rineanna. Principal industries include bacon-curing, flour milling, production of condensed milk and butter-making, and clothing manufacture.

Limerick was founded by the Danes about a thousand years ago on a site occupied from much earlier times. Brian Boru finally drove them out a century later. Captured by the Anglo-Normans towards the end of the twelfth century, it was re-captured by the O'Briens. King John of England visited it in 1210, and Edward Bruce occupied it for a short period in 1316. Parliaments were subsequently convened at Limerick, and trade prospered. In 1641 it was occupied by Confederate forces, and in 1651 by Cromwellians. Other sieges took place in 1690 and 1691, the latter being the date of the famous Treaty of Limerick.

In 1691 General Ginkell, from his victory at Athlone, attacked Limerick, then the last place of importance in Irish hands. Patrick Sarsfield, whose heroic efforts had led to the earlier withdrawal of William's forces, eventually came to terms, and the famous Treaty was signed on the Treaty Stone (p. 162). The civil articles of the Treaty were framed to protect the religious convictions and property of Roman Catholics. Though ratified by William, the promises were later repudiated by the dominant Protestant interest, and thus arose the term "The City of the Violated Treaty."

Close to the Station is **People's Park,** wherein is the **Museum, Library and Art Gallery** (*open week-days*), containing relics of the famous siege and some modern Irish paintings. Mallow Street runs into O'Connell Street, the city's principal thoroughfare and main shopping centre. In Lower Cecil Street, on the left, is the Post Office, and just beyond, the *Royal George Hotel*, with *Cruise's Hotel* farther along. Opposite, Sarsfield Street leads down to Sarsfield Bridge over the Shannon. Beyond *Cruise's*, Patrick Street continues to the **Town Hall,** containing a miniature art gallery of fine portraits. Almost opposite is the **Custom House,** built in 1769. *Mathew Bridge* crosses the Abbey river, the channel of the Shannon that forms King's Island, and by it one enters English Town. On the left are the precincts of St. Mary's Cathedral.

St. Mary's Cathedral (Church of Ireland)

The Cathedral was founded in 1168, but the fabric has been repeatedly altered and added to. The principal feature is the fine West Tower (120 feet), which has corner turrets with stepped battlements. Part of the west door is ancient. The interior, consisting of central and side aisles with chapels, is of little beauty. The oldest work is plain Norman.

There are, however, a number of interesting monuments, including those to the Limerick family in the Pery Chapel. Of special interest is one to Lord Glentworth (*d.* 1844). In the chancel is an elaborate monument to Donough O'Brien, Earl of Thomond (*d.* 1624). The misericords, fifteenth-century and with grotesque carvings in black oak are lone survivors of their type in Ireland.

From the cathedral Nicholas Street runs close to **King John's Castle** (*open daily*). This was erected in the time of King John to dominate the ford, and its exterior walls and towers are impressively massive. Beyond Castle Street is **St. Munchin's Church** (Church of Ireland), with a fragment of the old town wall nearby.

Thomond Bridge crosses the Shannon. It was rebuilt in 1839 and was the scene of the terrible massacre when Ginkell besieged the city. At the far end is the Treaty Stone (p. 161), a rough block of limestone on which the treaty of 1691 was signed. Close by is St. Munchin's Roman Catholic Church.

Returning across the bridge to Nicholas Street, and keeping straight on past the east end of the cathedral, right, and down *Mary Street*, we cross the Abbey river by *Balls Bridge* and enter Irish Town. Keep straight on along *Broad Street* and *John Street*, at the end of which is **St. John's Church** (Church of Ireland). A little farther on is a *Fountain*, and just beyond that **St. John's Cathedral** (Roman Catholic), with a lofty and graceful spire, 280 feet. Close at hand is the bronze *Statue of General Sarsfield*. From the Square, Gerald Griffin Street leads back to Parnell Street and the station.

Limerick to Tralee

There are two routes through the western half of County Limerick to Tralee—the inland road through Adare, Rathkeale and Newcastle West to Listowel, and the alternative road along the south side of the Shannon estuary *via* Mungret, Askeaton, Foynes, Glin and Tarbert to Listowel, whence the road becomes one to Tralee.

(1) Via Newcastle West

The main Cork road leads south-westward from Limerick to Patrickswell (6 miles), but our route leads now to the right, and in a further 5 miles Adare is reached.

Adare (*Dunraven Arms* (23 rooms)) is a village (population. 561) on the *Maigue*, a fair river for salmon and good for trout. Adjoining the village is **Adare Manor**, a fine limestone building in Tudor style, residence of the Earl of Dunraven. Within the estate (*grounds open*) is a 9-hole golf course. The Protestant church, near the bridge, was the church of an Augustinian Abbey founded in 1306. Cloisters and the old refectory (now used as a school) still remain. The Roman Catholic Church, near the entrance to the park, belonged to a Trinitarian Abbey founded in the thirteenth century.

Desmond Castle, on the banks of the Maigue, is a large and imposing ruin comprising an outer and inner ward, with a lofty keep, the view from which is worth the ascent. The beautiful ruins of the *Franciscan Abbey* founded in 1465 are in the park across the river. Noteworthy are the east window of the choir, the chapels adjoining the transept, and the cloisters on the north side of the church.

At **Clounanna,** 4 miles north of Adare, is held the annual Irish Cup (greyhound) Coursing Meeting (November), an outstanding event of the Irish coursing calendar.

Rathkeale, the next place on the Tralee road, is a small agricultural town on the *Deel* river, which has fairly good salmon fishing and beyond which the main road runs in 8 miles to Newcastle West. Newcastle West can also be reached by a fork right shortly out of Rathkeale, *via* **Ardagh,** a tiny village famous for the *Ardagh Chalice*; this was discovered in an old ring fort here in 1898, and is now in the National Museum, Dublin.

Newcastle West (*Central* (14 rooms)) is a busy market town (population 2,483; 9-hole golf course), the centre of a prosperous dairy farming district. The town takes its name from a (restored) twelfth-century castle built by the Knights Templar.

The country becomes hilly about Barnagh, then the road descends through desolate country to the Feale valley and **Abbeyfeale** (*Leens* (14 rooms)) at the foot of the Mullaghareirk Mountains. In the *Feale* there is salmon and trout fishing, much of it free. Continuing down the valley, the road enters Co. Kerry, to Listowel (*see* p. 164).

(2) Via Foynes and Glin

The alternative road from Limerick is *via* **Mungret** (3 miles), where there are remains of the old Mungret Abbey, erected on the site of an earlier monastery founded by St. Patrick. By the abbey are two ruined churches and remnants of a castle. Three miles to the west is *Carrigogunnell Castle*, prominent on a volcanic crag. Erected in the fourteenth century, it was blown up by Ginkell in 1691. Beyond the *Maigue*, crossed by a drawbridge, is Kildimo, and then comes **Askeaton**, a quiet town on the *Deel* river. **Desmond Castle,** on a small island in the river here, is of fifteenth-century date; it has vaulted rooms beneath, and a small chapel at the south end. Its Great Hall is well preserved. Askeaton in the fifteenth and sixteenth centuries was the home of the earls of Desmond. On the river bank are considerable remains of a Franciscan Friary, founded by James Fitzgerald, 7th Earl of Desmond. It has a beautiful cloister with marble arcading.

Foynes lies a few miles farther west along our road, where it meets the coast. At one time famous as a seaplane base and terminus of transatlantic air services, the port now serves local mining. A sheltered strait between the shore and Foynes Island provided an ideal site for the terminus, but it has been superseded by Shannon Airport on the other side of the estuary. The strait now serves as a safe anchorage for yachts and other small craft. Behind the village, on a hill, is a huge limestone cross commemorating Stephen E. Spring-Rice (1814–1865).

South of Foynes is **Knockpatrick Hill** (570 feet) on the summit of which are fragments of an old church. Farther south is **Shanagolden,** east of which are extensive ruins of the *Old Abbey*, an ancient Augustinian house. The pigeon loft and the west door of the ruined church should be noted. To the west of the Ardagh road is **Shanid Castle,** once a fortress of the Desmonds.

A good coast road runs west from Foynes to Glin and Tarbert, affording good views of the estuary and of the Co. Clare shore beyond.

Glin (*Conway's* (10 rooms); *Youth Hostel*) is a small village in a district busy with dairy produce. On the west is **Glin Castle,** seat of the Knight of Glin of the Fitzgeralds who have held it for over 700 years. Of the earlier castle only a ruined keep survives.

Four miles beyond, our road crosses the border into Co. Kerry and reaches **Tarbert.** For Listowel, the road turns due south through uninteresting country; alternatively, Listowel may be reached by a detour through **Ballylongford** (birthplace of Lord Kitchener) and lively **Ballybunion** (*see* below).

Listowel

Distances.—Abbeyfeale 10, Adare 34, Ballybunion 10, Belfast 247, Cork 74, Dublin 167, Glin 15, Limerick 44, Tralee 17.

Early Closing.—Monday.

Hotels.—*Stack's* (16 rooms), *Central* (9), *Listowel Arms* (20).

Population.—2,822.

Listowel is a thriving country town but has little of interest for the visitor. The castle was the last to surrender in the Munster War (it belonged to the Lords of Kerry), but now only two towers remain to be seen. Just outside the town is a *Racecourse* with an annual meeting in late September.

Ten miles north-west of Listowel, and connected with it by bus, is Ballybunion.

Ballybunion

Access.—From Dublin (Kingsbridge) by rail to Limerick, then bus. Bus connections with all main centres. By road *via* Nenagh; from Cork *via* Nenagh; from Cork *via* Macroom and Tralee.

Angling.—On the Feale, between Listowel and Abbeyfeale. Sea-fishing for pollock, bream, mackerel, plaice and bass.

Bathing and Boating.—A long stretch of sand provides safe bathing. Good diving at Black Rocks. Indoor heated sea-water baths. Boats for hire.

Dancing.—Dances nightly during season: Central Ballroom, Hibernian Ballroom.

Distances.—Abbeyfeale 20, Cork 84, Dublin 175, Glin 20, Killarney 42, Limerick 52, Listowel 10, Shannon Airport, 65.

Entertainment.—Cinemas and concert performances and numerous local functions. Dancing.

Golf.—18-hole championship course south of town. Weekly open tournaments during July, August and September.

Hotels.—*Castle* (41 rooms), *Marine* (22), *West End* (22), *Central* (23), *Mountain View* (12), *Greenmount* (10), *Hibernian* (13), *Imperial* (13).

Population.—1,160.

Blessed with particularly fine sands, Ballybunion is one of the most popular seaside resorts on the west coast of Ireland.

There is good provision for all types of holiday activity. To the north are richly coloured cliffs rising sheer from the water, with caverns and caves and successive sandy bays. From the top the view extends south to Kerry Head and the Dingle Peninsula, and north, far away, to the long, undulating arm of Co. Clare, ending in Loop Head.

On a projecting cliff near the church is a single lofty wall, only remaining fragment of the castle built by the Fitzmaurices. One mile north is **Doon Bay,** an attractive little bay with extraordinary rock-scenery. Farther along is **Lick Castle,** an old stronghold of the Fitzgeralds.

Three miles inland is **Knockanore Hill,** rising to 880 feet and giving good views over the Shannon estuary. Across the Feale estuary is **Ballyduff,** near which is the **Round Tower of Rattoo;** this rises to a height of 92 feet and is one of the best preserved of its kind.

Listowel to Tralee. The main road to Tralee skirts the *Stack's Mountains* and is uneventful. An alternative but longer road leads through **Lixnaw** and **Abbeydorney.** At the latter is the ruin of a Cistercian abbey. A few miles west of Abbeyderney is **Ardfert,** where are extensive ruins of a Franciscan abbey founded in 1253 and supposed to occupy the site of a monastery established by St. Brendan. The ruined **Ardfert Cathedral** is of thirteenth-century date. The choir has a fine east window with three lancets. In a niche is the figure of St. Brendan, to whom the cathedral is dedicated. The see dates from the sixth century and is now joined with Aghadoe to Limerick.

On the remaining stretch of road to Tralee there are views on the right of Tralee Bay and Caherconree, the apex of the Slieve Mish range. For **Tralee,** *see* p. 156.

TO KILLALOE AND LOUGH DERG

There are two roads from Limerick to Killaloe, one on either side of the Shannon. The main road (T 5. Bus service), to the south of the river, is *via* Castleconnell and Birdhill, whence a smaller road branches left for the village of Ballina and for Killaloe.

The other road, after crossing the Shannon, runs north through **Ardnacrusha** and the great Shannon Hydro-Electric scheme, completed here in 1929. Visitors are permitted to view the power station on week-days and on summer Sunday afternoons. The Shannon scheme was built by a German company and involved the building of a dam at Parteen, at the foot of

165

Lough Derg, an 8-mile long canal between O'Briensbridge and Ardnacrusha, and power house and locks at Ardnacrusha. A 90-foot fall at the Ardnacrusha end of the canal drives the turbines. An interesting hydraulic fish lift facilitates the migration of salmon and elvers.

At Clonlara a road leads off to the river close to the *Falls of Doonass*, a long stretch of shallow water pursuing a troubled course over boulders.

Beyond O'Briensbridge, with its bridge linking with Mont-pelier village, the river widens.

Killahoe (*Lakeside, Ballyvally*) is finely situated at the southern end of Lough Derg, which on its western side is dominated by the Slieve Bernagh range. In recent years it has become popular as a good sailing and water-skiing centre. C.I.E. run summer cruises on the lake and launches, cruisers and other craft may be hired. There is good fishing, both for trout and pike. Killaloe was the site of a church founded in the sixth century by St. Molua, and at one time was the seat of the Dalcassian kings.

The **Cathedral**, built about 1215, has a richly carved Roman-esque doorway in the south-west corner inside the building. Notice also a fine east window. The ancient church of St. Flannan (11th c.) is in the graveyard to the north of the cathe-dral. It has a remarkable steep stone roof. Above the town is the site of the Kincora palace of Brian Boru, now occupied by the town's Roman Catholic church. The smaller St. Molua's Church of tenth-century origin, was removed here from Friars Island during the making of the Shannon hydro-electric scheme.

Patrick Sarsfield, on his ride in 1690 to intercept the arms train of William at Ballyneety, during the siege of Limerick, crossed the Shannon at Killaloe.

Lough Derg. Immediately north of Killaloe is Lough Derg, largest of the Shannon lakes. It is 24 miles long and has an average width of about 2½ miles. The scenery at the southern end and the western end (Scarriff Bay) is very fine. Indeed, the circuit of the Lough *via* Mountshannon, Portumna and Nenagh makes a wonderful excursion. Motor launches and other craft are available at both Killaloe and Portumna.

A winding road runs close by the shore of the Lough, from Killaloe northwards through **Tuamgraney** and **Scarriff**, presenting fine views, to **Mountshannon**, a tiny one-street village with a fair lakeside harbour and a *youth hostel*.

Holy Island (Inishcaltra), of about 35 acres, lies a mile offshore

166

opposite Mountshannon, and contains the ruins of St. Caimin's church on a monastic site founded in the seventh century. There is also a *Round Tower* (80 feet), but the upper part has fallen.

The road northwards from Mountshannon passes Whitegate and then crosses the border into Co. Galway, at the eastern end of the Slieve Aughty mountains.

Portumna (*Clonwyn* (10 rooms); 9-hole golf course) is at the northern end of Lough Derg. A bridge crosses the Shannon, its centre section on an island in the river. The charming little town preserves some fragments of a Dominican Priory founded by Murchadh O'Madden in 1426. The Portumna demesne, just outside the town, includes a few ruins of the former Portumna Castle destroyed by fire. A still older castle here was the seat of the Clanricarde family, the largest landowners in Ireland. Sir Henry Segrave, the racing motorist, was born at Portumna.

To Nenagh, Roscrea and Birr

The main road (T 5) mentioned in the foregoing excursion follows the Shannon on the south side to **Castleconnell** (*Worrall's*), an attractive place pleasantly situated on the east bank of the river. There is some excellent salmon fishing (apply Shannon Fisheries, Thomond Weir, Limerick), at one time adversely affected by the hydro-electric development but now considerably restored. At **Birdhill** a road comes in from O'Briensbridge and shortly after leaves again for Ballina and Killaloe. Our road then continues through the valley between the Arra and Silvermines mountains to Nenagh.

Nenagh

Distances.—Belfast 178, Birr 23, Cork 88, Dublin 98, Killaloe 13, Limerick 25, Roscrea 21.
Early Closing.—Wednesday.
Fishing.—Brown trout in the Nenagh river. For Lough Derg, *see* p. 166.
Golf.—Nenagh Golf Club, 9-hole golf course on Birr road, at Beechwood (4 miles).
Hotels.—*Carmel* (10 rooms), *O'Meara's* (32), *Ormond* (18), *Central* (7), *Hibernian* (14).
Population.—4,542.
Swimming Pool.

Nenagh is an important agricultural town in County Tipperary, but there is little of antiquarian interest other than the "Nenagh Round," a fine Norman keep and sole remnant of the castle of the Butlers. The keep is about 100 feet high and the diameter at the base measures 55 feet.

Portroe, on Lough Derg, is 7 miles west of Nenagh. Slate is quarried from the Arra Mountains shielding the village on the south. **Dromineer,** beyond Youghal Bay, is well known for its snipe shooting.

There is a direct road from Nenagh to **Birr** (*see* below), but the main Dublin road goes eastward, passing **Toomyvara** village, with views of the Devil's Bit Mountains, to **Roscrea.**

Roscrea

Distances.—Belfast 159, Birr 12, Cork 95, Dublin 77, Galway 68, Kilkenny 38, Limerick 46, Nenagh 21, Portumna 26, Tipperary 46.

Early Closing.—Wednesday.
Golf.—9-hole course.
Hotels.—*Central* (15 rooms)), *Pathé* 23).
Population.—4,000.

About the end of the sixth century St. Cronan built his great church here, where he had one of the most famous schools in Ireland. The Protestant Church represents this foundation, and retains the eleventh-century doorway with niches of the Augustinian monastery. To the north-west of the church is a Round Tower about 80 feet high, minus its cap. The Roman Catholic church consists in part of the church of a Franciscan Friary, founded here in 1490. The Cistercian monks (*see* p. 91) have an establishment here in *Mount St. Joseph Abbey* (3 miles west). Amongst the antiquities in Roscrea is the square keep of **Ormonde Castle** (King John's Castle).

Birr, once called Parsonstown, north-west of Roscrea, is a busy town with some good accommodation (*County Arms, Dooly's*). The demesne of *Birr Castle* (*grounds open*) belongs to the Earl of Rosse. The third earl, William Parsons, in 1842 was the builder of what was then the world's largest telescope (now in a London museum). There is a golf course at Birr.

North-east of Birr on the Dublin road is **Tullamore,** chief town of Co. Offaly (Hotels: *Hayes* (38 rooms), *Bolger's* (23 rooms)) with a population of 6,654. It is a busy market centre, has an open-air swimming pool and a good 18-hole golf course in Brookfield Park, just outside the town. The picturesque Charleville Park is a little to the south of the town. At one time, 1798, Tullamore was the terminus of the Grand Canal, the extension westward to the Shannon being completed six years later.

On the Canal is **Srah Castle,** an Elizabethan ruin. Farther west along the Canal is **Rahan,** site of an ancient monastery founded by St. Carthach, Bishop of Lismore, in the sixth century. Little of it remains. In the church is a unique rose window.

On the Kilbeggan road north of Tullamore is **Durrow Abbey,** founded by St. Columba. Of it little trace remains, but the tenth-century High Cross can be seen in the churchyard. The famous "Book of Durrow," now in Trinity College Library, was written here in the seventh century.

For **Ballinasloe,** north-east of Birr, *see* p. 177.

COUNTY CLARE
✤✤✤✤✤✤✤✤✤✤✤✤✤✤✤✤

Limerick to Ennis — Gort — Kilrush — Kilkee — Ennistymon — Lisdoonvarna—Ballyvaughan

The western counties of Ireland each have a strong attraction for the tourist. Though Co. Clare may lack the wild and beautiful inland scenery of Donegal, Mayo, Galway and Kerry, it nevertheless has a coast line of sheer cliffs quite different from any other part of Ireland—indeed of the British Isles, with the exception of the Orkney Islands. The cliffs are of red sandstone or millstone grit which has the peculiarity of dropping to the sea perpendicularly without any footing of loose scree. The cliffs of Moher, 7 miles from Lisdoonvarna, are the most perfect cliffs in Ireland—much less in height than Slieve League in Donegal or Croaghaun in Achill, but unlike those so-called cliffs, which drop to the sea at an angle of 45 degrees, absolutely sheer. From Doonbeg (6 miles north of Kilkee) to Loop Head (12 miles south of Kilkee) the coast is of continuing interest. There is no finer place for bathing than Kilkee— better even than Portrush—while Lisdoonvarna, despite disappointing surroundings, is certainly healthy and popular. The southern boundary of the county forms the northern shore of the Shannon, which, westward of Limerick, widens into a 60-mile estuary to meet the Atlantic.

Limerick to Ennis

The road from Limerick westwards along the northern side of the Shannon estuary enters County Clare after 3 miles. A mile and a half beyond this point lies **Cratloe Castle,** built in 1610, with the wooded Cratloe hills rising behind. Oak trees from these woods went to the making of the roof of Westminster Hall in London, and the City Hall, now the Royal Palace, of Amsterdam. Beyond the Bunratty river (hump-back bridge) is **Bunratty** (*Shannon Shamrock Inn* (50 rooms)).

Bunratty Castle (*open daily*) stands on the northern shore of the Shannon and is the most complete medieval castle in Ireland. At least three castles preceded it, built on what was once an island, and dominating the mouth of the Shannon as well as the surrounding countryside. Thomas de Clare, son of the Earl of Gloucester, erected the first stone castle here, in 1277, which was finally destroyed by the Earl of Thomond in 1332.

169

The present castle was built in the middle of the fifteenth century by Sioda Mac Conmara, passing into the hands of the O'Briens in the sixteenth century, the Kings (and later) Earls of Thomond; the fourth earl made the main structural alterations to the castle of that century, most of which have now been removed during the recent restoration by the Office of Public Works and Lord Gort, who has also furnished it with late fifteenth-century furniture throughout.

The castle, with its dungeons, its chapel and solar room, the private apartments of the earl, etc., is worth exploring throughout, though the Great Hall is its most magnificent room, 48 feet high and long, by 30 feet wide, with a frieze on the north wall similar to that in Wolsey's closet at Hampton Court. It is here that the "Medieval Banquets" are held, organized by the Shannon Free Airport Development Co. Ltd. who manage the castle, and run in conjunction with one-day "Medieval Tours," starting at Shannon Airport, visiting various places of interest in Co. Clare and culminating in the banquet in the Great Hall of the Castle. Here fifteenth-century dishes are served by costumed Irish girls, and eaten with the aid of daggers, mead and claret are drunk, and singers, dancers and musicians, also in costume, entertain. In the grounds is an interesting Folk Park.

Beyond Bunratty, a road leads off to the left for Rineanna and Shannon Airport.

Shannon Airport (bus connection to and from Ennis and Limerick) is owned and operated by the Minister for Transport and Power. It is equipped and serviced to cater for all types of aircraft and air services operating to and from Europe and North America. Shannon became the world's first customs-free airport in 1947 since when aircraft and goods arriving from abroad in transit or intended for re-exportation are not subject to customs examination. Facilities include accommodation, a restaurant, spectators' lounge and a duty-free shop.

The Shannon Free Airport Development Company Ltd, a State-sponsored body, are developing an industrial settlement on the outskirts of the airport.

Newmarket-on-Fergus, the next place on the Ennis road, is a small town close beside tiny Lough Cash. *Dromoland Castle Hotel* (with stone fort in grounds) is seen just before the road crosses the *Ardsollus* river to run through **Clarecastle** to Ennis.

Clarecastle takes its name from a castle that stood on an island in the River Fergus. *Clare Abbey* (National Monument), with a lofty tower, was founded for Canons Regular about 1190 by Donall O'Brien, King of Thomond.

An alternative road from Limerick to Ennis branches right from Cratloe to **Sixmilebridge,** Kilmurry and Quin.

Quin Abbey. Founded for Franciscans in 1402, the buildings date from 1433, when Macon Dall Macnamara settled Observatines (reformed Franciscans) here. The monastic church consists of nave with south chapel, central tower, and chancel with a north chapel. A former castle on the site was incorporated in the abbey, and traces of this remain. The monastic buildings are north of the church. The abbey was suppressed in 1541, but the Franciscans subsequently returned, only to be driven out again in 1641, though they remained in the vicinity.

Ennis

Distances.—Ballyvaughan 34, Belfast 205, Cork 86, Ennistymon 17, Galway 42, Kilkee 35, Killaloe 31, Kilrush 27, Limerick 23, Shannon (Airport) 15.
Early Closing.—Thursday.
Fishing.—The Fergus river holds salmon in the spring, and numerous brown trout (free). The Ardsollus river is preserved through the Dromoland demesne, but the remainder (salmon and trout) is free.
Hotels.—*Old Ground* (65 rooms), *Queen's* (25), *West County Inn* (40).
Population.—5,834.
Sport, etc.—Tennis courts, 18-hole golf course, cinema, dancing.

Ennis, county town of Clare, is a busy and cheerful town on the Fergus river. Principal objects of interest to the visitor include the handsome *Court House*, a classical building of

ENNIS

1850, a *column* in the centre of the town to the memory of
Daniel O'Connell (the Liberator), the large *Roman Catholic
Cathedral* (SS. Peter and Paul), and a fine *Protestant Church*.

Ennis Abbey was founded in 1241 by Douchadh Cairbreach
O'Brien shortly before his death. It was subsequently added
to, and the ruins now present a somewhat mixed bag. The
abbey is noted for its sculptures of fourteenth- and fifteenth-
century date. A fine five-light window dates from 1287.

Ennis to Gort and Galway

Beyond Ennis the country becomes stony and is dotted with
rushy pools. On an island in one of the largest, Lough Inchi-
cronan, are the ruins of O'Brien Abbey. Beyond **Crusheen**
for 5 miles there is little of note, except that in crossing the
Moyree river the road enters Co. Galway. Further along there
is a tract of bog on the right of which is **Loughcutra Castle**, on
the shore of Lough Cutra (*Daily 10–6*.) The castle was built in
1811 for the first Viscount Gort, to the design of John Nash.
The Gort river flows out of this lough, and at a romantic glen
known as the "Punchbowl" about a mile distant falls into a
deep, rocky abyss, disappearing underground until it reaches
Cannohoun.

Gort (*Glynn's* (12 rooms)) is a neat town of just under a
thousand inhabitants, with a triangular market place.

Kilmacduagh Church and Round Tower are 3½ miles south-west of Gort.
The former retains the cyclopean doorway (closed) of the seventh-century
church of St. Colman. The Round Tower leans some way from the perpendicular.

For **Galway,** *see* p. 179.

ENNIS TO KILRUSH AND KILKEE

Ennis to Kilrush by the inland road *via* Darragh and Liscasey, 27 miles.
By the coast road *via* Kildysart, 34 miles.

Three miles south of Ennis is **Killone Abbey**. At first the
road is dull, but the scenery soon becomes attractive, and is
particularly so at Edenvale. In the limestone crags round
Edenvale are numerous small caves that have yielded interesting
finds of both human and animals remains. Killone Abbey is

172

prettily placed on the shore of Lough Killone. It was founded by O'Brien about the same time as Clare Abbey. The ruins include a crypt. Nearby is a holy well to which pilgrimages are sometimes made. The coast road continues with views of the Fergus and Shannon to **Kildysart,** a small seaside resort. In 22 miles comes **Labasheeda** and then **Knock.**

Kilrush (*Riverside* (18 rooms)) with a population of 2,734, is the main marketing centre of south-west Clare. It boasts a fine harbour, but its former port activity has declined. There are tennis courts, a 9-hole golf course and a cinema.

Scattery Island. Boats may be hired at Carragh Pier. Scattery Island, a mile and a half offshore from Kilrush, is a mile long and half a mile wide. Its interest arises from the fact of its having been a sacred spot from the earliest times of Irish Christianity. St. Senan, who died in 554, made it his retreat, and founded a monastery. Besides a well-preserved *Round Tower* (125 feet), unique in that its doorway is at ground level, there are traces of five early churches.

From Kilrush a fine road leads through Moyasta to Kilkee.

Kilkee

Early Closing.—Wednesday.
Distances.—Belfast 240, Cork 120, Dublin 180, Ennis 35, Ennistymon 30, Galway 77, Kilrush 8, Lahinch 28, Limerick 57, Shannon Airport 50.
Golf.—9-hole course on north side o town.

Hotels.—*Hydro* (77 rooms), *Victoria* (24), *Strand* (29), *Esplanade* (15), *Roya Marine* (41), *Thomond* (17), *Atlantic* (95), and others.
Population.—1,377.

Beautifully situated on the west coast of Co. Clare, Kilkee is a popular seaside resort. It has a horseshoe bay of firm sand providing excellent bathing, some magnificent coast scenery, and facilities for numerous holiday pursuits. Set in a corner of Moore Bay, the town is protected to some extent by a long reef known as **Duggerna Rocks** on the north-east. Next to its bathing and the attractions of the golf course, Kilkee's fine cliffs are an immense draw to visitors. These, though lower and less impressive than the cliffs of Moher, are very beautiful and even more varied in the picturesque combinations they present.

Kilkee to Loop Head (16 miles). This coast walk provides some magnificent views. From the town we pass above the Duggerna Rocks, a short distance beyond which is the *Amphitheatre*, with tiers of limestone, and the *Puffing Hole* where, in rough weather, the waves sweep in beneath and spring up through it in a cloud of spray. Close at hand are the Diamond Rocks, Intrinsic Bay, and Look-out Hill (217 feet), from which there is a good all-round view. Rocky

173

islets lie close almost beneath, and, about ¾ mile away, with level, grassed surface is **Bishop's Island.** Upon it are remnants of an oratory ascribed to St. Senan, Bishop of Scattery. The next point is *Foohagh Point*, standing 185 feet above the sea, and a little inland is a chalybeate well—Foohagh Spa.

On Castle Point (131 feet) are fragments of *Doonlicky Castle,* and then the road keeps close to the cliff edge. Farther on the road from Carrigaholt comes in, and the next place on the route is the village of **Cross.** Then, after touching the shore of the Shannon Mouth at Kilbaha Bay, the road reaches **Kilbaha,** the last village, 2 miles short of Loop Head.

Loop Head Lighthouse is 500 yards short of the end of the promontory, which seaward presents fine cliffs. The view from the lighthouse is very fine and stretches north to Slyne Head, with the Connemara Mountains to the right of it and the Aran Islands midway. Southward the prospect includes Kerry Head and the whole of the Dingle promontory, culminating westward in the fine summit of Brandon Hill. To the left, on the far horizon, are the Reeks, including Carrantuohill.

Separated from the Head by a narrow channel called the *Lovers' Leap* is an insulated cliff known as *Dermot and Grania's Rock*. Walkers can be recommended to follow the cliffs 3 or 4 miles northward from the Head in order to see the fine natural bridges formed by the action of the water against the lower part of the shale cliffs.

Ennistymon (population, 1,091; *Falls* (32 rooms)) is prettily situated on the *Cullenagh* river, here crossed by a bridge. Below this the river forms a cascade, which is a grand sight when in flood. For visitors there is dancing, tennis, cinema and other recreations, with good brown trout fishing in the **Cullenagh** and the **Dealagh.**

Two and a half miles from Ennistymon is **Lahinch,** on Liscannor Bay.

Lahinch

Distances.—Ballyvaughan 20, Belfast 224, Cork 105, Dublin 164, Ennis 19, Ennistymon 3, Limerick 42, Lisdoonvarna 10

Golf.—18-hole course and 9-hole course on north side of town.

Hotels.—*Aberdeen Arms* (60 rooms), *Claremont* (37), *Atlantic House* (26), *St. Anthony's* (13) and guest houses.

Population.—465.

Entertainments Centre and Swimming Pool.

Lahinch, with a fine sandy beach, is a bracing resort popular for its bathing and golf. Splendid excursions may be made, and the place is within easy reach of Hag's Head, at the southern end of the impressive cliffs of Moher (*see* p. 175).

Southward along the coast is **Milltown Malbay** (*Central* (10 rooms)) and **Spanish Point,** with a 9-hole golf course and some good sands.

Lisdoonvarna

Distances.—Ballyvaughan 10, Cork 110, Ennis 24, Galway 41, Lahinch 10, Limerick 47.

Hotels.—*Hydro* (46 rooms), *Imperial* (53), *Royal Spa* (26), *Keane's* (16), *Lynch's* (23), *Spa View* (28) and many others.

Lisdoonvarna is the most popular of Ireland's spas and is well provided with accommodation. There are several springs, including sulphurous and chalybeate, rich in iodine, and treatment available is up-to-date. At the Gowlan Spa there are good bathing facilities. A full programme of entertainment is provided during the season.

The situation of Lisdoonvarna (about 500 feet above sealevel) is rather bleak. It is almost on the dividing line between the limestone of the north and the millstone grit of the south of the county. In the shallow defiles, where the springs run, there are a few trees, but elsewhere the surface is bare.

Of the antiquities in the neighbourhood by far the most interesting is the sixth-century **Church of St. Cronan,** about 8 miles east, in the parish of Carran. At **Kilfenora,** 4½ miles south-east from Lisdoonvarna on the road to Corofin, is a fine twelfth-century *Cross* in the churchyard.

There are several fine excursions available, the most popular being to the Cliffs of Moher (below), and to Ballyvaughan down the "Corkscrew Road," returning *via* Black Head.

Cliffs of Moher

The range of cliffs is 4 miles long, at its north end 660 feet high and dropping to 440 at Hag's Head, near its southern end. Its impressiveness is mainly due to the continuous line of sheer rock forming a succession of sharp promontories against which the Atlantic waves break with grand effect. The rock is horizontal layers of sandstone, which taken piecemeal will crumble in the hand, but which in the mass can withstand the force of the waves.

A good view point on the cliffs is **O'Brien's Tower,** built as a castle or observatory by Cornelius (Corney) O'Brien in 1835.

The road inland from O'Brien's Tower leads in 1½ miles to the **O'Brien Monument,** tomb of the O'Brien family, and, close by, **St. Bridget's Well.** The cliffs may be regained or the road followed onwards to Liscannor and Lahinch.

From O'Brien's Tower the cliff line may be followed all the way to **Hag's Head** over almost level ground. The surface of soft turf is characteristic of this formation of rock.

Ballyvaughan is a neat village in the southernmost recess of Galway Bay. The low hills around are almost paved with blocks of limestone, and the general appearance is somewhat barren. Ballyvaughan is reached from Lisdoonvarna by the road that runs north-eastward across the barren plateau of the *Burren* and then descends the "Corkscrew Road," with a fine view across Galway Bay, with Galway town and Lough Corrib beyond it.

Ballyvaughan to Lisdoonvarna by Black Head (16 miles). This route follows the coast closely till within 3 miles of Lisdoonvarna. It affords excellent views of the Connemara Mountains—especially of the Twelve Pins—across Galway Bay, and a broadside one of the Aran Isles. The chief gap in the Connemara range marks the valley in which lies Lough Inagh, the hills to the east of which form the Mamturk range. **Black Head** (6 miles), the north-western corner of Co. Clare, is a low-lying promontory with limestone hills sloping up from it and almost bare of vegetation. With Slieve Elva (1,109 feet) well to our left, we strike inland up a long hill at the top of which, finely situated on a crag, stands **Ballynalackan Castle**, in situation not unlike Blarney Castle. It is then a straight run into Lisdoonvarna.

Ballyvaughan to Galway

Eastward of Ballyvaughan the road follows the shore of the promontories pointing northward into Galway Bay, passing on the left a fragment of *Muckinish Castle* with its slender tower. At **Bell Harbour** the road turns left to round the point of Burren. Close to the village of **Bealaclugga** is—

Corcomroe Abbey. Founded for Cistercians in 1194 by Donald, King of Munster, the abbey, called "The Abbey of the Fruitful Rock," was made subject to Furness, in Lancashire, in 1249. The remains of the monastery are considerable. They consist of nave and chancel extending together to a length of about 120 feet, side aisles and the stump of a central tower. The chancel, the finest part, has three narrow pointed windows at its east end, with one above, and a groined roof with herring-bone and other mouldings. On both sides are sedilia.

North of the choir is the huge recumbent effigy of Donough O'Brien, King of Thomond, killed in battle in 1267. The head is damaged. Close by is the tomb of O'Loughlin, King of Burren, and on the north wall a brass of a bishop.

At the next cross-roads on our road we enter Co. Galway at **Corranroe**. Three miles farther is **Kinvara** (*Winkles* (6 rooms); Doorus Youth Hostel, 2 miles N.W.), a seaport village on a small arm of Galway Bay and birthplace of Francis A. Fahy (1854–1935), who wrote the ballad *The Old Plaid Shawl*. Good quality oysters are cultivated here, and there is an annual festival. On the shore is the ruin of **Dungorey Castle**, a onetime fortress of the O'Heynes.

Five miles east of Kinvara is **Ardrahan**, on the Ennis–Gort–Galway main road. The same road, however, may be reached at **Kilcolgan** by bearing left just after Kinvara. Galway is then gained *via* Clarinbridge and Oranmore.

Clifden, Co. Galway

A Connemara Road

Ballina, Co. Mayo

Dooagh, Achill Island

DUBLIN TO GALWAY
✠✠✠✠✠✠✠✠✠✠✠✠✠✠✠✠✠✠✠✠✠✠

Distances.—Maynooth 15, Kinnegad 38, Moate 68, Athlone 78, Ballinasloe 94, Athenry 119, Galway 133.

The first part of this route, westward from Dublin to Athlone, is described in connection with the Westport–Dublin route on p. 191. For Athlone, *see* also p. 191.

Sixteen miles south-west of Athlone is **Ballinasloe** (*Hayden's* (50 rooms), *Ciul na Greine* (10 rooms); 9-hole golf course), a market town of 5,828 inhabitants on the river *Suck*, which divides Co. Roscommon from Co. Galway. It has not much to attract tourists except on the first Tuesday in October and the four following days each year, when an important cattle and sheep fair is held. Adjoining the town on the west is Gerbally Park, formerly property of the Earl of Clancarty and now a Catholic college (*public admitted*).

The direct Galway road from Ballinasloe passes in 6 miles **Kilconnell Abbey**, founded for Franciscan friars by William O'Kelly in 1400, and restored in 1460. The ruins of the church, which is cruciform and has a central tower and small foreign-looking cloisters (48 feet square), are well preserved.

Over a featureless district, the road continues to **Athenry** (*Hanberry's* (11 rooms), *Athenry* (10 rooms), *Western* (10 rooms)), a town of 1,333 people, with little of interest except to the antiquarian.

Still an important junction today, Athenry was a post of some importance at the time of the Norman conquest of Ireland, and the *Gate-Tower* at the town entrance is part of the original defences, which, together with the *Castle*, date from that time. The castle consists mainly of an oblong keep (1238) with gable ends. The church of the former *Dominican Friary*, founded in 1241 by Meyler de Bermingham, is represented by the ruins of its nave and transept, in which are some tombs of the Bermingham family. The Protestant Church is built on the site of the chancel of the old Franciscan Friary, founded in 1464. There is an interesting old cross on steps in the market place.

Four miles beyond Athenry is **Derrydonnell Castle,** on the left of the road, and then Galway is approached *via* **Oranmore,** where the main road from Ennis and Gort comes in from the left, close to a creek of Galway Bay. *Oran Castle*, at the head of the inlet, was built by the Earl of Clanricarde.

From Ballinasloe there is an alternative, though longer, route to Galway *via* Aughrim and Loughrea. **Aughrim** is famous as the scene (July 12, 1691) of the crushing defeat of the Irish under St. Ruth (who was killed) by Ginckle. The Irish were positioned on the east slope of Kilcommedan Hill, a ridge to the south of the village. William's army was at Ballinasloe the night before.

Loughrea (*Commercial* (8 rooms), *Railway* (12 rooms), *Lake Villa House* (5 rooms)) is a pleasantly situated town (population, 3,000) on the north shore of the small Lough Rea, beyond which rises the Slieve Aughty range. In the town are some remains of a Carmelite monastery and of a castle, both founded or built by Richard de Burgh, Earl of Ulster, about 1300. On Monument Hill there is a good stone circle.

Three and a half miles north of Loughrea is **Ballaun** where is the famous *Turoe Stone*, with its rich La Tine style sculpturing. It is thought to date from about one hundred years B.C.

North of Athenry, 17 miles, is **Tuam** (*Imperial*, 26 rooms; population, 3,624) a busy farming centre with an ancient cross in the market square. It is of importance ecclesiastically, being the seat of a Protestant bishop and a Catholic archbishop. The Protestant Cathedral retains its original chancel arch, a fine example of Hiberno-Romanesque work. The Catholic Cathedral, on the outskirts of the town, is modern.

GALWAY
❀❀❀❀❀❀❀

Access.—Good rail and road connections with all principal centres in Ireland. There are local bus services and bus and coach excursions to centres in Connemara, to Portumna on Lough Derg, Spiddal, Oranmore, Ballina, Roscommon, etc. There are limited aircraft facilities at Oranmore, 6 miles east.

Bathing.—Excellent bathing on sandy beach.

Churches, etc.—*Roman Catholic, Church of Ireland, Methodist* and *Presbyterian.* Also *Roman Catholic* at Salthill.

Distances.—Athenry 15, Athlone 56, Ballinasloe 40, Ballyvaughan 31, Belfast 190, Cork 128, Dublin 133, Ennis 42, Leenane 40, Limerick 65, Loughrea 23, Rosslare Harbour 169, Shannon Airport 57, Sligo 86, Westport 52.

Early Closing.—Monday.

Fishing.—Good sea fishing for pollock, mackerel, sea bream, etc. Boats available. Excellent salmon fishing on River Corrib. Much of the river is preserved but fishing in Lough Corrib is free.

Golf and Tennis.—Galway Golf Club (18 holes) and Galway Tennis Club at Salthill.

Hotels.—*Great Southern* (114 rooms), *Ardilaun House* (18), *Imperial* (50), *Skeffington Arms* (14), *American* (18), *Atlanta* (15), *Gibbin's* (10) and many others. *See also* under Salthill.

Information Office.—Victoria Place.

Population.—24,597.

Post Office.—Chief office in Eglinton Street.

Racing.—Three-day meeting at end of July and two-day meeting in September.

Steamers.—Services to Aran Isles daily in summer.

Galway, together with its holiday suburb of Salthill, is both the principal city of Connaught and one of the most interesting places in Ireland. It stands on both sides and near the mouth of the River Corrib, which flows from the lough of that name to the sea at Galway Bay.

The city is a progressive business centre, and to visiting fishermen is renowned for its salmon, which in spring provide an extraordinary sight close to the weir on the Corrib.

In the mid-thirteenth century, the Anglo-Norman invaders, under Walter de Burgh (Burke), Earl of Ulster, conquered the district, and what had previously been little more than a fortified port rose to be a prosperous colony with a substantial foreign trade, chiefly with Spain. Among the settlers, the principal families bore the names of Blake, Bodkin, D'Arcy, ffrench, Lynch, Martin, etc., and their descendants in the seventeenth century came to be spoken of as the "tribes" of Galway, on account of their clannishness; hence the name still sometimes heard, "the city of the Tribes".

During the troubles between Charles I and Parliament, a Catholic rising involved Galway, and when Cromwell crushed the insurrection hundreds fled and joined the armies of Spain, France, etc. The place thereafter declined in prosperity. In 1691 it sided with the Jacobite party, but capitulated to Ginckle after the disastrous defeat at Aughrim had made the Irish cause hopeless.

The city is today regaining much of its former prosperity, and there are a number of successful industrial activities, including chemicals, metal work, engineering, china, textile printing and fertilizer manufacture.

179

The railway and bus terminus look on to Eyre Square, where there are a number of the principal hotels. Here, too, is the *O'Conaire Monument* by Albert Power, commemorating Padraic O'Conaire, the Gaelic writer; the seventeenth-century *Browne Doorway*; and the memorial to Liam Mellowes, the 1916 patriot. In Eglinton Street, north-east of the square, is the chief post office. The continuation of Williamsgate Street is the aptly named Shop Street, the city's principal thoroughfare, wherein are the best shops. At the corner of Abbeygate Street the bank occupies a fine old mansion, once, as **Lynch's Castle**, the residence of the Lynch family. It retains mullioned windows and is ornamented with various coats of arms.

Turning from Shop Street is Lombard Street, where is the—

Church of St. Nicholas. It is a large cruciform building dating from 1320. Externally, the most noteworthy features are the west doorway and the dripstones of the aisle windows; the south porch, vaulted, with parvise over; the south aisle windows and gargoyles; and the curious-looking steeple of Irish oak. The interior, 152 feet long and 126 feet wide, is unusual in that the aisles are wider than the nave. There are some memorials of the Lynch and O'Hara families in the south transept, where also is the tomb of Mayor Lynch (1644).

Set in the graveyard wall, actually part of the old prison, facing Lombard Street on the north side of the church, is the **Lynch Stone**, bearing a skull and cross-bones, and a tablet with the inscription:

This ancient memorial of the stern and unbending justice of the chief magistrate of this city, James Lynch Fitzstephen, elected mayor A.D. 1493, who condemned and executed his own guilty son, Walter, on this spot, has been restored to its ancient site, A.D. 1854, etc.

The son's crime was the murder of a young Spaniard. When the time of execution came, the prisoner's mother raised the town to save her son, but in vain. The father, finding the usual place of execution unattainable, hanged him from a projecting window of the prison. Peculiarly, the father's high repute saved him from being himself "lynched" in the American sense.

A little to the north, in Francis Street, is the **Franciscan Friary,** successor to one founded in 1296, with some interesting memorials, including that to "Sir Peter French." There is a De Burgo tomb slab bearing shield, sword and dated 1645, with an inscription round the border.

Northernmost of the three bridges crossing the *Corrib* is the Salmon Weir Bridge, leading from the handsome **Court House** (1800) to the west side.

University College was founded as Queen's College in 1849, and now forms part of the National University of Ireland.

The Tudor-Gothic building is close to the west bank of the river. In the Library are the Minutes of the Galway Corporation from 1485–1818. The earliest entry was made in 1485. A map of the city in 1640 is of interest. The college is a centre of Gaelic culture, and a large number of the students are native Irish speakers who take their degrees in Irish.

The city's main bridge, the O'Brien Bridge, is farther south, and south again is the Wolfe Tone Bridge, giving acces to the area known as the **Claddach,** the former fishermen's quarter. At one time it was a network of little streets of whitewashed and thatched cottages, but they have now been replaced by modern houses.

Salthill is the seaside suburb of the city. (Hotels: *Eglinton* (55 rooms), *Banba* (36 rooms), *Golf Links* (21 rooms), *Rio* (42 rooms) and many others). There is some good bathing at Black Rock and at the Silver Strand. The Galway Golf Club have an 18-hole course here, and the Galway Tennis Club have courts in Threadneedle Road, where visitors are welcomed.

Seasonal events in Galway include the fantastic sight of hundreds of salmon lying in the bed of the Corrib below the weir at Salmon Weir Bridge, this providing the only means of access to west Galway's lakes; the annual Blessing of the Sea, when the local herring fleet moves out into Galway Bay, headed by a specially decorated boat; and the Galway Race Meeting, at the end of July, which attracts race-goers from many parts; the Galway Oyster Festival for three days towards the end of September.

Galway to Spiddal, 11 miles; and Costelloe, 23 miles. This is a beautiful drive along the north shore of Galway Bay, and is comparatively unfrequented. **Spiddal,** where there is an Irish College, has a sandy beach and good bathing and boating. **Costelloe** is at the head of Cashla Bay. Both are excellent centres for the fishing in the rivers and loughs, among the best in Ireland.

THE ARAN ISLANDS
✤✤✤✤✤✤✤✤✤✤✤✤✤✤✤✤✤✤✤✤✤

Access.—From Galway there are sailings on two or three days a week, augmented to a daily service during the season. C.I.E. vessels land passengers at Inishmore from where connection with the other islands is by curragh. Side cars for hire.
Accommodation.—
   On Inishmore: *Kilmurvey House* (10 rooms).
   On Inisheer: *Ard Muire* (9 rooms) and *Teach Ui Congaile* (6 rooms).

The Aran Islands, three in number, lie 30 miles south-west from Galway, at the mouth of Galway Bay. Inishmore or Aranmore (Great Island), the largest, is 9 miles by 2 miles at the widest part, Inishmaan (Middle Island) 3 miles by 1½ miles, and Inisheer (South-east Island) 2 miles by 1½ miles. Together they form a natural breakwater to Galway Bay, and extend in the above order from north-west to south-east.

The ground is covered with slabs of mountain limestone and the scenery is therefore somewhat desolate and bare. A few trees grow only in sheltered spots. There are fewer than 2,000 people in the islands who make their living by farming and fishing. For the most part the people are Gaelic-speaking, and all wear the homespun "bawneens" or coats and "pampooties," sandals of rough hide. For fishing the islanders use home-made curraghs (or coracles) of wood slats and tarred canvas.

The highest ground, 460 feet above sea level, is on Inishmore, while along the western side of the island is a range of fine cliffs of geological interest.

It is however on account of their ancient forts, cromlechs and cloghauns (stone-roofed houses) and very early Christian ruins that the Aran Islands are most famous.

Enna or Enda, chief of the Oriels in the mid-fifth century, abandoned his secular rule when he was converted to Christianity. He later received from Aengus, King of Munster, his brother-in-law, a grant of the Arans and he established an important monastic school at Killeany. Nine other schools were established on the island, and Inishmore became *Ara-na-naomh*, Aran of the Saints. Up to the time of Cromwell, the shell at least of the church at Killeany survived, but much of its material was then, in 1651, taken and used to repair the adjoining sixteenth-century castle of Ardkyn, now itself in ruin. The date of the various stone forts is not known, but tradition assigns Dun Aengus and Dun Conor, the two largest, to the first century A.D.

Inishmore (Aranmore). Inishmore is the largest and most westerly of the group. Towards its eastern end in Killeany Bay is **Kilronan,** the chief village and at which the Galway boats call. In the same bay is **Killeany** (1 mile) behind which can be seen the outline of *St. Enna's Church*. On the hill is a remnant of a round tower and a little to the west the striking ruin of *St. Brennan's Church* (*Teampull Bennan*). The 15-foot-high gable walls and the side walls are very thick. Close by are remains of ancient stone-roofed huts.

Facing the Atlantic, at the eastern end of the island, is *Black Fort*.

From Kilronan, a road runs north-west to Kilmurvy, passing close to a number of the island's other antiquities. On the right in about a mile is *St. Kieran's Church*, while on a hill to the left in another half mile is *Dun Oghil*, a well-restored stone fort. In 4 miles, at **Kilmurvy,** a village at the head of the bay, is *Teampull Mac Duagh Church*. Its original masonry consisted of some huge stones, 9, 10 and even 17 feet long.

About three quarters of a mile across the island on the south coast is *Dun Aengus*, a vast castle or hill-fort with triple line of ramparts occupying an angled projection of the sheer cliff. Little remains of the outermost defence which originally embraced an area of up to 30 acres. The middle and inner lines, more or less horse-shoe shaped, both begin and end close to the edge of the cliff. Alike for the 18-foot walls and the grand cliffs, the expanse of ocean and the sterile inland scene, this is one of the most impressive sights in Ireland.

A short distance north-west of Kilmurvy is *Dun Onaght*, a nearly circular fort on ground rising sharply from the plain of limestone flags. At the north-west end of the island, near Anaght village, two of the Seven Churches, *Teampull a Phoill* and *Teampull Brecain* may still be seen.

Inishmaan, or middle island, is separated from Inishmore by a mile wide strait, and is reached by curragh. The island contains two antiquities of interest, *Dun Conor*, a well-restored fort, and *Teampull Cananech*, a small church.

On **Inisheer** are traces of a round tower and a ruined church, *Teampull Caemham*, named after St. Cavan, brother of St. Kevin of Glendalough. From the south side of the island there is a fine view of the cliffs of Moher, 7 miles away.

CONNEMARA
♣♣♣♣♣♣♣♣♣♣♣♣♣

The district known as Connemara lies west and north-west of the town of Galway. It extends from the Twelve Bens on the north to the Atlantic on the south and west. Between it and the town of Galway is the district of Iar-Connaught, while from Lough Mask, on the east, to the south side of Killary Harbour lies Joyce's Country. Generally however the entire area west of the great Lough Corrib and Lough Mask is spoken of as Connemara, even to include Murrisk, in the corner of Co. Mayo between Killary Harbour and Clew Bay.

The scenery of the various and distinct parts of this area is varied, though everywhere it is wild and austere. The Twelve Bens are a fine group of mountains, and they dominate a plateau made up of many small loughs. Iar-Connaught is desolate with few heights exceeding 900 feet, while Connemara has an undulating plateau broken up by innumerable loughs and a bold group of mountains, some with summits over 2,000 feet. The lough region stretches inland for several miles, the mountains occupying the northern inland part. Joyce's Country, except for the Maam valley, is entirely mountainous, with the Maamturk range averaging 2,000 feet on the west, and the Partry range on the north. Murrisk, north of Killary Harbour, includes Mweelrea (2,688 feet) and many other summits of similar height.

Galway to Clifden

The main road (T 71) leaves Galway by University Road and gives good views of Lough Corrib on the right and then Lough Ballycuirke. In 7½ miles is **Moycullen** where the left turn leads to Spiddal on Galway Bay. Two miles straight ahead is Ross Lake with a distant view on the left front of the Twelve Bens. On the right is Aughnanure Castle, a former stronghold of the O'Flahertys.

Oughterard (*Corrib* (19 rooms), *Oughterard House* (23 rooms), *Egan's Lake* (25 rooms), *Connemara Gateway Motor Inn*) is a pleasant little village on the *Owenriff*, a stream flowing from Lough Bofin through the village to enter Lough Corrib three-quarters of a mile below. The village is well known as a fishing centre and many fine excursions can be taken. There are two holy wells in the village. The road now crosses a desolate plain of lough-dotted moorland. It continues by the north side of Lough Bofin and in another two miles Lough Ardderry to reach the road junction of **Maam Cross.**

The road northward leads in 4½ miles to **Maam** (*see* p. 190) passing Loughanillaun and Lough Maamwee, and at the foot of the descent from the gap crosses the *Failmore* river at Teernakill Bridge. The road south from Maam Cross crosses low-lying ground to **Screeb** and runs by many loughs and inlets to Cashla Bay. Three miles west of Screeb is Gortmore. Here a road branches south to **Rosmuck,** where is the *Pearse Memorial Cottage.* Padraic Pearse, the Irish leader, stayed in Rosmuck while studying Gaelic.

From Maam Cross the Clifden road skirts the south side of Lough Shindilla and then the north bank of Lough Oorid. The **Corcogemore** Mountain (2,102 feet) on the right, with the Maamturk range behind, is our first glimpse of the Connemara mountains proper. Ahead the Twelve Bens, beautiful in shape and colour, stand out prominently as in company with the *Recess* river we reach Recess.

Recess is finely placed among lough and mountain scenery, and is in fact one of the grandest of Connemara's beauty spots. To one side of the road is Lough Glendalough and on the other Lough Derryclare. To the north Lough Inagh stretches up Glen Inagh, the great rift between the Maamturk hills and the Twelve Bens. Immediately north of Recess is **Lissoughter** with a height of 1,314 feet and fine views.

Recess to Kylemore. The road northward from Recess along Lough Inagh, is unmistakable. As it reaches the far end of the lough, *Letter-breckaun* on the right rises to 2,193 feet, the highest point of the Maamturks. Beyond, the range recedes on that side and the low watershed is crossed about a mile short of the main road, left, through the Kylemore Pass (p. 187). For Kylemore, *see* p. 187.

Recess to Cashel Bay and Carna. A little over 2 miles along the Clifden road turn left across a channel between two parts of Lough Nacoogarrow. Beyond two small tarns on the right, the road passes through a gap in the hills and the sea comes into view ahead. Forking right after the gaps our road leads to Cashel in about a mile. **Cashel** (*Zetland* (18 rooms)) is a good fishing centre and resort on Cashel Bay at the head of the larger Bertraghboy Bay. The hotel is within easy reach of the Ballynahinch fishing. Fishing is available on the Gowla and Lough Curreel, etc. There is a fine view from Cashel Hill (1,024 feet). **Carna,** farther south, on Mweenish Bay, is another good angling resort.

Recess to Roundstone. Roundstone (*Seal's Rock* (21 rooms)) may be reached either *via* Cashel or *via* Canal Bridge on the main road by Lough Ballynahinch. Beyond Toombeola Bridge we pass the remnants of *Toombeola Abbey,* a Dominican Friary founded about 1427 by O'Flaherty. Urrisbeg, the height to the west of Roundstone, is easy to ascend and gives views of the water-studded country around. Roundstone has a reputation for its lobsters. Clifden may be gained from Roundstone by taking the coast road which continues round by Dogs Bay to Ballyconneely on Mannin Bay

and turning left 4 miles farther on at Ballinaboy Bridge at the head of Ardbear Bay.

Recess to Clifden direct. The main road continues westward beyond Canal Bridge, and along the north shore of Lough Ballynahinch. On the far shore is *Ballynahinch Castle Hotel* (28 rooms; fishing on lough and river), at one time home of the Martin family, virtual rulers over the country lying between Ballynahinch and Galway. A well-known member of the family, Richard Martin (1754–1834), founded the R.S.P.C.A. The road beyond Ballynahinch is comparatively uninteresting. The *Owenglin*, rising in the Twelve Bens, is crossed at Waterloo Bridge, and in a further 1½ miles Clifden is reached.

Clifden

Bathing.—About a mile west of the town there are fine sandy beaches and coves providing safe bathing.

Distances.—Ballynahinch 14, Cork 177, Galway 49, Leenane 21, Oughterard 32, Westport 41, Dublin 182, Belfast 226.

Early Closing.—Thursday.

Fishing.—The Clifden Trout Anglers Association issues permits for angling in local loughs. Good sea fishing in Clifden Bay. Good lobster fishing.

Hotels.—*Clifden Bay* (50 rooms), *Celtic* (11), *Rock Glen Country House* (17), *Ivy* (7), *Clifden House* (24), *Alcock and Brown* (20).

Population.—986.

Clifden itself has little of note, but is visited principally for its setting and excellent situation for exploration of the surrounding country. Fine bathing is close at hand, and also fishing and shooting.

Seven miles north-west is **Cleggan,** a little fishing port with some good bathing strands; from here a boat may be taken to

Inishbofin (2,312 acres) 6 miles offshore. There is an hotel (*Days*) on the island.

CLIFDEN TO WESTPORT

A little out of Clifden the road passes through a gap in the hills to the tiny Lough Breenbannia and then descends to Streamstown Bay with the village of **Streamstown** at its head. Leaving the Cleggan road on the left we bear right past Lough Tanny and descend towards **Moyard,** a village on picturesque Ballynakill Harbour. More hilly ground is crossed and then we reach the shore at Bernaderg Bay, a short distance beyond which is Letterfrack.

Letterfrack was founded about 1850 by a Quaker family. It is a pleasant little village convenient for excursions. Good bathing, boating and fishing are close at hand in Bernaderg Bay, a land-locked inlet of Ballynakill Harbour. Renvyle Hill (1,172 feet) and Diamond Hill (1,460 feet) are easy and rewarding climbs, while the 20-mile round by the coast road *via* Dawcross Bridge and Tully on to **Salruck** and back by Kylemore is well worth while.

Eastward from Letterfrack the road enters the **Pass of Kylemore,** a fine ravine flanked on the right by the northern peaks of the Twelve Bens and on the left by deep-coloured crags. *Kylemore Abbey,* a rather huge mansion, is now a school run by Benedictine nuns.

At the far end of Lough Kylemore, the road (described in the reverse way p. 186) to Recess by Lough Inagh leads off on the right, and the Maamturk range appears ahead as a giant wedge. In another mile the Salruck road *via* Lough Fee goes off on the left. As the road rises, there is a full-length view of Killary Harbour with Mweelrea rising high behind it to the left and Bengorm to the right.

Our road keeps above the bay for a while and then with **Devilsmother** (2,131 feet) ahead, falls sharply past Derrynacleigh (Public House) to the shore at Leenane.

Leenane (*Leenane*; *Roberts*) is one of the most delightful village-resorts of Connemara. It is famous as an angling centre and many fine excursions are available. The fiord-like Killary Harbour is excellent for boating and swimming. Close at hand are the lofty heights of Joyce's Country and of Murrisk.

A mile east of the village the road for Maam Cross and Cong leads off southward. It is described in the reverse direction on p. 190.

187

The direct road for Westport continues along the fringe of Killary Harbour and branches right in 2 miles at Ausleagh Church, beyond which begins the ascent of the Erriff Valley. On the right **Benwee** (2,239 feet) and **Maumtrasna** (2,207 feet) in the Partry mountains present fine fronts till in 6 miles **Erriff Bridge** provides a change of scene. Srahlea Bridge, Lough Moher and Liscarney are passed in monotonous surrounds, though Croagh Patrick (2,510 feet) dominates the view on the left. As the road approaches Westport there is a magnificent view of Clew Bay. For **Westport,** *see* p. 195.

Leenane to Westport via Louisburgh

The alternative but longer route to Westport bears off left at Ausleagh Church and shortly after passes the waterfall on the **Erriff.** Then the north shore of Killary Harbour is skirted to Bundorragha where the road strikes inland in company with the Bundorragha river to *Fin Lough* and passes **Delphi·** at the foot of Dhu Lough. The north-west side of the latter is followed to Glencullin Lough, the stern recess under Benbury (Glencullin, 2,610 feet) being noteworthy. Onwards to **Louisburgh** (sandy beach at Cloghmoyle) and along south of Clew Bay there is little to commend the scenery until **Murrisk** (p. 184) is reached. The last few miles into Westport are the best.

For **Clare Island,** *see* p. 195.

Galway to Cong

This route crosses the *Clare* river and follows closely the eastern shore of Lough Corrib to Headford (17 miles). Close to Ross Abbey the *Black* river separates Co. Galway and Co. Mayo. At Cross (24 miles) the forward road continues to **Ballinrobe** (*see* p. 194) but we bear left and in 3 miles reach Cong. For motor boat trips between Galway and Cong see local announcements.

Lough Corrib. Lough Corrib, one of the largest loughs in Ireland, is a shallow depression which has been formed by the solution of the limestone by the carbonic acid in the water. The lough is about 27 miles long and except in the northern part nowhere over 20 feet deep, and in many places less than 4 feet. Between Inchagoil and Cong, however, depths of over 150 feet have been recorded. Its breadth varies from $\frac{1}{2}$ to 7 miles, and for the most part its shores are low and indented. The lower end is broad and unbroken, then it narrows and there are innumerable small islets. Lough Corrib provides some of the best fishing (*free*) in the British Isles, holding salmon, trout, pike, rudd, perch and eels.

Motor boats start from Galway and 2 miles up the Corrib river pass *Menlough Castle* into a short canal connecting with the lough. On the east bank is Annaghdown, with a number of ecclesiastical ruins. Where the lough narrows is **Kilbeg**, with road connection with Headford. Next is seen on the right *Annagkeen Castle* and, opposite, *Aughnanure Castle*, an old stronghold of the O'Flahertys. Larger islands come into view as the lake expands, including Inchshamboe, "Isle of the White Cow," and Inchagoill, "Strangers' Isle," on which are ruins of two small churches. An inscribed stone here, the *Lugnaedon Stone*, is one of the oldest inscribed stones of the Early Christian period in Ireland. On the northern shore close to Cong are the extensive grounds of the Ashford estate.

Headford, on the Galway–Ballinrobe road, is a neat little town (*Anglers' Rest* (14 rooms)). A mile and a half north-west on the south bank of the *Black* river is the fine ruin of **Ross Abbey,** a Franciscan Friary founded about 1350. The ruins comprise the great church, cloisters, and a complete group of domestic buildings.

From Headford to Cong (10 miles) the road crosses high ground and commands good views of Lough Corrib and Lough Mask with the Maamturk and Partry Mountains on their far side.

Cong

Angling.—Fishing is free on both Lough Corrib and Lough Mask. Fishing on Lough Corrib for brown trout only. Boats and boatmen available.

Distances.—Ballinrobe 7, Belfast 186, Castlebar 25, Clifden 40, Cork 155, Dublin 145, Galway 27, Headford 11, Leenane 22, Westport 28.

Hotels.—*Ashford Castle* (40 rooms), *Ryan's* (18), *O'Connor's* (13).

Population.—175.

Shooting.—Good shooting in neighbouring woods for woodcock, pheasant and duck but is mostly preserved.

Cong village, a good sporting centre, derives its name (*Cunga* — a neck) from its situation on the narrow strip of land between the two large loughs Corrib and Mask. In the centre of the village is a copy of a fourteenth-century cross formerly standing here; the base is original. Adjoining the village is the extensive Ashford estate, including the *Ashford Castle Hotel*, formerly the mansion of the Earl of Iveagh. The public are admitted to the grounds on payment of a small charge. The grounds contain a farm, ornamental gardens and maze. Tennis and bathing is reserved to resident guests.

Cong Abbey. The present ruins date from the end of the twelfth century and are of an Augustinian establishment founded by the father of Roderic O'Conor (*d.* 1198), last native king of Ireland, who spent the last fifteen years of his life in it. The ruins occupy the site of an earlier foundation by St. Fechin in the seventh century. After Cromwell's time it became a ruin until considerably restored by Sir Benjamin Lee Guinness in the nineteenth century. There are some good doorways, while a feature of the north wall of the chancel is an East window of three pointed lights, lofty and narrow.

189

Curiosities at Cong include the dry Canal connecting the two loughs. The large scale work was undertaken during the famine of 1846–7 to promote employment and to provide a navigable channel through to Lough Mask. Owing to the porous nature of the limestone rock, however, the canal never held water. The two loughs are nevertheless connected by an underground stream to which access can be gained through a series of deep holes, the one most visited being the *Pigeon Hole*.

Cong to Maam and Leenane, 22 miles. The delightful scenery of the Joyce Country, named after the Joyces who settled here from Wales in the thirteenth century, can be enjoyed on this route. The road skirts the Ashford estate and the shore of Lough Corrib, passing between the latter and **Benlevy** (1,370 feet). In 8 miles **Cornamona** (*Oaklands* and *Corrib View* guest houses) stands at the head of the Dooras peninsula. On an island beyond Claggan, 2 miles farther, are fragments of *Hen's Castle*, which according to legend, having been built in a night by a witch and her hen, was presented with the hen to the O'Flaherty with the promise that if he was attacked the hen would lay enough eggs to enable him to hold out. In a display of temper, O'Flaherty killed the hen and paid the penalty. Soon after, the lough dwindles into a sluggish stream and we reach **Maam Bridge**. Beyond Maam the Leenane road ascends gradually a wide valley in the middle of which is the minor hill of Knocknagur (971 feet). Hills to both sides gradually become greener and less bold and the gap ahead is filled by Bengorm (2,303 feet), rising from the north shore of Killary Harbour. From the watershed, 250 feet above the sea, the steep run down to Leenane is one of the finest scenic runs in the district.

The above route from Cong can be varied to include **Clonbur** (*Fairhill Guest House*), a Gaelic-speaking hamlet and popular anglers' resort on Lough Mask. Three miles beyond, the road crosses the bridge separating the lough from its western arm and then runs parallel with the river *Finney* to the foot of **Lough Nafooey**.

From here a steep road drops down through the hills to the head of the Derrypark inlet of Lough Mask. There is then a fine drive along the lough to Tourmakeady and on to Partry at the northern end.

The Leenane road runs along the full length of Lough Nafooey passing round the head and disclosing the picturesque gorge down which the Fooey tumbles into the lough. Ascending in a large loop, it falls again to Griggans to join the Maam-Leenane road 5 miles short of Leenane.

For **Ballinrobe**, described in the route from Claremorris, *see* p. 194.

DUBLIN TO WESTPORT
❖❖❖❖❖❖❖❖❖❖❖❖❖❖❖❖❖❖❖❖❖❖❖❖❖

By this route the distances are: Maynooth 16, Edenderry 38, Tullamore 60, Athlone 83, Roscommon 103, Castlerea 120, Claremorris 144, Castlebar 162, Westport 173 miles.

The first part of this westward route is by the main (T 3) road *via* Lucan and Leixlip to **Maynooth,** all described on pp. 43–4.

Westward from Maynooth, road, rail and the Royal Canal keep close company to **Kilcock** on the border of Co. Kildare. After Kilcock the country is flat to Enfield, where there is a choice of route. Our road bears left (T 41) for Edenderry and Tullamore. Beyond Johnstown Bridge is the hamlet of **Carbury** where Carbury Hill commands an extensive view. The castle on the north-east side of the hill has graceful chimneys and gables of the Elizabethan period. On the other side of the hill at Trinity Well is the source of the river Boyne, which flows to the sea at Drogheda. Onward 4 miles our road reaches **Edenderry,** a pleasant town in a low-lying region close to the Bog of Allen. **Daingean,** 12 miles beyond, was in former days the seat of the chiefs of Offaly. There are remnants of a six-teenth-century castle. The place was originally called Philips-town after Philip II of Spain, consort of Queen Mary. Ten miles west is **Tullamore,** described on p. 168.

The Athlone road from Tullamore goes north-westward for 7 miles to **Clara** (*Mill House* (9 rooms)), a town of mills and jute works, to join the Athlone–Dublin road (T 4) at **Moate** (*Kelly's* and *O'Grady's Commercial*). An important market town, Moate is the centre of a rich cattle-raising area. There is a 9-hole golf course just outside the town.

Athlone

Angling.—Good trout fishing in the Shannon, especially below the weir. In Lough Rea for trout, pike, perch, rudd and bream.
Distances.—Ballinasloe 16, Belfast 136, Cork 134, Dublin 78, Loughrea 35, Moate 10, Mullingar 29, Sligo 73, Tullamore 25.

Early Closing.—Thursday.
Golf.—18-hole course of Athlone Golf Club at Hodson's Bay, 3 miles.
Hotels.—*Prince of Wales* (45 rooms), *Shamrock Lodge* (42), *Hodson Bay* (18), *Royal* (43), etc.
Population.—9,623.
Cruising.—Craft for hire.

Athlone is an important road and rail junction on the Shannon about two miles from the foot of Lough Ree. The principal town of Co. Westmeath, it was long a military town, but is now actively engaged in numerous light industries. Overlooking the bridge is **Adamson Castle**, erected in the thirteenth century but much repaired. The present bridge was opened in 1844, replacing an old historic structure. In 1691 Van Ginkel, William III's commander, bombarded the town, but the bridge was only taken after a heroic defence by the Irish army under St. Ruth. On the same side of the river is the **Church of SS. Peter and Paul**, an impressive building (1937) with twin spires and graceful dome.

Excursions from Athlone

Moydrum Castle, 3 miles east, dates from the early nineteenth century. Facing the castle is a Radio Eireann transmitting station.

Glassan, 6 miles north-east, known as the "village of roses".

Auburn or **Lissoy**, 3 miles north of Glasson, was the boyhood home of Oliver Goldsmith.

Clonmacnoise and the Seven Churches, 9 miles by river, 13 by road. By road *via* Ballynahown and Ballaghurt. Clonmacnoise, "the meadow of the sons of Nos", has been holy ground since St. Kieran founded an abbey here in 548. It soon became famous as a place of learning and was richly endowed. Throughout the years however it was frequently plundered and finally ruined by the English at Athlone. The Feast of St. Kieran is held annually on 9th September and the Sunday following.

On the bank of the Shannon are the fragments of the *Bishop's Palace* or *Castle* founded in 1214 and later destroyed by Cromwellians, and about 300 yards to the south-east is *St. Kieran's Well*. Close to the ecclesiastical ruins is *O'Rourke's Tower*, a 60-foot-high roofless round tower. The doorway is 12 feet above ground. The external diameter is 18 feet at the base with 4-foot-thick walls. O'Rourke was king of Meath about 960.

The *Great Cross*, 15 feet high, with faint inscriptions and sculpture, commemorates King Flann (*d.* 915) and Abbot Colman (*d.* 924) who are said to have founded the *Cathedral* or Great Church which stood immediately to the east. The present structure, *Teampull McDermot*, was a rebuilding in the fourteenth-century and probably incorporates the original capitals of the west doorway of the older foundation. The north doorway is elaborately sculptured with representations of St. Patrick between St. Francis and St. Dominic. Opposite, to the north, is the ninth-century *North Cross* of which only the shaft remains. *Teampull O'Kelly*, thought to have been erected by Conor O'Kelly in 1167, is represented by fragmentary foundations only. *Teampull Ree* (O'Melaghlin Chapel) and *Teampull Hurpan* have little of interest, but the *South Cross* close to the latter is a fine example of a ninth-century High Cross, covered with panels of interlacing scrolls and ornaments. Set apart on the east is *Teampull Kieran*, probably only an oratory. *Teampull Conor* to the north was built in the tenth century for King Cathal of Connaught but has been restored to serve as the Protestant parish church. *Teampull Finian*, the last of the seven churches, was built by Fineen McCarthy in the thirteenth century. It has

Benbulben, Co. Sligo

Lough Gill, Co. Sligo

Glen Lough, Co. Donegal

Errigal, Co. Donegal

an interesting chancel arch. From the chancel a doorway leads to the attached *McCarthy's Tower*, 55 feet high but with the door level with the ground.

A gateway in the east wall of the cemetery leads by the Pilgrims' Way past the "Cairn of the Three Crosses." Here are the remains of a chapel of a Nunnery founded by Devorgilla, daughter of O'Melaghlin, King of Meath, in 1168. There is little to see other than a beautiful chancel arch.

Lough Ree

Two miles north of Athlone the Shannon opens into Lough Ree. The south or main portion of the lough is about 6 miles long by 4 miles broad. North of that it sends out a great arm eastward to meet the Inny river, while a still larger northern arm 11 miles long stretches to the inflow of the Shannon at Lanesborough. At its south-east corner is the land-locked Lough Killinure. Near to the southern shore is *Hare Island*, with a ruined ancient church, and farther north the larger *Inchmore*. Over on the Roscommon bank is *Rindown Castle* (eleventh century) with little more than its keep remaining. The island of *Inchcleraun* contains several ruins including a square-towered church.

Our route for Westport is continued from Athlone by the road along the west shore of Lough Ree to Roscommon.

Roscommon (*Royal* (15 rooms), *Abbey* (10), *Grealy's* (16), *Central* (11)) is the chief town of the county (population 2,729) and has little to interest except remnants of a once stately castle and of a thirteenth-century Dominican friary. The *Castle* was built in 1269 by Robert de Ufford, justiciary of Ireland. One of the largest in the British Isles, it consists of a great quadrangle with a round tower at each angle and a gatehouse. The *Friary* was founded by Felin O'Conor, king of Connaught, in 1257. Most of the remnants, however, belong to a rebuilding of 1453. In the choir is a curious tomb with a damaged effigy said to be that of the founder.

Beyond Roscommon on the Westport road, is **Oran,** with ruins of a round tower and a holy well. Between it and Bally-moe, 5 miles on, is a turning right for **Ballintober** where, a short distance north of the village, is the huge **Ballintober Castle,** chief seat of the O'Connors of Connaught up to the eighteenth century. The ruins form a quadrangle similar to that at Roscommon, but with polygonal towers at the angles.

Five miles north of Ballymoe is **Castlerea,** situated on the river *Suck* where Sir William Wilde, surgeon father of Oscar Wilde lived for a time. At **Ballinlough** the rather featureless Lough O'Flyn is on the right. **Ballyhaunis** (*Central* (16 rooms);

9-hole golf course) is an attractive place, contrasting with its dreary surroundings.

Claremorris (*Central* (18 rooms)), though a busy traffic junction, has little beyond its 9-hole golf course to attract visitors. The Westport road now continues north-west over the plains of Mayo, *via* **Balla** and **Manulla** to Castlebar.

Castlebar (*Travellers' Friend* (22 rooms), *Imperial* (28 rooms), *Erris* (9 rooms), and several guest-houses) is the county town of Mayo. The busy town (population 5,629) is situated on the *Castlebar* river connecting Lough Cullin with Castlebar Lough just west of the town. There is a 9-hole golf course close to the town and hunting and other sports may be enjoyed. A popular excursion is to Ballintober Abbey (*see below*).

Ballintober Abbey, founded in 1216 by Cathal, king of Connaught, for Austin Canons, lies about 8 miles south of Castlebar. The beautiful church (N. Mon.) has an early Gothic nave and a Transitional Norman choir. Features of interest are the groined roof of the choir and beautiful mouldings of the east windows. South of the choir is a chapel with an interesting altar-tomb and a fine doorway.

Ballinrobe (*Railway* (13 rooms)), a town of 1,240 people, conveniently reached from either Castlebar or Claremorris, is situated on the *Robe* river about 2 miles east of Lough Mask. As a good headquarters for angling in the lough, the town is well known.

From Castlebar the road runs south-west past Castlebar Lough and Islandeady Lough on the right, with a distant view of Nephin (2,646 feet) behind. Ahead can be seen Croagh Patrick as we near **Westport.**

WESTPORT
❀❀❀❀❀❀❀❀❀❀❀❀

Distances.—Aile Cavern 6, Ballina 33, Ballinrobe 21, Ballintober 9, Belfast 186, Belmullet 51, Castlebar 11, Claremorris 28, Cork 180, Dublin 161, Galway 52, Mulrany 19, Murrisk Abbey 6, Sligo 65.
Early Closing.—Wednesday.

Fishing.—Good sea fishing; boats at Westport Quay.
Golf (9-hole course), shooting, tennis, etc.
Hotels.—*Jeffer's Railway* (19 rooms), *Grand Central* (24), *Royal* (20), *Clew Bay* (18), *Rosbeg Guest House* (7).
Population.—2,927.

Situated at the head of one of the many little inlets to Clew Bay, Westport is an attractive town. Its main thoroughfare, the Mall, is planted with trees, while a stream crossed by two picturesque bridges, runs down the centre. Between the town and the shore is *Westport House* and grounds (*open summer, 2–6, charge*) belonging to the Marquis of Sligo. The pretty Protestant church, set in the woods, is modern, as also is the rebuilt Roman Catholic church on the Mall. The late Canon Hannay, who wrote under the name of G. A. Birmingham, was rector at Westport between 1892 and 1913. At Westport Quay, just over a mile to the west, boats may be hired for boating and fishing in Clew Bay.

Ascent of Croagh Patrick (2,510 feet), about 2 hours from Murrisk Abbey, 6 miles from Westport on the Louisburgh road. The track up Croagh Patrick is opposite that to the abbey. *Murrisk Abbey* was an Austin Friary founded by the O'Malleys in 1457. Its principal feature is a good east window. The way to the summit is to cross the east foot of the cone and take the winding path on the far side. The view from the top is wide, embracing the island-dotted Clew Bay immediately below, Nephin to the north-east and, beyond the bay, Achill with Slievemore, and left of that, Croaghaun. A little out to sea is Clare Island. South-east are Mweelrea and Benbury and many other heights.

The south face of the cone is precipitous. It was here that St. Patrick rang his bell and flung it from him, only to have it returned to him by an invisible hand, while at each ring of the bell, toads and serpents fled from the Island of the Saints. March 17th was originally observed as a holy day on the mountain, but this has since been changed to the last Sunday in July when many pilgrims ascend to the summit.

Clare Island. Boats available from Westport Quay and from Louisburgh. Landing is made in a sheltered bay at the south-east end of the island. Close to this is *Grace O'Malley's Castle*, a sixteenth-century tower. Grace or Grainne O'Malley was a daughter of

195

Owen, chief of the Western islands, on whose death she assumed sovereighty over the region. Her exploits both on sea and in marriage have given her a place in history. A mile and a half west of the castle, on a hillside, are ruins of a *Carmelite Friary* of the same period.

The island, about 3,000 acres and very fertile, supports a population of just over 160 people.

Westport to Achill Island

The road (bus service) north from Westport follows the eastern short of Clew Bay and in 8 miles reaches **Newport** (*Anglers'* (8 rooms), *Newport House* (30 rooms), *Abbey Ville* (12 rooms)), a little port at the mouth of the *Newport* river. It is visited mainly for its sea and fresh-water fishing, the latter in Lough Beltra, six miles north-east. The dominant feature of the village is the Irish-Romanesque Roman Catholic Church with its high square tower.

Beyond Newport the road follows the curve of Clew Bay and passes over the *Burrishoole* river, outlet of Lough Furnace on the right and the larger Lough Feeagh beyond. Near the bridge are *Carrigahooley Castle*, where Grace O'Malley is said to have defied her husband, and the remnants of *Burrishoole Abbey*, a Dominican foundation of the fifteenth century. With views seaward and of **Cushcamcarragh** rising to 2,343 feet on the right, the road continues to Mulrany.

Mulrany (or Mallaranny) (*Great Southern* (70 rooms), *Avondale House* (5 rooms)), is a picturesque resort on the narrow strip connecting the Curraun Peninsula to the mainland. There is a fine beach for bathing, and boating, fishing and other sports are available. The Mediterranean Heath (*Erica*) grows to profusion here and is a blaze of colour in April and May.

The **Curraun Peninsula** provides a splendid round trip of about 20 miles. In the centre is the Curraun mountain (1,784 feet) giving some fine views. Just offshore from **Curraun** (Youth Hostel) at the south-west tip, is the small **Achilbeg Island.**

Northward from Mulrany a road skirts the shore of Bellacragher Bay to Castlehill, with views on the right of Nephin Beg and ahead on the left, of Blacksod Bay. **Ballycroy** is an anglers' resort in a lonely district. After crossing the *Owenduff* river, the main road strikes north-east for **Bangor Ennis** (6 miles) to join the Crossmolina–Belmullet road. The left turn passes Carrowmore Lough to enter Glencastle ravine with, beyond, the narrow isthmus joining the Mullet Peninsula to the mainland. For **Belmullet** *see* p. 200.

Achill Island

Bus service from Mulrany and Newport.

Achill, the largest of the islands off the west of Ireland, is connected to the mainland by a bridge across Achill Sound. It consists of two arms, each 12 miles long, at right angles to each other like an inverted L. The inland scenery is of no special note, being mostly bog and heather, but the island is renowned for its magnificent cliffs. There are three mountains—*Slievemore* (2,204 feet), *Croaghaun* (2,192 feet) and *Minawn* (1,530 feet). **Achill Sound** (*Achill Sound* (9 rooms), *Sweeney's* (8 rooms)) is the principal shopping place and has bathing, boating and fishing facilities.

Dugort (*Strand* (11 rooms), *McDowell's* (10 rooms)), 8½ miles from Achill Sound, on the north coast under the shadow of Slievemore, is a good bathing resort. The modern part of the village, referred to as "The Settlement," was originated in 1834 by the Rev. E. Nangle who founded here a Protestant Mission and set up a press to issue a controversial newspaper, *The Achill Herald*. Immediately west rises **Slievemore** (2,204 feet), a mass of quartzite rock and mica. Extending into the cliff below are the **Seal Caves**, much visited by boat. Close to the old village of Slievemore are remnants of a dolmen and stone circles.

Three miles away on the south coast is **Keel** (*Achill Head* (30 rooms), *Amethyst* (21 rooms), *Mulloy's* (10 rooms)), situated at the west end of a magnificent 2-mile strand which curves away eastward to the impressive Minawn Cliffs, which rise sheer from the sea to 800 feet at one point. There is good bathing, a 9-hole golf course, and excellent trout fishing in Lough Keel, a little inland. The so-called **Cathedral Rocks** adjoin the east end of the strand.

Two miles beyond Keel is the old village of **Dooagh** (*Wave Crest* (15 rooms), *Atlantic* (9 rooms)), again with a fine bathing strand. Three miles westward is **Keem** on a beautiful inlet, with a sandy beach sheltered by the steep Moyteoge Head. Immediately north is **Croghaun Mountain** (2,192 feet), occupying the western extremity of Achill Island. The ascent is dull, but the summit provides a magnificent seascape. There is a 4-mile line of cliffs. At one point the mountain drops to the sea in a sheer precipice of 2,000 feet. **Achill Head,** the western extremity of the island, consists of a double range of cliffs back to back and surmounted by an edge 378 feet above the sea.

BALLINA AND NORTH MAYO

❊❊❊❊❊❊❊❊❊❊❊❊❊❊❊❊❊❊❊❊❊❊❊❊❊❊❊❊❊

From Westport we retrace the Dublin road to Castlebar. Just beyond, a scenic road leads off left to run up the western shores of Lough Cullin and the larger Lough Conn to Crossmolina. The main road, however, keeps right for **Ballyvary** and **Foxford,** passing, mid-way between them, *Strade Abbey*, originally founded in 1252 by Franciscans but later transferred to the Dominicans. Adjoining the abbey is a burial ground with the grave, marked by a memorial cross, of Michael Davitt (1846–1906), founder of the Irish Land League.

Foxford is a small township on the *Moy* river. It has an active woollen industry and has attractions for the angler. Besides the upper reaches of the Moy river, and Lough Cullin and Lough Conn, there are sizeable trout to be caught in the smaller Loughs Callow and Lough Muck, 2 miles to the east. *Cromwell's Rock* is said to have been the point where the Protector and his army crossed the river. Westward from Foxford the road leads to **Pontoon,** where a bridge spans the connection between Lough Cullin and Lough Conn.

Lough Conn is about 9 miles long and 2 to 3 miles wide and has a number of small islands. It is separated from the smaller but more attractive Lough Cullin by two peninsulas joined by a short bridge giving its name to nearby Pontoon. Fishing on both lakes is free for trout and the small gillaroos (white trout).

Ballina

Cinema and Dancing.

Distances.—Ballycastle 17, Belfast 163, Belmullet 39, Castlebar 22, Cork 199, Dublin 150, Foxford 10, Galway 71, Pontoon 11, Sligo 37, Westport 33.

Early Closing.—Thursday.

Fishing.—On the *Moy* river for salmon (permits) and trout. Trout in Lough Conn, etc.

Golf.—9-hole course.

Hotels.—Downhill (81 rooms), *Imperial* (49), *Moy* (19), *American House* (12), *Glencairn House* (17) *Grovedale* (8).

Population.—6,084.

Ballina is the largest town in Co. Mayo. It is situated on the *Moy*, a broad tidal river crossed by two bridges connecting the main part of the town with the Ardnaree suburbs on the east bank. The Roman Catholic Cathedral is a handsome modern building. Close by are remnants of fifteenth-century Augustinian friary. Though not of great attraction in itself, Ballina is a good centre for excursions in the northern part of the county.

198

Excursions from Ballina

The most interesting objects near to Ballina are the ruins of Rosserk Abbey and Moyne Abbey, both of which can be visited on the way to Killala and Ballycastle, while the latter is convenient for Downpatrick Head. **Crossmolina** is on the *Deel* at the head of Lough Conn, and Nephin, with grand views, is easy to reach from the road between it and Newport.

The road westward to Belmullet affords good views of the wild mountainous area of West Mayo, but the road north-eastward to Sligo is disappointing at least until Sligo itself is reached.

To **Rosserk Abbey,** 5 miles; **Moyne Abbey,** 8 miles; **Killala,** 10 miles; **Ballycastle,** 17 miles. The main road north from Ballina to Killala misses Rosserk and Moyne, but they may be reached by taking the minor road nearer to the west bank of the river Moy. This road crosses a stream near Belleek, about 4 miles from Ballina, and then it is a little walk to Rosserk Abbey on the Moy bank, a short way north of the mouth of the stream. The Franciscan abbey, established by the Joyce family early in the fifteenth century, has a lofty tower.

Returning to the road, it is 2½ miles on to **Moyne Abbey,** facing a small bay separated from Killala Bay by the long, low Bartragh Island. Moyne was founded in 1460 and the ruins have been restored. The church has a lofty tower. The windows display some good tracery and the cloisters, plain pillars in pairs, are nearly perfect.

Killala is a little place on Killala Bay and was at one time the seat of a bishopric believed to have been founded by St. Patrick. The see is now united with Tuam, and the former cathedral, rebuilt about 1670, serves as a parish church. Close by is a fine Round Tower which suffered damage by lightning in 1800, but has since been repaired.

On August 22, 1798, the French sent three ships from Rochelle with 1,100 men under General Humbert, to assist the United Irishmen. They made a successful landing at Kilcummin to the west of Killala Bay, but were too late to be of use to the rebels, whose rising had been crushed. Humbert, though victorious at Castlebar over General Hutchinson, was forced to surrender at Ballinamuck in Co. Longford.

Beyond Killala the road passes the head of two inlets and in 3 miles reaches **Palmerstown,** with its long bridge over the *Cloonaghmore* river.

For **Rathfran Abbey** there is a turn to the right just beyond the bridge. The ruins of the Dominican establishment, founded in 1274, are close to the shore just beyond the point where the road turns away from the water.

The forward road from Palmerstown bridge makes some sharp turns and then ascends for **Ballycastle** village a short distance from rocky Bunatrahir Bay. From the village a minor road leads off to the right to within a short walk of **Downpatrick Head** (126 feet), a fine bold sandstone cliff jutting out to sea. Just off the end is the detached *Doonbristy Rock*.

Ballina to Belmullet

The *direct* road from Ballina is *via* Crossmolina and Bellacorick, to join up with the road from Mulrany at Bangor. It then crosses the *Munllin* river at the foot of Carrowmore Lough and beside Glencastle Hill, to thread the isthmus separating Broad Haven from Blacksod Bay, for Belmullet. The bridge in front of the generating station at Bellacorick is of interest. Musical tones can be produced by rubbing stones along the length of one parapet.

The *route via Ballycastle* is as above. Beyond Ballycastle the road keeps close to the coast as far as Belderg then cuts across wild and lonely country descending by the Glenamoy to Glenamoy Bridge. Two miles farther Bellanaboy Bridge is crossed to overlook Carrowmore Lough and to meet the sea again at Barnatra. Three miles farther we meet the Crossmolina road on to which a right turn is made for Belmullet.

Belmullet (*Healion's* (10 rooms), *Walshes'* (10 rooms)), with a population of 742, is situated on the canal-cut isthmus joining the mainland with the Mullet peninsula. This wild and windswept area does not attract many visitors, though there is a 9-hole golf course close to Belmullet and fishing and shooting facilities are excellent.

The North Mayo Cliffs. The range of cliffs along the Mayo coast from Bunatrahir Bay to Benwee Head are best inspected by boat, for the cliff-top walk is extremely rough and would occupy many hours of hard work. The grandest scenery is west of Belderg, particularly at Glinsk, Doonmara and at Benwee Head. These cliffs form the north flank of a narrow ridge which rises in Glinsk to a height of 1,002 feet, and about Doonmara, to 761 feet. Inland from the ridge the ground is made up of low bog which drains into Broad Haven. The cliffs throughout are superb precipices of countless shapes and colours. The bold rocks seen out to sea north-westwards are the *Stags of Broadhaven*. **Portacloy** has a delightful little harbour beneath towering Benwee Head, a magnificent headland (829 feet) with cliffs descending almost sheer from the summit.

DUBLIN TO SLIGO
❀❀❀❀❀❀❀❀❀❀❀❀❀❀❀❀

I.—Route via Mullingar, Longford and Carrick-on-Shannon

Distances.—Mullingar 51, Longford 78, Carrick-on-Shannon 101, Sligo 136.

This, the shortest road route (136 miles), follows close to the rail-way line throughout. We leave Dublin by the north bank of the Liffey, and after passing the southern fringe of Phoenix Park, cross the river at **Chapelizod,** the birthplace of that journalistic prodigy, Lord Northcliffe. Continuing *via* Palmerston, we reach **Lucan,** which at one time developed as a spa, but is now mainly residential. *Lucan House,* once inhabited by the Earl of Lucan, is now the Italian Embassy. A short distance farther upstream, we cross the river at **Leixlip.** The name means "salmon leap," but since the construction of the 80-foot dam in 1949, the leap has been replaced by an ingenious fish-pass. The road then crosses both railway and canal, passes the entrance to the park and mansion of *Carton,* the former seat of the Dukes of Leinster, and enters the small town of **Maynooth,** described on page 43.

Our road continues westward, past Kilcock, Cloncurry, Enfield and Moyvalley, to **Clonard** (33 miles), once the seat of a bishopric founded in 520 by St. Finian. A few miles farther on **Kinnegad** is passed, and the right-hand fork leads to **Mullingar,** the county town of Westmeath, and a busy market-town of some 6,471 inhabit-ants. (Hotels: *Greville Arms* (29 rooms), *Broder's* (19 rooms), *Lake* (19 rooms), *Connolly's* (6 rooms)). It has a few old public buildings of merit, and a very striking **Cathedral,** built in 1936.

From Mullingar the road to Longford runs north-west, passing **Lough Owel** on the left, and crossing the *Inny* at **Ballinalack. Edgeworthstown** (also called Mostrim), a few miles farther on, was the home of the Edgeworth family, one of whom was Maria Edge-worth, the novelist, who died in 1849. **Longford** (*Annaly* (36 rooms), *Longford Arms* (54 rooms)) is a county town, but has little to interest the visitor. From here we take the road running northwards to Newtown Forbes and on to **Dromod,** where the Shannon widens to form *Lough Bofin,* noted for its trout. After crossing the Shannon at the pretty village of **Drumsna,** and recrossing at **Jamestown** (formerly a walled town) we arrive at **Carrick-on-Shannon** (*Bush* (33 rooms), *County* (16 rooms), *Church's* (9 rooms), *Cartown* (8 rooms)), the county town of Leitrim, and a good centre for fishing. **Leitrim** village lies 4 miles to the north, and is the site of the Castle of O'Rourke of Breffni, traces of which still remain.

From Carrick we now head westward to **Boyle,** on the river of that name. Nearby are the ruins of a *Cistercian Abbey,* founded in the twelfth century; the remains of the church, guesthouse and kitchen are well worth visiting. Running north-west from Boyle our road crosses the ridge of the *Curlew Hills,* the scene of many historic encounters, to **Ballinafad,** on the shore of *Lough Arrow.* Three towers still stand of *Ballinafad Castle*; near here, in 1599, a desperate battle was fought between Irish and English, at which Sir Conyers Clifford, Governor of Connacht, was killed.

To the west of *Lough Arrow,* are the **Bricklieve Mountains,** with **Keshcorran** (1,183 feet); on the slopes of these hills are the Carrowkeel passage-graves, dating from 2000 B.C. A little farther west is **Ballymote,** an ancient small town which has the ruins of a castle built in 1300 by Richard de Burgo, the "Red Earl" of Ulster.

The main road continues from Ballinafad, *via* Castle Baldwin, and shortly before Collooney, *Markree Castle* is passed, a seventeenth-century mansion in a beautiful, wooded demesne. **Collooney,** on the *Owenmore* river, is a busy junction of roads, and was the scene of a skirmish in 1798, when the Limerick militia were defeated by General Humbert's French troops that had landed at Killala. Two miles on, at the estuary of the *Owenmore* lies **Ballysodare,** famous for its salmon fisheries. From here the road runs northwards, with pleasant views of **Knocknarea** (1,078 feet) on the left, and of the hills about *Lough Gill* on the right, until, after 5 miles **Sligo** is reached.

II.—Route via Drogheda, Clones and Enniskillen

This is a rather longer route of about 163 miles. We leave Dublin by Amiens Street, taking the main Balbriggan road through Santry, leaving **Collinstown Airport** on the left, to **Swords,** with its *Round Tower* and ruins of the thirteenth-century *Archbishop's Castle.* Our road then crosses the river known as *Broad Meadow Water,* and continues to **Balbriggan,** a small town noted for its fine hosiery. From here we go north-west, passing **Julianstown** on the river *Nanny,* with the castellated *Ballygarth Castle* on the right, to **Drogheda,** 29 miles from Dublin. Drogheda is described on pp. 49–52.

We continue northwards to **Newtown Monasterboice,** where, a little to the left of the road, are the ancient ruins of *Monasterboice,* including a round tower and three very notable carved stone crosses, said to be the finest in Ireland (*see* p. 53). Continuing through Dunleer and Castlebellingham, we come to **Dundalk,** an important railway and shipping centre with a good harbour opening into Dundalk Bay. From here we turn inland 15 miles to **Carrickmacross,** a small town noted for its fine lace. Our road runs north-west through Ballybay, and thence westward to **Clones** (two syllables), a small hill-side town with a *Round Tower* of rough masonry and a tenth-century sculptured cross. A few miles west of Clones, after passing the Northern Ireland frontier post at **Clontivrim,** we come to the customs post at **Newtownbutler,** where in 1690, the Enniskilleners defeated the native Irish with great loss.

About 3 miles to the west, on a peninsula jutting into *Upper Lough Erne,* lies **Crom Castle,** the seat of the Earl of Erne. In the grounds are the ruins of the old castle, and the oldest yew tree in Ireland.

Continuing from Newtownbutler, we pass *Lisnaskea* and take the left fork to **Enniskillen** (*see* p. 228).

We leave Enniskillen by the A 4, and after a few miles see *Belmore Mountain* (1,312 feet) rising to the right of the road. From its summit there is a wonderful view, and there are a number of interesting prehistoric remains. To the left of the road is *Lower Lough Macrean.* At **Belcoo,** between the upper and lower loughs, there is an interesting spring, the *Holywell,* and at **Blacklion,** just beyond Belcoo, is the Republic frontier post. Our road, now the T 17, passes **Glenfarne** and reaches the Republic Customs Station at **Manorhamilton,** a road junction surrounded by hills. Here the T 17 continues, due west, through fine scenery, until *Glencar Lough* is seen on the right, with the **Dartry Mountains** beyond. Here the road turns southwards and descends to **Sligo.**

SLIGO

♣♣♣♣♣♣

Banks.—*Bank of Ireland,, Hibernian National, Provincial, Royal and Ulster, Northern.*

Distances.—Ballysodare 5, Ballina 37, Ballyshannon 27, Belfast 127, Bundoran 22, Cork 207, Dublin 136, Enniskillen 40, Galway 86, Londonderry 85 Longford 58.

Early Closing.—Wednesday (all day).

Hotels.—*Great Southern* (60 rooms), *Clarence* (20), *Grand* (53), *Imperial* (40), *Central* (16), and others.

Information Office.—Stephen Street.

Population.—13,424.

Sport, etc.—Fishing, Golf, Hunting, Shooting, Bathing, Tennis, Dancing, Racing, Cinemas.

Sligo—in Irish, *Sligeach*, "the shelly river" is the chief town in north-west Ireland. It is built mainly on the south bank of the *Garavogue* river which connects Lough Gill with the sea. Its appearance is striking when viewed from neighbouring hills, and its chief attraction is its position on a wooded plain, in beautiful and interesting surroundings of lakes, trees, glens and encircling mountains. The 3-mile estuary of the river forms the port, and the harbour is sheltered by a long quay.

The importance of the town is largely due to its position: at one time there was a ford across the narrowest part of the river, and this was guarded by a fortress, traces of which can still be seen near the bridge; all traffic between north and south had to ford the river here. Today, the main route from the west to Donegal passes through Sligo.

The first historical mention of Sligo concerns a battle fought in A.D. 537, between the south and the north. In 807 it was plundered by the Vikings, and thereafter little is known of it till 1245, when Maurice Fitzgerald, Earl of Kildare, built a castle. This became a focal point both in the Anglo-Irish struggles of the thirteenth century, and later for local rival clans. In 1641, Sir Frederick Hamilton sacked the town, burning the abbey. Four years later, Sligo was retaken by Sir Charles Coote, commanding the Parliamentary troops.

The main part of the town lies south of the river Garavogue. A long road on the north side runs from east to west, starting as *The Mall*, in which stands the **Calry Church of Ireland,** a Gothic building erected in 1823. It then becomes *Stephen Street*, where there is a fine **Museum** (*Wednesday and Saturday, 3–5 p.m.*), containing archaeological exhibits, others of local interest dating back to pre-Christian times, the Yeats Memorial Collection, and a number of interesting historical documents. To the east of the Museum, *Bridge Street* crosses over the river, beyond which *Abbey Street* on the left leads to **Sligo Abbey.**

Sligo Abbey

The original church was founded by Maurice Fitzgerald, Earl of Kildare, for the Dominicans in 1252. The building was then accidentally destroyed by fire in 1414 and rebuilt in 1416. In 1641, it was partially destroyed during the sack of Sligo. The remaining ruins are in a good state of preservation and consist mainly of central tower, nave and choir. Remains of the thirteenth-century church can be seen on the south side of the choir, where there are eight deeply-splayed, Early Pointed windows. Under the fifteenth-century east window is a carved altar of nine panels, dated 1506, and on the south wall a mural monument (1623) to O'Connor Sligo. Three arches remain on the south side of the nave, and its north wall contains the ornate tomb (1616) of the O'Creans. The central tower is small, with lofty arches and a groined roof. From the north of the nave, a doorway leads to the **Cloisters,** the finest part of the building. On three sides they are almost intact, with beautiful arches and coupled pillars. On a projecting corbal of the north side, is a pulpit once connected to a passage above the cloisters.

Westward, Abbey Street leads *via Castle Street* and *Grattan Street*, to *John Street*, where stands **St. John's Church** with its massive tower. Founded in the seventeenth century by Sir Roger Jones, whose tomb (1657) is at the west end, it is the most ancient of Sligo churches. Adjoining is the fine **Roman Catholic Cathedral** (1869–1874). Other buildings worthy of notice include the attractive **City Hall** in Quay Street, the **Courthouse** in Teeling Stret and **Summerhill College** which overlooks the town.

East of the town is the fine, municipally-owned **Doorly Park,** with its Racecourse.

Excursions from Sligo

(1) To Lough Gill

One of the most attractive excursions is the 3 miles to Lough Gill, which can be reached by river or road. The river trip is recommended for the 2½-mile stretch of water between Sligo and Lough Gill, where the river flows between wooded banks and delightful parkland. On the east bank is the beautiful estate of *Hazelwood*, now municipally owned, and noted for its fine timber and its variety of evergreens. On the west side is the cliff well of *Tobernalt*, surrounded by stations of the cross and an altar. A pilgrimage is held annually on the last Sunday in July. Above is *Cairns Hill*, topped by cairns, cashels and a stone circle.

The lough, 5 miles long and 1½ miles wide, contains several islands. On both **Cottage Island** and **Church Island** there are ruins of ancient churches; nearby is the minute islet of **Innisfree**, made famous in Yeats' poem. **Dooney Rock,** also immortalised by Yeats in his poem, "The Fiddler of Dooney," is a good viewpoint at the eastern end of the lake.

The road route from Sligo, by the L 16 (24-mile circuit), runs north of the Lough, and forks, the road to the right being the shore road; the left branch gives good views of a pleasant region of ferny glens and small hills, and passes near Colgogh Lough. Near Fermoyle, some 4 miles from Sligo, on the top of a hill, is an immense megalithic tomb, a group of stones in an oblong site, measuring 150 feet by 50 feet. There is a large central chamber, with smaller enclosures at the east and west ends. In $8\frac{1}{2}$ miles we pass into Co. Leitrim and reach the sixteenth-century ruin of *Newtown Castle*. The road then passes the east end of Lough Gill before ascending to **Dromahair** (*Abbey Hotel*), a quiet village on the river *Bonet*, in historic surroundings, linked up with fortresses of the O'Rourke clan. On the site of Breffni Castle, once a fortress of the O'Rourkes, is the *Old Hall*, built by William Villiers in 1626. Opposite are the well-preserved ruins of **Creavelea Abbey,** founded early in the sixteenth century by Owen O'Rourke and his wife for Franciscan friars. The abbey has a fine east window, a large south transept and a small cloister. The return route (11 miles) to Sligo is *via* the road running due west from Dromahair.

(2) To Strandhill

This is one of the best short excursions from Sligo. **Strandhill** (*Golf Links* (11 rooms), *Baymount* (10 rooms), *Kincora* (10 rooms), *Sancta Maria* (9 rooms), *Strand House* (16 rooms)) is a coastal resort 5 miles west of Sligo, beautifully placed on the peninsula between Sligo Bay and Ballysodare Bay. Its fine beaches, with facilities for fishing and bathing, its attractive golf course, roller-skating rink and dance hall, all combine to make it a very popular resort. There are fine walks and climbs to panoramic views, especially from the summit of **Knocknarea Mountain** (1,078 feet), an easy ascent. Archaeologists climb to the top to see the gigantic cairn, over 600 feet in circumference, called *Misgaun Meadhbh*. It is a monument to Maeve, Queen of Connaught, who lived in the first century A.D. Midway between Sligo and Strandhill, on the south-east side of Knocknarea is the largest group of megalithic remains in the British Isles. This is on the low hill of **Carrowmore,** where there are 60 or 70 stone cairns, dolmens and stone circles, spread over an area of about two miles. They are said to be sepulchres of the warriors of the legendary battle of North Moytura. At **Cloverhill**, nearby, there is another carved monument, probably dating from the Bronze Age.

The *Glen of Knocknarea*, on the south-west of the hill, is a deep limestone fissure, 1 mile in length and 30 feet wide, covered with foliage. North of Strandhill, on the shore, is the ancient church of *Killaspugbrone*, the "Church of Bishop Bronus," a disciple of St. Patrick.

(3) To Rosses Point

Rosses Point (*Yeats Country* (100 rooms)) is a popular seaside resort situated 5 miles from Sligo, on the north shore of Sligo Bay. It is much frequented by golfers, as the course is one of the best in Ireland, and in addition is beautifully situated, with magnificent views. There are 3 miles of sandy beach with safe bathing; dancing and tennis are available. Between Strandhill and Rosses Point is **Coney Island**; when the tide is out it is possible to get to the island on foot or by car from the Strandhill–Sligo road. Otherwise there are frequent boat excursions.

(4) To Enniscrone

A longer excursion is to **Enniscrone** (population. 553; *Killala Bay* (16 rooms), *Atlantic* (18 rooms), *Benbulben House*) situated 35 miles west of Sligo. Leave Sligo by the T 3 running south and giving attractive views of the hills and Lough Gill, to **Ballysodare** (*Dun Maeve* (10 rooms)) on the Owenmore river, famous for its salmon fisheries. The ruins on the bank are those of the seventh-century *Abbey of St. Fechin*. From Ballysodare, follow the T 40 to Skreen (15 miles) which was once an important religious centre and has a well and monument dated 1591. A little north of the village is the ruined *Castle of Ardnaglass*, owned by the O'Dowd, and then by the MacSweeney clan. Twenty-three miles from Sligo, **Dromore West** is reached, a pleasantly wooded village with a rushing stream and a waterfall. The road forks here, the left hand road going to Ballina, but the coastal road should be followed to the small resort of **Easkey.** In the neighbourhood are forts, a large dolmen and a curious Split Rock, a relic of the Ice Age. The road then crosses the coastal plain to **Enniscrone,** a very popular seaside resort, with a fine, long, sandy beach, where surf-bathing may be enjoyed. There are two establishments for saltwater and medicinal baths, and facilities for golf (9-hole course), tennis and dancing;

there is also good fishing in the bay and many attractive walks can be made in the vicinity.

(5) To Bundoran and Ballyshannon

We leave Sligo by the Markievicz Road, which at first follows the estuary and then runs northwards for 5 miles to **Drumcliff,** where the stream from Glencar Lough runs into the sea. Here was once a monastery founded by St. Columba, though all that now remains is a fine carved cross, 13 feet high, and the lower part of a Round Tower. In the churchyard is the grave of W. B. Yeats.

At **Cuildrevne,** near Drumcliff, in A.D. 561 occurred the "Battle of the Books." This was the result of a dispute between the followers of St. Columba and of St. Finian. St. Columba had made a copy of a psalter borrowed from St. Finian, who claimed the copy rightfully belonged to him. The dispute was judged by Diamuid, King of Ireland, who supported Finian's claim, "To every cow its calf, and to every book its copy." St. Columba refused to accept the verdict, and sought to enforce his claim by going to war. In the ensuing "Battle of the Books," 3,000 men were slain, and as penance, St. Columba was exiled to preach to the heathen in Scotland.

From Drumcliff the main road (T 18) continues north, with the curiously formed **Benbulben Mountain** (1,722 feet) rising on the right, to **Grange** (16 miles).

An alternative, but longer, route is to follow the coast road from Drumcliff, past Carney, to **Lissadell,** the demesne of the Gore-Booth family. On the shore are the ruins of a *castle,* and nearby, some prehistoric remains. Beyond is **Raghly,** a fishing village on a headland in Sligo Bay, where there is the seventeenth-century *Ardtermon Castle,* once owned by the Gore family. Northward from Lissadell, the road goes to **Streedagh,** where are the ruins of *Staad Abbey* on the strand, a mile from the main road. Here three ships of the Armada were wrecked, and over a thousand corpses washed ashore. At Streedagh or Grange (where the coast road joins the main route) a boat may be hired to visit **Inishmurray Island,** 4 miles north-west of Streedagh Point. This island, one mile long and half a mile broad is uninhabited but interesting for its antiquities, enclosed by a great wall. There was originally a pagan stone fort here, converted into a monastery by St. Molaise in the early sixth century. There are beehive cells, altars, two wells and a sweat house, and more important, the three oratories of *Teach Molaise,* the larger *Teampull Molaise,* and *Teampull-na-Teinidh,* or Church of Fire, *c.* fourteenth-century construction.

From Grange, the main road runs north-eastwards, passing the pleasant village of **Cliffoney** (from here a road to the left

runs to the small coast resort of **Mullaghmore**, with its excellent bathing beach) and **Tullaghan** with an ancient cross, to Bundoran, 22 miles from Sligo.

Bundoran

Early Closing.—Thursday.
Hotels.—*Great Southern* (107 rooms), *Central* (29), *Hamilton* (38), *Murray Arms* (23), *Atlantic* (27), *Imperial* (22), and many others.
Population.—1,400.

Bundoran is a thriving seaside town with a fine southern situation on Donegal Bay, thus providing lovely views. It has one long, irregular street, running parallel with the seashore for nearly a mile. As a holiday resort it is very popular, for it has excellent bathing, rock pools, sandy beaches, swimming pools, diving platforms and a concrete pool for children. There are also facilities for tennis, boating and dancing, a good 18-hole golf course, a cinema and other entertainments. *Lough Melvin*, 2½ miles south-east, provides excellent fishing for salmon, trout and char. The cliff walks are especially interesting on account of the curious formation of the cliffs.

By walking along the promenade to Rogey, and along the cliffs of Aughrus Head to Tullan Strand, we pass the rock arches known as "*Fairy Bridges*." One of them has a natural arch with a 24-foot span. There are caves to be explored at the southern end of the Strand, and there is another, large one, known as the **Lion's Paw Cave**, under the cliffs west of the town.

From Bundoran, our road, bordered by sandhills, leads to—

Ireland (o)

Ballyshannon

Distances.—Belfast 114, Bundoran 5, Donegal 14, Dublin 139, Enniskillen 28, Londonderry 58, Sligo 27.
Early Closing.—Wednesday.

Hotels.—*Royal Millstone* (17 rooms), *Sweeney's* (14), *Imperial* (10).
Population.—2,233.

This is one of the largest towns in Co. Donegal, and is situated on steep slopes overlooking the River Erne. The name is derived from *Beal Atha Seanaigh*—"the mouth of Shannagh's ford." The ford, 300 yards above the old town bridge, was the principal crossing-place over the Erne before there were any bridges. The *Castle* of O'Donnell was built in 1423 to command the ford. In 1597, Hugh O'Donnell defeated and slaughtered an English force besieging the castle. Only scanty ruins now mark the site. One mile north-west of the town a few fragments remain of **Assaroe Abbey**, a Cistercian foundation of the twelfth century. About 50 yards from the abbey is a cave at one period used for the celebration of mass. It contains an altar and two hollowed stones believed to have been used as a baptismal font and a holy water stoup. **Assaroe Lake** was constructed above the dam as a reservoir in 1948–52, during the hydro-electric development of the Erne. The two power stations then constructed are open to the public on *week-days, 10–12 and 2–4*. Just below the Assaroe Falls is the islet of **Inis Saimer**. In 150 B.C., a Scythian, called Partholan, landed here, according to legend, to start the colonisation of Ireland. The favourite dog of the Queen of Scythia was called Saimer, and was killed by Partholan, the island being named after him.

Also of interest is **Mullaghnashee**, a rounded hill on the north side of the town. Here, in pre-Christian times, was a Royal Palace; the site now occupied by St. Anne's Church and graveyards. A large stone coffin was unearthed in 1887, believed to have contained the body of the old high king. The grave of the lyrical poet, William Allingham, adjoins a path to the south of the church. Allingham was born in Ballyshannon; a tablet marks his birthplace in The Mall.

To Rossnowlagh (*Sand House, Strand View, Warren*). The "Forked Headland" of Rossnowlagh lies 5 miles north-west of Ballyshannon. A bus service operates in summer to this pleasant coastal resort with its excellent beach, backed by an expanse of lawn and low hills. The modern Franciscan Friary has a museum of archaeological and historical interest, and is surrounded by beautiful grounds. There is a 9-hole golf course and there are also walks over the sand dunes and cliffs. One pleasant 2-mile walk is along the shore, past the village of **Coolmore** to *Kilbarron Castle;* a return can be made by road. The ruins of this once extensive thirteenth-century fortress overlook Donegal Bay. A short distance along the return road, are the ruins of the thirteenth–fourteenth-century *Kilbarron Church.*

COUNTY DONEGAL
✿✿✿✿✿✿✿✿✿✿✿✿✿✿✿✿✿✿✿✿✿

In the north-west corner of Ireland is County Donegal, with scenery unsurpassed by any elsewhere in the country. Measuring only 86 miles in length and 46 miles in breadth, it has a 200-mile coast line of rugged cliffs with lovely bays and long fiord-like inlets. There are deep glens, heather-clad moors, bogs, many lakes and high mountains. It is a strange and wild area endowed with fascinating names. Among these are Greencastle and Moville, Lough Foyle's famous watering places. Moville has acquired fame as the home town of Field Marshal Viscount Montgomery of Alamein. Then, on Lough Swilly with the reflection of the hills on its shadowed waters, are Fahan (pronounced *fawn*) beside Lisfannon's golf links; Buncrana, Letterkenny and Raphoe, names famous in Irish history; Culdaff, a place of infinite peace; Rosbeg, Portnoo, Dungloe and Gweedore, for mountain lake and glen; Falcarragh, for mountain climbing; then for golf (amongst others) Rosapenna, Portsalon and Rathmullen.

There are the glens too—the Poisoned Glen, Glen Lough, picturesque Glen Veagh and many others. The county of Donegal is noted for the abundance of its lakes, nearly all naturally wild in character; some are melancholy tarns, others sunlit expanses of water backed by wooded slopes, or dotted with islets. The extensive Lough Derg with its romantic and tragic history is famous for its pilgrimage of St. Patrick's Purgatory; the Dunlewy Lough is one of the most beautifully situated. Fishing centres are numerous; among them are Lough Fern, Gartan Lough, Kilmacrenan, Rathmelton, Dungloe and Crolly, Ardara, Glenties and the Gweebarra; also worth visiting are Glencolumkille, Killybegs and Malinmore, Mountcharles, Pettigo and Rossnowlagh, and Ballyshannon. Any of these is worth the trip to Donegal. On the other side of the Killybegs the making of the famous Donegal carpets can be seen.

The oldest rocks in Ireland are those found in the mountains of Donegal, and there is a great variety of geological formations. Archaeologists and historians will be attracted by the Druidic remains, prehistoric forts and cromlechs; there are also many sculptured crosses, pillar stones, places of pilgrimage, and

several Round Towers dating from the ninth to the thirteenth centuries.

The climate is invigorating on the coast, but soft and equable inland. As the coast is bathed by the Gulf Stream, the temperature of the sea never falls below 41° F.

Politically, Donegal is not included in Northern Ireland and in some districts of the extreme west Irish is generally spoken. The county of Donegal (formerly called Tyrconnel) once belonged to the O'Donnell clan, lords of Tirconaill.

Donegal

Banks.—*National, Royal Bank of Ireland, Ulster Bank.*
Cinema and 9-hole Golf Course.
Distances.—Ballyshannon 14, Belfast 114, Bundoran 19, Cork 247, Dublin 153, Enniskillen 42, Killybegs 18, Londonderry 44, Pettigo 17, Sligo 41.

Early Closing.—Wednesday.
Hotels.—*Central* (44 rooms), *National* (16), *Abbey* (13), *Barnsmore* (8), *White Gables* (5).
Population.—1,507.
Youth Hostel.—Ball Hill, 3 miles south-west.

Donegal "*Dun-na-n Gall*" the "*Fortress of the Foreigners*" is a pleasant market town at the mouth of the river *Eske* on Donegal Bay. It was the capital of the land of the O'Donnells (Tyrconnel) who once occupied Donegal Castle, which was almost entirely rebuilt by Sir Basil Brooke in 1610. The *Castle*, close to the market square, is now a picturesque Jacobean ruin with a massive gabled tower, two turrets, some fine mullioned windows and, alongside the tower, a Jacobean wing.

On the shore on the other side of the town from the castle

are the remains of **Donegal Abbey.** This was a Franciscan Friary founded in 1474 by Nuala, wife of Red Hugh O'Donnell. Hugh, his wife and son were buried in the abbey precincts. English troops twice occupied the abbey at the end of the sixteenth century. During a siege in 1601, several barrels of gunpowder blew up, and the building was almost entirely destroyed. The remains are mainly those of the choir, the south transept and arched cloisters. It is believed it was in this monastery that the famous *Annals of the Four Masters* were compiled (1632–36). These annals give the history of Ireland for over 3,000 years to A.D. 1616. In "The Diamond" is the **Four Masters' Memorial, a** fine obelisk 25 feet high on which are carved the names of the Four Masters and a Gaelic inscription. East of the town is **St. Patrick's Memorial Church of the Four Masters.** It is an imposing structure, built of Barnesmore red granite in the Irish-Romanesque style. Most of the rest of the town clusters round the quay, the centre taking the form of a wide triangular space named "The Diamond" where the three main roads from Derry, West Donegal and Sligo meet.

DONEGAL TO LONDONDERRY

Route via Ballybofey

For the direct route to Derry (42 miles) follow the main road (T 18) from Donegal. In 4 miles on the left will be seen the lovely **Lough Eske,** fringed with trees and backed by the Blue Stack Peak of the Croaghgorm Mountains. If time permits, the 6-mile drive around the lake is recommended for the delightful views of forest slopes and mountains. On an islet at the southern end of the lake is a ruined tower, all that remains of a prison used by the powerful O'Donnell clan. From Lough Eske Station, the main road continues in a north-easterly direction and mounts through the Barnesmore Gap. This pass, the valley of the river Lowerymore, extends for 3 miles and was at one time the haunt of highwaymen. Emerging from the Gap, Lough Mourne is passed on the right, and the road steadily descends to Ballybofey (17 miles). **Ballybofey** (*Jackson's* (26 rooms)) is a good centre for tourists, as it is well placed near the junction of four main roads; it has salmon and trout fishing facilities and a 9-hole golf course. The route leads over the arched bridge to **Stranorlar** (*Kee's* (19 rooms)), with its fine modern church. From here, there are alternative routes to Londonderry.

Route 1 follows the main road, running east alongside the river to **Castlefinn,** and then bearing left to **Lifford,** the administrative town of County Donegal. There is a Republic Customs Station here, then the road crosses the river Foyle and the frontier to **Strabane,** the Northern Ireland Customs Station. Leaving Strabane, turn left along T 3 which runs alongside the right bank of the Foyle for 15 miles to Derry.

Route 2. From **Stranorlar,** take the left branch of the fork T 59 to **Kilross,** where it is joined by the L 30. Bear right along the L 30 which in 5 miles reaches **Convoy** on the river *Deele,* a village busy exporting woollen goods. On the left are the Donegal mountains as we travel the 4 miles to Raphoe. **Raphoe** (*Central* (10 rooms)) is a small pleasant town in the centre of a mixed farming area. In the sixth century, St. Columba here founded a monastery, which was converted into a cathedral by St. Eunan three hundred years later. The present Gothic building has early eighteenth-century transepts and tower, and adjoins the ruins of the Bishop's palace. Near Raphoe is a Prehistoric Stone circle. The L 30 continues to the Customs station of **St. Johnston.** Beyond this is the Republican frontier post of **Carrigans,** and then the Northern Ireland frontier post of **Mullenan.** Here the L 30 becomes the A 40 which leads in 4 miles to Derry.

LONDONDERRY

Distances.—Antrim 58, Belfast 75, Coleraine 31, Donegal 44, Dublin 151, Greencastle 22, Letterkenny 25, Limavady 17, Portrush 37, Portsalon 46, Raphoe 16, Rosapenna 48, Strabane 14, Stranorlar 26.
Early Closing.—Thursday.
Golf.—18 hole course at Prehen, 1 mile from city on Strabane road.

Hotels.—*City* (75 rooms), Foyle Street; *Broomhill House* (20), *Melville* (51), Foyle Street; *Woodleigh* (15), Asylum Road; *Quigley's* (12); and several guest houses.
Population.—56,300.
Bowls in Brooke Park.
Tennis.—Brooke Park and St. Columbs Park.

Londonderry was originally called Derry, meaning "oak grove," and is in fact still generally known by this name throughout Northern Ireland. St. Columba founded his first monastery here, in the year 546, on a hill rising from the river Foyle, at times practically an island. The settlement, like many others that combined safe harbourage with church treasures, was periodically plundered by the Danes.

Later came the Normans, with an almost equal inclination to plunder, and in the early fourteenth century the town was granted to Richard de Burgo, who strengthened the fortifications. In Elizabethan days the O'Neill chieftains rebelled on several occasions, and an English garrison was established at Derry; but in 1608, the town was captured and devastated by Sir Cahir O'Doherty, and stronger measures were deemed necessary. The "Plantation" system, or Colonization of Ireland, had been started in Tudor days, but now the responsibility for Derry and the surrounding district was placed on the City of London, through "the Honourable the Irish Society" established by Royal Charter of James I and later confirmed by Charles II. The town (and county) were re-named **Londonderry** to mark this change, and to this day the Irish Society still carries out its charter obligations, with special reference to local development, education, and charities.

The first step of the Irish Society was to strengthen the town's defences, and the mile-long walls then built still survive in their entirety. Peace was soon disturbed by the Civil War, in which the town supported Parliament, and withstood a siege by the Royalists. The most famous siege of Londonderry, however, was that of 1689. James II, before fleeing to France in December 1688, had endeavoured to make Londonderry a refuge for English Roman Catholics, and when the celebrated "thirteen apprentice boys" locked the gate against the approach of a Roman Catholic regiment, the City authorities followed suit and declared for William of Orange. The dethroned James arrived with an army in April, 1689, laid a boom across the river, and the long siege of 105 days began. The privations suffered and the heroism displayed have been graphically described by Macaulay. Ten thousand people perished within the walls, mostly from famine and disease. Finally a desperate attempt by the relief ships sent by William under General Schomberg succeeded in breaking the boom, and the siege was raised.

Since then Londonderry has pursued a more peaceful existence, except that during the Second World War it became an important base in the "battle of the Atlantic." In 1945, more than 60 surrendered U-boats were brought in to Londonderry.

Within the Walls

The walls of Londonderry, built in the early seventeenth century, still completely encircle the old city. They are flanked by bastions and form a promenade that is continuous, unlike the walls of York, Chester and Canterbury. Since the walls were built, Derry has grown ten-fold. The area within the walls, however, still forms the hub of the city, and remains the chief shopping and commercial centre, as well as being the most interesting to the visitor.

From the **Shipquay Gate,** nearest to the river, the attractive **Shipquay Street** ascends steeply to the centre of the walled area—the open space known as the **Diamond.** Farquhar, the Restoration dramatist, was born in Shipquay Street, which still contains many fine Georgian buildings.

The Diamond is a square laid out as a garden, with the fine **War Memorial** at the centre. Formerly it was the site of the "Town House" from which municipal affairs were conducted. From the Diamond four streets run off at right angles, each reaching the wall at a gate of similar name. Continuing the line of Shipquay Street is **Bishop Street,** and the cross streets are called **Butcher Street** and **Ferryquay Street.**

The second turning to the left off Bishop Street brings one to—

216

St. Columb's Cathedral

the Anglican Cathedral erected by the Irish Society; it dates from 1633, with later additions and restorations of the nineteenth century. It is a plain building with a lofty spire, from the tower of which, 300 feet above sea level, is a fine view. In the vestibule at the western end is a shell which landed in the churchyard during the Great Siege. It was found to contain the surrender terms demanded by the besieging general, and the reply, "No Surrender," has remained the motto of Derry ever since. There is a fine peal of 13 bells.

Near the Cathedral is the **County Courthouse,** a fine building of white sandstone modelled on the Erechtheum at Athens. On the other side of Bishop Street is the **Freemasons' Hall,** formerly the Bishop's Palace.

A picturesque street is **Linen Hall Street,** which descends from Ferryquay Street towards the river, the lower portion being so steep that it is stepped.

Round the Walls

The tour of the walls extends for approximately one mile, and a convenient starting place is the **Shipquay Gate,** opposite the Guildhall. On the section of the wall parallel with the river, there are still a number of the guns used during the Siege, and that nearest the Shipquay Gate bears the date 1590.

The bastion at the corner north-west of the Shipquay Gate was known as **Coward's Bastion,** since being almost surrounded by water it was less liable to attack. Proceeding along the wall, one reaches first a modern opening, **Castle Gate,** and comes to **Butcher's Gate,** at the end of Butcher Street. Farther on is **Royal Bastion,** with a 90-foot column bearing the statue of the Rev. George Walker, who was one of the two joint Governors during the siege. Where the wall turns again at right angles is the **Double Bastion.**

The next gate, in the middle of the southern section of the wall is **Bishop's Gate,** which in 1789 was rebuilt as a triumphal arch in memory of William III. From here one can see the **Court House** within the walls, and the **Gaol** outside. **Church Bastion** marks the next turn in the wall, and half-way along the final stretch is **Ferryquay Gate,** the gate that was closed by the thirteen apprentices against the Earl of Antrim's regiment in 1688. From here riverwards the wall has suffered modifications and is of less historic interest.

Outside the Walls

The spread of the city has been mainly to the north, and across the river to **Waterside,** an area which now houses about one fourth of the population. Quays extend along the riverside, and the port was much enlarged during the Second World War.

Between the Shipquay Gate and the river Foyle (which once extended to the walls) is the **Guildhall,** a striking Gothic building dating from 1890, and reconstructed after being largely destroyed by fire in 1908. It contains much interesting stained glass by local craftsmen, including a window representing the Coronation of George V. In the Council Chamber are displayed the treasures of the Corporation, including a two-handed Andrea Ferrara sword said to have belonged to Sir Cahir O'Doherty. The tower contains a peal of bells, and a clock.

From the Guildhall a bus goes to **Waterside,** crossing the river by the **Craigavon Bridge.** This fine bridge has a 60-foot wide upper deck for vehicles and pedestrians, and a lower deck once for the railway but now converted for road traffic.

To the north of Waterside are several service establishments. At the bend of the river is **St. Columb's Park,** in which may be seen some of the oldest ecclesiastical remains in the district.

Returning to the Guildhall, passing *via* Waterloo Place into the **Strand Road** which runs northward, the first turning to the left past the bus station is **Great James Street.** This long and steep road leads to the **Roman Catholic Cathedral of St. Eugene,** which like St. Columb's Cathedral has a lofty spire. Beyond this is **Brooke Park,** with ornamental gardens, tennis courts and bowling greens. Here also is the famous old gun known as **Roaring Meg,** for long on the town walls. Following Strand Road farther northwards, the **Technical College** is passed. Nearby, in the Northland Road is the **Magee University College,** with close links with Trinity College, Dublin and Queen's, Belfast.

The industrial development of Londonderry has been continuous. Shirt-making has long been one of the main local industries, and to this has been added the manufacture of tyre fabrics, together with bacon-curing and the various engineering industries to be expected in a large port. More recently the **Maydown Industrial Site** has been developed on the shores of Lough Foyle, just outside the city. Here is a factory for the production of Neoprene synthetic rubber, a plant for acetylene manufacture, and a new Power Station

EXCURSIONS INTO DONEGAL
♣♣♣♣♣♣♣♣♣♣♣♣♣♣♣♣♣♣♣♣♣♣♣♣♣♣♣♣♣♣

From Londonderry many pleasant car excursions can be made into Donegal. It must be remembered that this is "over the border," into Eire, and tourists should ensure that they have their cross-border documents in order. The most fertile part of Donegal is the Foyle basin. Other parts are predominently rock areas, with numerous signs of glacial deposition or erosion. Western Donegal is somewhat treeless, but has a magnificent coastline.

I. THE INISHOWEN PENINSULA

The circular trip here described is about 66 miles, with 18 miles more added if Malin Head is visited. Leaving Derry by Strand Road, we skirt the shores of Lough Foyle, and in 2 miles pass **Boom Hall,** which marks the point at which the river was blocked by a boom during the great Siege. At **Culmore** is the Northern Ireland frontier post, and 6 miles from Derry one enters Eire at **Muff.** Here the road, with mounrains rising on the left, continues to **Moville** (*Keaveney's* (20 rooms), *McKinney's* (10 rooms), *Prospect* (5 rooms)), a small seaside resort very popular with Derry residents. It may be of interest to those who fought under Field Marshal Viscount Montgomery to know that Moville was his "home town".

A diversion from the tour may be made here by continuing along the coast road through **Greencastle,** with its 9-hole golf course and ruins of a castle built in 1305, (*Castle Inn*) to **Inishowen Head,** 6 miles beyond Moville. From this rocky headland, one can see to the east *Giants' Causeway,* and at times, the coast of Scotland.

The main road turns inland from Moville, and follows the **Bredagh Glen,** bearing left to **Gleneely** and thence to **Culdaff,** a secluded village with a good bathing beach. The area has much to interest the student of archaeology. From Culdaff, the road runs westward to **Malin,** an attractive village with a green and a ten-arched bridge.

From here, if time permits, one can extend the tour 9 miles northwards to **Malin Head,** the most northerly point of Ireland. There are fine sea views from the headland, though the cliffs here are less lofty than those to the east. On **Inishtrahull,** a small island 6 miles from the shore, there stands a lighthouse. Near to Malin Head is a curious rock chasm known as *Hell's Hole,* through which the tide surges with great force.

Continuing from Malin, we cross the bridge and bear south for **Carndonagh,** a busy, small agricultural centre with a notable modern granite church, dedicated in 1945. Half a mile away is the **Donagh Cross,** said to be the oldest low-relief cross in Ireland. The main road now runs west to **Ballyliffin,** a mile or two to the north of which is **Pollan Strand,** a fine stretch of sand several miles long extending northwards to the ruins of **Carrickabraghy Castle.** A few miles beyond Ballyliffin we come to **Clonmany,** a pleasant village surrounded by hills, notably **Raghtinmore** (1,657 feet) to the west. Eleven miles farther south, by way of **Drumfries,** where **Slieve Snaght** (2,019 feet) may be seen to the left, we reach **Buncrana.**

An interesting but rather longer alternative route from Clonmany to Buncrana is by the road that follows more closely the line of the coast and crosses the **Gap of Mamore,** where the gradients are steep but the views magnificent.

Buncrana (*Lough Swilly* (47 rooms), *Atlantic* (8 rooms), *Central* (16 rooms)) is the chief town of the peninsula, and has some 2,896 inhabitants. It is a popular summer resort, being situated on the eastern shore of Lough Swilly, and sheltered by hills on the inland side. Golf, tennis and other amusements are catered for, and the sandy beaches offer good bathing. By *Castle Bridge*, to the north of the town, there stands the square keep of the castle of the O'Dohertys, built in 1430. Nearby is the eighteenth-century mansion known as *Buncrana Castle.*

From Buncrana, the road skirts the strand of *Lisfannon* with its 18-hole golf course, and brings us to **Fahan** (pronounced *fawn*) a small seaside resort pleasantly situated in a wooded valley. From Fahan there is a ferry service across the lough to **Rathmullen** (*see* p. 221). The road now turns inland and in 10 miles comes to **Bridgend,** at which is the Republic frontier post.

From Bridgend one may visit the **Grianan of Aileach,** 3 miles to the southwest. This is a circular stone fort standing on the eminence known as **Greenan Mountain** (802 feet), which commands views over both Lough Swilly and Lough Foyle. A circular central area, 77 feet in diameter, is enclosed by a stone wall, 17 feet high, and outside this are concentric ramparts of stone and earth. The fort, much restored in 1874, is certainly of great age, though there is considerable doubt about the story that it dates from 1700 B.C. and was originally a temple to the sun. It was, however, occupied by the early kings of Ireland long before the sixth century.

Continuing from Bridgend, we soon reach the Northern Ireland frontier post at **Gallach,** and re-enter Derry by the Strand Road.

II. DERRY TO CREESLOUGH AND RETURN TO DERRY

This tour, excluding the diversions indicated, is of about 85 miles. We leave Derry by the Foyle Road, and soon turn away from the river to pass the frontier posts at **Killea** and **Kildrum** respectively. After leaving the small *Port Lough* on the right, we pass through **Newtowncunningham** and Lough Swilly comes in sight. Soon after **Manorcunningham** (14 miles) our road is joined at **Pluck** by the road from Strabane; it then crosses the Swilly at *Port Bridge* and enters **Letterkenny** (*Central*, (7 rooms), *Gallagher's*, (16 rooms), *McGarry's* (16 rooms)), a town of some 5,000 inhabitants and spreading from one long main street on the hillside. From the high ground above the town there are fine views to be had, and the modern *St. Eunan's Cathedral* has many features of interest.

Our road now runs north-east for 8 miles to **Ramelton** (or Rathmelton), a noted angling centre on the shores of Lough Swilly.

From here a diversion may be made by taking the lough-side road for 6½ miles to **Rathmullen** (*Fort Royal* (22 rooms), *Pier* (10 rooms)), a popular small resort with a fine beach, good fishing and golf, and the ruins of a fifteenth-century Carmelite priory. To those interested in Irish history, Rathmullen has a number of associations, including those it has with Wolfe Tone, who with captured French forces was brought here after the French frigate, *La Hoche*, had been intercepted in Lough Swilly in 1798.

Our route follows the second turning to the right after leaving Ramelton, and leads to **Milford** (*Milford* (18 rooms)), an angler's resort beautifully situated at the southern end of **Mulroy Bay.**

From Milford, a longer diversion is possible if one takes the road running up the eastern shore of the bay, through **Carrowkeel** (or Kerrykeel) and leaving the **Knockellan Mountain** (1,203 feet) on the right, to **Portsalon** (10 miles). This is a noted resort on the western shore of Lough Swilly, with a fine 18-hole golf course in beautiful surroundings. Between here and **Fanad Head** at the northern end of the peninsula is some wonderful cliff scenery. First come the rocky tunnels known as the *Seven Arches*, then the *Great Arch* at **Doaghbeg**; and at the *Bin*, shortly before the lighthouse at Fanad Head is reached, the cliffs are 350 feet high.

Continuing our main route from Milford, we cross the little *Bunlin* river and proceed along the western shore of Mulroy Bay. After *Cranford Bridge*, there are fine views of the bay, and the road turns westward to **Carrigart.**

A short distance away is **Rosapenna** (*Rosapenna*) with its famous 18-hole golf course, and **Downings** (*Beach* (19 rooms)), an attractive resort of increasing popularity.

From Carrigart the road to Creeslough runs south-west.

About one mile from Carrigart a minor road runs off to the left to the village of **Glen** (6 miles) at the head of the long and narrow *Glen Lough*. But we continue on the main road to **Creeslough.**

This is a convenient centre for the ascent of **Muckish** (2,197 feet), the mountain lying several miles to the south-west. Near Creeslough, also, at the head of *Sheep Haven*, are the remains of **Doe Castle,** a former stronghold of the MacSweeney (or Mac-Suibhne) clan, and the scene of many desperate sieges. In the adjoining graveyard there is a carved slab of great antiquarian interest, the only similar slab being found at Killybegs. Still farther north, on the *Ards Peninsula*, is a Capuchin monastery in surroundings of great beauty.

Our road from Creeslough now runs south-east, crossing the *Owencarrow* river at **New Bridge,** and ascending to the rocky **Barnesbeg Gap,** with *Salt Mountain* on the left; thence to **Termon,** and down to **Kilmacrenan** in the valley of the *Lenan* river. Here is a prominent church tower, and the ruins of a fifteenth-century Franciscan friary on the site of an earlier abbey founded by St. Columba. From Kilmacrenan the road rises to give a fine view of the Donegal Mountains, and then descends to **Letterkenny,** whence we return to Derry by the route taken on the outward journey.

III. DERRY TO GLENTIES VIA RAPHOE AND STRANORLAR

From Derry to Glenties by the most direct route is 51 miles. We leave by Foyle Road, continuing along the line of the river to the frontier posts at **Mullenan** and **Carrigans.** After leaving **St. Johnston,** we take the right fork to **Raphoe** and **Stranorlar** (*see* p. 213).

From Stranorlar (24 miles) we cross the *River Finn* to **Ballybofey** and here take the right fork, following the river and crossing after several miles to its opposite bank. Near **Brockagh** there is a salmon-leap, and about 8 miles farther on we come to **Fintown** at the end of the narrow *Lough Finn*. The road continues along the shores of the lough, with **Aghla Mountain** (1,961 feet) visible on the far side, and descends to **Glenties** (*Highlands*, 15 rooms), a thriving township set in picturesque and well-wooded surroundings. The rivers *Owenea* and *Stracashel* converge here, and together with the lakes nearby afford excellent fishing. On the Owenea river is the *State Hatchery*. Glenties has a busy industry in glove-making and hosiery.

IV. THE COASTAL AREA BETWEEN CREESLOUGH AND DONEGAL

The remaining coastal area of Co. Donegal can be visited from Creeslough, Glenties or Donegal, to which routes from Derry have already been described.

From **Creeslough,** the road runs northwards *via* **Ballymore** to **Dunfanaghy,** both coastal resorts with excellent sandy beaches. From Dunfanaghy, a walk of a few miles to the north brings one to **Horn Head,** with cliffs that are 620 feet high and noted for their variety of sea-birds. Dunfanaghy has an 18-hole golf course, tennis courts, and other amenities for visitors. From here the road runs west to **Falcarragh** and **Gortahork.** In the grounds of Ballyconnell House, near Falcarragh, is the *Stone of Cloghaneely*, on which the giant Balor, who ruled over *Tory Island*, is said to have decapitated the mainland chieftain, MacKineely. The alleged bloodstains that still remain are probably iron-ore.

From Gortahork, the shortest road to Gweedore is that which runs due south, until, with **Errigal** (2,466 feet) on its left, it bears westward and is joined by the road from **Dunlewy.** The longer route is that running parallel with the coast, towards **Bloody Foreland** and then circling round *via* **Derrybeg,** and turning left at Bunbeg to Gweedore.

Gweedore is a small place, and the famous hotel built there some hundred years ago by Lord George Hill is now closed. The district is famous for its fishing and its scenery. A few miles to the east is **Dunlewy Lake** at the far end of which is the **Poisoned Glen** (*Youth Hostel*), penetrating into the Derryveagh Mountains. From **Dunlewy** one can make the ascent of **Errigal** (2,466 feet), from which in clear weather there is a fine view.

From Gweedore, we cross the *Clady* river by **Bryan's Bridge,** and, 3 miles farther on, the *Gweedore* river by **Crolly Bridge.** From here, the left-hand fork is the most direct route to Dungloe, passing **Lough Anure** on the left. The right-hand fork takes a much longer route, following the coast, *via* **Burtonport** —from which it is 2½ miles by boat to **Aran Island**—and the shore of **Lough Meale. Dungloe** is a small town of no great interest, but the coast between here and **Croghy Head,** about 5 miles to the south-west, is very picturesque. There is a curious landslip formation known as the *Talamh Briste*, or "broken earth"; near the headland is sandy **Maghery Bay.**

The main road runs south-east from Dungloe and then

223

branches right from the **Doocary** road. Some 10 miles farther on, it crosses the *Gweebarra* estuary by a long bridge, turning inland at **Maas** to **Glenties,** 16 miles from Dungloe (*see* p. 222).

A few miles west of Maas are the adjacent small resorts of **Narin** and **Portnoo** (*Portnoo* (20 rooms), *Rankin's* (22 rooms), *Ardmore* (10 rooms), *Glebe House* (8 rooms)). Here is good bathing and a 9-hole golf course, and the district has become a favourite for caravan holidays. Nearby there are two old forts at **Dunmore Head**; and a little to the south is **Doon Lough,** in the centre of which is an island with a circular stone fort.

Six miles to the south-west of Glenties is **Ardara,** a village (*Nesbitt Arms* (22 rooms)) in a valley at the mouth of the *Owentocker,* and noted for the manufacture of homespun Donegal tweeds. It is an excellent angling centre with fine coastal scenery. From Ardara a narrow peninsula runs out into the bay, culminating in **Loughros Point** (6 miles) which makes a pleasant excursion. A few miles along the main coast-line to the west of Ardara, are the **Maghera Caves,** which can be explored at low tide, and the beautiful **Essaranka Waterfall** is nearby. Still farther west is **Slievetooey** (1,458 feet).

From Ardara the road runs south, following the river valley, and is joined by the road from Donegal 2 miles before Killybegs is reached. **Killybegs** (*Ben View* (14 rooms), *Quinns'* (6 rooms)) is a fishing port in a fine natural harbour, and a centre for the manufacture of Donegal carpets. It is also a good centre from which to visit the magnificent scenery of south-west Donegal. In the Church of St. Mary's is a remarkable carved slab in memory of Niall Mor MacSuibhne.

Westwards from Killybegs a road goes to **Fintragh Bay,** with **Crownarad** (1,621 feet) rising on the right. The road then turns inland to **Kilcar,** a pleasant village from which one may visit **Muckross Head** and the remarkable **Muckross Caves,** 2 miles to the south. Beyond Kilcar is **Carrick,** (Youth Hostel), where the *Glen* river runs into the long and narrow **Teelin Bay.** This is a good point from which to make the ascent of **Slieve League** (1,972 feet) whose rocky slopes drop steeply to the Atlantic. At **Bungloss** at the southern end of the range, the cliffs rise sheer to 1,024 feet, and between here and the highest point runs the narrow *One Man's Pass.* Six miles to the north-west of Carrick is **Glencolumbkille** in the valley at **Glen Bay.**

From Killybegs eastward to Donegal, our road crosses the *Oily* river at Milltown, and soon reaches **Dunkineely,** 1½ miles south of which are the ruins of the old castle of the Mac-Suibhnes of Banagh. Four miles beyond Dunkineely is the small fishing village of **Inver,** and as far again we come to **Mountcharles,** a hill town commanding views of Donegal Bay to the south and of the mountains to the north. Another 4 miles brings us to **Donegal** (*see* p. 212).

DERRY TO ENNISKILLEN VIA STRABANE
AND OMAGH

The 61-mile drive from Derry to Enniskillen is along excellent roads of recent construction. Leave Derry by the A 5; in 4 miles this forks to become the T 3 which runs parallel with the *River Foyle* through broad river meadows. At **Magheramason,** we leave Co. Derry for Co. Tyrone. This county is now well-cultivated, arable land, but up to the seventeenth century, it was thickly wooded. Once known as the strong kingdom of Tir-Eoghain, it refused to recognize England as its conqueror until the reign of Henry VIII, when the reigning O'Neill exchanged his sovereignty for the position of Earl, and accepted English law. The kingdom was divided into three counties: Armagh in the south, Coleraine (now Londonderry) in the north and Tyrone in the middle. The Sperrin Mountains form part of the boundary between Tyrone and Londonderry. The T 3 follows the bend of the river and in 5 miles on the farther bank can be seen the ruined tower of **Montgevlin Castle** where James II resided in 1689 during the siege of Derry. Fifteen miles from Derry is the Northern Ireland frontier post of **Strabane** (*Abercorn Arms* (21 rooms), *Commercial* (21 rooms)). The town (population, 9,800) is the centre of a large agricultural district, but apart from a pleasing road bridge, is of little architectural interest. It is situated on the river Mourne, noted for its salmon. Several distinguished men who figure in Canadian and American history were natives of Strabane, one being Lord Dorchester, Governor of Quebec, 1766–96 and Commander-in-Chief in America, 1782–83.

A mile to the south-west is **Carricklee** (B 85) popular for point-to-point races. We continue along the west bank of the Mourne to **Sion Mills,** where there is a flourishing linen industry, a model village and an interesting parish church. Also new R.C. church. At Victoria Bridge, 3 miles farther on, there is a choice of routes to Enniskillen, but we follow the main trunk road, T 3, to **Newtownstewart** (*Castle* (4 rooms)), named after William Stewart, ancestor of the Lords Mountjoy. This is a paradise for anglers and attractive to historians for the ruined castles in the district. One of the most conspicuous is **Harry Avery's Castle,** ½ mile south-west of the town. After the Siege of Derry, James II retreated through Newtownstewart and ordered the destruction of bridges and castles. Several roads radiate from Newtownstewart.

A digression may be made from the main route by going 2 miles south-west along B 84 to **Baronscourt**, the palatial home of the Duke of Abercorn, formerly Governor of Northern Ireland. The chief glory of the well-wooded estate are the terraced Italian gardens which extend from the mansion to one of a chain of islet-studded lakes which intersect the park. Near the large and magnificent house is an extensive plantation of evergreens and many varieties of giant rhododendrons. The picturesque walks and drives extend for nearly 30 miles. The Duke of Abercorn is head of one branch of the Scottish family of Hamilton, and descended from the fourth son of the second Earl of Arran, whose son was created Baron Abercorn in 1693.

Our road (A 5) from Newtownstewart runs southward alongside the *River Strule*, noted for its trout and its mussel pearls. Hills loom up on either side—**Mary Gray** (828 feet) on the left and **Bessie Bell** (1,387 feet) on the right, so named after the ladies in a ballad written by a Scottish lord of Newtownstewart. Ten miles south is Omagh.

Omagh

Access.—Bus connection with Belfast, Dublin, Londonderry, etc. U.T.A. bus services to many points.

Angling.—For salmon and trout in the Strule and subsidiary streams. The Camowen for 6 miles upstream to Leap Bridge is controlled by Omagh Angling Association.

Distances.—Ballyshannon 41, Belfast 73, Dublin 117, Dungannon 30, Enniskillen 27, Londonderry 34, Newtonstewart 10, Pettigo 25, Strabane 20.

Early Closing.—Wednesday.

Golf.—9-hole course, ½ mile from town.

Hotels.—*Melville* (17 rooms), *Royal Arms* (29), *Silver Birch* (31).

Population.—10,000.

County town and administrative centre of Tyrone, Omagh has a population of just over 10,000. It stands at the junction of the *Drumnagh* and *Camowen* rivers which unite to become the *Strule*, and is the centre of a large agricultural area. In the town are a two-steepled Roman Catholic church, the Church of Ireland, and an attractive courthouse, where the assizes are held. The Royal Inniskilling Fusiliers have their regimental headquarters at Omagh with which town they have had a long association.

Omagh is a good centre from which to explore the wild scenery to the north-east. The B 48 runs 8 miles north to **Gortin Gap,** where there is a Youth Hostel. The road passes between the high hills of **Mullaghcarn** (1,778 feet) on the right and **Curraghchosaly** (1,372 feet) on the left, to the pretty village of **Plumbridge**, nestling in the mountains. At Plumbridge, turn left along the B 47 which goes through the beautiful Corrick Glen to Newtonstewart where it joins the A 5 for Omagh. The drive can be extended north from Plumbridge by keeping to the B 48 which traverses *Butterlope Glen,* through attractive scenery to **Donemana,** where there is a picturesque ruined castle named Earl's Gift. Scottish people settled at Donemana and there is still a distinct trace of Scottish words and forms of speech among the inhabitants.

From Omagh to Enniskillen the most direct route (*bus*) is the T 10 which runs south-west to **Dromore** (*Commercial,* (9 rooms)), a typical Tyrone village, where St. Patrick is said to have founded an abbey. The next village we pass through is **Trillick,** backed by the **Brougher Mountain** (1,046 feet). Two miles beyond is **Kilskeery,** dominated by its tall steeple, and in 1 mile we cross into Co. Fermanagh by the A 32 which descends to Ballinamallard and Enniskillen.

ENNISKILLEN AND LOUGH ERNE
❧❧❧❧❧❧❧❧❧❧❧❧❧❧❧❧❧❧❧❧❧❧❧❧❧❧❧❧❧❧❧❧❧❧

Enniskillen

Access.—Bus connections with Omagh, Clones, Belfast, Ballyshannon and Bundoran, etc.

Angling.—Permits for trout in Lower Lough Erne from Board of Conservators, High Street, or at Post Office.

Cattle Market.—Thursdays.

Distances.—Armagh 50, Ballyshannon 28, Belleek 24, Belfast 86, Cavan 42, Cork 215, Donegal 42, Dublin 111, Dungannon 43, Londonderry 61, Omagh 27, Sligo 40.

Early Closing.—Wednesday.

Golf.—9-hole course on Dublin road, 1 mile.

Hotels.—*Imperial* (70 rooms), *Celtic* (14), *Railway* (28), *Royal* (11), *Killyhevlin* (10), *Manor House* (24) and several guest houses.

Population.—8,877.

Enniskillen, the chief town of Co. Fermanagh, occupies a most attractive position on the *River Erne*. For the most part it is situated on an island between channels of the river which separates the two lakes, Upper and Lower Lough Erne. Bridges connect the island to east, north and west banks.

It is a thriving market town in the centre of Northern Ireland's principal stock-raising county, and a large cattle market is held every Thursday. This county town commands the direct route to the west and also that serving the shipping ports of Belfast and Derry. It has an excellent shopping centre, and although not a town of great antiquity, it has one or two buildings of interest.

The Parish Church in the centre of the town was raised to the dignity of the *Cathedral of St. Macartin* in 1924. The building dates from 1840, built on the site of an earlier church of 1637, of which only the tower remains, surmounted by a spire of 1841. Some objects of historical interest are preserved in the interior. The *Pokrich Stone* (1628) is a slab inscribed to the memory of Richard Pokrich, who was possibly one of the founders of Enniskillen. It is near the door of the west wall of the church. There is also a slender, beautifully carved font, dated 1666. The chancel is adorned with the regimental colours of the Inniskillings.

The other churches in the town are of modern construction, as also is the imposing Town Hall with its domed tower.

Enniskillen Castle is in the barrack yard at the bottom of Castle Street. The remaining ruins are those of a fifteenth-century keep, and a water-gate of the sixteenth century, near which is a defence earthwork, locally still referred to as "The Sconce." There was probably a castle on this site before the sixth century, when the first christian missionaries came to the county.

The first historical record of Enniskillen Castle is in the time of the Maguire clan early in 1439. It changed ownership several times, until 1607, when it was finally captured by the English and handed over to Sir William Cole, who contributed much to the founding of Enniskillen: the castle was rebuilt, a charter established, and lands were assigned for a royal school, later founded by James I.

In 1641, the colonists and settlers valiantly defended the town, and again in 1689, Enniskillen joined with Londonderry in repulsing the rebels. After the Siege of Londonderry, the defeat of James II's army was turned into a rout by the men of Enniskillen, who struggled through bogland to challenge and rout an Irish force double their strength. It was during these troublous times that the two great regiments, the Inniskilling Dragoons and the 27th Inniskillings (now called the Royal Inniskilling Fusiliers) were formed from the horse and foot soldiers commanded by private citizens. Since then, the men have won fame for their regiments and Enniskillen, by their gallantry in every major war in which the British army has taken part. These regiments have now been granted the Freedom of the Borough of Enniskillen.

Overlooking the eastern end of the town are the **Forthill Pleasure Grounds.** Delightful gardens flank a very tall column erected to the memory of Sir Galbraith Lowry-Cole, one of Wellington's generals in the Peninsular War and a Governor of Cape Colony. A spiral staircase leads to the top, from which wonderful views are obtained in all directions.

South-east of the town on the A 34 is **Castlecoole,** the seat of the Earls of Belmore. Built in the Doric style by James Wyatt (1720–98), this is one of the finest eighteenth-century mansions in Ireland, and contains fine plaster work by Joseph Rose. In the grounds is a lake sanctuary for wild fowl, and there are many unusual trees and shrubs. Castlecoole is now in the care of the National Trust. (*Admission charge, on Tuesday, Wednesday, Friday, Saturday and Bank Holidays. 2–6 from April to September; Sundays from July to September.*)

Lough Erne

The River Erne has a navigable course of over 50 miles through rivers and lakes. Rising in Co. Longford, it flows northward through Co. Cavan, unites with other rivers and enters Co. Fermanagh. Here it spreads into **Upper Lough Erne,** 15 miles long and 4 miles wide, with a maze of inlets, bays and small islands. At the northern end of this upper lake, the river narrows and passes either side of the island on which Enniskillen stands, and then again unites. In one and a half miles it expands into the wonderful sheet of water known as **Lower Lough Erne,** 7 miles wide and 18 miles long. Lough Erne, with its legendary associations, its beautiful setting, wooded islands, ruined castles and fascinating wild life, provides delightful excursions for the tourist.

Most interesting of the many islands in Lough Erne is **Devenish** (*Daimh Inis,* the isle of oxen), two and a half miles north of Enniskillen (*boats from West Bridge*). The island is celebrated for its group of ecclesiastical remains on and close to the site of a monastery founded in the sixth century by St. Molaise. Best preserved is an 82-foot *Round Tower,* among the finest and largest in Ireland, and notable for its finely sculptured cornice. An ascent can be made from the inside of the tower which was originally divided into five storeys. Of the *House of St. Molaise,* the most ancient building, only foundations and parts of the walls remain, its disintegration being hastened by vandals. The *Great Church,* or *St. Molaise's Church,* much ruined, retains an interesting Romanesque window. Higher up the hill, *St. Mary's Abbey* was a house of Canons Regular of St. Augustine. It is a Gothic structure erected *c.* 1449 on the site of an earlier foundation. A stone stairway leads to a quadrangular belfry tower, and the groined vault and pointed door in the north wall are interesting. The sacristy door has decorations of foliage and a bird. To the south, in the Abbey cemetery, is a 7-foot cross of unknown date, decorated with intricate carvings.

Round Lough Erne

The favourite excursion is the 57-mile drive round Lough Erne. Leave Enniskillen *via* West Bridge and the A 46. On the right we pass *Portora Royal School,* founded in 1608 under Royal Charter, and originally situated at Linaskea. Among famous pupils, were the first Lord Plunkett, the Rev. H. F. Lyte (author of "Abide with Me"), Archbishop Magee of Dublin and Oscar Wilde. A little beyond are the ruins of **Portora Castle,** built by Sir William Cole in 1615. A barrage has been constructed across the Narrows as part of the Erne hydro-electric scheme, and during the excavations, many stone and bronze-age weapons were uncovered. Four miles along the route is the well-wooded estate of *Ely Lodge,* residence of the Duke of Westminster. Near the lake are the scant remains of *Castle Hume.* Three miles to the west of this, on rising ground, is ruined *Castle of Monea* (1618). In the church a mile north of the castle, is a fifteenth-century window taken from the Abbey at Devenish in 1630. The road runs inland a little, but out on the lake we can see the island of **Inishmacsaint** (the isle of the plain of sorrel). On this island a monastery was founded in the early sixth century. Close to the ruins of its thirteenth-century parish church is a 13-foot-high cross of early date. Shortly after Tully Bay a cart-track leads off to the right to the ruins of *Tully Castle,* the scene of a treacherous massacre and fire in 1641.

The road hugs the lake shore to Rosscor Bridge, where a road to the right leads to the return road, A 47 along the north shore of the lough. But it is worthwhile to continue for another 4 miles, along A 46, to **Belleek,** famous for its trout fishing and its hand-made Parian porcelain. From Belleek, if time permits, an excursion can be made southward along the B 52 for 4 miles, to the pretty village of **Garrison** (*Melvin, Casey's Lake*). It is at the eastern end of *Lough Melvin*, and is very popular with fishermen, for Gillaroo trout abound here.

At Belleek we turn sharp right, along A 47, for the return route to Enniskillen, *via* the northern bank of Lough Erne, passing *Castle-caldwell*. The district supplies the clay for the Belleek ware, but the castle is now a ruin. It is notable for its fiddle-shaped stone of 1770, at the entrance gate, on which the inscription reads:

> "On firm land only exercise your skill,
> There you may play and safely drink your fill."

The main route crosses to **Boa Island,** 4 miles in length, and affording wonderful views of the Lough.

The alternative but longer route, by B 136, crosses into Eire to the frontier town of **Pettigo** (*Flood's* (7 rooms)), part of which is in Co. Donegal and part in Co. Fermanagh. From Pettigo, L 84 runs northwards for 4½ miles to Lough Derg, a place of pilgrimage from June to August each year. On **Station Island,** in the lake, St. Patrick had his vision of Purgatory. Pilgrimages have been made since about 1150, and there is a hospice to accommodate pilgrims on the island, and a large church. Farther north in the lake is **Saints' Island,** where exist the remains of a monastery founded by St. Daveog, a disciple of St. Patrick. From Pettigo, A 35 joins A 47, which has traversed the length of Boa Island, at Bannagh Bridge, and continues to **Kesh,** where the road, B 4, to the left, leads to the hillier regions of **Ederny** and **Lack.**

We continue along the A 35 for 3 miles, until it bears left for Irvinestown to Enniskillen. Here we fork right, on B 82, to keep close to the lough and its picturesque views. **Crevenish Castle** is passed—a fine example of a seventeenth-century plantation residence —then White Island, situated in Castle Archdale Bay. **White Island** is interesting for its twelfth-century church and its carvings. This is a small building, partly in ruins, with a Romanesque doorway and windows. Inside are curiously carved figures built into the wall, and probably dating from the seventh to ninth centuries, though their history is unknown. Seven of the figures were discovered during repair work in 1928, and the eighth thirty years later. The shore road skirts the grounds of **Castle Archdale** (caravan park); erected in 1773, on the site of the original plantation castle, it served as an important R.A.F. headquarters during the Second World War, when the bay was used as a flying-boat base. In about 5 miles from Castle Archdale, we come to *Killadeas* (*Manor House*), which was also an R.A.F. base, and is now a popular resort with anglers. Killadeas church is worth visiting for its curiously carved stones. The shore road soon unites with the A 32, and in 4 miles reaches Enniskillen.

Upper Lough Erne

Several interesting excursions lie to the south of Enniskillen. Upper Lough Erne is a shallow lake 4 miles in width and extending nearly 10 miles towards Newtownbutler and Belturbet. The low shores are much indented, and the lake is dotted with at least a hundred islets, so that exploration of the lake itself is best done by boat. One of the most beautiful of the islands is **Bellisle**, at the eastern end of the lough and connected to the mainland by a bridge. Some of the roads round the lough cross and recross the frontier, and others are not suitable for motor traffic. There is a fine view of the lough from the rock of Knockninny, 10 miles south of Enniskillen.

Six miles south-east of Enniskillen, *via* the A 4 and the A 32, is **Florence-court**, the estate of the Earl of Enniskillen. The lovely eighteenth-century mansion is noted for its fine plasterwork and the Florencecourt Yew. It is now in the care of the National Trust. (*Open Tuesday, Wednesday, Friday, Saturday and Bank Holidays, 2–6, April to September; also Sunday, 2.30–5.30, July to September.*)

Three miles farther along this road is the **Marble Arch Glen.** The arch, in the lovely Cladagh Glen, marks the mouth of an underground river, which flows through several caves. These caves can be explored, preferably with a guide.

West of Enniskillen, the A 4 leads in 25 miles to Belcoo, where there are many prehistoric monuments and an ancient church. **Boho**, nearby, has some interesting caves. Towering above is **Belmore Mountain** (1,312 feet) where there are several giants' caves, cairns and other prehistoric monuments. From the summit there is a wonderful view embracing lakes, mountains and rivers, and in the far west, a glimpse of the Atlantic.

DERRY TO COLERAINE
❀❀❀❀❀❀❀❀❀❀❀❀❀❀❀❀❀❀❀❀❀❀❀

For the 31 mile run to Coleraine road and rail keep close
company along the southern shore of Lough Foyle. Londonderry is left by the A 2 over Craigavon Bridge, which after
Faughan Bridge becomes the T 7. In 4 miles a road turns off to
the right for Muff Glen and **Eglinton,** a delightful village that no
one should miss. Here there are some magnificent trees, flower-
filled cottage gardens, and the beautiful *Muff Glen* which
extends over Highmoor to the grand waterfall of the Burntollet
river. Beyond the Eglinton turn the main road passes the tiny
village of **Ballykelly** which has an attractive church and a
fortified mansion built in 1619 by the London Fishmongers'
Company. Three miles eastward is—

Limavady

Distances.—Ballymoney 20, Belfast 63,
Coleraine 14, Dublin 142, Londonderry 17, Portrush 20.
Angling.—Good fishing for salmon
(mostly grilse) and sea trout in River Roe.

Early Closing.—Thursday.
Hotel.—*Alexander Arms* (9 rooms).
Population.—5,500.

The name Limavady is derived from *Lim-an-nhadadh* (fort
of the dog leap). According to tradition, the dog of O'Cahan,
the chieftain, jumped the River Roe and conveyed a message to
Dungiven summoning help from the clan there. A castle was
built on the site by the O'Cahans and the town grew up around
it. At the Plantation of Ulster Sir Thomas Phillips was given
the district and he moved the site of the town from O'Cahan's
castle; thus Newtown Limavady as the place is often called.

Roads run south from Limavady on both sides of the beautiful valley of the *River Roe* (red river). Roe Park lies between
the town and Dog's Leap. In the park at Mullagh Ridge is the
mount of *Drumceat*, thought to have been the gathering place
of the great religious convention of A.D. 574 under the presidency of St. Columba. One of its decisions had widespread
consequences, in that Western Scotland (which had been
colonized by the Irish and given its name of Scotia) should be
given Home Rule and be independent of Ulster. Thereby
Ireland gave Scotland its Parliament. It was at Limavady in

1851 that Miss Jane Ross heard a strolling fiddler play the haunting melody which later became famous as the "Londonderry Air." It is believed to have been composed by a famous chief of the north—Rory Dall O'Cahan, "Lord of the Route and Limavady." Thackeray wrote his poem "Sweet Peg of Limavady" in the town, and here too W. F. Massey, Premier of New Zealand, was born.

The *direct* route to Coleraine from Limavady presents alternative roads: the first right turn (T 7) out of Limavady or in a further 2 miles another right turn (B 201) on to the old hill road. These roads pass either side of **Bolea,** an attractive hamlet in the valley of the Curly Burn. In the surrounding area are the Dooans, site of ancient funeral rites, and a rare example of the "sweathouse," an ancient Turkish bath by the stream. Both roads mount to over 800 feet on the shoulder of a hill giving fine views of mountain, moor and sea. The old road crosses **Sconce Hill** (900 feet) on the top of which was the fortress of the Red Branch Knights (*Dun Ceithern*). The T 7 passes through **Macosquin** where a Cistercian monastery was founded in 1172 and whose abbot became Bishop of Derry. Both routes then descend to the valley of the Bann and into Coleraine.

The longer coast route from Limavady (A 2) runs north to skirt the base of **Benevenagh Mountain,** a fine basaltic peak, 1,260 feet high. Several picturesque waterfalls cascade down its wooded slopes where grow alpine plants, and where the raven and peregrine nest. Road and rail then cross the flat *Magilligan Peninsula* to **Downhill** (*Downhill* (13 rooms)), on the coast. *Magilligan Strand* is a raised sandy beach backed by sandhills. The beach provides a wealth of seashells and extends for 6 miles to the mouth of Lough Foyle at Magilligan Point where a ferry crosses the 1 mile gap to Greencastle. There is an old tower or fort at the Point.

Close neighbour to Downhill is **Castlerock** (*Castlerock* (6 rooms), *Golf* (11 rooms)) noted for its excellent golf course (18 holes) and good rock and surf bathing. It is a quiet seaside resort and a centre for the ornithologist and antiquarian. The former Downhill Castle here was built by the Earl of Bristol (1730–1803), bishop of Derry and insatiable traveller after whom many Continental hotels are named. Close to the cliff is the *Mussenden Temple* (1783; National Trust) built by the Earl as a library but later dedicated as a memorial to his cousin, Mrs. Mussenden.

From Downhill the main road leads away from the shore to **Articlave,** a hamlet once subject to frequent invasion from the Danes, and in 6 miles it reaches Coleraine.

234

Coleraine

Road and Rail connection with London-derry, Belfast and all neighbouring places.
Boating.—Boats available for the Bann.
Distances.—Antrim 38, Ballycastle 19, Ballymena 27, Ballymoney 8, Dublin 142, Belfast 55, Limavady 14, London-derry 31, Maghera 21, Portrush 6.

Early Closing.—Thursday.
Angling.—Good fishing for salmon and trout in the Bann; also some coarse fishing.
Hotels.—*Westbrook* (21 rooms), *Gorteen House* (12).
Population.—13,500.

Coleraine (*Cuil Rathain*, corner of the ferns) with its several modern industries, is one of the most prosperous business and market towns in Ulster. It is situated on the *River Bann* some 4 miles from the river mouth at Ballyaghran Point. The town is an excellent centre for touring the neighbourhood. The Bann provides good sport with salmon (permits locally), sea trout and brown trout. There are a rowing club and an annual regatta, tennis courts and bowling green, cinemas and two fine parks. The golf courses at Castlerock, Portstewart and Portrush are within easy reach. Rail and bus services are good, and roads radiate in all directions.

Coleraine is very ancient, for its old fort, *Mountsandel* was the seat of Rory Mor, king of the Picts about 100 B.C. and the capital of their territory. From A.D. 1100 to 1424 there were frequent raids, battles and sieges and much of the town was destroyed. In the sixteenth century it was occupied by English troops and in the seventeenth century received its first charter. The Irish Society of London helped to colonize the area with English and Lowland Scots to help keep the Irish clans in check. The Irish Society has been responsible for the fine public buildings, and for encouraging a high social, educational and cultural level of life. The name of the town is familiar to many from the song title "Kitty of Coleraine," originally published in a Waterford Chapbook of 1810. Coleraine was the home of the Lawrences, of Indian Mutiny fame.

The open square in the centre of the town is known as the "Diamond" and most of the town's traffic converges at this point. Overlooking the Diamond is a fine Town Hall erected in 1743. Just off the square is the parish *Church of St. Patrick* built in 1884 on the site of a fifth-century church burnt down in 1177. At the end of Bridge Street leading off the square the *Bann* is crossed by a bridge from which there are some excellent views of the river. To the north of the bridge is the small harbour busy with river traffic.

A pleasant walk southwards for about a mile and a half along the west bank of the river leads to the *Salmon Leap*, a barrier of rock some 12 feet high over which salmon and eels hurl themselves to reach the spawning grounds in the upper reaches of the river towards Lough Neagh.

For **Portstewart,** 6 miles north of Coleraine, *see* p. 274.

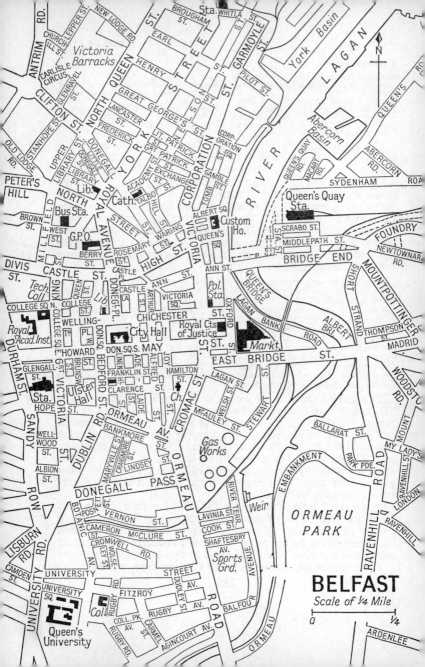

BELFAST

Scale of ¼ Mile

0   ¼

BELFAST
✹✹✹✹✹✹✹✹✹

Airport.—Belfast Airport is at Aldergrove, 12 miles west of the city. There is an air terminal at Glengall Street.

Angling.—Best rivers in vicinity are the *Crumlin, Glenavy, Comber* (preserved), and *Lagan.* Excellent fishing (particularly for brown trout) is to be had in the Belfast Water Commissioners' reservoirs, by licence.

Buses.—Good local services linking the city and suburbs, while *Ulsterbus Ltd.* services provide connections to all major towns in Ireland.

Banks.—*Bank of Ireland, Belfast Banking Co., Belfast Savings Bank, Munster and Leinster Bank, National Bank, Northern Bank, Provincial Bank, Ulster Bank.*

Distances.—Antrim 17, Armagh 37, Ballymena 28, Bangor 13, Coleraine 55, Donaghadee 18, Dublin 103, Larne 21, Lisburn 8, Londonderry 75, Newry 38, Killarney 271, Cork 252.

Early Closing.—Wednesday and/or Saturday.

Entertainment.—
Cinemas. There are numerous cinemas. For programmes see local press.
Concerts. Ulster Hall, Grosvenor Hall, Sir William Whitla Hall, St Mary's Hall, Assembly Hall, King George VI Youth Centre, Wellington Hall.
Show Jumping. The Royal Ulster Agricultural Society's annual show is held at Balmoral in May.
Theatres. Group, Bedford Street; *Arts*, Botanic Avenue; *Opera House*, Great Victoria Street, *Grove*, 194 Shore Road.

Hotels.—*Grand Central* (170 rooms), *Midland* (63), *Belgravia Private* (170), *Kensington* (66), *Robinson's* (41), *Royal Avenue* (108), *Conway* (78), and many others. There are many boarding establishments. A full list of all grades may be obtained from the Information Centre, 6, Royal Avenue.

Information.—Northern Ireland Tourist Board, 6, Royal Avenue.

Places of Worship.—There are over 160 churches in Belfast and its immediate suburbs. Particulars of service times are given in local papers and announcements.

Population.—386,000.

Post Office.—General Post Office, Royal Avenue.

Sport.—
Athletics. Meetings at Balmoral, Paisley Park, Tillysburn, and Ormeau Park.
Bowls and Tennis. There are numerous courts in the public parks. Certain clubs make courts available to visitors.
Football. Association at Windsor Park, Lisburn Road; at the Oval, Grosvenor Park, Cliftonville and Seaview. Rugby at Ravenhill Park.
Greyhound Racing. Alternate evenings at *Celtic Park*, Donegall Road, and *Dunmore Park*, Antrim Road.
Golf. 18-hole courses include the *Balmoral*, Lisburn Road; *Belvoir Park*, Newtownbreda; *Fortwilliam*, Antrim Road; *Knock*, Stormont; *Malone*, Malone Road; *Shandon Park*, Knock Road; and the *Royal Belfast*, Craigavad.
   9-hole courses at *Cliftonville*, Westland Road and *Ormeau*.
Swimming. Baths at Grove, Ormeau Avenue, Falls Road and Templemore Avenue. Open air baths at Falls Park and Victoria Park.

With a population of 386,000, Belfast is the second city in size in Ireland. As seat of the Northern Ireland Government, with a cathedral and university and many thriving industries, it is of leading importance. Well situated on the River Lagan near its meeting with Belfast Lough, it has a fine harbour and its ship-building yards are world-renowned. Though it is true that Belfast made the Lagan, yet that service was reciprocated by the Lagan making Belfast. The name "Lagan" signifies "a hollow or narrow district between hills." The river rises in the Mourne Mountains and during the last quarter of its 46-mile course separates the Antrim and Down counties. Belfast proper is on the west side, while on the opposite bank, and connected by two bridges, is the part known specifically as **Ballymacarett** (*Bally Mac Art*, town of the son of the High Chief, O'Neill. O'Neill was King of Ulster in earlier times).

Belfast is not a difficult city to explore. Most of the hotels and restaurants, the main shops, public buildings and places of entertainment are located in a central area of about a mile square. Donegall Quay, where the cross-channel steamers berth, is little more than a stone's throw from **High Street,** Belfast's chief thoroughfare. High Street, rather conventional, merges at its westerly end into Castle Place, and terminates in **Castle Junction,** Belfast's hub.

Walk 1

Northward runs **Royal Avenue,** with the General Post Office, arge hotels, shops and the Central Public Library. We, however, take the opposite direction, down stately **Donegall Place,** leading past the *Titanic Memorial* to **Donegall Square** and Belfast's municipal palace, **The City Hall.**

Built in quadrangular form with an internal courtyard, it is a pleasing blend of seventeenth- and eighteenth-century Renaissance styles, covering about an acre and a half of space and bordering on four wide streets. It was designed by Sir Brumwell Thomas (1906) and occupies the site of the former Linen Hall. Towers at each of the four corners rise to a height of 115 feet, while a great central green dome, terminating in a stone lantern 173 feet above street level, dominates the whole of the city. Features of the interior include the Council Chamber, a noble Reception Room and Banquet Hall, and the magnificent Great Hall, occupying almost the whole of the east front of the building. Outside are attractive gardens and numerous statues, including those of Queen Victoria and prominent Belfast citizens.

Leaving the City Hall we turn up **Bedford Street** and find ourselves in the midst of Belfast's linen quarter. Bedford Street also contains the **Ulster Hall,** seating 2,000, built in 1862. It has housed many famous assemblies, and during recent years its Minor Hall has been Belfast's "**Group Theatre,**" well worthy of a visit.

At the beginning of Bedford Street a long thoroughfare —known in its different sections as **Grosvenor Road, Howard Street, Donegall Square South** (the rear of the City Hall) and **May Street**—extends in a straight line from west to east, from the distant hills right to the River Lagan.

We turn across the Howard Street part as far as **Great Victoria Street** (not to be confused with Victoria Street, a little nearer to the river), with its Rail and Road Terminal. Also in Great Victoria Street are the Opera House (Belfast's only legitimate theatre), the Odeon and the A.B.C. (combining variety with films and dining). Opposite the A.B.C. is the dignified pile of buildings, with its handsome pinnacled tower, that is the headquarters of the **Irish Presbyterian Church.** A little farther north, on the same side, is the Classic Cinema, famous as being the site of the house in which Lord Kelvin was born. (His father was mathematics master in the Academical Institution opposite.) The **Royal Academical Institution** was, prior to the establishment of Queen's College (now University) in 1847, Belfast's College, and its lustre as the leading public school has not diminished despite the passing of time, though its northern wing is now almost eclipsed by—

The City of Belfast College of Technology

Visitors may inspect the College on application at the General Office.

The College of Technology provides courses from elementary level to research work in craft subjects, leading to higher University degrees. It is closely linked with the Queen's University of Belfast, preparing students for internal degrees in Applied Chemistry and Pharmaceutics. Over 10,000 day and evening students are enrolled in it.

Leaving the Belfast College we may see in the adjoining **College Square East and North** some traces of what was prior to 1907 a pleasant Victorian square. Go eastward through the narrow **College Street** into a retail linen market where the economic housewife may pick up bargains in cheap remnants. From Fountain Street either the **Queen's Arcade** or Bird Cage Walk may be crossed to reach Donegall Place again.

Walk 2

From Castle Junction again, Castle Place leads eastwards past Corn Market to **High Street,** a few doors down which is **Crown Entry,** which was the meeting-place of the United Irishmen of the 1798 Rising in the North. A neighbouring shop was the house where Sir Samuel Ferguson was born, one of the greatest of Irish poets. Across the way is **Bridge Street** (here the open river was crossed), and in the entry almost opposite, the first number of the world-known *Bradshaw's Guide* was issued.

Lower down on the right side, though modestly set back is **St. George's Church**—perhaps the oldest as regards site among Belfast's 150 or more churches of all denominations. It was converted into a citadel by the Cromwellians, but reconverted with the Restoration. The present building, the third on the site, was erected in 1816. The stately pillars of its portico came from the palace at Ballyscullion of the erratic bishop, the Earl of Bristol, whose name is perpetuated in the Bristol hotels on the Continent.

As we turn to the right into **Victoria Street** we see the **Albert Memorial Clock Tower,** about 140 feet high, with its statue of the Prince Consort.

Behind the Albert Memorial is the **Custom House,** a large Italian building with handsome carved pediment having figures emblematic of peace, manufacture, commerce and industry. Here, Anthony Trollope, the novelist, and Allingham, the poet, were officials for a time.

Victoria Street continues from the north side of High Street into **Corporation Street** and terminates a mile away at the busy York Road Station. We turn along the south section, which continues into **Cromac Street,** close to the **Law Courts, Telephone House** and the Markets, and finally extends into the Ormeau Road.

The Royal Courts of Justice is a dignified building of the traditional Italian school after the Palladian style. Both internally and externally it is regarded as the most beautiful public building in Belfast. Certainly its central Court Hall, with its walls and floor of travertine marble, avoids the garish tinting that detracts from the similar chamber in Stormont. The main buildings house King's Bench Courts, the Chancery Court and the Court of Appeal, as well as the Bar library and necessary Court Offices.

Ann Street, which crosses Victoria Street at the High Street end, is the chief artery over the **Queen's Bridge** from industrial

Londonderry

East Strand, Portrush, Co. Antrim

Belfast City Hall

Ballyholme, Bangor, Co. Down

Belfast-across-the-river. We turn citywards up Ann Street, a modern, busy street, with few memories, save that a hundred years ago it was known as "the Back Green Street." There, in a small theatre in one of the abutting courts, the lady who lived to become Duchess of St. Albans once acted. At the city end of Arthur Street is **Arthur Square,** where was the *Theatre Royal,* in days past known to admirers of Sir Henry Irving, Ellen Terry, Benson, Beerbohm Tree, and many others.

We turn now to the left, along **Arthur Street,** and soon again we turn to the right and find ourselves in **Chichester Street**—a memory of Belfast's founder, as are Ann Street, Arthur Street, Donegall Place, etc. This is one of Belfast's pleasantest streets, leading up from the Law Courts, the city police courts, and the Fire Station, past the City Hall, where it is styled Donegall Square North. Here on the right is the **Linenhall Library,** with a fine collection of books relating to the linen industry as well as general and historical works.

Walk 3

This time we go northward along **Royal Avenue,** a thorough-fare which is living evidence of Belfast's forward march, for it seems difficult to imagine the rank slums that were here as recently as 1880. Taking the left side walk, we pass in turn the **Provincial Bank**—a fine building set back from the street—and then the **Ulster Reform Club,** a red sandstone edifice with domed tower and spire, the club of the leading businessmen. On the street floor of the Reform Club, at No. 6, is the **Northern Ireland Tourist Board.** The next block is the *Grand Central Hotel,* while on the opposite side is the *Royal Avenue Hotel.* The *Grand Central Hotel* derives its name from its erection on the site of an abortive Belfast central city tube railway.

By no means a very ornate building is the **General Post Office,** extending back considerably over a street at the rear into Smithfield Market, where the antiquarian or book-collector may find a bargain.

From here to busy North Street there is not much of interest beyond the attraction of well-filled shops. Continuing along the left-hand side of Royal Avenue we quickly reach the **Central Public Library**—well worth a visit, both upstairs and down. Next to the library is the home of the *Belfast Telegraph* and allied newspapers.

Arriving at the corner of Royal Avenue and Donegall Streets, we see the continuation of the first-named thoroughfare as **York Street**. Stretching as far as York Road Station with its *Midland Hotel*, it runs parallel to the river Lagan. Flanking it, is the extensive **Gallaher's Tobacco Factory.**

Crossing the junction of Royal Avenue with York Street is **Donegall Street** in the corner of which is the fine new Ulster College of Art and Design. The upper part of Donegall Street is traversed by all traffic going towards the suburbs by the Antrim, Crumlin and Oldpark Roads. A few minutes above Royal Avenue is **St. Patrick's Roman Catholic Pro-Cathedral,** which has its side chapel adorned by Sir John Lavery, R.A., who was born in North Queen Street, in this vicinity, and was christened here. We now take its lower portion for—

St. Anne's Cathedral

a commandingly noble edifice with imposing portals. It replaced in 1904 the old Belfast parish church built by the Marquis of Donegall in 1774–6 and dedicated to St. Anne in honour of his wife.

The first idea was to erect a building as large as St. Patrick's in Dublin, but this was abandoned in favour of a simpler and less costly scheme. A basilica type of building having been adopted, as in the case of the earliest Christian churches, there are fewer arches and a wider nave than the Gothic style would have allowed. In the words of the architect, "the plan and proportion of the church are singularly simple and arithmetical. A nave of 40 feet width, aisles of 20 feet width, six bays of the nave, each of 20 feet; the crossing, transepts, and chancel, each, within their piers, squares of 40 feet; the internal height of the aisle walls, 36 feet; and of the walls of the nave and its clerestory, 72 feet.

The completed portion of the scheme includes the Nave and its aisles, the Baptistry, the Chapel of the Holy Spirit, the Apse and the Ambulatory. While the general scheme was planned by Sir Thomas Drew, the western portals were designed by Sir Charles Nicholson as a war memorial and include carvings symbolic of Sacrifice, Victory, Christ in Glory, etc. The mosaic surmounting the west entrance represents the *Te Deum*. The Baptistry, designed by Mr. W. H. Lynn, has a floor of various Irish marbles and is decorated by heads of angels carved by Miss Rosamund Praeger, a gifted local sculptor, the mosaics—representing the four elements—being the work of Miss Gertrude Martin. The dome and walls of the Chapel of the Holy Spirit are particularly rich in mosaics and Irish marbles, while the magnificent windows of the aisle depict the Old Testament Prophets and the Building of the Temple.

The noble proportions of the **Nave** impress all visitors. The flooring of maple and Irish marble also includes a distinctive stone from each of Ireland's thirty-two counties. The fourteen capitals of the nine pillars symbolize industries and virtues and the corbels represent historic leaders of

242

the Irish Church, although curiously the most notable of all, Dean Swift, is omitted. The tomb of the Ulster political leader, Lord Carson of Duncairn (Sir Edward Carson), is in the Cathedral. The organ is a fine four-manual instrument.

A little lower down Donegall Street, and on the same side as the Cathedral, are the offices of the *Belfast News Letter*, which has been issued continuously since 1737 and is the oldest Irish newspaper.

Here at the convergence of five streets—North Street, Donegall Street, Waring Street, Bridge Street and Rosemary Street—stands the **Belfast Bank** (the Irish component of the Midland Bank of England).

NEAR BELFAST
❦❦❦❦❦❦❦❦❦❦❦❦❦

The immediate surrounds of Belfast are picturesque and varied. Strung along the shores of Belfast Lough are a dozen seaside resorts; some are quiet villages in beautiful surroundings, others are alive with crowds and gaiety. Only a few miles from the City Hall are the lonely moorlands and silent valleys of the ring of mountains encircling the city, and the wide, thinly populated plain that slopes down landward to the chain of clean hamlets fringing Lough Neagh.

I. Bellevue and Cave Hill

Belfast citizens are justly proud of their **Bellevue.** It is a resort for people of all tastes, and within twenty minutes from the heart of the city. Even the approach to it is of much charm.

The routes converge near the **Waterworks,** now utilized as a pleasure ground with model yachting and boating ponds, since Belfast gets its water from the distant Mourne Mountains, 50 miles away in Co. Down. Then, to the left, is the **Cavehill Road,** one way of ascent to the Hill, but rather tedious. However, this junction commands a very extensive and delightful view, **Divis Mountain** (1,564 feet) **Squire's Hill** (1,237 feet) and **Cave Hill** (1,188 feet) presenting themselves with Ligoniel snuggled in the dip of the hills and only betrayed by its smoke. Down a short street on the opposite side is the entrance to **Alexandra Park,** with its 20 acres of bowling green, tennis lawns, pond and grasslands. Still farther along, we come on the right to the entrance to **Fortwilliam Park**—a tree-fringed residential thoroughfare leading to the Shore Road. A few yards more bring us to **Chichester Park.**

Now onwards we are in an area of comfortable spaciousness, with cheering peeps at the pretty tree-clad Cave Hill on our left, while down below through the avenues and trees we get views of Belfast Harbour and the busy shipyards.

Belfast Castle was built in 1867, in Scottish baronial style, by the third Marquis of Donegall (who was the Earl of Shaftesbury's grandfather), and it was occupied by the Shaftesbury family until 1916 or so. In 1934, however, the Earl decided to live permanently in England, and the castle and grounds were gifted to the city. Thus, with the adjacent Hazelwood and Bellevue pleasure gardens, they

244

form a public park of 350 acres unique in the British Isles. In July, 1937, part of the Castle was opened as a ballroom and café.

At the turn of the road we traverse a vantage-point with a really glorious view of Belfast Lough and the northern area of County Down, where to the left may be discerned **Helen's Tower** (*see* p. 277), and to the right **Scrabo Tower** (*see* p. 282) at the head of Strangford Lough. Then a few yards farther and we are at **Hazelwood,** the southern entrance to—

Bellevue

—a name literally descriptive of the magnificent panorama of land and sea afforded by this broad shelf on the escarpment of the mountain. From the Terrace, or better still from the hillock at Hazelwood, the vista is exceedingly comprehensive, Bellevue combines three sections: (1) the Belfast Castle and grounds of 200 acres; (2) **Hazelwood,** 44 acres, the miniature Switzerland, with its Floral Hall, Tea and Dance Hall, miniature golf links and pond; and (3) Bellevue proper, 32 acres, with its Grand Staircase, Noble Terrace, Amusement Park, Zoo and Rock Gardens. All tastes are catered for.

The **Zoo,** of approximately 13 acres extent, is entirely modern. Almost all the animals are in open air. The animals bred in Belfast's Zoo so far have been very numerous, including lions, wolves, llamas, etc.

There is the hustle and bustle of a fun fair at the Amusement Park, but for others the Rockery may be more acceptable. There is dancing in the **Floral Hall** in the Hazelwood section and at Belfast Castle. Those who want to return through the Belfast Castle grounds should continue along the path to the left, at the base of the Hazelwood cliffs.

Cave Hill

Cave Hill may be ascended by way of the steps through the rustic glen and hazel grove beside the stream separating Bellevue from Hazelwood. Visitors are recommended to cross the stream and stroll to the left along the cliff-tops as far as **M'Art's Fort** (1,100 feet), which was the crater of a volcano belching forth—like the lesser **Carnmoney** crater across the Glengormley valley—the lava which cooled as the basalt hills and plateaux of County Antrim. The view from this altitude is very fine. From an elevation a little behind M'Art's Fort and rather more northerly may be seen four Loughs—Strangford to the south over the Co. Down hills; Belfast below us; Larne (a peep) to the north-east; and the wide expanse of Lough Neagh westward.

Those whose time is limited should descend by the **Sheep's Path,** immediately below the Fort, to the Antrim Road bus, or to the Belfast Castle Grounds, within forty minutes or so. Those with, say, a further couple of hours to spare may continue along the breast of the Cave Hill for another mile or so, and then take the leisurely path descending to the **Quarries** and subsequently down to the Cave Hill road bus. If time still permits go directly west from behind M'Art's Fort along the stream, and half an hour will bring the walker into the **Hightown Road**—a mountain pass whose wildness seems absolutely incompatible with the immediate vicinity of a large city. Yet it is almost within Belfast's municipal boundaries. Here we may bear to the right and, after reaching the cross-road half a mile north, turn again right and within half an hour or so arrive at **Glengormley** terminus.

Energetic walkers can be recommended to continue directly westward across the Hightown Road, through a small meadow, and so ascend the slope of **Squire's Hill**. It is not a very long detour, merely a leisurely tramp, of say, 1½ hours all told, but the view from the top (150 feet higher than Cave Hill) is magnificent. The country to the south-west is obscured by **Divis** (1,564 feet)—the highest mountain of the Belfast range—but in the opposite direction the prospect extends as far north-east as **Knocklayd**, rising above Ballycastle and Slemish, the mountain on which St. Patrick was a swineherd; towards the north-west, through a gap in the Sperrin Mountains of the Counties Tyrone and Derry, we glimpse "Ould Donegal" in the tip of Slieve Snaght in Innishowen Peninsula. We make our descent easily, across pastureland to the bus terminus at the top of **Ligoniel** village (1 mile).

II. Queen's University—Botanic Gardens Park—Ulster Museum

From Donegall Square, it is an easy run (bus) *via* Bedford Street and Dublin Road, to University Road, on the left of which is—

Queen's University

Admission.—Enquiries should be made at the steward's office, at the right side of the main entrance hall.

The Queen's University of Belfast received its Charter in December 1908 and its first session began in October 1909. Its history, however, is really continuous with that of Queen's College, Belfast, which was founded in 1845. Queen's Belfast was linked with two other Queen's Colleges at Cork and Galway in the Queen's University in Ireland, which was established in 1850. The Queen's University was dissolved in 1879 and replaced by the Royal University of Ireland. The Royal University was itself dissolved in 1908 and replaced by two Universities, the National University of Ireland with its seat in Dublin and constituent colleges in Dublin, Cork and Galway, and the Queen's University of Belfast, which was, in effect, Queen's College raised to University rank.

Queen's University has now about 6,500 full-time students, this representing an increase of almost 100 per cent over the past ten years. To improve its facilities the University has planned a large building programme on which progress continues.

The architect of the original portion of the main buildings, including the Tudor-Gothic façade, was Sir Charles Lanyon, who although eminent primarily as a civil engineer (he engineered the Antrim Coast Road) had exceptional talent in designing buildings in a variety of styles. His many other creations include Assembly's College, the Customs House and Belfast Castle.

Apart from the imposing Entrance Hall with its memorial stained-glass windows, the most notable feature of the interior of the main front is the Great Hall with its leaden mullioned windows, its oak beams and vaulted roof. The large painting in the Hall is a copy of Titian's "Assassination of Peter the Martyr." The original constituted the altar-piece of the Church of SS. Giovanni and Paolo in Venice, but since it was destroyed by a fire which burned down that Church in 1867, this copy has enormously increased in value.

The University library possesses about 520,000 volumes, most of which are housed in the main library (1967) and Science library (1969). The main library contains a number of valuable special collections. There are separate branch-libraries for Medicine and Agriculture.

The Sir William Whitla Hall (1949), a memorial gift of Sir William Whitla, M.D., who also presented to the University his residence, Lennoxvale, for the use of the Vice-Chancellor, is now the University's Assembly Hall. Adjacent to this hall is the new Extension (1962) to the Physics Building (1913).

So great have been the demands on the main University site that it has been necessary to utilize other sites. Buildings for Agriculture (1928) and Geology (1954) have been erected in Elmwood Avenue and a new Students' Centre, comprising Union, Refectory and Debating Hall, has been built nearby. The David Keir Building (1958), the largest building project in the University's history, lies a few minutes' walk from the University between the Stranmillis and Malone Roads, and houses many departments in Science and Applied Science and Technology; it also has a branch library and an interesting Zoology Museum with an extensive collection of specimens, some of them of great rarity. This museum has a particularly fine skeleton of the giant Irish Deer. Adjacent is the new Mechanical and Electrical Engineering Building (1964). The Institute of Pathology (1933), Institute of Clinical Science (1954), and Microbiology (1965) lie in the grounds of the Royal Victoria Hospital some two miles from the University. A new Medical Biology building stands on the site previously occupied by the Deaf and Blind School at the west end of Elmwood Avenue. The University's playing fields have been developed in the former Malone Golf Course at Upper Malone. The Physical Education Centre is at Sans Souci Park, Malone Road, although a new building, with swimming pool attached, is planned for a site in the Botanic Gardens obtained from Belfast Corporation. Certain other University departments are in converted houses within the general University area. Halls of residence lie off the Malone Road.

In proximity to the University are (1) the **Assembly's College** (for training students for the Ministry of the Presbyterian Church) which, prior to the opening of the Stormont administrative buildings, served to house the Northern Ireland Parliament and Senate for ten years; and (2) the **Methodist College,** one of Belfast's leading secondary schools for boys and girls. The former is located somewhat to the rear of the University,

247

while the gates of the latter face the main entrance to the Botanic Gardens in University Road.

The Botanic Gardens

(Open daily from 8 a.m. till sunset.)

The Botanic Gardens has immense fascination because its infinite variety leads the visitor to imagine its area to be vastly over its 38 acres—for it extends down to the Lagan. Planted artistically so as to present picturesque vistas at every turn, it includes palm houses and conservatories, lawns, playing fields, rock gardens and rose terraces. The **Tropical Garden** or fernery, wherein tree ferns, india-rubber trees, palms, fig trees and bananas flourish abundantly, must certainly be seen. Great antiquarian interest attaches also to that "living fossil," the Ginkgo or Maiden-hair tree, which, although first brought to Britain about Queen Anne's day from the Far East, is no longer to be found growing wild anywhere—even in China.

The Ulster Museum

This, the State Musuem of Northern Ireland, is situated in Botanic Gardens Park, and was opened in 1929 by His Grace The Duke of Abercorn, K.G., K.P., Governor of Northern Ireland. The building is in Government control, under a Board of Trustees.

Ground Floor. To the right is the Old Belfast exhibition room with prints, drawings, portraits, maps, and objects relating to civic history; coins and medals. Here are main offices and a students' library, with a lecture room where frequent lectures and films are given through the winter months.

First Floor. The first two rooms contain collections illustrating natural history of the Ulster region, including the William Thompson collection of birds, a fine example of the Irish wolfhound, and special exhibits in season. The next room is devoted to Ethnography and to selected aspects of Ulster History, including exhibits of Irish Harps, Irish Volunteer and Constabulary materials, and Belleek Pottery. Farther on is a representative collection of Irish Antiquities, illustrating life in Ireland, but with special reference to Ulster from the Mesolithic to the Plantation; among the most important exhibits here are the Downpatrick Gold Hoards, the Early Celtic decorated sword-scabbards from Lisnacrogher, the material from the Early Christian Monastery of Nendrum, and the Inauguration Chair of the O'Neills of Clandeboye and a full-size reproduction of the High Cross of Muiredach of Monasterboice. There is a gallery for local industries, including the development of the linen industry; also of interest are the Horner Collection of Spinning Wheels, the T. Edens Osborne Collection illustrating the evolution of the bicycle, and a reconstructed Saddler's shop.

Second Floor houses the **Art Gallery.** In the corridor is exhibited sculpture, glass, ceramics and embroideries; Irish historic silver includes the Adam Loftus Great Seal Cup of 1593, also the Dopping and Freke Porringers of

1685. In the various rooms the visitor should from time to time find most of the following available for inspection: an excellent representative collection of British watercolours from the eighteenth century to the present day; the Sir R. Lloyd Patterson collection, chiefly of British artists of this century, including Sickert, Steer, Matthew Smith, and Stanley Spencer; modern works, including paintings by Kenneth Noland, Helen Frankenthaler, Vasarely, Appel, Tapies, Francis Bacon, William Scott, Victor Pasmore and Bernard Cohen; paintings by Irish artists; old masters, including works by Peter Breughel the Younger, Jan Breughel, Pannini, Sebastiano Ricci, Turner and Lawrence. Frequent loan exhibitions of both old masters and modern art are held and necessitate the temporary removal and rearrangement of the permanent collection.

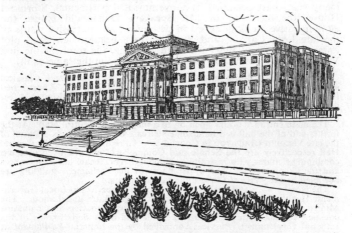

III. The Northern Ireland Houses of Parliament

Admission.—Monday to Friday, 9.30–4.30, except when House is sitting, when it is 9.30–1.30. Closed on Saturdays and Sundays. The Houses usually sit from mid-October to mid-July with short intervals at Christmas and Easter.

Buses.—No. 22 bus (from High Street, or Chichester Street) and No. 23 bus (from Chichester Street) take passengers to the building itself; No. 16 (Dundonald) and No. 17 go to the main entrance of the estate only.

On the journey to Stormont the buses cross either the **Queen Elizabeth Bridge** or the **Albert Bridge,** both spanning the River Lagan, which flows into Belfast Lough. On the right, about 2 miles from the city centre, visitors will see the **Belfast Ropeworks,** the largest of its type in the world. The works cover some forty acres and employ more than 1,500 workers. Buses 22 and 23 approach the Stormont grounds by way of Massey Avenue, named after William Ferguson Massey, a native of Limavady, Co. Londonderry, who became Prime Minister of New Zealand.

The Parliament Building

The dignity and impressiveness of the Parliament Building are at once apparent from the entrance to the main **Processional Drive** or from the Massey Avenue gates. The Stormont Estate, most attractively laid out, is 300 acres in extent. Within it, besides the Parliament Building, are Stormont Castle (formerly the official residence of Viscount Craigavon, first Prime Minister of Northern Ireland, but for many years past occupied by Government departments), Stormont House (the residence of Mr. Speaker), Dundonald House (an administrative block designed in two units), an impressive statue of the late Lord Carson, and, standing in a beautiful enclosed plot immediately east of the Parliament Building, the tomb of the first Viscount Craigavon (Lady Craigavon is buried in the same vault).

The Parliament Building, completed in 1932, is in the Greek Classical style, and the architect was Sir Arnold Thornley, F.R.I.B.A. Approached from the south by a flight of wide granite steps, it is 365 feet long, 164 feet deep, and 70 feet high, rising to 90 feet in the "crested attic" over the pediment.

The main entrance doors open on to a magnificent Central Hall. At the farther end of the hall is a handsome staircase on which stands a statue of the late Viscount Craigavon in Court dress. To right and left of the Central Hall respectively are the Senate and Commons Chambers, each of them combining richness with restraint and dignity. The Senate has 25 members and the Commons 52. The upper floors of the Parliament Building are occupied by the staffs of Government departments.

The Northern Ireland Parliament controls such services as Local Government, Health, Housing, Education, Police, Agriculture and Labour. The Ministry of Commerce deals with trade and industrial matters and maintains constant contact with the Board of Trade and other departments of the Imperial Government. Services controlled by the Imperial Parliament at Westminster, in which Northern Ireland has a representation of 12 members, include Defence, Inland Revenue, Customs and Excise and the Post Office.

At the opening of each Session of the Northern Ireland Parliament the Queen's Speech is read by His Excellency the Governor. The Governor resides at Government House, Hillsborough, Co. Down.

By the Processional Drive, we reach the main road and stroll a few paces outwards, beyond the Stormont Estate and the bus terminus at Dundonald (*dun Domhnail*, fort of Donal) to the *Elk Inn*, where the road forks to left and right. The left branch leads to Newtownards, Mountstewart (*see* p. 283), Greyabbey, Portaferry and the Ards Peninsula, forming the eastern shores of Strangford Lough; the road to the right goes to Comber (4½ miles south-westerly), Killyleagh, Downpatrick, and the western shores of the Lough.

IV. Ormeau Park

From Donegall Square *via* Ormeau Avenue and Ormeau Road (bus).

Formerly the property of the Marquis of Donegall, the estate came into the market in 1869 and Belfast Corporation seized the opportunity of acquiring its 174 acres at a rental which is more than compensated by the ground rents from merely a portion of it let to builders and the Ormeau Golf Club. It is well laid out, with broad avenues and areas for bowling, football, tennis and cricket, and an athletics track. Adjacent are golf links.

From the eastern end of the Park the Ravenhill Road (bus route) proceeds countrywards to a junction with the Ormeau Road.

The vicinity of the **Ormeau Road** bus terminus has its memories, too, for the widowed mother of the great Duke of Wellington lived here and was visited by the Iron Duke during his holidays.

The inviting road on the right at Ormeau Road terminus leads in about fifteen minutes to the picturesque hamlet of **Newtownbreda**. With its cottages embowered in honeysuckle and roses, it suggests Devonshire rather than Down.

Turning again townwards it is not necessary to board the bus here, but bearing to the right along **Rosetta Park Avenue** we reach in ten minutes the Cregagh Road terminus, at the base of the **Castlereagh Hills** ("the grey castle," the historic stronghold of the O'Neills, Chiefs of Ulster), and a pleasant run of thirty minutes will bring us to the heart of the city again.

Belfast Airport

The new civil airport at Aldergrove, fifteen miles from Belfast, was opened in 1963 and supersedes the former airport at Nutts. Corner. There are two 6,000-foot runways. Facilities include restaurants, lounges and bars and an open-air spectators' observation platform. A former operational station of the R.A.F., it is now controlled by the Board of Trade (Civil Aviation Department). The airport now handles over a million passengers annually.

251

ANTRIM AND LOUGH NEAGH

✸✸✸✸✸✸✸✸✸✸✸✸✸✸✸✸✸✸✸✸✸✸✸✸✸✸✸✸✸✸✸✸

Route Belfast to Londonderry via Antrim, Maghera and Dungivan

This road route is by the Antrim road out past Bellevue and Cave Hill (1,188 feet), Glengormley and Templepatrick. To the right of the road, beyond Templepatrick, is Donegore Hill, while on the left is **Muckamore** with its trout stream and old abbey site.

Antrim

Distances.—Belfast 17, Ballymena 11, Dublin 113, Larne 22, Londonderry 58, Portadown 28, Randalstown 5.

Early Closing.—Wednesday. Market Day.—Thursday.

Hotels.—*Halls* (35 rooms), *Massereene Arms* (10).

Population.—4,500.

Sports.—Golf, tennis, cricket; sailing and fishing on Lough Neagh, and in Six mile-water and Antrim Reservoir.

Antrim is a small but fast developing town on the north-east of Lough Neagh, at the mouth of Six Mile Water. In recent years new trades have grown up alongside the traditional industries with large factories such as those of British Enkalon and the Michelin Tyre Co., providing further employment. A new motorway, planned to link the town with Belfast and ultimately Londonderry, will greatly speed its development.

The parish church dates from 1596. It contains some good glass windows and a memorial to the Massereene family.

North of the station is Antrim's famous **Round Tower** in the grounds of the Steeple estate, now the council headquarters.

There are few more perfect specimens of the famed Irish round towers than this, which is 93 feet high, about 50 feet in circumference at its base and then gently tapering upwards. The entrance door, facing north and only wide enough to admit a single person, is about 7 feet from the ground, and here the walls are about 3 feet 9 inches thick. Four windows near the summit face the cardinal points of the compass.

These windows had a definite use, for sentinels there, viewing an enemy far off, could ring a bell and alarm the monks. A few minutes sufficed for the brethren to ascend the ladder to the door in the tower and, with the sacred missals and other treasures now placed therein, to draw up the ladder. Here they found security for themselves and their treasures, for food and water were always stored ready for such emergencies. By these round towers —often referred to as "cloc tees," or bell-houses—the traditional culture of Irish art and religion were preserved through the dark ages. Curiously,

Co. Armagh has no round towers, although almost eighty can be traced elsewhere in Northern Ireland, and Scotland has only three. They always adjoined monasteries.

At the northern end of High Street is Massereene Park, the grounds of Antrim's Castle, now a ruin. Extending for two miles along the shore of the Lough, the grounds are very beautiful, with many fine old trees, rhododendrons and flowering shrubs. The original castle was built in 1662; its successor burnt down in 1816. The last building was burned down in 1922.

As originally designed, Antrim Castle was a quadrilateral pile three storeys high, enclosing a small courtyard and flanked at the angles by square towers. With its site where the Six Mile Water river enters Lough Neagh, some idea of its strength may be gathered from the fact that its walls were 6 feet thick. Originally it was intended as a fortress, which Sir Hugh Clotworthy, a Somerset gentleman who accompanied Essex, was compelled to erect by the Ulster Plantation enactments. Sir Hugh's son, Sir John Clotworthy, who figured in the Parliamentary Wars, enlarged the Castle and still further improvements were made in 1813 by Chichester, fourth and last Earl of Massereene. Sir John Skeffington, son-in-law of Viscount Massereene, succeeded him by special remainder, and his great-grandson received an Earldom, which lapsed in 1816. The only daughter married the second Baron Oriel, son of the Hon. John Foster, Speaker in Grattan's Irish Parliament. These peerages are now held by the descendant, the present Viscount Massereene and Ferrard.

A legend of Antrim Castle is that so long as a stone wolf-hound on the battlements remains intact a direct heir to the Massereenes will never be lacking. The legend runs that while an ancestress was walking by Lough Neagh, a wolf attacked her, but she was saved by a hound. In gratitude the hound was taken to Antrim Castle and cared for. Suddenly it vanished, but late one night the Castle was aroused by a fierce barking and when the alarmed people rushed to the Castle gates they found the dog killed by a mob who had meant to murder the Massereenes. Simultaneously with its slaughter, however, the stone hound appeared on the Castle.

Lough Neagh

Lough Neagh occupies a considerable area almost in the centre of Northern Ireland. It is the largest fresh-water lake in the United Kingdom, 17 miles long, 11 miles broad, 100 feet deep in one section, but only 46 feet above sea-level. No fewer than five of the six counties comprising the Ulster unit contribute to the 80-mile borders of its area of 157 square miles, i.e. about seven times larger than the area of Belfast city. It contains a good supply of fish, considerable quantities of eels, trout and pollan (fresh-water herring) being sent to market. The water is said to have petrifying qualities, but the process is very, very slow, and confined to the eastern area, at the Crumlin and Glenavy rivers.

253

SHANE'S CASTLE

In ancient times this region provided much of the oak for British battle-
ships and Lough Neagh had its own naval flotilla. One of the titles of the
sixth Marquess of Donegall is "Hereditary Lord High Admiral of Lough
Neagh." The title seems Gilbertian but it must be remembered that in
A.D. 832 the Norsemen ventured from the Atlantic up the river Bann, and
for 150 years made Lough Neagh their operational base. During World
War Two Lough Neagh and nearby Crumlin were the busy scene of many
aircraft of all types. The area was virtually "occupied" by thousands of
American troops and used as a vast training and assembly ground for the
invasion of North Africa and Europe.

Ram's Island, situated in Sandy Bay, about 2 miles from
the shore and 4 miles from Glenavy. About 25 acres in area, it
has the ruins of a round tower and remains of an old cottage
which was the old summer residence of the O'Neill family. It is
the haunt of many varieties of birds including ring doves, black-
birds, larks and thrushes. In summer undergrowth is extensive
making access difficult.

On the eastern shore of the lough is the pretty 9-hole Massereene golf course.

The road north-westward from Antrim leads in 5 miles to
Randalstown, passing, on the left—

Shane's Castle.*

The Old Castle and part of the estate is open Weds. and Suns. 2–6,
and Sats. 11–6. Part of the shoreline of Lough Neagh bordering the
area is a Nature Reserve run in co-operation with the R.S.P.B.

Shane's Castle is the residence of the O'Neills of Clannaboy. The
ruins are of the sixteenth-century castle destroyed by fire in 1816. The
later house was burnt during the "troubles" in 1922 and the present
house (*not open*) was completed in 1958.

Although the oldest part of the Castle is a ruin, a Terrace and
Conservatory, which were added early in the nineteenth century, are
preserved.

The Conservatory houses a fine collection of camellias, and the
Terrace is equipped with 21 old Naval cannons pointing out over
Lough Neagh. One of the corner stones in the square south tower
bears the black head of the O'Neills. According to tradition, the
end of the O'Neills will come should it fall. As the visitor will probably only see Shane's Castle in daytime, he is unlikely to encounter the
family "banshee", with which every Irish castle is honoured.

It may be pointed out that Shane O'Neill, the great Prince of Ulster
(who spent some years at the Court of Queen Elizabeth), had nothing to
do with Shane's Castle, its building or occupation, though he may have

* Not to be confused with Shane's Castle, Ardglass (*see* p. 292).

254

camped near it, at Edenduffcarrick. Shane's Castle was not built until many years after Shane's death in 1567.

Mrs. Siddons, the great actress, visited Shane's Castle in 1783 and has recorded that here also as guest was the ill-fated Lord Edward Fitzgerald, "the most amiable, honourable and misguided youth I ever knew." She tells also that "the luxury of the establishment was beyond words, really an Arabian Night's entertainment. . . . A fine band of musicians played during dinner. The guests plucked their own dessert fruit from the exquisite trees of the conservatory, the foot of which was washed by the waves of a superb lake, and the cool and pleasant zephyrs came therefrom to murmur in concert with the harmony from the band."

The O'Neills were raised to the Irish peerage in 1797. Strangely enough, the O'Neill of that day was a supporter of the Irish Volunteer movement, but opposed to secret societies, and met his death in the Battle of Antrim (1798) from the United Irishmen.

In visiting Shane's Castle the interested sightseer may observe that the badge of the O'Neills (and of Ulster concurrently) is the red right hand and not the left as is erroneously displayed on the Ulster Hall and other Belfast buildings. It appears correctly at the Randalstown gate especially. Confirmation is given also in the right hand underneath the right bar of the Cross of Monasterchoice replica in Belfast Museum. This uplifted right hand ("the hand of God") was the usual gesture of witnesses when taking their oath at Ulster courts.

Randalstown is a small town with linen and carpet works. It has a long history, but little of antiquarian interest.

Three miles west, a road leads off to the shores of Lough Neagh at **Cranfield**, (*Creamh-coille*, "wood of wild garlic"). Its church dates back to 1258 and its Holy Well is still a perennial venue for pilgrims.

In a further 2 miles along our route is **Toomebridge** at the northernmost tip of Lough Neagh, where the Bann river quits the loch for **Loch Beg** and then on to the Atlantic. The scenery of Loch Beg is very fine. There is excellent fishing for perch and pike here and in the lower reaches of the Bann, where salmon also can be had. On Church Island are some ancient ruins and a fairy thorn and holy well.

From Toomebridge our road ascends to **Maghera,** a typical town of this area, and shortly enters the **Glenshane Pass** in the wild grandeur of the **Sperrin Mountains** (*Carntogleer*, 1,521 feet, on the right, and *White Mountain*, 1,774 feet, to the left). Next comes the market town of **Dungiven** with a population of a few over 500. At the entrance to the town, opposite the church, is the fortified mansion built in 1618 and granted to the Skinners' Company. To the south, on a cliff overlooking the *Roe*, are the ruins of *Dungiven Abbey*, founded *c.* 1100. The remains consist of twelfth-century church and a nave of later date. Of interest is the recumbent effigy of *Coo-ey-na-gall*, chief of the

255

O'Cahans, founders of the abbey. On the front of the tomb are six more figures armed with helmet, sword and spear.

From Dungiven there is a choice of route, the main road branching off south-westward through **Banagher,** which has an ancient church with a quaint west door, square-headed outside, semicircular-arched inside. In its churchyard is the church-like tomb of the founder, Muiredach O'Heney. At **Feeny** the road from Tobermore comes in on the left, and beyond **Claudy** the road descends the pretty Faughan Valley to the *Foyle*, with Derry on the opposite bank.

The Antrim Coast Road

Newcastle, Co. Down

Mourne Mountains from Dundrum Bay

Rostrevor, Co. Down

THE ANTRIM COAST
✠✠✠✠✠✠✠✠✠✠✠✠✠✠✠✠✠✠✠✠✠

**Carrickfergus—Whitehead—The Gobbins and Island Magee—
Larne—The Antrim Coast Road—Glenarm—Carnlough—
Garron Point and Tower—The Glens (Glenariff)—Cushen-
dall—Cushendun—Ballycastle—Torr Head**

Railways.—The main Belfast to Portrush line runs directly from south to north, while from its easterly side extends a branch running to the sea to Whitehead and Larne. Then northerly at Coleraine the main trunk divides into—(a) the short direct northerly branch to Portstewart and Portrush; (b) the westerly branch to Londonderry.

Buses.—There are daily excursions at moderate rates both to Glenariff by the coast and also traversing the entire coast to the Giant's Causeway and Portrush, returning by the inland road. The intending visitor is advised to obtain Ulsterbus timetables and special pamphlets setting out full particulars.

It is a long coastline from Belfast round to Portrush, over 120 miles, and yet it is margined by a road, the well-surfaced A 2, all the way. Unlike County Down, Antrim has considerable level areas. Extending right along almost the entire coastline of Antrim is a high rampart of mountains, and from their westerly side the land slopes down in well-tilled farms to become level as far as Lough Neagh. This coast rampart, however, is broken by a series of valleys—the **Nine Glens of Antrim** (*see* p. 262)—debouching on the sea, and of these Glenariff almost bisects East Antrim.

For the opening of the journey between Belfast and Whitehead, we travel along within view of Belfast Lough and the wooded slopes of County Down. And on the landward side the grandeur of the Cave Hill from this aspect will not be missed, especially if it is autumn, when the heather and woods are a mass of glory. At **Whiteabbey,** Anthony Trollope wrote his *Autobiography*. Knockagh Hill (938 feet) on the landward side is topped by the *County Antrim War Memorial* obelisk.

About 10 miles from Belfast we reach—

Carrickfergus

Distances.—Belfast 11, Antrim 19, Dublin 114, Londonderry 77.
Early Closing.—Wednesday.
Golf.—18-hole course.

Hotels.—*Coast Road* (20 rooms), *Dobbins Inn* (15).
Population.—14,000.
Tennis, bowls, sailing, fishing.

Carrickfergus, 11 miles north along the coast road from

Belfast, is a busy resort and popular yachting centre. It is an ancient town and was of great importance when Belfast was only a small hamlet. In 1669 it was the largest town in Ulster. Its population is now 14,000.

Remains of the ancient walls and fortifications may still be seen. The North, or **Spital Gate,** is nearly perfect, and the **Castle** (*small charge*) for three centuries the only English stronghold north of Dundalk and the key to the north-east of Ulster, is one of the most perfect of Ireland's fortresses. The inner ward of the castle was built in 1180 by John De Courcy and additions made in the thirteenth and sixteenth centuries. It stands on a basaltic dyke on the rocky shore. On three sides it has the sea. On the town side are two half-moon towers; and between them is another, protecting the entrance gateway. The keep, 90 feet high with walls 9 feet thick, is in good preservation. Entry to the Castle, outer court and walls is permitted (*fee*).

Prince (afterwards King) John resided here in 1210. During the rebellion of 1641 the colonists made the Castle their stronghold. The soldiers of King James II held it for a time against Duke Schomberg in 1689. The French Commodore Thurot besieged and captured it in 1760—unique in English history as the only French victory in the United Kingdom. Curiously, too, Thurot was Irish by descent, his real name being Farrell.

A little beyond the Castle entrance is the **Harbour.** At the end of the quay which divides the old harbour from the outer basin is the stone on which King William III is said to have stepped when he landed in Ireland on June 14, 1690.

The names "Scotch Quarter," and "Irish Quarter," still given to certain streets, recall the segregation of the inhabitants, who were obliged each night at curfew, to retire to their respective regions.

The **Parish Church** of St. Nicholas is one of the most interesting churches in the diocese from an antiquarian point of view, and certainly repays a visit. The sister church is St. Nicholas in Galway. Much of the old stonework has recently been uncovered, and there is a beautiful monument to Sir Arthur Chichester, first English Governor of Ulster, his wife and son. The Church is believed to date from the twelfth century.

Whilst the railway hugs the shore, the road leaves the coast and passes through **Eden** and **Kilroot** before regaining the shore at Whitehead.

Whitehead

Amusements.—Yachting, swimming (pond and open sea), bowls, tennis, golf (9-hole course), putting, sea-fishing.
Early Closing.—Thursday.
Distances.—Belfast 16, Carrickfergus 5, Larne 9, Dublin 118, Londonderry 82.

Hotels.—*Royal, Royal George* and guest houses.
Churches, etc.—*Presbyterian, Episcopalian, Methodist, Roman Catholic.*
Population.—2,742.

Of comparatively recent growth, Whitehead is today a modern seaside resort with numerous amenities and facilities for holiday recreation. It has a fine Esplanade, with seats and shelters, facing the sea and giving an interesting prospect of ships and yachts as well as of Bangor, Belfast Lough, the County Down coast and the Copeland Islands. The beach is pebbly, but there are sandy parts and bathing is safe. The town is the head-quarters of the County Antrim Yacht Club, and there is a good 9-hole golf course. The seaward extension of the Esplanade is the promontory called Blackhead, with its lighthouse. A circular walk embracing the base and summit of the cliffs can be made in about an hour. There is a good view from the top of the cliffs, and along the shore are many fine glacial boulders. The town's past history is centred in the ruins of its old square fort, Castle Chichester, built by Sir Moyses Hill in 1604.

Island Magee

From the Belfast–Larne road high above Whitehead the observer can see how the town is located on a narrow neck of land between two inlets of the sea—Belfast and Larne Loughs—while the peninsula on the sea side of the latter was once really an island, as its present name Island Magee implies. In fact, it has its geographical parallel south of Belfast Lough in the Ards Peninsula. Deriving its name from a family, the Magees, and its entrance once guarded by Castle Chichester, it extends north-westerly for about 7½ miles. Buses traverse it from Belfast, Whitehead and Ballycarry to **Brown's Bay**, a delightful sandy cove at the mouth of Larne Lough, and Portmuck. The Larne Golf Club is near Brown's Bay.

Just north of Blackhead is a road junction from which a road runs to the Gobbins, a bold, precipitous range of great cliffs. The cliffside path has fallen in many places and is extremely dangerous. The **Man o'War Rock**, a great sea stack with water foaming at the base, is reached by a steel bridge 70 feet long. The pathway continues to one of a group of caves known as the **Seven Sisters,** and the upper road can then be regained by a zigzag path beyond this. Island Magee produces good potatoes and a race of magnificent sailors. Visitors who do not want to walk back can meet the bus at Duff's Corner. Others can go on to **Brown's Bay** and from there walk 1 mile to the *Larne Ferry* at Ferris's Bay.

Magheramorne

From Whitehead the main Larne Road continues north along the western side of Larne Lough, passing through **Magheramorne**, where was born St. Comgall, who brought Christianity to Eastern England, and whose name is still perpetuated by St. Gall in Switzerland. In 1836 the lime-works here were so flourishing that the trade kept 459 ships going; now it is one of the busy branches of the British Portland Cement Corporation.

A couple of miles north we come to the immaculate village of **Glynn.** The name Glynn is, of course, a variant of the Scottish word Glen and its southern Irish form *glan* ("a valley"). Glynn has some ecclesiastical history, having had a church founded by St. Patrick. Some 3 miles inland is the extremely picturesque **Glenoe** village, almost hidden between two wooded green banks through which gurgles a sparkling stream having a waterfall and a couple of cascades.

Soon we come to view the open sea where Larne Lough expands after escaping from the sickle-shaped peninsula, the *Curran* ("reaping hook"). **Larne Harbour** is the Irish port of the short-sea crossing route Larne and Stranraer.

Larne

Access.—By rail, 40 minutes from Belfast. There are two railway stations *Larne Town* and *Harbour* (1 mile distant). Buses run frequently between the Town and Harbour and also between Larne and Ballymena (21 miles), Larne and Belfast (several routes), and also between Larne and Glenarm, Garron Tower, Waterfoot (for Glenariff), Cushendall, Cushendun, Ballycastle, Giant's Causeway and Portrush.

Amusements.—Tennis, bathing, dancing, fishing, sailing, cinemas, bowls and golf (2 courses).

Bus Depot.—In Narrow Gauge Road; for information about tours to Mournes, Carlingford Mts., and Dundalk, also Bellevue and Bangor.

Distances.—Belfast 21, Antrim 22, Ballymena 21, Carrickfergus 14, Cushendall 26, Dublin 124, Londonderry 75, Whitehead 9.

Early Closing.—Tuesday.

Ferry.—From harbour station to north end of Island Magee.

Hotels.—*McNeill's* (68 rooms), *Laharna* (150), *King's Arms* (32), numerous guest houses.

Churches, etc. — *Church of Ireland, Methodist, Presbyterian, Baptist, Congregational, Roman Catholic.* Services usually at 11 and 7.30.

Population.—17,250.
Steamer Trips by the Stranraer steamer to Ayr, Newtownstewart, Portpatrick in Scotland.

Larne is a name of comparatively modern date and a contraction of **Latharna** (a reputed son of a prehistoric chieftain). While the name of Larne is now given to the district, it was originally applied only to the strip northward along the open coast; and from the sixth to the twelfth century the bay was known as Ollarba and the hamlet on its river mouth was *Inver*.

The town does not risk putting its eggs into one basket, for while Nature has been liberal in endowing her with charms, the enterprise and industry of the people have made it a town of manufacturers. Occupations include linen weaving, engineering, turbo-generator plant, telephone equipment, etc.

Larne has a great many attractions and the visitor who happens to be there when the musical and dramatic feis is held will delight in the folk dancing and music by the inhabitants of the Antrim Glens.

Rambles over the ring of hills forming Larne's background, together with jaunts out to Glenoe Waterfall (3 miles), Glynn and the Sallagh Braes (3 miles north), or to Brown's Bay, Druid's Altar, and Portmuck in Island Magee, are all well worth doing. The Sallagh Braes are especially interesting. They are easily reached at about 3 miles from the town and extend northerly above the coast. Aloft in Cairn Dhu, "the Black Rock," the visitor can see magnificent views of the Irish channel, with Ailsa Craig, in the Clyde estuary, in the distance, and nearer at hand a long stretch of the Antrim hills. The return to Larne may be made by bus along the main Coast Road.

Few places in the British Isles have such ancient history as the present peninsula containing the steamer wharf. Although the town now has varied peaceful industries, its prehistoric staple product was flints for arrow and spear heads, as well as skin scrapers and other tools; and it supplied many western European peoples with them. Only a few years ago an archaeological expedition unearthed near the ruins of **Olderfleet Castle** about 10,000 worked flints. Probably both Phoenicians and Norsemen came here. The latter called the Lough Ulfrek's Fiord and English traders and invaders during later years varied the name to Wulfrickford (A.D. 1210), Wolderfrith, Wolverflete, and eventually Olderfleet, as the old castle is still called. The remains of Olderfleet Castle stand on the Curran, a long gravel spit curving sickle-shaped from the town at about 12 feet above water mark.

Westward of Larne, a good road gives connection with Antrim *via* **Ballyclare** (9-hole golf course; angling), a busy market town on the Six Mile Water. At **Ballyeaston**, 1½ miles north, was the home of the U.S. President Andrew Johnson's grandfather, who emigrated to America in 1750.

261

THE ANTRIM COAST ROAD

This is one of the most remarkable and interesting roads in Europe. From Larne to Cushendall is 25 miles, yet during the entire distance we are so close to the sea that we might at any time flick a pebble into it. Passing the Antrim Glens, with each bend it becomes more beautiful. Even the names of the nine Antrim Glens are melodious as rustling brooks—Glenarm, Glenariff, Glen Ballyemon, Glenaan, Glencorp, Glenshesk and Glentaise.

Two miles from Larne is the **Blackcave Tunnel,** where the road thrusts through the rock which on its sea side has been hollowed by the waves into the **Devil's Churn,** round which the water surges noisily. On an isolated rock stood the ruins of **O'Halloran's Castle,** built in 1625, probably by one of De Courcy's knights, but tenanted in later times by an Irish poet, Agnew. Four miles from Larne is **Ballygalley Head,** a fine promontory 250 feet high, with great basaltic pillars called the Corn Stacks. Close at hand is *Ballygally Castle Hotel*, originally built in 1265 and an interesting example of the chateau style of architecture introduced in the time of Mary Queen of Scots. There is also a *Youth Hostel*. Six miles out at sea are the **Maiden Rocks,** the scene of many shipwrecks; close at hand is a beautiful sandy beach. A little short of Glenarm is an opening in the rocks which goes by the name of the **Madman's Window.**

The picturesque unspoilt village of—

Glenarm

is on the south side of a river which runs down through a pretty wooded glen. On the other side of the stream, crossed by a bridge, is **Glenarm Castle** and its beautifully wooded grounds (Earl of Antrim). The Castle was built in 1636 by the first Earl. *The grounds are open free to those who obtain a permit from the Estate Office, Glenarm.*

There is good bathing at Glenarm, and some sea fishing, and the place is a favourite one for picnic parties.

Occasionally the Coast Road has its landslips, for the chalk portion rests on slippery Lias clay, and a hamlet at Straidkelly Point, midway between Glenarm and Carnlough, is still known as "the Slipping Village." **Carnlough** is a perfect heaven of peace, only troubled by the soft lapping murmur of wavelets on its sandy beach. Besides facilities for safe bathing, fishing and boating there are many pretty walks and drives. Near Carnlough is **Dungallon,** the last fort held by the Danes.

Ahead now is **Garron Point,** a bold bluff headland looming above the road. On the lofty plateau forming a broad shelf on the mountains are pleasant pleasure grounds and a school. Originally it was the home of the Marquis of Londonderry.

Onward by Ardclinis we view the wide expanse of Red Bay (so called because of the red sandstone so plentiful here, in contrast with the chalk) and the Layde Peninsula beyond Cushendall, bounding the northern horizon. The famed Glenariff Valley slopes to the sea at the picturesque little village of **Waterfoot,** and the road thereto branches on the left from the Coast Road to run inland parallel with the river to Parkmore, at the top of the valley, a distance of about 5 miles.

The Vale of Glenariff

Access.—There are daily excursions by bus from Belfast, Bangor, Larne and Portrush, the valley being approached from inland and 1 to 2½ hrs. being allowed for passengers to walk down Glenariff and then rejoin the buses at the lower gate.
Admission.—Charge. Refreshments can be had at Glenariff Café.

It is decidedly preferable to enter Glenariff by the upper gate, at the picturesque Parkmore Post Office, for then as background the sightseer has always the expanse of emerald sea into which the valley seems to dissolve so imperceptibly. Paths traverse both banks, the path on the left continuing all the way down the glen, that on the right only part of the way. Both are beautiful. So, indeed, is every spot in the glen. It abounds in wild flowers, the sides are clothed with trees, and over rock and boulder rush two mountain torrents, making a most romantic and picturesque combination.

In the courses of the streams are many falls and cascades. The finest of the waterfalls are **Ess-na-larach,** "the fall of the mare," and **Ess-na-Crub,** "the fall of the hoof." The former is the upper and higher of the two. At its foot is a bridge, and close by it is Ess-na-Crub, a fine fall 40 feet high, well seen from the rocks underneath or from the rustic bridge at the top. It is formed by the rivers Glenariff and Inver.

Regaining the Coast Road at Waterfoot we keep to the left and go under an arch of old red sandstone beneath *Lurigethan* (1,154 feet) with the ruins of **Red Bay Castle** above. Its history dates back to the Bissets between 1200 and 1300; in 1561 a MacDonnell, its occupant, defied Queen Elizabeth, and Shane O'Neill on her behalf laid the Castle in ruins.

263

Cushendall

Early Closing.—Tuesday.
Golf.—9-hole course.

Hotels.—*Glens of Antrim, Cushendall.*
Youth Hostel.—*Moneyvart,* Layde Road.

Cushendall, "the end or foot of the River Dall," is in the words of Joxer, in *Juno and the Paycock*, "a darlint village," sheltered by high hills and embowered by some of the loveliest spots in Co. Antrim. Nearly all tastes can be satisfied here. There is bathing, boating, fishing (free in three rivers), climbing, a delightful combination of hills, woods, glens, waterfalls, and sea all quite close together—everything to please a nature-lover, while botanists, geologists and antiquaries will find much to interest them.

The beauty of the Antrim Glens is here at its finest, and the historical associations are legion. On the mountain shoulder, at Lubietavish, a half-circle of stones marks the reputed grave of Ossian, the pagan warrior and poet (about A.D. 430); Turnley's Tower in Cushendall derives its name from its founder, the son of a worthy, wealthy Belfast brewer, who designed it over a century ago as symbolic of Evil in a terrestrial paradise.

Leaving Cushendall, there is a choice of three roads northward. No. 1 is the road direct down from the town to the lovely beach and so across the **Layde Peninsula** for 3½ miles into Cushendun. But the bus (or main) road turns inland for a couple of miles up the vales of **Glenaan** ("the glen of the proverb") and **Glencorp** ("dead man's glen") whose two rivers contribute to the Dall. Then we branch off coastward to traverse the lower reaches of **Glendun** ("the brown glen") and soon are entranced again by the glorious vista of open sea which beckons us into—

Cushendun

("the end or foot of the River Dun"). Cushendun (Hotels. *Bay, Glendun,* Angling) is a trifle more idyllic and just a shade more modest and retiring than Cushendall. The name has become more widely known by the title (Lord Cushendun) which was taken by one of its sons, the late Ronald McNeill, on his elevation to the peerage. Cushendun is the favourite haunt of artists.

From Cushendun three roads are available. One very interesting route, if you can face the steep hairpin descent of "Dan Nancy," is to keep by the coast northward over Tornamoney Headland. Passing the reputed burial cairn of Shane O'Neill the Proud, the road runs practically along the top of the cliffs, affording a magnificent view from the Green Hill of the Scottish isles of Jura and Islay, with Rathlin and the North Channel in the near distance. The little bays of **Loughan** and **Portaleen** are delightful, as is **Tor Head,** beyond which the road bears westward to join the main highway at **Ballyvoy.**

No. 2 route is to return again inland a couple of miles by the Cushendall Road, *via* Knocknacarry, and then at the junction turn to the right by the main Antrim coast road. After a gradual ascent it crosses the Dun river and Glen by the Cushendun Viaduct and then traverses the spiral way through Craigach Wood to come out into the open mountainous moorland. And hereabouts the No. 3 direct road, leading from Cushendun up the left hillside of the valley, converges.

It is a vivid change to this high-up moorland track from Glenariff and from the coast road on the southern side of Cushendall. There is about this region the desolate and peaceful beauty of an uninhabited world. It is wild moorland with neither house nor tree, and hardly a human being, unless it is turf-cutting time. There at the summit of the pass is the lonely roadside lake of **Loughareema,** which Moira O'Neill not inaptly calls "The Fairy Lough." Onwards on our left the district shows small farms, shallow valleys, white houses and even occasional clumps of trees. The region of **Corrymeela,** located between the main Antrim Coast Road and the coast, is immortalized in the *Songs of the Glens of Antrim*, by Moira O'Neill.

At Ballyvoy, almost within sight of Ballycastle, located below in the broad valley of the Glenshesk ("Glen of the Sedges") a road branches eastward to the right, soon forking again to the right to Tor Head and Cushendun (*see* p. 264); and direct ahead to—

Fair Head

or Benmore, 3 miles to the east, the most northerly point of County Antrim. A jaunting car, or motor, can be taken most of the way from Ballycastle, but many people will prefer the ramble by the shore, passing the old coal mines and then over the lesser intervening headlands.

It is a jaunt well worth any trouble, and those who take the ramble will find it pure joy—especially on a clear day. A lofty basaltic promontory, the Head towers 636 feet skywards, the upper part being perpendicular for some 400 feet and then at its base sloping into the sea—so steep, indeed, that a stone can be dropped, not thrown, from the summit to the talus far below. Its basaltic columns are four times higher than those of Staffa, and more numerous. From this grand pinnacle is one entire scene of enthralling beauty.

Romance is kindled by the two small lakes or mountain tarns—**Lough Dhu** ("the black lake"), with its outlet over the cliffs, and **Lough-na-Crannoge** ("Lake of the Island"), with a small artificial island, or crannog, on it. These lake dwellings are frequent in Ireland—the lake at Bellevue, Belfast, is another example—and in Switzerland, and go back to the Bronze Age.

Probably they were safety retreats and even dwellings, and this one had a stone wall round it. Spears found here are in Belfast Museum.

At our feet is an artist's delight, **Murlough Bay,** with its regularly formed semicircular cliff walls. Close at hand is a chasm in the cliffs with one long column of basalt fallen across it, the so-called **Grey Man's Path,** by which one may scramble carefully—it is not dangerous—down to the beach. From Murlough Bay a path leads south to **Tor Head** (5 miles' stiff walk), a bold headland, and the nearest point to Scotland, which is only **12 miles** off. At the cottage on beautiful Murlough Bay it is always possible to get tea and, perhaps, fish fresh from the sea, while similar refreshment is always available at *Cross*, a farm on the road from Fair Head, on the return to Ballycastle.

Ballycastle

Amusements.—Golf (18-holes), fishing for trout and salmon; also sea-fishing, tennis, cricket, hockey, bowls. Good bathing.

Buses to Ballymoney, Belfast, Coast Road, Portrush, Carrick-a-rede and Giant's Causeway.

Churches.—*Episcopalian* (2)—11.30 and 6.30. *Presbyterian*—Noon and 6.30. *Roman Catholic*—8, 9.30, 11 and 7.

Distances.—Belfast 55, Antrim 38, Ballymoney 16, Cushendall 17, Dublin 150, Larne 42, Londonderry 50.

Excursions.—Fair Head (5 miles); Rathlin by motor-boat; Glenshesk, Murlough Bay, Carrick-a-rede, etc., by bus, also to Londonderry, Belfast, Bangor, Donegal, etc.

Early Closing.—Wednesday.

Hotels.—*Marine* (78 rooms), *Antrim Arms* (22), *Royal* (10).

Population.—3,500.

Youth Hostel.—North Street, at Ballyvoy and at White Park Bay, Ballintoy.

Ballycastle has a charming, wide, semicircular, sandy bay between Fair Head and Ballycastle Head. Its annual Tennis Tournament week—Ulster's Wimbledon—is a festival of beauty and gaiety. Moreover, while the town itself lies about half a mile from the sea front, the two are connected by a stately avenue, **Quay Road,** lined with leafy sycamore trees, and every house is colourful with its flower gardens.

The town and bay lie in wooded surroundings at the foot of **Knocklayd** (1,695 feet). It is a convenient centre for excursions. In addition to hotels, there are numerous guest houses and private houses where accommodation can be found. The ancestral home of U.S. President McKinley—a whitewashed, thatched farmhouse—is at **Dervock** (4 miles distant).

Near the shore, to the right of the golf links and just off the Fair Head and Cushendall Road, are the ruins of **Bonamargy Friary,** a Franciscan friary, dating probably from the fifteenth century. In the nave of the church is the tombstone of *Sorley Boye* ("the yellow-haired"), who after much fighting, first with other Irish tribes and then with the English, finally made his peace with Elizabeth. His son was the first Earl of Antrim.

Inland from Ballycastle is another of the Antrim Glens, **Glenshesk,** a fine wooded dale running for 6 miles to **Armoy,** where a good Irish Round Tower may be inspected. From here return can be made by bus. Then northward from Ballycastle on the cliffs is **Clare Park,** with the ruins of **Dunaneanie Castle,** the early residence of the MacDonnells and where Sorley Boye died. Still farther northwards is **Kenbane Head**—ideal for a picnic (*see below*).

Rathlin Island. Invitingly placed 7 miles from the coast is Rathlin Island more correctly Raghery, or *Rechra.* There is a motor-boat service to it, and a sailing-boat can also be taken across that usually rough sea called the *Brochan* (or "boiling porridge pot"). Embarking at the little port of Ballycastle, one wonders how Sir Walter Raleigh once landed 300 men here. Church Bay, the Kingstown of Rathlin, has some accommodation.

Rathlin is a twentieth-century Treasure Island—with castles, caves, and history. Pliny and Ptolemy knew Rathlin centuries ago, and Charles Kingsley mentions Rathlin in *Westward Ho!* describing it as like "a drowned magpie," because of its alternate white and black cliffs.

Here Robert Bruce learnt from the spider how to "try, try again," and triumphed later at Bannockburn.

The population of about 100 is mainly engaged in farming and fishing.

Rathlin is a delight for the bird-watcher and botanist, and the couple of lakes teem with fish. At the south-east extremity near Doon Point (and opposite Fair Head on the mainland) is a miniature Giant's Causeway formation.

Now we head north for the Giant's Causeway. For the first few of the 13 miles the road runs at some distance from the open sea; and about 2 miles out, by turning down a lane to the right, we may reach **Kenbane,** or *Ceanbane* (the "White head," from its limestone cliffs), with its castle ruins, caves and waterfall. Curiously, the basalt here is below the chalk. Elsewhere during volcanic eruptions the flowing lava spurted upwards through the chalk to cover it with basalt, but at Kenbane, the liquid basaltic lava lifted the chalk upwards bodily. During storms the Head vibrates. Nearby is **Grace Staples Cave,** with all the columnar beauty of Staffa; it is approached at low water. Then 2 miles farther, at the school house, the road branches coastwards to—

Carrick-a-rede. The name means "the rock in the road," *i.e.* the road of the salmon, and is applied to the isolated rock divided from the mainland by a chasm through which the sea tumbles tumultuously. Over this chasm, 60 feet wide, swings a narrow, frail-looking cable bridge, quite 90 feet above the sea. The chasm is a good salmon run.

There is a splendid view from Carrick-a-rede, and you may continue along the cliffs to the old-world village of **Ballintoy** (1¼ miles), where there is good sea-angling from the rocks, and a *Youth Hostel.* Downing College, Cambridge, was endowed by a Ballintoy landlord and its oak panelling and stairways came from a former Ballintoy Castle. The quaint harbour is ideal for a dreamer. **Whitepark Bay** (*Youth Hostel*), with its golden strand and magnificent amphitheatre, holds wonderful treasures in shells, bronze, stone and flint implements, pottery, etc.

At the branching of the roads is **Lisnagunogue,** and we still keep to its coast arm, passing **Port Braddon** and its salmon fishery. A good road now runs from **Dunseverick** village, at the east end of the Giant's Causeway cliff ridge, along the sea margin close to a very beautiful shell strand and bathing gully, down to an ideal holiday corner. There we gaze at the scant and lonely remains of **Dunseverick Castle,** perched on a cliff summit. Next we are at **Portmoon,** with its pretty bay; and 3 miles farther is our destination, with **Bengore Head,** 367 feet high (12 miles from Ballycastle), and **Benbane** intervening as mile-posts.

THE GIANT'S CAUSEWAY
🍀🍀🍀🍀🍀🍀🍀🍀🍀🍀🍀🍀🍀🍀🍀🍀🍀🍀🍀🍀🍀

Access.—Bus trips to the Causeway from Belfast, Larne, Portrush and all neighbouring centres daily. The Causeway and approaches are the property of the National Trust, and are freely accessible to the public.
Amusements.—Splendid beach-bathing at Runkerry and Portallintrae sands. Golf Links (9-holes) at Bushfoot, 1½ miles away.

Cars can be hired to Carrick-a-rede.
Guides and Boats.—Guides and boats available for hire (see notices).
Hotel.—*Causeway* (29 rooms). Spacious restaurant and tea facilities, cloakrooms, etc., are provided. Accommodation also at neighbouring farmhouses.
Post Office at the Causeway. Telegraph Office at Bushmills.

The Giant's Causeway, one of Northern Ireland's greatest and best-known curiosities, may be at first sight disappointing to some visitors, partly since it is almost impossible not to think it largely artificial, partly because the Causeway itself is small and lies so low that the pillars form the beach, or rather tessellated pavement, upon which one walks. Yet such high-sounding names have been given to various parts that one expects something gigantic. The longer it is examined, however, the more one realizes that it is indeed the greatest natural marvel of the country.

The cliffs, 200 to 360 feet high, extend some miles from Portmoon to beyond Bengore Head, enclosing with their precipitous sides a series of seven bays. From the top there is a good view of the three main projections: (1) the triangular one to the left, known as the **Little Causeway**; (2) the **Middle Causeway**, or Honeycomb; (3) to the right and protruding seaward for 700 feet or so, the **Grand Causeway** itself.

The path down was formerly called the "Onion Trap," where the basalt in cooling formed curiously into spheroid masses. But the Causeway itself, although also due to a volcanic outflow, exhibits another different phase. The peculiar columnar formation was caused by the slow cooling in the centre of a great basalt lava flow, the bottom and top of which had cooled more rapidly. Thus was irregularly created what was known to old geologists as "starchy trap." As a matter of fact, those who have watched starch cooling in a basin, its drying surface showing hexagonal cracks, have had an illustration of the making of the Causeway, which evolved by the similar cooling of lava from an adjacent volcanic eruption. On the path down a section may be seen where the two planes of cooling meet.

269

Observing the cliff in **Portnoffer,** pay attention to the horizontal red band half-way up, since it represents the old land surface of the Lower Basalt. On it trees grew and animals lived in the long interval before the Upper Basalts were poured out from the volcanoes to extinguish all life in the area they covered. This area extends over most of North-east Ulster, even into Benevenagh (*see* p. 234) in Co. Derry. The Cave Hill cliff, Belfast, forms the southern escarpment of the Basaltic Plateau of Co. Antrim.

This red band across the Portnoffer cliff plainly proves the existence of two beds of columnar basalt. They spring from the sea here, and rise on the face of the cliffs towards Bengore Head. There the lower bed attains a height of 189 feet above the sea; but both beds fall again to reach sea-level at Portmoon, about 2 miles east of Portnoffer. The lower bed at its western outcrop forms the **Grand Causeway,** a natural mole about 210 yards long, 50 yards wide at the land end and tapering to about 10 yards wide at the sea end. Its centre is about 40 feet high and the surface slopes gently to the sea. This mole or causeway is entirely composed of columnar basalt, the columns set nearly perpendicular to the horizon. The upper portion has been washed away, so that the exposed ends form a pavement of irregular polygons closely fitted together. The great majority of the columns are six-sided, but there are some of three sides, and some with five and seven. Just two—**the Key Stone** and the **Wishing Chair**—have eight sides.

The surface as a whole is not flat like the tiles in a conventional pavement, for some of the polygons are hollow or concave, while others are rounded or convex. This is occasioned by the peculiarity of the cross fractures which divide each column into several sections of various lengths, from 12 inches up to 6 feet. The Causeway columns are divided up into rather shorter sections. Those on the east side, at the Giant's Loom, are, however, about 32 feet long and divided into sections of only 12 inches or so; but joints as long as 6 feet have been quarried near Ballintoy without showing any tendency to break off into shorter lengths.

Naturally the varying shapes and heights of the columns result in fantastic arrangements, and these have names, *e.g.* the **Wishing Chair**, in which you sit and have three wishes, the **Giant's Horse Shoe**, the **Giant's Pot Lid, My Lady's Fan**, the **Giant's Loom**, the **Giant's Coffin**, and on the cliff face, the **Giant's Organ**. Round the corner, by the **Shepherd's Path**, we go to the **Giant's Amphitheatre**, a perfect section of a colosseum, with its 80-foot-high pillars and broad benches for the Cyclopean guests, as they might sit with their backs against the 350-foot-high cliffs. The name of the next bay, **Port-na-Spania** ("Port of the Spaniards"), reminds us that here was lost in November, 1588, the Spanish galleon *Gerona*, with 260 lives, including its Rear-Admiral, Alonzo De Leya, of the Great Armada. Actually, however, this lordly ship came ashore among the cliffs nearer Port Ballintrae, where the *River Bush* runs into the sea. This is a good salmon river but largely preserved; there is also brown trout angling.

Two miles inland from the Causeway is **Bushmills,** with a distillery long famous for its whiskey. By the footbridge, we come on the *Bushfoot Golf Links*. Then ten minutes' walk farther along the cliffs and we are in **Port Ballintrae,** a seaside resort of unique tranquillity and beauty, and with hotels and several good boarding-houses (*Bayview, Ballintrae House, Bayhead House*). From Port Ballintrae across the fields, by the path, and we join the main Portrush Coast Road, at a bus halt.

For Dunluce Castle, 1½ miles west, *see* p. 273.

PORTRUSH AND PORTSTEWART

❀❀❀❀❀❀❀❀❀❀❀❀❀❀❀❀❀❀❀❀❀❀❀❀❀❀❀❀❀

Portrush

Access.—By rail: Portrush is 66¼ miles from Belfast, usually 80-minute journey. By road: From Belfast by direct road, 61 miles, by coast, 98 miles.

Amusements.—Two first-class golf links (18 holes), where championship matches are decided. Recreation Gardens at Ramore Head, with bowling greens, tennis courts and putting green. Frequent tournaments. Beach and swimming facilities at all tides, on both sides of town. Sea fishing: brown trout angling in nearby reservoirs. Dances daily. Cinema in Main Street and theatre in Town Hall.

Buses.—A great variety of tours throughout Ulster and Donegal are available from Portrush and Portstewart. Frequent local services for Giant's Causeway, Dunluce Castle, Portstewart, etc.

Churches, etc.—*Church of Ireland*, Main Street; *Methodist*, Main Street; *Presbyterian*, Main Street and Glenmore Road; *Roman Catholic*, Causeway Street; *Gospel*, Portstewart Road; *Baptist* at Town Hall.

Distances.—Ballycastle 18, Ballymena 33, Bushmills 6, Belfast 61, Dublin 147, Causeway 8, Londonderry 37, Portstewart 4.

Early Closing.—Wednesday.

Golf.—*Royal Portrush Golf Club*, two 18-hole courses and pitch and putt course.

Hotels.—*Northern Counties* (91 rooms), *Skerry-Bahn* (66), *Kiln-an-Oge* (24), *Fawcett's Royal Portrush* (130), *Eglinton* (40), *West Bay View* (53), *Alexandra, Clarence, Esplanade, Moorings, Seabank;* and many others. Many guest houses, etc.

Population.—4,263.

Post Office.—Causeway Street.

Portrush, situated on a bold promontory less than half a mile wide, and projecting almost a mile into the Atlantic, is one of the leading holiday resorts of Ireland. It is virtually an island, since it is only connected to the mainland by the railway and the coast road, which is a continuation of the Antrim Coast Road from Larne and the Giant's Causeway to Portstewart, 3 miles more westerly.

The magnificent bays on either side, with their beautiful sandy beaches, provide pleasures for all tastes. These beaches provide excellent bathing, as also does the famous Blue Pool on the east side. Portrush (*Port ruis:* "harbour of the promontory") is a paradox: simultaneously popular and exclusive, fashionable and democratic. Moreover, although so far north, with latitude 55.4 N. (compared with London's 51 N.), even in winter it is warmed by the Gulf Stream and is always of equable temperature.

Portrush is famous as the home of the *Royal Portrush Golf Club* which has two 18-hole courses—the Dunluce Championship Course and the Valley Course—and a 9-hole pitch and putt course.

272

Those who have been interested in the geology of the Giant's Causeway and the Antrim Coast Road will find something further in the rocks in the vicinity of the Blue Pool and Ramore Head, which were originally soft Liassic clays and shales of the kind that are so abundant on the English south coast and cause serious landslips and cliff falls. Here, however, the clays have been baked as hard as flint by the great heat of the lavas poured out red or white hot from soft earth rifts, and their mass formed **Ramore Head,** on which the older part of Portrush stood.

The **Skerry Islands,** a mile offshore, form a natural breakwater to the west bay (once planned as an Atlantic harbour), and are a favourite resort for bathing, fishing and picnics. They are reputed to have been the last nesting-place on this side of the Atlantic of the greak auk, a sea-bird now extinct, and tradition asserts that a notorious Scottish pirate, Tavish Dhu, was buried there. There is a well of beautiful water and visitors find both Castle and Long Island a delightful rendezvous.

Two miles east of Portrush are the **White Rocks Caves** which are seen to best advantage from a boat. Farther east is—

Dunluce Castle (*small charge*) once the favourite residence of the Earls of Antrim. Dating back to the fourteenth century at least, it covers the site of an older castle, and rears itself on a bold black headland, over 100 feet high, overhanging the sea. It is connected with the mainland by a very narrow bridge, and all its rooms, halls and courts can still be traced. It was held by Sorley Boye MacDonnell until the English took it in 1585. Romance and story are enshrined in every grey stone of its walls.

Built probably between 1315 and 1350 and well named *Dun-lis* ("the strong fort") the Castle was lost by the Bissets (or McQuillans) to the

MacDonnells, who in their turn lost it to Shane O'Neill, who threatened to starve his prisoner, Sorley Boye MacDonnell, to death. Even the English could not hold it, for fifty of the Irish entered it by a rope one night. Then in 1630 another MacDonnell, the first Earl of Antrim, brought here his bride, the widow of that Duke of Buckingham who was assassinated by Felton in Portsmouth. In 1639 a great storm caused the collapse of much of the Castle into the sea below and while nine of the servants went with the wall, the "Tinker's Window" still remains to tell of how a tinker sitting there escaped. Monro captured Dunluce in 1648 and subsequently the Marquis of Antrim removed the family seat to Glenarm (p. 262).

Four miles west of Portrush is—

Portstewart

Amusements.—Two 18-hole golf courses: Town Links extending east of the town towards Portrush, and the Strand course to the west, at Agherton Strand, ¾ mile from town. Tennis, bowls, bathing, boating, fishing, cinema.

Bus services.—Portrush (3 miles), Coleraine (4 miles).

Churches.—*Church of Ireland*, The Diamond; *Baptist*, Coleraine Road; *Methodist*, Heathmount; *Presbyterian*, Church Street; *Roman Catholic*, The Crescent.

Hotels.—*Carrig-na-Cule* (35 rooms), *Windsor* (30), *Strand* (80), *Montagu Arms* (39), *Links* (14), *Golf* (20), others and many guest houses.

Population.—4,300.

Situation.—56½ miles from Belfast, 39 miles from Derry.

The ancient name *Port-na-Binnie Uaine* ("the port of the green headland") still describes this twin sister to Portrush, though she does not display her charms so flamboyantly. The headland under the lee of which lies the harbour—a real fishing harbour—is not the least of Portstewart's features.

Portstewart is particularly pleasing and picturesque, the

274

town girdling a crescent bay extending from the neat little
fishing harbour to the old rock-perched **Castle**—once the home
of the O'Haras but now a convent school—while from the
terrace above peeps another arc of fine houses. There are
up-to-date hotels and boarding-houses, bathing for all ages,
two golf links, and the best of both rock and boat fishing.

The views along the coast looking seawards are charming,
either from the Promenade or from the cliff walk westerly
round to the magnificent **Agherton Strand,** stretching 2½ miles
to the Barmouth, where the Bann meets the ocean. In the near
distance, across that river, are **Castlerock,** a quiet resort, with
an 18-hole golf course, and **Downhill Strand** which continues
for miles westward as far as **Magilligan,** at the entrance to
Lough Foyle and with a ferry across to **Greencastle** (*Fort
Hotel*).

Portrush to Belfast via Ballymoney and Ballymena

The inland road between Portrush and Belfast strikes southward towards **Coleraine** (*see* p. 235) and **Ballymoney,** a market
town and a centre of the linen industry (*Manor Hotel*; Population, 3,409; Early Closing, Tuesdays). A minor road striking
north to **Dervock** passes in 3 miles the hamlet of *Conagher*,
former family home of U.S. President McKinley.

Ballymena

Distances.—Belfast 28, Antrim 11, Ballymoney 19, Dublin 123, Cushendall 20.

Population.—14,740.
Hotels.—*Adair Arms, Clarence, Crescent.*
Early Closing.—Wednesday.

Situated in the Braid valley, Ballymena is a busy marketing
centre, owing its prosperity to the linen and tobacco trades.
There are tennis courts, a 9-hole golf course, bowling green,
cinema, etc., and fishing in the rivers Main, Braid and Clogh,
and the Kells Water. There is little of note in the town but there
are a number of interesting places in the vicinity. To the west is
Galgorm Castle, built in 1618 and now restored. Beyond the
demesne is *Gracehill*, a Moravian Settlement with a central
square. To the north-west is **Cullybackey,** where the father of
U.S. President Chester A. Arthur, 1830–1886 was born.
Eight miles east of Ballymena, beyond **Broughshane,** is the
prominent height of **Slemish Mountain** (1,437 feet), traditionally
the scene of St. Patrick's youthful slave years.

Southward, our route continues straight for Antrim (p. 252)
whence the road to Belfast is described in p. 252.

EASTWARD FROM BELFAST
✠✠✠✠✠✠✠✠✠✠✠✠✠✠✠✠✠✠✠✠✠✠✠✠✠✠

Crossing the *Lagan* by Queen's Bridge the A 20 goes due
eastward for Dundonald and Newtownards (p. 283). Two
miles from the city, however, just after the Ropeworks, a left
fork (A 2) is taken to skirt the eastern shore of Belfast Lough
and its pleasant resorts. Cave Hill stands out prominently in
the view across the water.

Holywood

Location.—6 miles east of Belfast on A 2.
Trains from Queen's Quay station.
Buses from Oxford Street (Queen's
Bridge end).
Amusements.—Boating, tennis, cinema,
bowls and yachting.
Golf.—18-hole course at Demesne Road.

Hotel.—*Strathearn, Central* and guest
houses.
Early Closing.—Wednesday.
Places of Worship.—*Episcopalian, Meth-
odist, Presbyterian, Unitarian, Roman
Catholic, Plymouth Brethren.*
Population.—8,250.

Pleasantly placed on Belfast Lough, about 6 miles from the
city, and with a genial climate due to its sheltered position at
the foot of high hills, Holywood is the home of many Belfast
business people. Unlike the American Hollywood, the Ulster
Holywood has an honoured history dating back for centuries.
Here St. Laserian founded a church A.D. 600–700, and the
mound in the grounds of the Motte, 100 yards south of the
Maypole, was called after the saint's name. The townland
was *Ballyderry* (the town of the oaks) until the Normans
invaded it and changed the name to *Sanctus Boscus*—the
Holy Wood.

The first monastery was destroyed by the Danes during
one of their invasions. Restored by one of the early English
landowners, this establishment continued until 1572, when
it was burned by O'Neill, Lord of Clandeboye, during his
insurrection against Queen Elizabeth, to prevent the English
from fortifying it.

The most outstanding object in Holywood today is the
tall **Maypole** at the intersection of its chief streets, probably
the only maypole in Ireland and still decorated on May Eve.

In the early nineteenth century Holywood was Belfast's
beloved seaside resort, as its lay-out suggests, and it was like-
wise the birthplace of Irish golf; but now its chief features are
its military depot and the pleasant walk which runs by the sea
for 8 miles or so to Bangor. There is good brown trout fishing
in the Council's reservoirs at Creighton's Green and Church
Road.

On the outskirts of Holywood are the seaside suburbs of **Marino** and **Cultra** ("the corner of the strand"). Cultra is of geological interest as one of the few spots in Ireland where Permian rocks are exposed. Cultra Manor has been developed as the new *Ulster Folk Museum*. The *Royal Northern Yacht Club* have headquarters at Cultra. At Craigavad ("rock of the boat") is the *Royal Belfast Golf Club*.

Helen's Bay, $3\frac{1}{2}$ miles eastward, is a bathing-place on a little inlet of the Lough. It has charming coast scenery and a good 9-hole golf course. Adjoining the station is an **Avenue**, 3 miles long, constructed by the late Lord Dufferin and extending from Clandeboye House to the coast, which is within ten minutes' walk of the railway. On the shore to the right are the shingle and sand of Helen's Bay; on the left are the copses and rocks of **Grey Point**, a headland which affords a beautiful view of the Lough and its shores. Steamers on their way to and from Belfast pass near the headland, as the water off it is very deep.

The headland and property at Helen's Bay is private.

It is a pretty walk of 4 miles by the coast from Grey Point to Holywood, and an even more attractive stroll of 3 miles, in the opposite direction, seaward to Bangor.

About two miles inland from Helen's Bay station is—

Clandeboye

the seat of the Marquis of Dufferin and Ava. It can be approached by the main Belfast–Bangor highway, or by the road through the small but delightful village of **Crawfordsburn**, with its picturesque *Old Inn*. There is an 18-hole golf course at Clandeboye.

In the beautiful demesne **Helen's Tower** stands on high ground some 2 miles beyond Clandeboye mansion.

It can be reached only by a stony path leading from the little village of Conlig (on the Bangor–Newtownards bus route and about 2 miles from the former town) through a wood directly to the summit. *Visitors may approach the tower only by printed permit issued at the Estate Office.* The building is three storeys high. The topmost chamber is an octagon boudoir, with groined roof and oaken panels; in letters of gold are the lines addressed by his mother, Helen Selina, Lady Dufferin, to the builder of the tower, the fifth earl, later to become the 1st Marquis, when he reached his twenty-first birthday (1847). The tower was built in honour of this Lady Dufferin. She was the gifted granddaughter of Richard Brinsley Sheridan, the dramatist. Lord Dufferin was in succession Governor-General of Canada, Ambassador at St. Petersburg, Ambassador at Constantinople, and Viceroy of India.

The fame of the tower was sung by Tennyson and Browning, and their verses, on plates mounted in panels, are displayed in the reception room,

277

East of Helen's Bay is **Crawfordsburn Glen**—leading up to Crawfordsburn village—a beautiful ravine containing trees, ferns in abundance, shady walks and a stream on its way to the sea. Visitors, however, must ask permission from its owner to walk through it.

Continuing by the shore we quickly come to **Carnalea** and its fine golf links (18-hole), on high ground overlooking the sea. Just below the club-house, where teas, etc., are available, is a bathing-place usable at all states of the tide. The path onwards for about a mile crosses **Strickland's Glen,** and then rounding **Wilson's Point** we have the spacious panorama of Bangor Bay with the town as an amphitheatre looking over it.

Bangor

Access.—Bangor is 14 miles N.E. of Belfast. By train from Queen's Quay (12¼ miles). By bus, from Oxford Street terminus.

Amusements.—Band performances, carnivals, dancing, bowling, tennis, cricket, yachting, football, boating, Lough trips, sea-bathing, sea-fishing, motor rally, cinemas and drama and variety shows.

Early Closing.—Thursday.

Golf (Bangor).—18-hole course. Open to visitors. Sunday play.

Hotels.—*Ballyholme* (49 rooms), *Royal* (46), *New Savoy* (160), *Queen's Court* (60), *Redcliff* (24), *Mayfair* (18), *Sefton* (18). There are many guest houses.

Inquiries.—Town Hall, The Castle.

Places of Worship.—
Parish Church, Presbyterian Churches (six), *Methodist* (four), *Baptist, Roman Catholic* (two), and *Plymouth Brethren.*

Population.—About 31,000. Fourth largest Ulster town.

Regattas.—*Royal Ulster Yacht Club* in July, *Juvenile* in August, and *Ballyholme Yacht Club* in July.

Excursions.—Whole day tours start from the Esplanade for: (1) Portrush, Giant's Causeway and Antrim Coast; (2) Lough Erne and Donegal; (3) also other routes as programmed. Half-day tours include: (1) Glens of Antrim; (2) County Down, circular journey; (3) Mountains of Mourne; (4) Shane's Castle and Lough Neagh; (5) Ards Peninsula; (6) Mountstewart Gardens, Millisle and Donaghadee, as well as afternoon and evening novelty trips. The proximity of Belfast to Bangor and the facilities in early and late trains also enable visitors staying at Bangor to engage in all the tours from Belfast, as well as the County Down and other Railway excursions therefrom.

Bangor is the largest resort in Northern Ireland and also serves as a dormitory town for a large number of business and professional men in Belfast. A frequent and fast service of modern diesel trains connects Bangor with the capital and, in addition, there is a supplementary service by bus.

Bangor has almost doubled its population in the post-war period and is now the fourth largest town in Northern Ireland, being exceeded only by Belfast, Londonderry and Newtownabbey.* The sea-front extends over 4 miles around Smelt Mill Bay to the west, Bangor Bay, and **Ballyholme Bay** to the east.

* Newtownabbey is the collective name given to the area north of Belfast consisting of Whitewell, Whiteabbey, Whitehouse, Jordanstown, Glengormley, Greencastle etc. which have merged into an urban district with the entitlement to the term "town."

Although the town is of ancient origin, its growth coincided with the development of modern transport, thus slums are practically non-existent. Large spaces have been reserved for parks and sports. There are hotels, boarding houses and restaurants, to suit the requirements of all.

There are two golf courses, three municipal bowling greens and one privately owned, tennis courts available to the public and first-rate facilities for yachting, boating, sea-angling, putting, miniature golf, bathing, walking, etc. On the entertainments side, drama and variety theatres operate throughout the season. There are cinemas, several ballrooms and a host of special events, including regattas, swimming galas and the like, horse shows, Highland Gathering, fancy-dress parades, sand-designing competitions, golf, hockey, tennis and bowling weeks, and drama, music and folk dance festivals.

The swimming pool at Pickie is the largest enclosed open-air pool in Ireland, whilst beach bathing may be enjoyed from the sands at **Ballyholme Bay**.

The **Marine Gardens** extend from the western boundary of the borough to the centre of the town by the sea and provide a sheltered, sunny rendezvous. Adjoining the Marine Gardens are **Strickland's Glen** and **Connor Park**.

Ward Park, situated in the centre of the borough, extends over 56 acres and encloses one of the most varied collections of wild fowl to be seen in the British Isles, aviaries, flower gardens, shrubs and playing fields.

Castle Park extends over 150 acres and includes a forest are of some 15 acres. It includes a nature trail of about $1\frac{1}{2}$ miles. Facilities for football and hockey are to be found in Castle Park as is also **Bangor Castle**, originally the home of the Clanmorris family, but today a fine Town Hall.

A portion of the wall that separates the old Abbey Church from Castle Park is reputed to date back to the twelfth century and is the only tangible relic of Bangor's ancient ecclesiastical history.

Bangor to Donaghadee is a popular excursion. The places are not connected directly by rail, but buses run almost continuously from the Esplanade and Railway Station. The distance is $7\frac{1}{2}$ miles by Coast Road.

At first the road skirts **Ballyholme Bay,** separated from Bangor Bay by a promontory covered with villas. The eastern inlet has a long beach of sand and shingle bordered by attractive houses and sheltered from easterly winds. The road goes over a ridge to the little

fishing village of **Groomsport,** 3 miles from Bangor. The foundation
on which its Quay is based is the old quay built by the Danes centuries
ago. With its grassy slopes, liberal sailing and bathing facilities and
clean sandy bay, Groomsport village is a fascinating place. Buses
link it on either side with Bangor and Donaghadee.

A mile and a half beyond Groomsport the road ascends a ridge
that ends in **Orlock Point,** where uptilted rocks form rugged ridges
and hollows, here plunging down into deep water, there forming a
foaming reef. Beyond Orlock Point the road strikes the shore, and
follows it closely for the rest of the way.

There is much pretty coast scenery ahead. Seaward are the Copeland Islands (p. 281), while beyond parts of the Scottish coast are
visible. Inland may be seen the huge carpet-making factory of a
well-known company.

Donaghadee

Access.—Ulsterbus direct from Oxford
Street; or by rail from Queen's Quay
to Bangor, and thence by bus to
Donaghadee.

Amusements.—Bathing, boating, fishing,
golf, sea cruises and launch trips to
Copeland Isles and Bangor, bowling,
tennis.

Hotels.—*Imperial* (21 rooms), *Copelands*

(15), *Dunallen* (16), *Mount Royal* (16),
etc.

Population.—3,649.

Early Closing.—Thursday.

Places of Worship.—
Church of Ireland.—11.30 and 7. *Presbyterian* (two).—11.30 and 7. *Methodist.*—11.30 and 7. *Roman Catholic.*—
8, 9 and 12 noon.

Donaghadee, 22 miles east of Belfast, is situated on the
open sea-coast, beyond Belfast Lough. It is the nearest spot to
Scotland. The Irish end of the submarine cable to Portpatrick
(in Wigtownshire), with the cable-house, is just outside the
town on the south side. Its fine sandy beach, good bathing
facilities, golf links (18-hole), small rainfall and salubrious
climate have made Donaghadee a favourite health resort.
The town has two main streets, one of which sweeps round
the bay. At the southern end is the harbour.

For a long period Donaghadee was a mail-packet station, the boats
running to and from Portpatrick, 21 miles distant. The service was transferred to Larne and Stranraer in 1865 on account of the superiority of their
harbours.

While Donaghadee enjoyed the privileges of a packet station, its good
natural harbour was improved by the erection of two stone piers and
breakwater, which enclose a large bay. At the seaward end of one pier is a
lighthouse showing a fixed light.

The derivation of the name is not clear. One suggestion is that it comes
from the Gaelic *donagh dith*, "church of loss," but more probably it was
Down-da-ghee, "the mound of two heroes." Its huge Dun (*dune*) or fort
still remains (*see below*). The town faces north-east and by reason of its
geographical location has the lowest rainfall in Northern Ireland.

The beach consists of stretches of sand, pebbles and rocks.

At the *Quarry Hole*, near the bus depot, and at the *Warren*, at the opposite end of the town, ample provision is made for bathers. On the shore at the northern end of the town is an 18-hole **Golf Course,** with club-house, and there are tennis courts, bowls and putting greens south of the pier.

A great attraction to visitors is a huge rath, or mound, locally called **The Moat,** crowned with an old powder magazine, at the back of the town. It is 140 feet high, with a circumference at the base of 480 feet, and commands a magnificent view of Belfast Lough, the Scottish coast and the Isle of Man.

The antiquarian will find much of interest in the **Parish Church** with its 600 years' history and its seventeenth-century tombstones, one of which perpetuates Jean Machgwear, who "lived well and died well." Here, by the way, Donaghadee is given as "Donoudie."

Among favourite short walks from Donaghadee is that to **Bangor,** by the shore road described on p. 279, and that to **St. Patrick's Well,** a mile southward from the town by the Mill Isle Road, beyond the cable-house. The water is reputed to be a cure for headache.

Opposite Donaghadee are the—

Copeland Islands

A visit to these makes a pleasant and interesting boating excursion. They are three in number. The largest is about a mile in length by half a mile in breadth and separated from the mainland by a channel a mile wide at its narrowest point.

The little cemetery contains traces of a chapel (one of the adjuncts of the great Abbey of Bangor) and the adjacent inlet is known as Chapel Bay. The Copeland Islands take their name from an English family who settled in the Ards during the early invasions.

A pillar box on the Island still bears the inscription: "E.R. VII."

A mile farther out to sea is the **Lighthouse Island.** The only valuable part of its surface is about 40 acres of grazing ground. The building to which it owes its name has been superseded by one on **Mew Island,** a low rock of 26 acres lying close to the eastern side of Lighthouse Island. Its lantern, 121 feet above high water, contains one of the most powerful lights (1,210,000 candle-power) in the world and forms a guide to the entrance of Belfast Lough. Each half-minute it shows four short white flashes. In thick weather, a diaphone gives four short blasts every thirty seconds. Mew Island is a great resort and breeding-place of the tern or sea-swallow.

THE ARDS PENINSULA
✿✿✿✿✿✿✿✿✿✿✿✿✿✿✿✿✿✿✿✿✿✿✿

Served by bus from Belfast *via* Newtownards, Grey Abbey, Kircubbin and Portaferry.
To Ballywalter from Newtownards *via* Carrowdore and to Ballyhalbert *via* Kircubbin.

The Ards Peninsula is a tract of low, hillocky, fertile land, about 20 miles in length and from 3 to 5 in breadth, between Strangford Lough and the Irish Sea. There are raths, many ruins of abbeys, churches, castles, etc, so that the district is of great interest to archaeologists. Naturalists and geologists also find here much of special interest. The Scottish accent is very marked in this district.

The roads are excellent. To go down one side of the peninsula to Portaferry and back by the coast road is a run of some 73 miles from Belfast.

County Down

There is some similarity between the shore contours of the adjoining counties of Antrim and Down. Each has its distinctive lough or sea-inlet north and south of busy Belfast Lough, Larne Lough on the north providing the Island Magee Peninsula and Strangford Lough on the south giving the similar Ards Peninsula. Each, too, has its hills fringing the sea, though in Co. Down they are not so pronounced except in the south by the Mourne Mountains. However, Down is an exceedingly hilly county.

The bus crosses the Lagan by Albert Bridge and follows the Dundonald bus route to the outskirts of the city. Then we pass through the roadside village of **Dundonald,** near which is an Anglo-Norman motte. Just over a mile to the east is the *Kempe Stone dolmen.*

Southward extend the glistening waters of **Strangford Lough** —originally called Lough Coyne or Cuan (the "harbour lake"), but renamed by the Norsemen Strang Fiord, the "violent inlet," because of its strong tides. Newtownards and Comber are at its northern head, while between these twin towns rises a lofty crag, **Scrabo** (the hill "of the cows"), crowned by a monument to the third Marquess of Londonderry, a remarkable man, though not so well known as his relative, Lord Castlereagh. At the foot of the hill is Scrabo Golf course (9 holes).

Looking northwards from this point, we get a glimpse of **Helen's Tower** (*see* p. 277).

282

Newtownards

is a prosperous industrial town—the Ards capital—with about 13,090 inhabitants, flourishing engineering, nylon and woollen factories, and an **airfield** close by.

Originally it was known as Villa Nova de Blaethwych, the New Town of Blaethwych, but later (probably because of its geographical location) the "New Town of the Ards," implying that there was probably a very much older predecessor around the ancient **Movilla Abbey** ("the plain of the old tree"), 1 mile east. Here Finnbarr—the St. Finian famous also in Cork's history—founded a church about A.D. 540. Some beautiful window tracery and ancient slabs dating earlier than the Norman invasion are still preserved in Movilla.

Walter de Burgo also founded a Dominican monastery at Newtownards in 1244; and, after the Bruce invasion of 1316, the town seems to have fallen into the hands of O'Neill, who built a castle. However, although the castle has long ago disappeared the ruin of the Abbey remains, with its light graceful arcade and its square tower later erected by Sir Hugh Montgomery in the reign of James I. The town cross, erected in 1636, also bears the arms of the planter Montgomerys.

For 5 miles we follow the shore beside a silent sea, well named "the harbour lake," owing to the general absence of shipping. Midway is marked by *The Butter Lump*, a huge boulder of 130 tons on the lough shore, carried here by a glacier.

Mount Stewart

Admission.—Gardens open in summer, daily except Mondays other than Bank Holidays, from 2 p.m. *Charge.*
Buses from Belfast to Grey Abbey, etc., stop at Clay Gates entrance.

If in life realization seldom balances anticipation, here in Mount Stewart Gardens is the notable exception. There are rock gardens gay with colour, woods of evergreen ilex, magnolias, auracaria and firs blending with the giant blue gums, cedars, Wellingtonia, stately beeches and leafy limes, parades festooned with a wealth of rambling red, white and purple roses, lakes, Spanish and Italian, as well as *"Tir n'an Oge"* (the Peter Pan) and bog gardens and pools resplendent with gold and silver fish and vivid green tree frogs. All the beautiful urns and masonry, with the statuary of Dodos and other famous fossil animals (including the now extinct Irish greyhound pig), are the workmanship of cottagers of the estate, while the mansion, classic in style, is built of sandstone from nearby Scrabo and floored with bog-oak found in the demesne. The mansion was planned in the early eighteenth century but not completed until eighty-five years later, and in it, in 1769, was born Robert Stewart, afterwards Lord Castlereagh, who was famous as the statesman who achieved the Union between Great Britain and Ireland in 1800. Later as Foreign Secretary he represented the United Kingdom in the negotiations of the Peace Treaty after Waterloo.

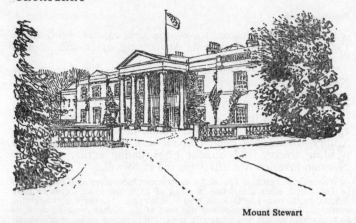

Mount Stewart

Grey Abbey

Two miles beyond Mount Stewart is **Grey Abbey** village, where many of its old-world cottages have given place to modern houses. At the top of the "High Street" a right turn leads to the ruins of the old—

Grey Abbey, dating back to Norman times, when the Normans held this part of County Down. Founded by the wife of Sir John de Courcy in 1193, it was destroyed with others by O'Neill in 1572 lest they should shelter Sir Thomas Smith's prospective English settlers. Later it passed more peacefully to the Montgomery family, who re-roofed the stout old walls in the seventeenth century, and until 1778 the nave was the parish church. Grey Abbey is remarkable for beauty and size. The great windows and very elaborate west door date back to A.D. 1250, and the two figures represent the foundress and De Courcy.

Here is a junction of the ways. Southward along the Lough side goes the bus route to **Kircubbin** (4 miles) and **Portaferry** (another 8 miles). Another bus route crosses the Ards Peninsula to the open Irish Sea at **Ballywalter** (*see* p. 286).

Portaferry

near the southern extremity of the Ards Peninsula, is a quaint little eighteenth-century town with a comfortable hotel (*Portaferry*), houses offering private lodgings and also a *Youth Hostel*. The derivation of the name is obvious, for here the broad waters of Strangford Lough narrow to a river-like width of half a mile; and through this bottleneck of 5 miles a tremendous tide rushes in and out. When the wind is from the east and the tide ebbing, the Strangford bar with its Angus Rock midway in the channel warrants its Norse name, Strang Fiord, the violent firth.

Portaferry, with one long main street parallel to Strangford Lough and a steep hill leading up from the Quay to the Square, was once a very busy shipping port, but now, detached from the world, it merely dreams of past days, and the population is only 1,406. Lace making is carried on on a small scale.

No prospect could be more pleasing and peaceful than that from **Portaferry House** grounds—of the crescent bay and the ancient fortresses in the lovely wooded grounds of Castleward across the straits.

For holiday-makers there is good bathing and sailing, delectable dishes of clams and lobsters, and everywhere the courteous hospitality of its kindly people.

Opposite Portaferry, and connected to it by ferry, is **Strangford,** one of the most charming villages in Ireland, with historical associations going back to the ancient Irish, who knew it as Cuan centuries before the arrival of the Norsemen. Overlooking the harbour is **Strangford Castle,** an ancient tower-house, now National Trust property and *open to the public.*

A mile to the west of Strangford is **Castleward,** built by the first Lord Bangor in 1765. The house and grounds, now National Trust property, are open from April to September, from 2 p.m. daily except Mondays other than Bank Holidays. *Charge.* Away to the right is the square keep of *Audley's Castle,* an ancient fortress. A little south of that is the ancient *Castle Ward,* a picturesque square battlemented tower surrounded by farm buildings.

After passing Castleward grounds, there will be seen, near the shore of the Lough, a modern castellated mansion called **Myra Castle,** with the ancient keep of Walshestown Castle close beside it. Then, on the left, is the little church of **Raholp,** locally known as Churchmoyley, founded by St. Patrick.

Topping a commanding hill at Saul is a 35-foot statue of St. Patrick, for it was here Ireland's patron saint landed and began his mission.

Still nearer Downpatrick is **Quoile Castle,** a small square tower, now in ruins.

Southward from Strangford there is a lovely sea coast and a good road for 6 miles to the quaintly picturesque port of **Ardglass** (*see* p. 291). This is a patch of charming marine scenery too often missed by visitors. From Ardglass one can go *via* Downpatrick to **Newcastle** and the Mourne District (p. 293) or return to Belfast direct. Or from Strangford, a bus may be taken to Belfast *via* Downpatrick (p. 288).

Portaferry to Donaghadee

Four miles to the south-east of Portaferry is **Ballyquintin Point,** the southern extremity of the Ards Peninsula and of interest chiefly to the geologist. The places to be seen along the *sea* side of the Ards Peninsula, which we have just followed by the inland or Strangford Lough road, are not of great interest. A mile and a half northward of the Point are a few remains of the ancient church of *Templecowey* and a fine souterrain. Half a mile farther north is **Tara Fort,** a circular earthwork on an isolated hill, and between half a mile and a mile farther are the remains of two stone circles. Next comes **Quintin Castle** ($2\frac{1}{2}$ miles to the east of Portaferry), so modernized that there is little in its appearance to show that it was erected in Queen Elizabeth's era.

And now we begin our journey northwards along the eastward, or open sea, shores of the Ards Peninsula. Three miles or so from Quintin Castle we reach **Cloughey** ("the stony place"), with its red-roofed bungalows grouped along a beautiful sandy bay. Half a mile inland are the remains of the castle and church of **Castleboy,** once held by the knights of St. John of Jerusalem. The next object of interest is **Kirkistown Castle,** erected in the early part of the reign of James I, and formerly the seat of the Savages of Kirkistown. The keep and surrounding bawn, or fortified yard, are still perfect. Here, also, is an 18-hole golf course, and a motor racing circuit.

On the coast is the village of **Portavogie,** with a modern harbour and a fishing station noted for its catches of herrings.

Continuing northward from Portavogie, the road follows the coast along to the small village of **Ballyhalbert,** where are a standing-stone, a tumulus, and the ruins of the old parish church.

For the rest of the route the road closely follows the coast line, along which rocky reefs and bays of yellow sand alternate. Four miles from Ballyhalbert is the small town of **Ballywalter** (*Sunnyholm Hotel*), a fine resort for sea-anglers. Adjoining it on the south is **Ballywalter Park,** the seat of Lord Dunleath, while half a mile towards the north-west are the ruins of *Templefinn*, the White Church.

Two miles inland is **Carrowdore** where the Carrowdore 100 Motor Cycle Race is held annually.

Another mile along the coast brings us to the sprawling bungalow suburb of **Millisle,** and beyond that is *St. Patrick's Well*, while $2\frac{1}{2}$ miles from Millisle is **Donaghadee** (p. 280), 23 miles from Portaferry by the route we have followed.

KILLYLEAGH AND DOWNPATRICK
❀❀❀❀❀❀❀❀❀❀❀❀❀❀❀❀❀❀❀❀❀❀❀❀❀❀❀❀❀❀❀❀❀❀❀❀

In the previous section the southerly protruding Ards Peninsula, separating the outside Irish Sea from the inland sea, if we may so dignify Strangford Lough, was examined. So now we are free to continue our explorations of County Down's main body, located on the west side of Strangford Lough and extending so far westerly as to even impinge on Lough Neagh.

To Downpatrick via Killyleagh

The route is as for Dundonald (*see* p. 282). Four miles farther south-east is **Comber** (from the Irish *comar*, a confluence; so obviously here the confluence of Comber river with Strangford Lough). In its square is an obelisk of a Comber native, Sir Robert Rollo Gillespie, who also earned a memorial in St. Paul's Cathedral. On the outskirts of Comber a left fork, signposted Mahee Island, follows the Comber estuary and then skirts the westward fringe of Strangford Lough, an area rich in ruins of Norman castles and churches. This road runs parallel with the direct road (bus) to Killyleagh, which walkers can quickly regain by several connecting roads.

From the main road picturesque views of the Lough and its many green islets can frequently be seen, and soon we are at **Ballydrain.** Here a road leads off for Ringneill, where the ancient ruins of a castle indicate the causeway connecting **Mahee Island** with the mainland. Here are the ruins of **Nendrum Abbey** ("nine ridges") which was established by Mochaoi, disciple of St. Patrick, and flourished from A.D. 450 until its destruction by the pagan Norsemen about A.D. 974. The view from the monastery site is delightful. Adjacent is Island Mahee golf course. Here, too, is the club-house of the *Strangford Lough Sailing Club*. The well-preserved **Castle of Sketrick,** on nearby Sketrick Island, calls for note.

Killyleagh

(*Dunmore Hotel*) is among the most interesting villages in Northern Ireland. There is some linen and port activity, though with its peaceful main street it would seem now somewhat dull. At one time it was represented by two members at the Irish

Parliament (1783–1800). Killyleagh was the birth-place (1660) of Sir Hans Sloane, the celebrated physician and naturalist whose famous collection of natural objects, books and MSS. formed the nucleus of the British Museum. At the top of the hill is the imposing **Killyleagh Castle,** originally built by De Courcy and remarkable in that it has been in constant occupation for thirteen centuries. A short way above the Castle and down a lane on the right is the stile on which Lady Dufferin based the song poem, "The Emigrant's Farewell." In the churchyard is the Dufferin vault, containing the remains of Vice-Admiral Sir Henry Blackwood, who was Nelson's colleague and friend.

There is good coarse fishing in the *Curigullion Lakes,* a few miles north-west of here.

Downpatrick

Access.—By road (bus service), from Belfast *via* Saintfield and Crossgar.
Angling.—In the *Quoile* and in nearby lakes.
Buses radiate from Downpatrick to (1) Tyrella Sands at Minerstown, Rossglass; (2) Killough and Ballyhornan, also on Dundrum Bay; (3) Strangford and (4) Dundrum and Newcastle.
Distances.—Ardglass 7, Belfast 22, Bangor 28, Dublin 96, Newcastle 13, Newtownards 22, Strangford 9.

Early Closing.—Wednesday.
Golf.—9 hole course.
Hotel.—*Denvir's* (7 rooms).
Places of Worship.—*The Cathedral* the *Parish Church, Methodist, Presbyterian* and *Unitarian Churches*—all at 11.30 and 7; *Roman Catholic*—7.30, 8.30, 10, 11, 12 and 7.
Population.—4,219.
Youth Hostel.—Nearest one at Minerstown, Ballyvaston.

This cathedral city, the County capital, though not now of great commercial importance is one of the most ancient places in the country, dating from a period long prior to the Christian era. It was at first called *Rath-Keltair*, the "fort of Keltair," a prince in very early days. It was also known as Dun-daleth-glas, or simply "Dun," because it was the principal fort in the district. This contraction, in the form of "Down," is still constantly employed and is also the name given to the county. In later times the name of the patron saint of Ireland was given to the fort, making the modern appellation Downpatrick or Dun Patrick.

Now located partly in a valley, partly on hills, it was originally entirely upon high ground and was surrounded with walls, but with the dawn of peaceful days its position was changed, and the chief business thoroughfares are now in the valley. The straggling town is pleasantly situated and picturesque in appearance, especially as seen from the road. Prominent on the left is the square pinnacled tower of the Cathedral; to the

288

right is the spire of the Roman Catholic Chapel, and farther right still the great pile forming the Mental Hospital.

The walk by the River Quoile towards Strangford Lough is pleasant.

Down Cathedral

The Cathedral is a fine, but heavy, specimen of the Pointed style, built chiefly of unhewn stone, and comprising a nave, choir and aisles. The lofty square tower, embattled and pinnacled, stands at the west end. On the external face of the wall at the east end are niches with battered effigies of SS. Patrick, Bridget, and Columba, found after the Cathedral had been destroyed by Lord de Grey.

On the site once stood an Abbey, generally said to have been founded by Saint Patrick, about A.D. 490, but it is not certain that the building owed its origin to him. There is, moreover, only questionable evidence that he was buried at Downpatrick. The first Abbey, as well as the city and district, suffered much from incursions of the Danes, being plundered eight times between the years 824 and 1111. In the latter year the invaders were defeated, and their king, Magnus Barefoot, was killed. The Abbey was repaired and adorned by De Courcy towards the end of the twelfth century, when he changed the dedication from the Holy Trinity to St. Patrick, but by charter of James I (1607) the original dedication was restored. In 1316, Downpatrick was sacked by Edward Bruce and the church burned to the ground. In 1538 it was destroyed by the Lord Deputy, Leonard de Grey, an act of vandalism which formed one of the articles against him when he was impeached and subsequently beheaded. For more than two centuries and a half the building lay in ruins. In 1790, through the exertions of the then Dean (the Hon. and Rev. William Annesley), its restoration was begun. The nave and transepts, however, were never rebuilt, and the present cathedral is really the choir of the earlier building. Some fine examples of Early English foliated capitals remain. The tower was completed in 1829.

In the graveyard on the south side of the Cathedral is what is reputed to be the **Grave of St. Patrick.** It is covered by an enormous block of granite, left in the rough, brought from the Mourne Mountains in 1900. Engraved upon it are a Celtic cross of early design and the word Patric in old Irish characters. However, while this belief is fostered by many, local people consider it a myth.

The grave is even reputed to contain also the remains of St. Bridget and St. Columba, said to have been placed there by De Courcy.

St. Patrick lived in the fifth century. His birth-place is uncertain. It was as a young slave that he first landed in Ireland, probably at Strangford Lough. Unauthenticated report states that he lived and tended swine on Slemish hill, near Ballymena, in County Antrim. There he had visions, and finally ran away and studied in France at the school of St. Martin of Tours. His heart, however, was set on returning to Ireland to teach and preach the Gospel he had learned to love. He therefore landed in this neighbourhood and travelled about Ulster for the purpose of bringing the people "by the net of the Gospel to the harbour of life." The distribution of copies of the Gospel and the Pentateuch was a special feature of his method. In 432 he met the King and the Druids at the royal hill of Tara in formal conference. He seems to have declined the honours of a bishopric until nearly fifty years of age. Various miracles are ascribed to him, among them the extirpation from Ireland of snakes and all venomous reptiles.

Beyond the east end of the Cathedral is a tenth-century granite cross which formerly stood in the centre of the town.

It was re-erected from scattered fragments in 1897. The carving is much defaced.

The mound, or **Dun,** from which the city derives its name, is on the north-west. It is easily reached from English Street by turning to the right of the Court-House, near the Cathedral, and crossing a couple of fields. By this approach, the visitor comes to a fosse about 40 feet wide and 9 feet deep with a steep rampart, 50 feet high, on the farther side. Beyond the rampart the ground drops 20 feet into a large enclosure, having on one side a mound 30 feet high, encircled by a ditch 10 feet deep. In olden days the fort was almost surrounded by the sea at high tide.

Inch Abbey.—North-west of Downpatrick, reached by turning left from the main Belfast road, is Inch Abbey, with its mile-long avenue. Here, on the north bank of the Quoile river, is a picturesque pile of buildings probably built between A.D. 1200 and 1300.

Inch, of course, means "island" and the site was originally insular. The first abbey was Celtic and was ravaged by the Norsemen in 1002, and so in 1180 John de Courcy founded the second abbey, bringing to it a company of monks from Furness Abbey in North Lancashire. Inch was undoubtedly a wealthy abbey. Its church, the three-pointed eastern windows of which still remain, was 170 feet long, and had transepts and side chapels. There was a tower at the crossing. Some beautiful stonework still remains, especially at the bases of the former pillars. The buildings were very extensive.

At **Struel** ("the Stream"), 1¼ miles east of Downpatrick, are **Holy Wells,** believed to have been blessed by St. Patrick. They are really pre-Christian, and may have been connected with Druid Worship. Near them are the ruins of a small chapel dedicated to St. Patrick; and on the face of Struel Mountain is a heap of stones called, like so many others, **St. Patrick's Chair.**

About 2 miles north-east of Downpatrick are the ruins of the **Abbey of Saul** (*Sabhal,* a barn), erected towards the close of the twelfth century by St. Malachy. It was built, it is believed, on the same spot as the barn in which St. Patrick held his first Christian service in Ireland. Part of the site of the abbey is now occupied by a church, built in 1933. From Saul we are directed by a sign past **Slieve Patrick.** On the hill is a memorial shrine, and in its proximity is a copy of an Irish round tower displaying a figure of St. Patrick.

At **Raholp,** 2 miles from Saul, is one of the oldest buildings in Ireland, now a sadly neglected ruin. This little church (known as *Church-moyley*), only about 33 feet long and built of rough stones held together by clay instead of mortar, was probably founded by St. Patrick, and here he received his last communion (*see also* p. 285). Nearby is a cromlech. The old mill at the base of the hill merits attention because of its Norman origin. St. Patrick is believed to have landed near here on his arrival in Ireland, as described in the *Book of Armagh*, compiled about A.D. 807. At the foot of Slieve-na-griddle is a little lake with water-lilies, and just beyond a stone circle with "fairy" bushes (thorns), which no one must touch, growing amongst the stones.

About 2¼ miles south of Downpatrick, and a mile or so west of the Killough road, is **Ballynoe,** near a substantial **Stone Circle.**

This antiquity is within five minutes' walk, along a lane that runs westward from the road. It consists of a complete circle of large stones enclosing an incomplete ellipse of smaller stones. The outer ring is about a hundred feet in diameter. The largest stone stands 6 feet 6 inches high. This Ulster Stonehenge is probably a funeral monument.

The Ardglass bus road reaches the coast 3½ miles farther, at—

Killough

a small, quaint bathing resort on Killough Bay. It consists of the usual broad street, planted with sycamore trees. The bay is spacious and known for fishing. Nearly in the centre of the harbour entrance is a rock, a thousand yards long, covered at high water. This serves as a breakwater to a good anchorage behind, but the harbour is used only by a few local fishing-boats.

It is a pretty walk of 3½ miles southward along the shore to St. John's Point, which forms the northern horn of Dundrum Bay. Here are the remains of an ancient church and a notable lighthouse. The tower rises 140 feet above the water. There is a fine view from the gallery. Note too the ruins by the roadside of the 1,300-year-old St. John's Church, only 24 feet by 17 feet in area.

A winding road runs westward for 9 miles from St. John's Point, along the northern shore of Dundrum Bay and through Minerstown and Tyrella to Ballykinlar, where a ferry crosses to Dundrum, connected by road (3½ miles) with Newcastle.

Going eastward, however, from Killough we skirt the bay and cross a narrow tongue of land, 2½ miles distant to—

Ardglass

Amusements.—Golf, bathing and sea-fishing.
Hotels.—*Ardglass Arms* (4 rooms), *Downs Guest House* (8).

Places of Worship.—*Church of Ireland, Presbyterian, Roman Catholic.*
Population.—735.

This attractive resort is situated at the head of a little creek, with high green hills on each side. These are known respectively as the **Ward of Ardglass** and the **Ward of Ardtole.** From the former the town takes its name, in English, "the green height." The site is highly picturesque, and the quiet little place has a fascinating appeal for the purity of its water, its bracing air, the sandy nooks along its rock-bound bay, and its host of castles —as well as for the golf and the picturesque bustle of the herring fleet. On the **Downs,** a high common along the coast, south of the town, is an excellent *Golf Course.* Here and there a reef of rock provides a formidable hazard. De Courcy built seven castles for the protection of the place, but those now in ruins are ascribed to a trading company established under a grant from Henry IV, and to subsequent traders. Curiously, Ardglass has still its Royal Harbour Master. The end of the harbour is a favourite spot for anglers.

Overlooking the harbour is **Jordan Castle,** alternatively **Shane's Castle,*** a slender tower 70 feet high, built in the twelfth century. It is said to have been named after Jordan de Sankvill, a member of a Norman family that settled in Ardglass in 1177. King John is reported to have stayed in it in 1210. During the Earl of Tyrone's rebellion in the reign of Elizabeth the castle withstood the onslaught of the insurgents for three years. Its stout defender was one Simon Jordan, who was at length relieved by the Lord Deputy and suitably rewarded for his valour. It was burnt in 1641 and long stood desolate. The battlements, hearths, etc., were preserved together with a nearly perfect columbary. Now tended by the Northern Ireland Government, *it is open to visitors*, and should not be missed.

On the left, just within the gates at the entrance to the Downs, is **Cowd Castle.** Within the grounds is **Ardglass Castle,** which dates back to 1790 when its resident owner was Lord Charles Fitzgerald. Before him the building was known, and indeed still is locally, as the New Works, and was in existence in 1427. The remarkable building is 234 feet long, with a tower at either end, and has eighteen arched doorways to as many rooms on the ground floor. It was probably a fortified warehouse in the period when Ardglass was a flourishing port with trading ships from most European cities. A more modern building here is **Beauclere's Castle.**

On the summit of the hill of Ardtole, north-east of Ardglass, stand the ruins of the ancient **Church of St. Nicholas.** It was formerly the parish church of Ardglass, but, as recorded in the Terrier of 1615, "wood kern of M'Cartane's country upon a time when the inhabitants were at mass killed them all; whereupon it was brought within the town."

Leading north-eastward from Ardglass is the road to **Strangford** and **Portaferry,** along the cliffs past **Ballyhornan** and **Gun's Island,** an enjoyable ride. Altogether this quaint and lovely area is to be recommended to those who want a restful holiday with a pleasant old-time flavour.

* There is another Shane's Castle on the shores of Lough Neagh (*see* p. 254).

THE MOURNE DISTRICT
❀❀❀❀❀❀❀❀❀❀❀❀❀❀❀❀❀❀❀❀❀❀❀❀❀

Newcastle—Kilkeel—Rostrevor—Warrenpoint, etc.

The region of the Mourne Mountains, so famous in song, is a tourist district entirely different from any other, and one that offers scenic attractions of a very high order. The principal resorts in the district are Newcastle, Rostrevor and Warrenpoint, and from each of these, as indeed from Belfast itself, there are good facilities for exploring the mountains.

Belfast to Newcastle

The direct road (A 24 *via* Carryduff) is through rolling countryside studded with small farms and everywhere affords different views of the extensive range of the Mourne Mountains. Soon we come (16 miles) to **Ballynahinch,** "town of the island," a town occupying exactly the centre of County Down, and having some good markets (hotel: *White Horse*). Several hills encircle it. In 2½ miles more is **The Spa** (*closed*), with chalybeate and sulphurous wells. There are golf links and angling and a fair amount of hunting.

Four miles south-west of the Spa is **Slieve Croob** ("the mountain of the hoof," 1,755 feet), the most northerly of the Mourne

chain and visible from many points in the streets of Belfast. On its western slope the River Lagan rises.

Beyond Spa there is a choice of route (buses serve both), the right-hand fork making for Castlewellan (below), the left-hand road leading through Seaforde and Clough along inner Dundrum Bay, and so to the old-world village of Dundrum. **Dundrum** (*Commercial Hotel*), with a population of a little over 600, is noted for the ruins of its stately old **castle,** or *fort on the ridge*, as the name Dundrum means.

It was built by Sir John de Courcy for the Knights Templar in the early part of the thirteenth century, and was occupied by them until 1313, when the order was abolished. A good example of Anglo-Norman, it stands on the site of the original *dun*, or primitive earthen fort. The castle was dismantled by Oliver Cromwell in 1652. The ruins include an unusual, if not unique, circular donjon keep, part of the enclosing walls, and barbican towers, also circular.

At **Slidderyford,** only a short distance off the main road to Newcastle, is a perfect *cromlech* standing in a field at the side of the road. The upper stone is about 7 feet square, and there are three supporting stones, the whole group standing about 8 feet high.

The alternative fork right from the Spa leads in a few miles to—

Castlewellan (population 1,241; *Commercial Hotel*), conspicuously placed on a high ridge from which it looks down on a plain extending from Dundrum's fortress-crowned knoll to the spot where the *Bann* flows from the side of Eagle Mountain. North and west are rocky hills and extensive woods in which is **Castlewellan Park** now developed as a public forest park with lake, a mile in length, and famous for its wealth of rare trees and shrubs.

Four miles from Castlewellan, the road reaches the coast at—

Newcastle

Amusements.—Golf, angling, bathing, boating, tennis, bowls, mountain climbing, cinema, concerts, etc.
Distances.—Belfast 31, Ballynahinch 16, Downpatrick 13, Dublin 87, Dundalk 35, Londonderry 105, Newry 22.
Early Closing.—Thursday.
Hotels.—*Slieve Donard* (111 rooms), *Avoca* (20), *Arkeen* (21), *Harbour House* (15), *Enniskeen* (15), and many guest houses.
Places of Worship.—*Church of Ireland, Methodist, Presbyterian, Roman Catholic, Gospel, Baptist.*
Population.—4,336.
Youth Hostel.—30, Downs Road.

In regard to location, no seaside resort is more favoured than Newcastle, nestling at the foot of Slieve Donard. One of the principal resorts in the north of Ireland, it is famous for its picturesque scenery, for the invigorating purity of its air, for

NEWCASTLE

its excellent golf links, and for the numerous facilities it affords
for recreation and amusement.

Newcastle is built facing the sea and stretches for almost
2 miles along the most westerly curve of Dundrum Bay. To
the north, beyond the huge Slieve Donard Hotel, with golf links
behind it, the broad beach of smooth sand, backed by sand
dunes, curves away for miles; to the west lie tree-covered hills,
while immediately south of the town tower the Mourne
Mountains, with Slieve Donard rising impressively in the foreground. At its foot lies the harbour with its two short piers
affording shelter for small boats, while the town creeps up its
steep, wooded slope. On the green strip, planted with trees,
which runs between the houses and the sea, there is a bandstand
for concert parties.

Newcastle received its name from a castle built near the
bridge crossing the Shimna river about the time of the Spanish
Armada, but every trace of it has disappeared.

Bordering the grounds of the Slieve Donard Hotel is the
Royal County Down Golf Club. The 18-hole course is of
championship standard. There is a second 18-hole course in
the town, while in Castle Park, off Shimna Road, are facilities
for tennis, bowls and putting, and a boating lake. Football
and hockey are played in Donard Park.

The sandy beach is shelving and safe, and in addition to the
open sea at the Harbour there is a large swimming pool at
Blackrock. Anglers have three good trout streams within as
many miles' radius; and for those sightseers who prefer riding
to walking, local coaches provide a great range of tours through
the Mournes and farther afield.

Two miles west of the town, beyond Bryansford, is **Tollymore
Forest Park,** formerly a seat of the Roden family but now freely
accessible to the public. Here there is a wonderful combination
of wooded mountains and running river, with banks of ferns
and other plants. Car parks and picnic spots are provided. The
Ulster Museum, in association with the Forestry Division,
Ministry of Agriculture, N.I. have set up an exhibition hall as
field or trailside museum of natural history with exhibits of
plants and animals of the Mourne district.

THE MOURNE MOUNTAINS

The name Mourne is derived from *Mughdhorna*, the tribal name of a section of the MacMahons, who, about the middle of the twelfth century, migrated from Cremorne, in Co. Monaghan, and settled in the south of the present county of Down. It is certain that from a very early period the district formed a little kingdom that played a considerable part in the history of Ireland.

The Mourne Mountains are a fine group occupying an elliptical area, about 14 miles long and 7 miles broad, immediately south-west of Newcastle. All parts are easily accessible from neighbouring resorts. At the base of Donard, at the northerly extremity, is Newcastle, while at the southerly tip is Rostrevor. To the north is Hilltown, midway between Newcastle and Rostrevor, which has a fine mountain road leading through the Spelga Pass and bisecting the mountain chain to connect with the sea at Kilkeel.

Of the score or more peaks in the area, eleven are over 2,000 feet high.

	Feet		Feet
Slieve Donard . . .	2,796	Slieve Muck . . .	1,931
Slieve Commedagh . .	2,512	Carn Mountain . .	1,919
Slieve Bignian . .	2,449	Finlieve . . .	1,888
Slieve Bearnagh . .	2,394	Slieve Maganmore .	1,837
Slieve Meelbeg . .	2,310	Pigeon Rock Mountain	1,749
Slieve Lamagan . .	2,306	Ott Mountain . .	1,724
Slieve Meelmore . .	2,237	Ben Crom . . .	1,721
Shan Slieve (above Tollymore		Rocky Mountain .	1,718
Park) . . .	2,204	Cock Mountain . .	1,662
Chimney Rock Mountain	2,152	Slieve Martin (above Ros-	
Eagle Mountain . .	2,084	trevor) . . .	1,595
Shanlieve . . .	2,055		

The range consists of a variety of volcanic rocks, chiefly granite, of uncertain age. The more interesting mountains and all the higher peaks are on the Newcastle side.

There is a good road round the group but, with one exception, in the Spelga Pass, no road penetrates the mountains. The mountains are not high, and none of them present any great physical difficulty to the climber. But there is something indefinable about them, beyond height or gradient. The valleys are sometimes rough, through being strewn with stones or containing rutty peat, but the ridges are usually smooth, so that it is generally more advisable to make a wide sweep round the bend of a valley than to cut across.

296

The Ascent of Slieve Donard (2,796 feet). One of the chief charms of Newcastle is its proximity to Slieve Donard. The mountain was originally called *Slieve Slainge*, after the bardic hero Slainge, who is said to have died "Anno Mundi 2,533" and to have been interred in a cairn on the summit. Towards the end of the fifth century A.D. St. Domhanghart, a disciple of St. Patrick, built a cell on the top of the mountain, which ever since has been called Slieve Domhanghart, or by contraction, Slieve Donard.

Slieve Donard, a huge dome of granite, is the highest mountain in Ulster. The best ascent is from Newcastle Harbour, *via* the *Quarries*, which are about 750 feet high and mark the first viewpoint. The ascent is continued with the streamlet still on the left. Gradually, however, the climber leaves the stream, and on the right front is seen the grand cone of Slieve Donard. The route lies then to the south-west. The slope is steep, but the stunted vegetation makes a surface that is easy to walk on. At a height of 2,720 feet, the Lesser Cairn is passed. A less difficult ascent is to follow the Glen river, and pass through the Pot of Pulgarve. There is still another route from Bloody Bridge (*see* p. 298).

The Ascent of Slieve Bearnagh, 2 miles eastward. The approach is by the Hilltown road, inland through Bryansford and past Tollymore Park. Then, keeping always left, cross the Shimna river and turn up a wild valley down which runs the Trassey burn. On the right will soon be seen a gigantic rock, the Spellack, and ahead the **Hare's Gap**, between Bearnagh and Slieve-na-glogh. There we have a magnificent view of the brown mountains and the top of the Silent Valley, but even this sight is surpassed when we climb by the right over the heather to the apex of Slieve Bearnagh itself. The descent can be made easterly, by the Diamond Rocks, on the southern side of Slieve-na-glogh.

Slieve Bignian (2,449 feet) and Blue Lough call for a good, fine, long day for their exploration. Proceeding from Newcastle southerly along the Kilkeel road, we quit the latter for a roughish road on the right, at Glasdrummon, and continue along it for 2 miles to Dunnywater Bridge over the Annalong river. We then ascend a barish patch to come up to the **Blue Lake**, a fairy-like tarn sandwiched between high cliffs on the left, and Slieve Lamagan (2,306 feet) on the right. From here the ascent is continued up the steep slope alongside the rushing mountain stream issuing from Lough Bignian.

The Silent Valley. *The works are open daily to 5 p.m.*

Most visitors will prefer to reach the Valley by motor, either from the Newcastle–Warrenpoint coast road, or better still, by descending to it from Hilltown or Castlewellan, across the Deer's Meadow (where the River Bann is in its infancy) and the Spelga Pass. Walkers cannot go wrong if they take the signposted direct road on the right, just before reaching Kilkeel from Newcastle, but they must be prepared for a 3-mile tramp before they reach the gates. The Valley lies 12 miles from Newcastle.

Intruding 5 miles into the mountain, the water area of the lake is 240 acres, the length almost 2½ miles, the depth 80 feet, and the length of the transverse embankment about a third of a mile. The construction began in June 1923, and was completed in October 1932. Concurrently two tunnels, 2 miles and 3 miles respectively, had to be pierced through the mountains, and two 35-mile-long conduits built to the service reservoir at Knockbracken, 4 miles south of Belfast's centre.

In 1952, a 2½-mile tunnel was driven through Slieve Bignian, thus diverting the water of the Annalong river from the parallel Annalong Valley into the Silent Valley Reservoir.

To allow for the storage displaced by this additional inflow, a second reservoir, Ben Crom, was built in 1957 in the Upper Silent Valley, about ½ mile above the tail of the existing reservoir.

The completion of these and other ancillary works marked the final stage in the development of the Mourne Scheme originally envisaged in 1890. It provides a supply of 30 million gallons of water per day to Belfast and its surrounding district. The total capacity of the two reservoirs amounts to 4,700 million gallons.

Newcastle to Warrenpoint by the Coast

By the coast road, which is followed by buses, the distance from Newcastle is 26 miles. The mountain road on the north side of the group is 3 miles shorter, but the coast road is often preferred.

Ascending rapidly from Newcastle the road winds along the shore of the bay, the ever-changing peaks of the Mourne Mountains overhanging it on the right, while on the left is the sea, with cliffs rising almost perpendicularly for more than 100 feet, and here and there indented by yawning caverns. Then comes **Maggie's Leap,** a chasm 90 feet deep, across which, as some say, a pretty girl with her basket of eggs sprang to escape the attentions of an unwelcome suitor. When the woods no longer obstruct the view, the summit of **Slieve Donard** is seen behind several shoulders which look equal to the peak in height but are really 1,000 feet below it. As the road takes a southward course there comes into view the quaint **Chimney Rock** (2,152 feet), so called from the granite tors that crown its long ridge-like summit. Rather more than 2 miles from Newcastle is **Bloody Bridge,** a picturesque, ivy-wreathed structure a little above the bridge now used. It derives its name from being the scene of the massacre of a number of Presbyterians in 1641. On a mound on the seaward side is the ruined eleventh-century **Church of the Pass** in the strange graveyard in which only the unbaptized or drowned were buried. Under the bridge a torrent rushes down the wild valley between Slieve Donard and Chimney Rock in a series of cascades and deep green pools amid rough brown heather, gorse, and huge blocks of grey granite. The ascent of Slieve Donard can be made from here also. As we proceed Slieve Bignian (p. 297) comes into view from behind Spence's Mountain. Seven miles from Newcastle is the straggling village of **Annalong** ("the ford of the ships") with a small harbour from which dressed granite is shipped. Here the *Annalong* river, which rises on Slieve Donard and runs southward through the grand valley, enters the sea. Between 2 and 3 miles farther is the hamlet of **Ballymartin.** where a long hill has to be ascended and the low point of Leestone may be seen running out into the water. Fresh mountains now come into view. In the centre of the group are the **Pigeon Rock Mountain, Slieve Maganmore,** and the **Eagle Mountain.** To the westward are **Knockchree,** the "hill of the deer," and the grassy pointed summit of **Knockshoe.** We cross the *Kilkeel* river, meandering through a deep flat valley, and at 12½ miles from our starting-point enter the little town of—

Kilkeel

Access.—By bus from Newcastle, as just described. There is a service between Kilkeel and Greencastle. From Greencastle, a ferry crosses Carlingford Lough to Greenore.

Amusements.—Golf Links (1 mile). Good bathing and fishing.
Early Closing.—Thursday.
Hotels.—*Kilmorey Arms* (12 rooms), *Royal* (15), and numerous guest houses.
Population.—2,490.

Kilkeel ("the narrow Church") is a substantially built and thriving place, with attractions for holiday makers. It is close to the open Irish Sea, has a beach of sand and shingle extending for miles north and south, and is backed by an amphitheatre of mountains that are singularly bare of trees. The town stands on both banks of the *Aughrim*, a pretty trout stream over which the main thoroughfare is carried by a stone bridge. The Aughrim is a tributary of the Kilkeel river, near the mouth of which is a harbour much frequented by fishing-boats and small coaster steamers, and with an export trade of granite and potatoes. In the vicinity are several cromlechs or dolmens.

In Bridge Street are the ivy-covered ruins of the old **Parish Church,** rebuilt in 1780 but said to have been originally built in the fifth century by St. Colman. In the graveyard is a rough granite cross of ancient pattern.

Continuing straight through Kilkeel's main street, we head for **Greencastle,** on Carlingford Lough coast, 5 miles from Kilkeel. It was for centuries the capital of the kingdom of Mourne, and later was one of the principal strongholds of the English in Co. Down. On a small peninsula is the keep of a **Castle** of great strength, erected by the Anglo-Normans in the thirteenth century. The ruin is a conspicuous feature of the coast, and is regarded as a remarkably fine specimen of the ancient Norman-Irish keep.

Two roads turn sharply to the right out of the main street of Kilkeel. The first runs north-westward through the Mourne Mountains to **Hilltown** (p. 303), and is the only highway which crosses them. The second road has a westerly direction and is the direct coach route to Rostrevor and Warrenpoint.

Close by the Roman Catholic church, about a mile from Kilkeel on the Rostrevor road, is a rath called the *Mass Fort*, because the Roman Catholics in the penal days held services here.

A mile or so farther we pass the entrance gates of **Mourne Park** (Earl of Kilmorey), through which flows the *Whitewater* (trout), with scenery as beautiful as that of the Shimna river in Tollymore Park. At the upper end of the park is an isolated eminence called **Knockchree** ("the hill of the deer"), 1,013 feet high.

Two miles farther we cross *Causeway Water*, and then have on our right the bare cone of **Knockshee** (1,144 feet), while on our left is Seafield (the parental home of the 1st Lord Russell, Lord Chief Justice of England). Two miles beyond Causeway Water bridge we reach the new and old Roman Catholic churches of **Killowen,** a hamlet farther ahead. The buildings stand near the junction of the old and new roads to Rostrevor.

Between the Roman Catholic churches and the white-washed cottages of Killowen we pass Ballyedmond Castle Hotel with grounds sloping down to the edge of Carlingford Lough. In the vicinity of the hamlet the old road mounts the hill slope and commands fine views of Carlingford Lough and Mountains on the left, and the Mourne Mountains on the right. Then, for a mile, trees arch the highway and cover the ground from the shore to a height of 1,000 feet. The wood ends at **Rostrevor Quay,** where are a pier and an hotel (*Great Northern*). The village itself is some ¾ mile farther along the coast. The hotel and the near-by group of buildings nestle among the wooded slopes at the foot of **Slievemartin,** 1,595 feet high, on a shoulder of which lies a huge boulder upwards of 40 tons in weight known as **Cloughmore,** a corruption of *cloch mor*, "a great stone." This block of syenite (a rock of a different kind from that of the rest of the mountain), perched at a height of 957 feet, is probably a survival of the glacial age; but local tradition declares that it was thrown there by Finn McCoul from the other side of the Lough as a challenge to a Scottish giant.

Continuing our journey along the main road for half a mile, we pass **Rostrevor Park** on the right, cross the Kilbroney rivulet by Rostrevor Old Bridge, and so, 23 miles from Newcastle, reach—

Rostrevor

Distances.—Warrenpoint 3, Kilkeel 10, Newcastle 23, Newry 9, Belfast 42, Dublin 74.
Early Closing.—Wednesday.
Hotels.—*Great Northern*, The Quay; *Roxboro House*; *Ballyedmond Castle*, Killowen.
Population.—1,260.
Youth Hostel.—Knockbarragh Youth Hostel, Lower Knockbarragh, 3¼ miles from Rostrevor.

This charming little watering-place, "an Old English village set in a Norwegian fjord," is delightfully situated on Carlingford Lough, with the Carlingford Hills on the opposite shore and a background of beautifully wooded mountains that completely shelter it from north and east winds.

Rostrevor was so called, some say, from a fortress of that name; others say the name comes from the Irish "Ros," a wooded point, combined with the family name, Trevor, of some English settlers who were connected with the place from Queen Elizabeth's time.

On a mound a quarter of a mile from the village towards Warrenpoint stands an obelisk to the memory of *Major-General Ross*, a native of the place who died shortly after the fall of Washington in 1814.

Half a mile or so farther northward are the ruins of **Kilbroney Church** and its churchyard. "Broney" is a corruption of Bronach, the name of a holy woman who established an abbey close by. Only parts of the nave and chancel remain, and within these, as in similar spots in Ireland, trees grow amid the tombs. There is also a curious small stone enclosure which may have been the cell of the saint.

A strange romance attaches to St. Brigid's Bell, now in the Rostrevor Roman Catholic Church. A genuine example of the earliest Christian bells known in Ireland, it was the gift in the fifth century of a young Mourne chieftain, Fergus, who had wrongly killed his rival in love. St. Brigid had the bell hung in the fork of a young tree near the convent. The Danes subsequently destroyed the convent but the bell remained hidden. For several centuries the bell was heard to toll through the valley on certain nights and many eerie stories of banshees, leprechauns and the wailing of the lost lover were told as explanation. Then early in the nineteenth century the bell became mute and mystery deepened. But in 1888 a giant oak fell in Kilbroney Churchyard and when it was sawn up the old fifth-century bell was found embedded in the hollow trunk. Thus was its silence for the previous seventy years or so explained. Antiquarians declare its value as priceless.

Close to Kilbroney cemetery is **St. Brigid's Well**—reputed to possess the powers of granting eternal youth and beauty to whomsoever wash their face on the eve of Bronach's feast.

A favourite walk near Rostrevor is through the **Fairy Glen**, the richly wooded valley through which the Kilbroney stream flows. A footpath alongside the stream is entered at Rostrevor Bridge.

The route westwards from Restrevor to Warrenpoint (2½ miles) is almost entirely along the edge of Carlingford Lough, by a delightful road affording an admirable view of the placid waters and the shores on the opposite side, with Carlingford, Calvary and Omeath basking under the high ridge of Slieve Foy and the Carlingford Mountains, which form the spine of the Cooley Peninsula of Louth, separating Carlingford Lough and Dundalk Bay.

Warrenpoint

Buses, etc.—There are good local services and ample coach tours to all neighbouring places.

Distances.—Rostrevor 3, Newry 6, Greencastle 9, Kilkeel 12, Newcastle 25, Belfast 41, Dublin 71, Londonderry 99.

Early Closing.—Wednesday.

Golf Links (18 holes).—Visitors welcome.

Hotels.—*Crown* (12 rooms), *Balmoral* (7), *Liverpool* (7), *Osborne* (8), *Fintemara House* (7), *Shimna* (10).

Places of Worship.—*Church o Ireland, Methodist, Presbyterian, Roman Catholic* and *Unitarian*.

Population.—3,500.

Recreation.—Bathing, boating, golf, steamer trips, tennis, trout-fishing, cinema, dancing, bands in Park, concerts in Town Hall, and variety entertainments in Pavilion and Municipal Gardens.

This restful seaside resort is charmingly situated at the head of the bay, where the Clanrye, or *Newry Water*, flows into Carlingford Lough. It is the principal centre for the many beauty-spots around the famous Carlingford Lough and Mourne Mountains districts, and is one of the best-planned seaside resorts on the east coast of Ireland. Warrenpoint, with its spacious tree-lined square and avenue, is Continental rather than Irish. It owes its name to the fact that at one time the site was an extensive rabbit warren. Running out from the esplanade is a short **Pier.** A constant ferry service connects Warrenpoint with Omeath, in the Republic.

The town has pleasant public gardens, a recreation ground, swimming pool and hot and cold sea-water baths. Fronting the Lough for about a mile, a fine promenade commands a superb view of its expanse, and of the Carlingford and Mourne Mountains. Thackeray described this view as "a world's wonder." At the western end of the esplanade is a large open square containing the principal shops, the harbour and railway station. Oysters from the estuary are a favourite local dainty.

About 2 miles from the town along the Newry road is **Narrow Water Castle,** with extensive and beautiful grounds (*admission charge*). The castle, originally built in the thirteenth century, was destroyed by a Parliamentary force in 1641 and rebuilt in 1663 by the Duke of Ormonde. The ruins show that it must have been a place of great strength. It consisted of one square battlemented tower built upon a rock which was at one time insulated, the tide flowing completely round it; but for many years there has been a broad causeway connecting it with the high-road.

Hilltown is a simple village of some 300 inhabitants on a ridge overlooking the River Bann and commanding a glorious view of the mountains. It has an hotel and is an admirable centre for the exploration of the Mourne group, and anglers get good trout-fishing in the waters of the Bann.

Kinnahalla Youth Hostel is only 2¼ miles away, on the road to the Spelga Pass.

Hilltown is reached by a road rounding the northern side of the Mourne Mountains. It runs into Rostrevor, and then leaves that village by the hilly road between the Episcopalian and Roman Catholic churches. Half a mile farther it forks. Both branches lead to Hilltown, but the one to the right is the more direct road.

The more direct route from Warrenpoint to Newcastle does not, however, pass through Hilltown, but leaves it on the left and then turns towards the sea, climbing above the valley of the Bann until, at **Fofanny** (the place of thistles), it has an elevation of 600 feet. When that point has been reached, the high eastern peaks become prominent objects in the landscape. Among the more noticeable are the long ridge of **Slieve Meel-more** (the big bare mountain), between 2 and 3 miles away, in a south-easterly direction; the cone of **Slieve Meel-beg** (the little bare mountain), a mile farther away and more nearly south; and, nearer the sea, **Slieve-na-glogh** (the mountain of stones). The road passes round the northern side of the long black ridge of **Slieve-na-man** (the mountain of the women), near which there is a *Youth Hostel*, 3½ miles from Bryansford, and then Castlewellan comes into view. Its appearance is quickly followed by that of **Lough Island Reavy**, a lake much nearer to the road. Some 2 miles farther eastward the road skirts Tollymore Park (*see* p. 295), with its splendid trees, and after running through Bryansford turns to the right and descends to **Newcastle**, 23 miles by this route from Warren-point. This road has a very good surface. Curiously enough, at the highest point there is a great sandpit, and the road and soil are nearly all sand from here onwards. There are glorious views by this route, of sea, mountains and woods and then of Newcastle below.

Newry

Distances.—Belfast 38, Dublin 65, Greenore 16, Warrenpoint 6, Newcastle 22, Kilkeel 18.
Early Closing.—Wednesday (all day).
Hotels.—*Boulevard* (20 rooms), *Imperial* (16) *Ardmorc* (28).
Places of Worship.—St. Mary's (*Parish Church*), John Mitchel Place; St. Patrick's, Stream Street; *Methodist*, Sandys Street; *Presbyterian*, Sandys Street and Downshire Road; *Reformed Presbyterian*, Basin Wall; *Roman Catholic Cathedral*, Hill Street, and *Dominican*, Dominic Street; St. Mary's, Chapel Street; *First Presbyterian* John Mitchel Place.
Population.—12,450.

Newry (an "inland sea-port," someone once called it), a thriving commercial and market town with port facilities, lies at the head of Carlingford Lough on the border of Co. Armagh and Co. Down.

The town contains a number of factories, and has an important agricultural market. Besides steamship communication *via* its sea-canal and Carlingford Lough with several ports in England and Scotland, it has many miles of inland navigation by means of its **Canal.** Although commerce on the canal is now merely fractional, the great numbers of wharves and warehouses are memorials of once busier times.

Newry is built on a sheltered site between the Mourne and Carlingford mountain ranges. Though it lies low, the town is well situated. On the north is a well-cultivated agricultural district with many handsome country houses, factories and bleaching-greens. On the south the mountain-locked bay stretches to the sea, looking like an inland lake amid the wooded mountains. There are quarries from which excellent granite setts and stone for building are hewn.

The history of the town dates from prehistoric days and was intimately connected with the introduction of Christianity into Ireland. St. Patrick and St. Brigid are said to have laboured here: the yew-tree from which the town derived its name (literally, "the yew-tree") was planted, it is said, by St. Patrick himself, and continued to flourish for 700 years after his time, when it was burned, together with a neighbouring monastery and its furniture and books. The monastery, which is supposed to have occupied the site of Hyde Terrace, was damaged by fire on more than one occasion, and was a place of distinction until Henry VIII appropriated its revenues. On account of its position, the town was much involved in the struggles to do with the establishment of the Pale (the English settlement comprising Armagh, Down and Louth, governed from Carlingford), being, indeed, more than once practically destroyed.

The **Roman Catholic Cathedral** is an imposing building of dressed Irish granite in the Gothic style, and has beautiful windows and good wood carving.

St. Patrick's, the oldest Protestant church in Ireland, was built in 1578 by Sir Nicholas Bagnal, Marshall of Ireland, upon whom, "for excellent services," Edward VI bestowed the privileges and possessions of the monastery suppressed by his father. Bagnal's arms are still prominent on its tower.

The first Presbyterian Church, in John Mitchel Place, was founded in 1615, on the site now known as "The Old Meeting House Green". The present building was erected in 1853.

In the old burying-ground lie the remains of John Mitchel, a leader of the Young Ireland Movement of 1848.

Three miles north-west of Newry is the "model" village of **Bessbrook**, a convenient angling centre, mainly for trout, but also for salmon. The village was founded by the Richardsons, a Quaker family, who are mainly concerned in the local linen spinning mills.

Newry to Belfast

From Newry the return to Belfast can be made by the fast A 1, the main Dublin–Belfast highway. In 14 miles we come to **Banbridge** (*Devonshire Arms*; 9-hole golf course), a linen centre well situated on a hill overlooking the Upper Bann. Its main street is on different levels, the side sections being connected by bridge. In the square is a statue of *Captain Francis Crozier* (1796–1848), second-in-command to Franklin on the North-west Passage exploration. In a further 7 miles is **Dromore** (*Commercial*), spread on both sides of the River Lagan. Bishops Bridge, over the river, bears a tablet to Bishop Percy, who occupied the episcopal throne from 1782–1811. He enlarged the Cathedral, now the parish church, originally built by Jeremy Taylor. Near the Church is an ancient cross on a granite pedestal. There are some old stocks in the market square. A quarter of a mile from the town is the fine Norman earthwork known as **Dromore Mound.** In a further 5 miles is the small town of **Hillsborough,** deriving its name from Sir Arthur Hill, who built the castle which stands in the park on the south side of the town during the reign of Charles I. Charles II made it a royal fortress and appointed Sir Arthur and his successors hereditary constables, with twenty warders. Though a bugler still carries on his traditional custom at the Parish Church on Sunday mornings, the warders have been replaced by a company of the Irish Guards. The **Castle** is now the official residence of the Governor of Northern Ireland. It was one of the resting-places of William III on his way to the Boyne, and, curiously, even now a Royal grant is given annually for its upkeep as a military fort. The Marquis of Downshire, to whom Hillsborough gives the titles of Earl and Viscount, is a descendant of Sir Moyses Hill, whose estates reached virtually from Lisburn to Newry. A statue of the third Marquis on an obelisk tops the hill overlooking the country. From Hillsborough the main road continues over the Lagan to **Lisburn** and **Belfast.**

ARMAGH
🍀🍀🍀🍀🍀🍀🍀🍀🍀

County Armagh, of gently undulating hills, is a pleasant county for holiday-makers, offering good opportunities for sport and relaxation in a land of considerable romance and legend. Besides the growing of barley and oats, there are rich apple-growing interests and mushroom enterprises.

Armagh

Distances.—Belfast 37, Banbridge 19, Dublin 80, Dundalk 28, Dungannon 13, Londonderry 73, Lurgan 16, Newry 20, Omagh 39, Portadown 11.
Early Closing.—Wednesday (all day).
Hotels.—*Beresford Arms* (20 rooms), *Charlemont Arms* (26), *Drumsill House* (8).
Museums.—*County Museum*, The Mall; *Military Museum*, Sovereign's House, The Mall.

Places of Worship.—St. Patrick's Cathedral, *Church of Ireland;* Roman *Catholic Cathedral* (St. Patrick's); St. Mark's Church; *Presbyterian Churches* (two); *Methodist.*
Population.—12,000.
Recreation.—Golf (9 holes), cricket, tennis, cinemas, hunting, shooting, angling, swimming pool, etc.

The city of Armagh is one of the oldest and, historically, most intensely interesting places in Northern Ireland. It is the ecclesiastical capital of Ireland, being the seat of the Archbishops of both the Church of Ireland and Roman Catholic churches. Here one is at the fountain-head of Ireland's early Christian culture, which illuminated in its time all Europe.

All, regardless of faith or politics, have had a common denominator in claiming Armagh as the ecclesiastical metropolis. The pen (or the pulpit) is mightier than the sword; so the fame of St. Patrick's teaching outlasts all memories of Brian Boru, Leary and Tara's kings. Patrick chose Armagh. Even before Patrick's time the place was noted because of the great palace-fort, Navan (the ancient *Emania*) (*see* p. 309), which was from 300 B.C. to A.D. 332 the capital of the kings of Ulster; and Macha, the warrior queen who founded the fort, has her name perpetuated in Armagh (*Ard-Macha*, "the height of Macha").

In legend and tradition Armagh district is peerless. Indeed, without disparagement to England it is actually of greater antiquity than Canterbury. Armagh church was founded in A.D. 445 and Canterbury not until A.D. 597.

Now Armagh snuggles in the folds of its seven green hills, with its twin cathedrals guardian angels on its highest peaks.

Although the atmosphere of its narrow streets is that of a restful city still unruffled by events since the early Georgian era, its citizens are not unmindful of its earlier traditions. As a potent reminder of this city's fame as a seat of learning we have that priceless volume, the *Book of Armagh*, which is little inferior to the world-famed *Book of Kells* in Dublin University and even contains St. Patrick's autobiography. The Bodleian

Library in Oxford prizes other similar Armagh MSS. While the famed *Bell of St. Patrick*—now in Dublin—survived fire and vandalism through long warring centuries, neither of the present cathedrals boasts great antiquity.

St. Patrick's Cathedral (Church of Ireland)

(Services: 10.15 or 11 and 3.15 on Sundays; 9.30 a.m. on week-days, Saturdays 10 a.m.).

The Church of Ireland Cathedral, built of red sandstone and dedicated to St. Patrick, marks the central point of the city. It has a stately attractiveness individualistic in character, and here, as at Lincoln and Durham, the city and cathedral seem to form a natural harmony.

A.D. 432 is generally accepted as the date when St. Patrick began his missionary labours here; some years afterwards, having obtained a site at Armagh from a chieftain named Daire, he founded a church which came to be the Metropolitan Cathedral. As far back as the year 830, the Cathedral is referred to as "the great stone church." It suffered frequently from fire, and in 1268 the then Primate started to rebuild it. The transepts which he added are practically the present ones. In 1367 the Cathedral was again restored and probably the side aisles of the nave were then erected. Some 200 years later, Shane O'Neill used the Church as a fortress during his rebellion against Queen Elizabeth, and ended by ruining and partly burning it. The building remained in this ruined condition until restored by Primate Hampton in 1613. During the next two centuries extensive alterations and repairs were made. In 1834 a complete restoration was begun, mainly at the cost of Primate Lord John Beresford, but unfortunately the characteristic Irish architecture was altered.

Although small and plain compared with English cathedrals, its solidarity and absence of ornament give it a reverend and solemn appearance. It is cruciform, 182 feet long, with a width across the transepts of about 100 feet. A tower, formerly surmounted by a spire, rises from the crossing to a height of 100 feet and provides a splendid viewpoint for the surrounding country. The tower, which in 1834 replaced the spire, contains a peal of eight bells.

The nave is separated from the aisles by five arches. Among statues here, notable are: *Sir Thomas Molyneux, M.D.* (d. 1733) by Roubillac, considered one of the finest works of this famous sculptor; and the reclining figure of *Dean Peter Drelincourt* (d. 1720) by Rysbrach, remarkable for the delicacy and accuracy of its work. Note also the statue of *Archbishop William Stewart* (d. 1822) by Sir Francis Legett Chantrey. The arches of the crypt are of very primitive formation and considered to be ninth or tenth century.

The stained glass in the Cathedral is modern, but unusually good. In the south transept is a richly-carved stone screen which until 1866 enclosed the choir and the easternmost arch of the nave.

In the south aisle are several memorials including a marble bust by Nollekins of Primate Robinson (1765–95), who presented to the city the Mall (a public park), built the Bishop's Palace and the Royal School, and founded an Observatory and Public Library.

The colours of the Royal Irish Fusiliers attest to the world victories of this famous regiment.

Opposite the north-west entrance to the Cathedral yard is the **Public Library** (*open 11–4, Saturday, 11–1*), first endowed by Archbishop Robinson. It contains some 21,000 volumes and is rich in rare works, especially those relating to Irish history and archaeology.

307

Beyond the Infirmary and Shambles Market is—

The Roman Catholic Cathedral

Dimensions. — The internal length is 208 feet; breadth across the transepts 120 feet; length of nave, 114 feet; length of chancel, 60 feet; breadth of nave and chancel, 75 feet; and the choir is a square of 38 feet. The external roof is 100 feet in height; the internal one, 81 feet.

This, like the Church of Ireland Cathedral, is dedicated to St. Patrick. It is an imposing modern structure on Knockadrain Hill, in the north-west of the city, and commanding picturesque views.

This great Church has to be reached by a seven-terraced flight of broad steps—225 feet long—which lead from the unecclesiastical-looking entrance gates and lodge to a spacious platform in front of the western doors.

The building was begun on St. Patrick's Day, 1840, but it was not until 1873 that it was dedicated, and it was 1904 before the interior was finished and consecrated. The walls are of limestone, quarried near the old Navan Fort about 2 miles west of the city, while the columns and arches are of freestone from quarries near Dungannon.

Built on the fourteenth-century style of Decorated Gothic, it is cruciform in plan, comprising nave, aisles and transepts, with chancel and choir. The interior is lofty, and of uniform height throughout. At each angle of the western front is a tower with a slender spire rising to a height of 210 feet and surmounted by a 10-foot cross. In the Bell Tower is a carillon of 39 bells, the largest weighing 2¼ tons.

The **Interior** is richly ornamented with marbles, mosaic and stained glass. The freestone columns and arches are almost the only parts of the original framework not covered with mosaic.

In the south transept is the *Sacred Heart Altar*, containing some of the most precious marbles in the Cathedral. The pulpit is beautifully sculptured and inlaid with various marbles.

The *High Altar* is of purest Carrara marble, and its frontal displays an alto-relievo representation of Leonardo da Vinci's "Last Supper."

The South Aisle of the Chancel, approached from the south transept, forms *St. Brigid's Chapel*, and is covered with mosaics illustrating her life.

The *Lady Chapel*, occupying the central part of the chancel, also contains some beautiful mosaics. The reredos is a fine specimen of Irish carving.

The north chancel aisle forms *St. Joseph's Chapel*. On the walls of the great north transept are medallions of Irish saints and a great five-light window.

Connected by a cloister with the north-east end of the Cathedral is a graceful and spacious two-storeyed building containing the **Synod Hall**, with its Chapter Room featuring portraits of previous Archbishops, and The Sacristy, with priceless plate and vestments.

The Cathedral terrace affords the best view of **Mount St. Catherine,** where is the *Convent of the Sacred Heart*, with a national and boarding school. A little way from the south-east side of the Cathedral is *St. Patrick's College* for clerical and lay students, and about as far from the seminary is the *Archbishop's House*, built in 1876–77.

On the east side of the city is **The Mall,** a wide, tree-planted public recreation ground some 7 acres in extent and overlooked by imposing Georgian houses. Close at hand is the **Presbyterian Church,** built of hard limestone from the near-by quarries. It has a beautiful spire. On the opposite side is the **County Museum,** with collections of pictures, costume and folklore.

To the north-east, off College Hill, is the fine **Observatory.** Here is a planetarium and one of the rarest clocks in the world. On the other side of College Hill is the **Royal School,** originally founded by royal charter in 1608.

Armagh's Royal Portrait Gallery.—It is not generally known that in the Primate's Palace, south of the city and located between the Newry Road on the east and the Monaghan Road on the west, is a remarkable collection of portraits of Kings and Queens of England, known as the Royal Portraits. Most of these pictures are by famous artists, including Sir Joshua Reynolds. (*There is no public admission.*)

Excursions from Armagh

St. Patrick's Well. West of the city, from which it is about fifteen minutes' walk by Navan Street and the old Callan Bridge. The visitor will be intrigued by the rags tied to the *Fairy Thorn* which overhangs the well. They—and pennies, too, occasionally—are symbols of gratitude in advance for the fulfilment of the prayers of the pilgrims.

Navan Fort or Emania. About a mile beyond St. Patrick's Well. Here, about three centuries before the Christian era, Queen Macha built the palace of Emania, where the kings of Ulster continued to reside for more than 600 years. As at Tara there are now no remains of the palace other than the great mound on which it stood and the earthen ramparts by which it was encircled. It must be remembered that in earlier days—even up to A.D. 1600—these royal palaces were constructed of perishable wood and often decorated with golden ornaments. Emania was in ruins even when St. Patrick came to Armagh about A.D. 445. In ancient times this was one of the most important of all Irish palaces. Here Cuchulain, the Red Branch knights, assembled to be trained in deeds of bravery and skill.

St. Brigid's Well. This is within the Church of Ireland Primate's demesne in a wooded hollow a few yards up the avenue from the Palace Row entrance The well is locked, but the water flows into a small exterior basin.

The **Franciscan Abbey.** This also is within the Church of Ireland Primate's demesne. It is on the city side of St. Brigid's Well—between that and the boundary wall. It was founded by Primate O'Scalan in 1263, and of the five abbeys of Armagh is the only one remaining. It is an interesting fragment of Celtic Romanesque.

King Niall's Grave. A burial mound beside the River Callan, a mile distant by way of Irish Street, Mullanstown and Rookford. It is the reputed resting-place of King Niall III, surnamed "of the Callan" because he was drowned in that stream while attempting to save one of his warriors. The Callan is a good river for brown trout.

Seven miles north of Armagh is the small village of **Charlemont,** connected by a bridge with the larger and very picturesque village of **Moy.** The former village is in County Armagh, the latter in County Tyrone. Between them flows the lovely *Blackwater*. **Loughgall,** more English than Irish in its setting, is another oasis of beauty in this vicinity.

Portadown

Ten miles north-east of Armagh is Portadown, with a population of 20,707. It is one of Northern Ireland's most prosperous towns, being especially noted for linen and for rose-growing. The town is the centre of the Armagh apple-growing district, and has a canning factory and other industrial activities. It has good recreational facilities for the usual sports, including a 9-hole golf course, and fishing for trout in the rivers Bann and Cusher. The old name, *Port-na-dun*, "Port of the fortress," was derived from the castle of the McCanns which formerly commanded the passage of the river.

Five miles on the Belfast road from Portadown is **Lurgan,** another important centre of the linen industry (population 20,677; 9-hole golf course). **Maghery** is a village on the shore of Lough Neagh, 8 miles north-west of Portadown. It is a good fishing spot, and boats may be hired for trips on the lough. Offshore is **Coney Island,** property of the National Trust.

The Sir Robert Mathew Report (1963) to the Northern Ireland Government envisages the amalgamation of the boroughs of Portadown and Lurgan and the creation of a combined new city with up to 100,000 population. There is a considerable diversity of industry being attracted to the district to provide employment.

Index

✤✤✤✤✤✤✤

INDEX

314

317